MARKETING

An Introduction for Irish Students

Donal Rogan

p60

Gill & Macmillan

Gill & Macmillan Ltd
Goldenbridge
Dublin 8
with associated companies throughout the world
www.gillmacmillan.ie

© Donal Rogan 2000

0 7171 2831 8

Index by John Loftus
Print origination by Andy Gilsenan

1 3 5 4 2

gift-
M. Shovelin This book is typeset in Goudy 10/12.5pt

658-80094l
ROG

To the memory of Ellie Rogan.

Contents

Preface

Marketing involves understanding needs. This book seeks to serve the needs of students of marketing by providing an introduction to marketing theory, illustrated, where possible, with examples of marketing practice.

Marketing continues to evolve: it is a dynamic discipline, and this book provides some insights into the ideas and concepts that have shaped and continue to influence it. As with the study of business in general, it is important to learn from marketing examples, which are all around us. As a result, this book includes a significant number of case vignettes in each chapter. In addition, each part is followed by a number of more extensive case studies; these relate to the material covered in the preceding part and should provide the reader with added insights and opportunities for analysis and discussion.

The book is written from an explanatory viewpoint. Topics are introduced and explained, hopefully in a clear and concise way. The emphasis throughout is on putting the customer at the centre of the business; this is the basis for making marketing decisions. The student of marketing should also appreciate the importance of monitoring forces in the environment that affect the firm. In Ireland we are fortunate that the news media and specialist business media provide extensive coverage of business and marketing-related topics, and many of the examples in the book have been obtained from these sources. This should also be an encouragement to students to look for such examples to increase their understanding of the business environment. While Irish examples dominate the book, it would be myopic to concentrate on them alone, and some examples from other countries are also used.

Technology, in many forms, will continue to be an influential force on marketers, and firms will therefore be more concerned with such issues as electronic commerce, the internet, and digital television, all of which, together with other technological developments, are discussed. In addition to its role in business, the internet will also be a more important source of information for students. This will make it easier for them to keep in touch with developments in marketing and to find illustrative examples.

The book is divided into five parts, designed to follow logically from each other. Parts 2–5 are completed by a case study or case studies, designed to integrate and build on the material covered in the preceding part.

Part 1 introduces the nature of marketing. This consists of two chapters, which explain why marketing involves putting the customer at the centre of the business and examine its role in developing the business. The nature of marketing and concepts of customer service, ethics, quality management and enterprise development are among the topics introduced.

Part 2 concentrates on the market. The forces in the marketing environment are described, and an introduction to the theories of buyer behaviour is given. The marketing research process is also introduced in a separate chapter. The important process of segmentation, targeting and positioning is described, and students are given examples to illustrate the link between them. Two case studies, the sun care market and Tesco Ireland, complete this part of the book.

Part 3 concentrates on the elements of the marketing mix, what are traditionally referred to as the 'four Ps'. The nature of the product is explained, and considerable attention is paid to branding, packaging, and new-product development. The chapter on pricing examines the decisions to be made in pricing products and services; pricing methods are described, and market influences that affect price are examined. Rather than use the term 'promotion', the chapter on marketing communication presents a broad profile of the components of this dynamic aspect of marketing practice. The communication model is explained, and the nature of advertising, public relations, sales promotion, personal selling and sponsorship is described and discussed. The chapter on marketing channels is also broader than the more traditional 'place' description. Issues in channel management, including distribution, logistics, transport, wholesaling, retailing, and franchising, are explained. Part 3 is completed with four case studies: Agfa, Keelings, Oki Ireland, and Smithwicks.

Part 4 comprises four short chapters on marketing applications. These seek to introduce marketing practice in the context of services, international markets, business-to-business markets, and non-profit organisations. Each chapter demonstrates how the principles of marketing are equally relevant, regardless of application, but also why adaptation may sometimes be required. Part 4 is completed with the Citygold case study.

Part 5 consists of a single chapter on marketing strategy and planning, which integrates the components of the previous chapters and emphasises the importance of planning for the business. This part is completed with the Cheeverstown Industries case study.

At the end of each chapter there are recommendations for further reading, selected to provide the reader with more detailed coverage of the material introduced in the chapter.

Acknowledgments

I would like to acknowledge the assistance I have received in writing this book. I am particularly grateful to my colleagues Patricia Medcalf and Adrian Payne, who contributed the Keelings and Oki Ireland case studies, respectively. They also reviewed parts of the text, and their comments and observations proved most useful. I would also like to thank Mr Robert Vervoort, managing director of Agfa-Gevaert, Mr William O'Connor, manager of passenger services, Inter-City, Ms Pauline Crowley, head of customer insight, Tesco Ireland, Ms Rosemary Fagan, marketing manager of Hawaiian Tropic (Ireland), and Mr John Madden, Cheeverstown Industries, for their co-operation in the development of case studies included in the book.

I would like to thank Ailbhe O'Reilly of Gill & Macmillan, who encouraged me to take on the writing of this book and provided continuous support during the process. I would also like to thank the managing editor, Deirdre Greenan, for her advice and assistance. In addition, the comments and suggestions made by Gill & Macmillan reviewers at the early stages of development were most useful and appreciated. Any defects or omissions remain very much my own.

PART 1

Marketing: The Customer and the Business

1

Putting the Customer at the Centre

Marketing is a subject that should be interpreted rather broadly. It is widely associated with business practice, but it should not be defined in a purely business context. In the business context it can be described as an outlook or way of thinking that puts the customer at the centre. It is based on understanding the needs of customers and serving those needs, competitively, at a profit.

There have been many definitions. Kotler (1987), a leading marketing academic, defined marketing as 'a human activity directed at satisfying needs and wants through exchange processes.' This definition illustrates the broad nature of marketing. The exchange processes may cover business and non-business transactions and activities. The individual does not have to exchange anything with a business to be involved in marketing: Kotler's definition covers exchanges between any individuals.

In this book, marketing is considered largely in the context of its role in business. The Marketing Institute of Ireland, a representative organisation for marketers and marketing practitioners, uses as its slogan 'Marketing is the business.' This demonstrates the important role marketing plays in business firms. All firms have to develop appropriate products to meet market needs and employ communication and distribution methods to reach the customer. In doing so they can learn from the experience of marketers in the business world. In the words of Kotler and Levy (1969), 'the business heritage of marketing provides a useful set of concepts for guiding all organisations.'

What does it mean to be marketing-oriented? The essential feature is putting the customer first. The customer is the reason the business exists: it is the customer who pays the wages. In his book *Crowning the Customer*, Feargal Quinn, one of Ireland's leading marketing practitioners, outlined his view of marketing. He developed what he described as the 'boomerang' approach: quite simply, keep customers happy and they will keep coming back. He also demonstrated the importance of listening to the customer. The policy certainly worked for him, with the Superquinn chain of supermarkets providing high standards of customer service, at a profit.

SUPERQUINN: PUTTING MARKETING INTO ACTION

The Superquinn chain has its origins in the Dublin suburb of Finglas, where Feargal Quinn opened his first shop in 1965. The chain grew and by the late nineteen-nineties had shops in Counties Dublin, Kildare, Carlow, Kilkenny, and Tipperary. Over the years the company has built a reputation for innovation. In 1973 it pioneered in-store bakeries, and it followed this by establishing a range of fresh food departments; these included delicatessens, pizza kitchens, pasta kitchens, salad kitchens, and even sausage kitchens, where sausages were made in the shop to a traditional recipe.

A central part of Feargal Quinn's retailing policy was an emphasis on customer service, founded on a determination to keep close to the customer and to build a firm that would always try to see things from the customer's point of view. This would also be a means of encouraging customer loyalty. Managers were encouraged to get out on the shop floor; this was helped by an instruction to architects to give them small, dingy offices. Quinn himself regularly appears in shops, talking to customers and packing bags for them. Every fortnight he holds 'customer panels', at which he listens to groups of shoppers, who tell him how they think the group could serve them better. Out of such encounters have come many innovations, such as play areas for children, an umbrella service on wet days, and a carry-out service to customers' cars.

Superquinn has also been innovative in the use of retail technology. It was the first Irish supermarket chain to introduce a loyalty card scheme and the first to experiment with self-scanning of goods by customers. The Superclub loyalty card scheme rewarded customer loyalty; by the late nineteen-nineties most other grocery chains had followed suit.

Feargal Quinn always believed that customers want a high level of personal service, and a kind of service that can be provided only by human beings, not machines. He proved that investment in people pays off in increased business, which pays for the additional staff costs. In other markets the perceived wisdom had been that a high level of service was something the customer had to pay for in higher prices, but in Ireland this was always impossible, because the grocery trade was so competitive.

Superquinn has been a consistently profitable firm. Profit figures are not released, but turnover was estimated at between £280 and £310 million in 1997. Profit margins in grocery retailing are estimated to be 2–3 per cent.

Sources: Quinn, 1991; Quinn, 1996; J. Lee, 'Service with a smile', *Marketing*, 28 November 1996; Business and Finance, *Top 1000 Companies*, 1997.

The Superquinn example demonstrates two other essential features of a marketing-oriented firm: repeat business and profit. It is considerably cheaper to hold on to existing customers than to find new ones. Businesses exist to make profits for their shareholders or owners; they should do so by meeting customers' needs. Firms that have satisfied customers and high levels of repeat business will tend to be profitable. Costs obviously need to be kept under control.

THE NATURE OF MARKETING

Marketing should permeate the whole operation of the company as it seeks to determine what to produce and how and where to sell it. It is a process that begins before the product or service begins and continues after it has been sold.

Kotler's definition of marketing indicated a number of related concepts that should be examined; these are illustrated in fig. 1.1.

Fig. 1.1: Core marketing concepts

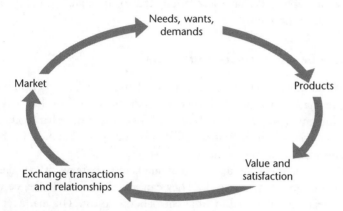

Source: Kotler et al., 1996.

NEEDS, WANTS, AND DEMANDS

Marketing begins with an understanding of human needs. *Needs* describe a state of felt deprivation. According to one theorist, A. Maslow (1943), human beings are constantly needing individuals. At a basic level we need air, food and drink, sex and shelter to survive; these are described as innate or primary needs. We may also need to feel secure, to belong, to acquire knowledge, to have power, and to be able to express ourselves. These needs are considered to be acquired, because they are influenced by our culture or environment. They are referred to as secondary needs.

All needs are motivational: in other words, if we feel the need for something we experience tension, and we will be driven towards reducing the tension by satisfying that need. At a basic level, if we are hungry we will reduce the tension by eating something. This could involve any number of possibilities, from preparing something at home to dining out in a restaurant. What we eat may depend on secondary needs: for example, we may eat with friends in a restaurant, making it a social occasion, or we may go to a fashionable café where we like to be seen and where we hope we will meet others.

Wants describes the form taken by human needs as influenced by culture and the individual's personality. We need clothing, but we don't all wear the same style of clothes. Individuals may want to follow a particular style or fashion or express themselves in what they wear.

Demand exists when people have the purchasing power to satisfy their needs. Few people will have the income to satisfy all their needs, so they will make trade-offs, buying products and services that give them the greatest amount of satisfaction they can get for their money. Understanding how these trade-offs are made is important for marketers; it also emphasises the significance of customers' needs in marketing theory.

Most marketing practitioners are concerned to generate and satisfy the demand for their products or services. Company growth, development and profitability are usually dependent on achieving sales growth. There may, however, be circumstances when the marketer wants to dampen and control demand; this has been referred to as *de-marketing* (Lawther, Hastings and Lowry, 1997). In the health area, for example, advertising campaigns have been conducted to discourage people from seeking drug prescriptions for minor ailments; similarly, they have also attempted to discourage people from using casualty departments in hospitals.

The difference between needs and wants

The terms *needs* and *wants* should not be used interchangeably. Every person has needs; some of these are innate. Wants are for specific products or services that will satisfy a need. If we are hungry, therefore—an innate need—we may want a bar of chocolate, a sandwich, or a four-course meal. Wants will depend on a combination of individual characteristics, on social and environmental influences.

An often-heard criticism of marketing is that 'marketers create needs to make money.' In reality, marketers cannot create needs. They can and do seek to influence wants. A hungry consumer can be influenced in what they choose to eat. The marketer did not, however, make the consumer hungry. We are familiar with advertising for food and drink products that promise different taste sensations, speedy preparation, or thirst-quenching properties. These are an attempt by the marketers of these products to encourage consumers to differentiate between alternatives, to satisfy a need by wanting a specific product or brand.

Products

Usually the term *product* is used to describe what is being exchanged by the marketer with the market. A product is anything that can be offered to satisfy a need or a want. It can include physical things, such as cans of Coca-Cola or bottles of washing-up liquid; these are described as tangible. Something is tangible if we can see, touch, hear, smell or taste it. Products can also be intangible, such as the experience of visiting a theme park or seeking financial advice from a bank. Intangibility describes experiences, feelings, or emotions.

Marketers therefore use the term *product* in a very wide sense. In between these categories there are many products that have a combination of tangible and intangible features, as demonstrated in the following panel.

PHONE CARDS FOR PROMOTIONS

The Phone Card Company produces a range of prepaid promotional cards that can be used to advertise products. The cards can be branded and credited with any number of units and can be used for long-distance and international calls. Logos, pictures and company names can be used. The concept is popular in Britain and the United States; for example, Coca-Cola gave away a million on the cover of a magazine. The cards are not inserted into a phone: instead, the user dials a freefone number and then enters the PIN on the back of the card. Each time the card is used the user is told how many units are left. Working in partnership with Global One (a joint venture between Deutsche Telecom, France Télécom, and Sprint), the Phone Card Company uses its fibre optic network.

The entrepreneurs responsible for the company, Mark Richardson and John McQuaid, developed the idea after they had completed an enterprise development course run by Dublin Institute of Technology.

Source: Christine Doherty, 'Promotional phonecards provide route to talkative consumers', *Sunday Business Post*, 22 February 1998.

The phone cards are tangible plastic cards that have a monetary value, in the form of the number of phone calls that could be made using one. The use of the cards for advertising demonstrates both tangible and intangible aspects. The illustrations on the card are tangible, while their effectiveness as an advertising medium would be more intangible. The convenience and ease of use of these cards would also be intangible factors.

Kotler and Levy (1969) contended that marketing is a pervasive social activity that goes considerably beyond selling tangible products, such as toothpaste or soap. They suggested that the term *product* could be used to describe physical products, services, people, organisations, and ideas. The following are some examples of each type of product:

Physical products: Crisps; beer; detergent; fertiliser.
Services: Holidays; insurance; a haircut; advice.
People: Politicians; journalists; actors.
Organisations: Irish Farmers' Association; political parties; charities.
Ideas: Energy conservation; anti-litter campaigns;
                       environmental awareness.

VALUE AND SATISFACTION

Whatever the nature of the product, it must be valued and must give satisfaction if it is to be demanded. Value and satisfaction can mean different things to different people, once again demonstrating the importance of understanding buyers' behaviour. To one consumer a product or service offering particular features and priced at a particular level may represent value and satisfaction, to another consumer it may not. Marketers must therefore understand the nature of the value and satisfaction consumers are looking for and tailor their products or product variations accordingly.

Customer value can be illustrated simply as:

$$customer\ value = \frac{what\ the\ customer\ gets}{what\ the\ customer\ pays}$$

The customer may do this calculation mentally, making a quick assessment of the value they get from products and services they buy or consider buying. They may also carry out a more detailed value analysis, assessing and evaluating all the factors that contribute to overall value. Value analysis is common in organisational buying, where buyers may assess value using mathematical models or formulas.

Customer value reflects a wide variety of factors, depending on the nature of the product. For consumers they could include

- the availability of information on the product to help the consumer make a decision
- the convenience of retail outlets
- how the consumer was treated by sales or customer service personnel
- ease of payment
- delivery
- operating instructions
- the performance and durability of the product
- the functions of the product
- maintenance cost.

For businesses, value would also be assessed on a variety of factors. These might include

- the length of customer lead time (the time it takes from the order to receiving the product)
- variation from promised delivery times
- the condition of the product on arrival
- sales calls and order initiation requirements
- credit, billing and payment procedures
- the effectiveness of after-sales support
- the manual and instructions accompanying the product
- the performance, fit and function of the product
- the frequency and duration of downtime
- maintenance cost and difficulty.

The lists above are not exhaustive, but they show that value can be measured in a variety of ways. Depending on the nature of the product or service, customers will assess value according to factors such as these.

The implications of this for the marketer are the need to understand how customers measure value, and how the marketer can maximise value for the customer. The designing, manufacturing, marketing and support processes that the firm engages in will be the main sources of value for the customer. Firms therefore engage in what we can describe as a *value-adding* process. From the buying of raw material to production, branding, distribution, image-making—in fact all the activities of the firm—we see the value-adding process in action.

Marketing involves adding value. The activities of marketers, such as researching new features and benefits, branding, and advertising, involve adding value. This book examines the different ways in which marketers add value.

EXCHANGE, TRANSACTIONS, AND RELATIONSHIPS

Marketing is an exchange process. Typically, we exchange money for products and services. However, not all exchange involves money. We can exchange anything that has value: for example, organisations such as the Samaritans do not charge for their service, which involve the exchange of time, advice, and counselling.

Bagozzi (1975) considers that there are three types of exchange: restricted, generalised, and complex. *Restricted exchange* refers to two-party reciprocal relationships, for example retailer-consumer. *Generalised exchange* involves univocal reciprocal relationships among at least three actors. This can be illustrated with an example. The National Tidy Towns competition is sponsored by the Super Valu retail chain. The Tidy Towns organisation negotiated sponsorship with Super Valu; it also liaises with local communities and encourages participation. If people from these communities patronise Super Valu outlets as a result, this would be a generalised exchange. The third type of exchange suggested is *complex exchange*, which refers to a system of mutual relations among at least three parties. A typical example of complex exchange would be manufacturer-retailer-consumer.

Transactions are a trading of values between two parties. While most transactions involve some form of monetary payment, this is not always the case. Bringing glass bottles to a bottle bank for recycling is a transaction, but it does not involve any monetary exchange between the consumer and the marketer. Transactions may also involve the customer trading in an older product in part-exchange for a newer one; this is common in the car market and has been used in electrical goods retailing. The important point is that in any exchange a value is placed on what is being exchanged.

The notion of exchange has been developed into the concept of *relationship marketing*. Relationship marketing implies that the firm attempts to build relationships between itself and its customers, suppliers, and distributors—in other words, with any individual or firm it exchanges or wishes to exchange with. The central idea is that these interactions should be viewed as relationships involving the exchange of value.

The concept of relationship marketing helps illustrate the nature of value. In the case of the marketer-retailer exchange, for example, the relationship does not simply involve physical distribution but also involves other factors, such as market development, co-operation in marketing and distribution campaigns, and mutual problem-solving. If the marketer and retailer view their arrangements as a relationship that can be developed to be mutually beneficial, it is more probable that improved performance and profitability will follow. If the relationship is viewed as confrontational, this may be less probable.

The development of relationship marketing theory gathered pace in the nineteen-nineties. The creation, development and quality of relationships are at the core of marketing.

This was well illustrated by the academic Christian Grönroos (1994) when he argued that relationship marketing was in effect a 'paradigm shift' in marketing theory. By this he meant that relationship marketing had led to a fundamental shift in the theory underlying marketing.

Many models and approaches were developed to help explain the concept of relationship marketing. A model developed by Evans and Laskin (1994), for example, proposed that there are three important elements to be considered: inputs, outputs, and assessment. The principal inputs were understanding customers' expectations, building service partnerships, empowering employees, and total quality management (TQM) schemes. The results of relationship marketing were customer satisfaction, customer loyalty, product quality, and profitability. The success of relationship marketing efforts could be assessed through customer feedback and by assessing how integrated the marketer's operations were as a result.

The theory of relationship marketing is a useful framework for understanding the concepts underlying marketing theory. It is also fundamental to the development of marketing practice. The Evans and Laskin model indicates the inputs, outputs and assessments that will apply, regardless of the nature of the relationship. The marketer can apply the principles of relationship marketing in dealing with suppliers, channel members, and customers. The concept of 'customer', therefore, applies not just to the final customer or consumer but to the other individuals or firms that the marketer deals with.

The marketer-customer relationship is a core aspect of relationship marketing. Viewing the customer as an individual with whom the firm wishes to develop a relationship encourages businesses to look beyond mere transactions. The customer is someone whose needs the firm seeks to serve again and again.

THE MARKET

The *market* describes the actual and potential buyers for the product. In this book we examine markets such as the consumer market, the business-to-business market, and international markets. These are descriptions of different types of market, but all markets have one thing in common: they involve relationships. Whether marketer-consumer, consumer-consumer, or business-business, markets represent a set of relationships.

Market profiling is an important aspect of marketing. Markets exhibit different characteristics and trends, and comprehending and monitoring these is a central aspect of marketing. Understanding the customer is guided by universal principles, but the customer must also be understood in the context of their environment. In the European market, for example, the Irish have the highest per capita consumption of soup but the lowest consumption of pasta, as table 1.1 illustrates.

Table 1.1: Soup and pasta: high and low consumption levels

Soup consumption per capita		Pasta consumption per capita (kg)	
Ireland	£8.08	Italy	25
Netherlands	£7.51	Greece	7.5
Belgium	£6.26	France	6.6
Austria	£6.14	Portugal	5.8
Britain	£5.53	Germany	4.8
Sweden	£4.74	Spain	4.7
Germany	£4.63	Belgium	4.4
France	£3.68	Netherlands	3.9
Finland	£3.06	Denmark	2
Italy	£0.48	Britain	1.5
Greece	£0.29	**Ireland**	1

Source: *Checkout Ireland*, January–February 1997, September 1997.

The different consumption patterns for these products can be explained by a combination of environmental factors and historical market conditions. Obviously, Ireland is a good market for soup marketers, and probably a market with potential for pasta marketers. The point for any marketer is that you must understand the profile and nature of the consumers in your market. Such understanding of the customer, their tastes and preferences, is what leads to successful marketing.

All markets are different. Chapter 3 describes the environmental forces that affect Irish marketers; chapter 12 demonstrates how other environments can be different and where marketing activities and practice may need to be modified.

THE EVOLUTION OF MARKETING

While there have probably always been marketers—though they may not have been described as such—the origin of contemporary marketing has more to do with the industrial revolution. The development of the factory system and the introduction of new forms of transport made selling products to a wider market more feasible. A central aspect of the factory system was large-scale, efficient production. This allowed companies to mass-produce products at attractive prices. The coming of the railways and improvements in shipping technology made possible the expansion of distribution networks. The development of advertising was also stimulated by the industrial revolution, as manufacturers needed to inform new and growing markets about their products.

Marketing evolved as a body of knowledge to meet a need. The growth in markets presented many challenges. Firms needed to plan, organise, develop, communicate and control in an integrated way. Over time, marketing theory developed and was refined to meet these needs; and it continues to develop. Needs change, markets change, and marketing theory is constantly subject to updating and addition. As a discipline, marketing is dynamic: it does not stand still.

With regard to guiding policies, the management of marketing is influenced by five alternative concepts: the production concept, the product concept, the selling concept, the marketing concept, and the social marketing concept.

The production concept

While the factory system did lead to the production and wider availability of products, in many cases it was company managers who decided what to produce; customers were not necessarily consulted. This meant that customers had no say in the process.

Firms that concentrate on production and distribution efficiency demonstrate the production concept. This holds that consumers favour products that are widely available and affordable. This approach is appropriate as long as what is produced is what the customer wants. If the customer wants something else and the firm cannot provide it, they may not buy, or may buy something else. In the air transport market, Ryanair could be considered to follow this approach. The company concentrates on producing a low-cost service. Unlike many of its competitors, it does not offer added benefits, such as in-flight meals or frequent-traveller schemes. The production concept works for this company: it serves a need for low-cost travel, and there is a sufficiently large market with that need.

The production concept may not work in markets where buyers require a high degree of customisation or additional benefits. If a business requires specialist financial advice, for example, it will not be able to buy a mass-produced service.

The product concept

The product concept holds that consumers favour products that offer the highest quality and the greatest number of performance and innovative features. As a result, manufacturers may spend considerable time and effort in improving products by adding new features or benefits. This can also be important in maintaining market share or in reacting to competitors; but improvements must be valued by the market.

As we saw earlier, consumers will make trade-offs. They may like products with many features and high performance levels, but such products may cost more, and the consumer may not be able to afford them. In the search to improve products or add new features, manufacturers or service providers should not lose sight of customers' needs. The launch of compact discs, for example, led to a significant decline in the sale of records. While there is still a small specialist market for records, producers knew that no amount of improvement or added features could save the product. These producers had to view their businesses not as record providers but as audio product providers. Needs changed, and firms in the industry had to react.

It can be shortsighted, however, to follow the product concept too closely, as it can lead to 'marketing myopia'. This implies that the business is concentrating too much on the product and not enough on market needs. The concept of marketing myopia was well illustrated by Theodore Levitt (1960), who used the example of railway companies in the United States, which defined themselves as being in the railway business. The problems with this definition became apparent when competition from road and air became more intense. Levitt argued that the railway companies should have defined themselves as being in the transport business. It would have been myopic for record producers, for example, to ignore the new CD technology and persist with the production of records. What is produced is ultimately determined by customers' needs. If those needs change, businesses have to adapt.

The selling concept

Often people use the terms *selling* and *marketing* as though they meant the same thing. Selling is a function of marketing. Firms seek to sell products and services to make a profit; what they sell should be what the customer wants.

The danger with the selling concept is that the firm concentrates on selling rather than on matching products with needs. It is possible to sell people products they don't need or want. This is not what marketing is about, nor indeed is it what good salesmanship is about. It is myopic to concentrate on getting the sale without worrying about the customer's needs or post-sales satisfaction.

The marketing concept and the social marketing concept

The marketing concept is based on understanding customers' needs and providing competitive products or services to meet those needs, at a profit. Marketing is therefore concerned with understanding the customer, being competitive, and making a profit.

The social marketing concept introduces the idea of being responsive to the well-being of society in general. We can elaborate on both these concepts by examining the role of marketing in the firm and in society.

Marketing plays a number of roles, both internal and external to the firm. It is inseparable from the creation and development of enterprises, whether profit-making or non-profit-making. Whether researching an idea, testing a concept, or launching a product on the market, marketing activities come into play. Marketing plays a role in the initial research and creation of a product; it also sustains and is used to develop the product over its lifetime. Marketing has helped to create many of the products and services we take for granted. It has also helped to create successful products that have become what could be described as consumer icons. Think of products such as Coca-Cola, the Volkswagen 'Beetle', or Nike sports wear: without marketing, would they enjoy the success they have experienced?

Marketing also plays a role in society. It facilitates exchange, leads to the development of products and markets, provides jobs, and is a body of knowledge that allows products, services, places and ideas to be taken from initial thoughts to commercial and profitable reality.

Taking all this into account, what actually makes a marketing-oriented organisation? It is really a combination of factors, but the following list probably sums it up.

A marketing-oriented organisation

- is customer-driven
- is centred on satisfying customers' needs

- has a competitive advantage
- is capable of change
- is responsive to the customer's needs before, during and after the sale of the product
- is profit-driven (whether in financial or non-financial terms)
- is responsive to society's well-being.

According to Quinn (1996), there are three essential questions to be answered: how to get every member of your team working to meet customers' needs (team members also include customers themselves); how to create a bigger and better marketing department than the competition's; and how to reward customer loyalty, as opposed to creating it. Superquinn seems to have managed to answer these questions: the business has grown, profits have increased, and the chain is widely recognised as providing high standards of customer service.

Centred on customers' needs

Being centred on customers' needs implies knowing what those needs are and attempting to serve them better than your competitors. Marketing research plays a role in finding out about customers' needs and monitoring how they change. Research will certainly be useful; it will also be useful to apply common sense. There really is no great mystery in understanding the customer: what is often more mysterious is the ability of firms, with all their resources, to get it wrong.

There have always been businesses that have remained close to their customers and that have always concentrated on customers' needs. In the case of Kelly's Resort Hotel (described in the following panel), this focus involved adapting over time to suit changing needs. This company has been putting marketing theory into practice for several generations.

KELLY'S RESORT HOTEL: LOOKING AFTER THE CUSTOMER SINCE 1895

Started as a tea-room to cater for Sunday beach-goers, Kelly's Resort Hotel in Rosslare has grown over four generations of the Kelly family to become one of the best-known family hotels in Ireland.

The coming of the railway at the turn of the century was a spur to development. Guests could travel from all parts of the country to the hotel. The changing needs of guests over time meant that the company had to react: guests required more than accommodation, food and beverage service. The hotel was the first in Ireland to build an indoor swimming-pool and tennis courts, and it established a strong reputation for its amenities. In addition to providing a high standard of facilities, the hotel also catered for special-interest segments and offered courses in sport, health and beauty, wine-tasting, interior design, and gardening

According to Linda Byron, a senior specialist at the Irish Management Institute, Kelly's is 'an Irish company that excels at looking after their customers and reaping the benefits.' The benefits are expressed in customer satisfaction and profitability. Sometimes up to 90 per cent of rooms are occupied by guests who have been to the hotel before. The organisational culture puts customers ahead of short-term profit; strong leadership is provided by the management; and there are good internal communications. The benefits are also expressed in a string of awards, including several National Hygiene Awards and the Egon Ronay Hotel of the Year award in 1995.

Sources: *Sunday Business Post*, 10 September 1994; *Irish Independent*, 2 March 1996; *Sunday Business Post*, 23 March 1997.

Competitive advantage

Having a competitive advantage means that the business has something with which to differentiate its product or service from that of competitors. Products or services must have *unique selling propositions* (USPs), otherwise customers may not be able to tell them apart. A competitive advantage is therefore a prerequisite of successful marketing. If the product or service is not better than that of competitors on criteria such as quality, price, availability, choice, or image, what is there to market?

Competitive advantage needs to be sustained: successful products and brands need to be kept up to date, and any new market potential needs to be examined. Consider the case of Yoplait yoghurt, a successful brand in Ireland since the nineteen-seventies.

YOPLAIT YOGHURT: STILL BRAND LEADER

Yoplait yoghurt first appeared on the market in 1974, and since then it has been the consistent national brand leader, commanding a 60 per cent share of the yoghurt and *fromage frais* market in 1997. Research on the brand demonstrates that it was consumed in equal proportions by children and young people. This was not surprising, as these were the segments that had always been aimed at. Research also demonstrated that the brand was perceived as the best on the market, and that people had taken ownership of it. They also considered it good for health, convenient, portable, and suitable for all occasions.

Yoplait decided to redefine its brand proposition to drive its usage occasion and to aim at children and adults. A new advertising campaign was created, the central message of which was that Yoplait was 'food for living'. The advertising emphasised that it was a health food with nutritional benefits; it also used strong life-style imagery.

Source: M. Brophy, 'Reid about yoghurt', *Checkout Ireland*, November 1997.

Marketing helps keep this brand in its number 1 position. Its competitive advantage derives from a number of sources. The product satisfies a need in the market and has been successful in responding and adapting to environmental forces, such as changing views on health and life-style. (In chapter 3 we consider the forces in the marketing environment that can present opportunities and threats for the marketer; these forces will affect the company's competitive advantage.) The Yoplait product is aimed at defined market segments, and the brand positioning has been carefully developed. (In chapter 5 we will explore the nature of market segmentation, targeting, and positioning; these play an important role in achieving competitive advantage.) The product, pricing, promotional and distribution strategies employed by the company have also proved effective. (In chapters 7–10 we will examine how these four factors, collectively known as the *marketing mix*, can contribute to competitive advantage.)

Achieving competitive advantage is therefore a significant goal for any business. It is necessary for survival, and marketing plays an important part in achieving it.

Capable of change

The Yoplait example demonstrates the need for change. The launch of a novel dairy product was successful; over time, the product was developed, and its market positioning was changed. Marketers need to be able to adapt to changes in the environment; this ability to change will be necessary to sustain competitive advantage. Change in response to environmental forces both internal and external to the firm will be necessary. These forces are considered in more detail in chapter 3; for the moment, change can be illustrated by examining one force that has affected marketing in many ways: technology.

Technology is a source of competitive advantage, not simply by adding value to the consumer with improved products and services but also through its role in the practice of marketing. Technology is also a threat: it can become obsolete, quickly rendering the firm's products, services and management practices uncompetitive. The nineteen-nineties saw increased attention paid to what was referred to as 'electronic commerce'—this describes sharing business information, maintaining business relationships and conducting business transactions by means of telecommunications networks (Zwass, 1996). The applications of electronic commerce in marketing are widespread. It was argued that they would have most impact in developing and maintaining customer relationships, direct marketing, finding new segments or markets, and linking the core business processes (Harrington and Reed, 1996). Obviously, the staff of a company need to know how to use this technology, which has implications for recruitment and the development of skills.

Information technology in particular has been very influential. The marketer's ability to gather information about customers and markets, generate data-bases, create management information systems and interact with other firms has developed significantly since the nineteen-eighties. Specific marketing practices such as direct marketing, data-base marketing and tele-marketing have all grown as a result. *Electronic data interchange* (EDI) has had particular application in marketing channels. (These marketing applications will be explored in chapters 9 and 10.)

In the late nineteen-nineties many organisations began to develop sites on the worldwide web and use of the internet increased. The internet allowed companies to communicate with existing and potential customers and also allowed them to offer new services.

INTERNET BANKING

In November 1997 customers of Allied Irish Banks who registered for 24-hour telephone banking could also sign up for internet banking. This allowed them, for the price of a local phone call anywhere in the world, to carry out transactions on their own accounts or between other AIB accounts. Balances could be viewed, and phone, electricity, gas and cable television bills could be paid. The service was considered very convenient for people who worked away from home a lot but also for customers who liked to keep a close eye on their spending or those who didn't live near an AIB branch.

The main barriers to greater use of the service were seen as the relatively high cost of internet access. The user would require a relatively high-specification computer, a modem, a telephone line, and an account with an internet service provider. As the internet diffused in the market, however, it seemed probable that costs would come down and that more customers would use internet services.

Source: AIB Bank, 1998.

Many commentators in the late nineties were enthusiastic about the internet and its potential as a global business medium. In 1998 it was predicted that the number of subscribers in Europe would grow from 7 per cent of the population to 13 per cent by 2001 (*Business Week*, 11 May 1998). Use of the internet would be most significant in business-to-customer communications and transactions. There also existed the *extranet—*inter-organisational networks, for example between a marketer and a retailer. This would have significant applications in business-to-business marketing (see chapter 13). *Intranets* are networks within an organisation, for example between departments within a large organisation. An intranet would therefore be useful for internal marketing applications (see chapter 3).

Responsive before, during, and after

Marketing is concerned with developing a relationship with the customer. This relationship begins before the product or service is sold; it may involve significant interaction during the sale, and it continues after the sale has been made. Marketers need to be just as concerned about post-purchase satisfaction as with the factors that precede the sale. Factors such as creating awareness or sales technique are important aspects of pre-sales activity; but marketing does not end there.

The development of relationships is at the heart of the theory of relationship marketing. Firms must manage a number of relationships. The marketer-customer relationship is the obvious one, but there also exist marketer-supplier, marketer-intermediary and marketer-marketer relationships. Whatever the nature of the relationship, it should be managed in such a way that it develops and will last.

In chapter 6 the factors that influence behaviour before, during and after the purchase are examined. It would be myopic for marketers to concentrate only on the actual purchase. There are many pre-purchase influences in the buyer's environment; equally, post-purchase factors such as satisfaction must also be considered.

Profit-driven

Profit, for most firms, is the reward for entrepreneurial effort and is required by investors and shareholders in the business. It is also required to ensure the continued survival of most businesses. For some organisations, profit may not be measured in purely financial terms. There are many non-profit organisations that measure success in more intangible ways. Charities and cultural organisations, for example, do not exist to make profits for shareholders: their success may be measured in aid provided, support given, or heritage protected. Marketing principles are equally relevant to these organisations, for they are also involved in exchanging something of value.

Responsive to society's well-being

Marketing activities are carried out within society. They should not do anything to damage that society. This demonstrates the importance of ethical marketing practice.

Ethics is defined as generally accepted views of what is right and wrong. Ethical practice requires the firm to be socially responsible. Marketers have to serve the needs of society, and activities that do not do so can hardly be described as customer-centred. There is certainly a paradox if marketing appears to be unethical when its objectives are concerned with responding to consumers' needs.

Given the nature of marketing practice and activities, it is not surprising that ethical issues have emerged. Typical issues include misleading advertising, dubious pricing practices, and sales approaches being made under the guise of market research. Relative to the consumer, the marketer is usually in a more powerful position. This means that if the business loses sight of the core marketing principle of serving the customer, the customer may be compromised.

Marketing is not a regulated profession in the same way that pharmacy or medicine are. But codes of ethics do exist in specific areas of marketing practice, such as market research and advertising. The Marketing Institute in Ireland also has a code of practice, which outlines the professional responsibility and conduct required of its members. This code provides a useful overview of the responsibilities, conduct and values that should be a feature of good marketing practice.

CODE OF PRACTICE OF THE MARKETING INSTITUTE

The code states that professional marketing executives have responsibility to their employers or clients, to customers, to colleagues, to the marketing profession, and to the public in general.

It describes the importance of professional conduct, obliging members to conduct themselves at all times as people of integrity and to observe the principles of the code. In this way the reputation of members of the institute, the institute itself and of marketing in general will be enhanced.

The code describes the nature of professional conduct with regard to the instruction of others, injury to other members, honesty, professional competence, conflict of interest, confidentiality, and the securing and developing of business. It also obliges members to be aware of and to comply with other relevant codes of practice in advertising, sales promotion, market research, public relations, and direct marketing.

The institute can investigate and take action against members where breaches of the code have occurred.

Source: Marketing Institute of Ireland.

There are also various laws and regulations that govern the way in which business is done (some of these and their implications are considered in chapter 3). These are part of the environmental forces that affect marketers. Very often it is the way in which business is done that comes in for criticism. Consider the case of 'alcopops', which caused a good deal of controversy in the nineteen-nineties.

ALCOPOPS

In 1995 alcoholic carbonated drinks or 'alcopops' were launched on the Irish market. They proved to be a controversial product category. The products, which had a sweet non-alcoholic taste and fashionable packaging graphics, were accused of encouraging under-age drinking.

The brand leader, Woody's, marketed by United Beverages, introduced a code setting out standards for packaging, labelling, merchandising, and advertising. In spite of this, some supermarket chains removed them from their shelves, Feargal Quinn commenting that 'there seems not to be enough mechanisms in place to prevent the sale of alcopops to under-age drinkers.' In 1997 the Minister for Consumer Affairs described them as 'insidious concoctions, cynically aimed at the impressionability of youth.' In response the Woody's brand had its packaging revised, with the removal of the frog image it had been using, and new, more adult graphics were added.

The controversy also encouraged the distributors of spirit-fruit mixes, such as Smirnoff Mule, Bacardi Breezer, and Pernod Hex, to distance themselves from the alcopops. They described their products as brand extensions in the 'spirit pre-mix' category, lest they were confused with alcopops.

In spite of the publicity and controversy surrounding the products, many drink retailers considered that it might be just a passing fad. Once the novelty appeal wore off the products, it was argued, they could even disappear.

Source: 'Retailers say that alcopops market is declining', *Checkout Ireland*, September 1997.

On occasion, marketing activities such as advertising or promotions are criticised. The following example outlines the criticism levelled at the Tesco supermarket chain and the petrol retailer Esso, which had joined forces in a promotion aimed at schools.

THE TESCO COMPUTERS-FOR-SCHOOLS PROMOTION

The Minister for Education criticised Tesco and Esso for hard-sell tactics in their computers-for-schools marketing promotion. The companies had sent letters to schools—to be forwarded to parents—asking them to buy Tesco and Esso products so as to earn coupons towards a computer. The National Parents' Council and the Consumers' Association also criticised the tactics.

Parents got one voucher for every £10 they spent in any Tesco shop or Esso service station. A school had to accumulate 15,000 vouchers for a computer. Tesco expected to distribute a thousand computers, worth a million pounds, through the scheme.

The minister had launched the scheme but stated that he was concerned about pressure being put on schools and parents to become involved in the marketing and promotion of commercial products. The National Parents' Council, while they considered that a letter home might serve a useful purpose in making parents aware of the promotion, drew the line at any pressure, however subtle, being exerted on parents to shop at particular outlets. The Consumers' Association warned parents to look carefully at the scheme.

Source: J. McManus, 'Irish rap Tesco tactics on computers-for-schools offer', *Sunday Times*, 5 April 1998.

In the late nineteen-nineties, ethics was a much-debated topic in Ireland. Ethical issues and dilemmas were raised in business, politics, sports, and religion; issues such as tax evasion, sexual abuse and fraud were given much media attention. It was not the first time that such issues had emerged, but that so many emerged in quick succession was a source of unease for many. In the business world, several cases were brought to notice, including that of National Irish Bank.

BANK ADMITS UNAUTHORISED TAKING OF CUSTOMERS' MONEY

In March 1998 National Irish Bank admitted that it took money improperly from some customers' accounts in the late nineteen-eighties and early nineties. It also admitted knowing about this since the early nineties, but it had not returned the money or informed the customers affected. The bank's admission followed allegations made by journalists working for RTE. The bank admitted that it had engaged in 'interest loading', or charging illegitimate interest on current accounts, in five of its branches. It stated that it would now seek to identify and reimburse those affected by sharp practice.

National Irish Bank had also come under the spotlight earlier in the year when it was claimed that some customers used offshore investment bonds to hide money from the Revenue Commissioners.

Source: *Irish Times*, 26 March 1998.

Given the complexities of business, the ethical issues and dilemmas raised can also be complex. By putting the customer first, however, it is less likely that a firm or its employees would engage in unethical practice. Firms should have a code of ethics, which would communicate what its priorities, values and expectations are. The code should be published and should send a clear signal to everyone in the firm that ethics are a priority. In the words of one commentator (Tierney, 1992), 'people weigh the ethical implications of their decisions not only by their personal values but also by the working environment created by the leadership.' The difficulty for a large firm such as National Irish Bank can be in ensuring that ethical practice prevails in all areas and at all levels in the company. The practices described above may have arisen in a small number of branches or cases, but they brought the entire firm into the spotlight.

Codes of ethics will be useful only to the extent that people can understand them. Some firms have therefore invested in training programmes. These can involve examining organisational values, presenting people with ethical dilemmas, analysing ethical issues, and weighing up the consequences of particular actions. Codes and training are important, but they also need to be implemented and adhered to. The values incorporated in the code can be incorporated in the firm's performance appraisal system. This would imply that the firm's marketing personnel, for example, would be evaluated not just on criteria such as sales or profitability but also on the ethical performance of their role.

MARKETING PRACTICE IN IRELAND

We have examined the nature of marketing and looked at how it has evolved as a theory. It is also useful to consider how marketing practice evolved in Ireland.

As in other countries, marketing as a specific function began to appear in Irish companies in the nineteen-fifties. The following table presents a chronology of some of the important developments since then. Marketing was not a completely new idea: there were many firms that had always been marketing-oriented; what was new for most firms was the establishment of a specific marketing function. This was spurred on by the post-war development of domestic and international markets.

Table 1.2: Some important developments in marketing in Ireland

1952	Córas Tráchtála established
1962	Marketing Institute of Ireland established
1965	Sectoral Committee on Industrial Organisation criticises marketing practice Anglo-Irish Free Trade Area Agreement opens the way for increased competition
1968	Federation of Irish Industry expresses concern about lack of prominence of marketing
1973	Ireland joins the European Economic Community, implying more competition
1982	Telesis Report on Industrial Policy considers marketing to be a major weakness in Irish companies

1984   *Ireland and Marketing* report leads to debate about the state of marketing practice.
1987   First Minister of State for Trade and Marketing appointed
1992   Culliton Report suggests specific marketing initiatives
1997   Research by the Marketing Institute demonstrates that marketing will become more influential in Irish companies

In 1952 Córas Tráchtála, which had been established to promote the export of Irish products, employed American consultants to assess the export potential of some firms. They concluded that the firms should not try exporting, because they had not got quality products and had no inclination to take risks. The report also identified marketing as a weakness in the companies they studied (Ward, 1987).

In 1962 the Marketing Institute of Ireland was founded as a representative body for marketing practitioners. Its role involved representing, lobbying, and developing marketing practice. A significant aspect was education and training; this was particularly necessary in the nineteen-sixties and seventies, when many managers had no formal marketing training or education. In 1965 the Sectoral Committee on Industrial Organisation confirmed this when it reported that there were management deficiencies in many firms, inadequate training, inadequate marketing, and poor marketing arrangements.

Also in 1965 the Anglo Irish Free Trade Area Agreement was signed. As a result, Irish firms had to deal with increased competition. Many were unable to cope.

Marketing was still a serious weakness. In 1968 the Federation of Irish Industry was expressing concern that marketing had not been given the prominence it deserved.

Ireland joined the European Economic Community in 1973. This resulted in more competition in the home market, and also opened up greater export possibilities. In the nineteen-seventies and eighties exports rose rapidly and firms came to appreciate the role of marketing and the need to keep in touch with the consumer, especially in markets both physically and culturally removed from the home market. They were reminded of this in the Telesis Report on Industrial Policy (1982), which identified marketing as a central weakness in Irish firms.

A Government report, *Ireland and Marketing* (1984), criticised poor marketing performance by companies and stated that Ireland needed to market its products more effectively for economic growth and survival. The report stated that the failure of firms to adopt a clearly stated strategic marketing orientation was a fundamental weakness in marketing practice. Following the publication of this report there was much discussion on the nature and role of marketing in Irish business (Condon, 1985; Cook, 1987). This was important, as it drew companies' attention to the importance of marketing and the role it should play in the firm. Interesting analogies were drawn; one leading academic asked the question, 'Where are our marketing samurai?' which reflected something of the state of marketing practice at the time and the need for change (Cunningham, 1987).

In 1987 the Government appointed the first Minister of State for Trade and Marketing. This was a recognition of the important role played by marketing. The Culliton Report (1992) emphasised the importance of developing marketing skills in Irish business and suggested that specific marketing initiatives be taken in the food sector.

In 1997 the Marketing Institute of Ireland commissioned research into companies' attitudes to marketing. This showed that more than 80 per cent of companies had a more progressive attitude towards marketing than what had existed five years earlier. As the following panel shows, most respondents considered that marketing would become more influential in the future.

IRISH COMPANIES' ATTITUDES TO MARKETING

The research was carried out for the Marketing Institute by Lansdowne Market Research among 650 senior marketing personnel in the top thousand companies. The response rate was 38 per cent.

Respondents were asked whether they felt marketing would become more influential; as the chart indicates, 81 per cent felt that it would.

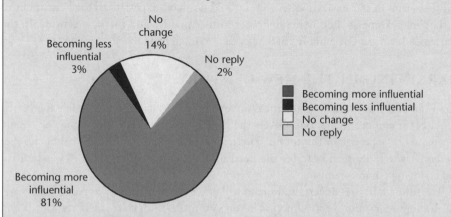

The study also showed that 73 per cent of respondents felt that marketing managers should spend more time listening to their customers. An increased emphasis on results-based marketing programmes by companies was reported by 86 per cent of respondents. Only 39 per cent of firms indicated that their marketing budgets were being increased over the rate of inflation (which in 1997 was 1–2 per cent).

The chairman of the Marketing Institute, Redmond O'Donoghue, chief operating officer of Waterford Wedgwood, expressed concern with this short-term profit approach rather than one of long-term investment. He indicated that Waterford Wedgwood spent 6 per cent of income on marketing, not including personnel costs. This is considerably more than most Irish firms but closer to international brands, such as Gucci and Ralph Lauren, which are believed to spend up to 12 per cent of income on marketing.

Source: F. Mulrennan, 'Survey shows major shift in companies' attitude to marketing', *Irish Times*, 8 August 1997.

The chronology of the development of marketing gives some idea of what has happened over time. It also emphasises the need for firms to keep abreast of change. Customers' needs can change, and firms must be able to change in response. Marketing is therefore a discipline that requires flexibility and adaptability, not least when it comes to planning for the future.

The Superquinn and Kelly's Hotel approach to business has not been replicated by all firms in Ireland. As various reports and commentaries have shown, Ireland has been slow to develop marketing practice. There are a number of reasons for this. Protectionism tended to result in a market with few competitors and limited consumer choice. Industrially there may have been an over-reliance on foreign direct investment and a slow development of indigenous industry.

Many foreign-owned companies established factories in Ireland but carried out their marketing activities elsewhere. As a result, there were few opportunities for managers to develop their marketing skills. Marketing education and training did become a strong feature of the third-level educational system and other relevant educators, such as the Marketing Institute and the Irish Management Institute, particularly since the nineteen-eighties. Firms in the sixties and seventies would not have experienced the benefit of this to the same extent as their contemporaries in the nineties and the new century. In the years ahead, what are the likely challenges that marketers will face?

MARKETING IN THE NEW CENTURY

The results of the Marketing Institute survey showed that respondents felt marketing would become more influential. Given the timing of this survey, this influence should become more apparent in the future. The review of marketing practice in Ireland over the last few decades demonstrates the need to develop marketing skills in competitive and changing environments.

The future is always uncertain. Ireland will enter the new century as part of a growing and strengthening European Union. The opportunities to develop markets within and outside the European Union are substantial. There will also be competitive threats; firms that cannot change and adapt will face difficulties. Those that maintain close links with their customers and markets should be better prepared for the challenges that will emerge.

It has been argued that in the eighties and early nineties marketing lost some of its strength by overt functionalism and a concentration on the tactical rather than the strategic (Doyle, 1995). While it is important that marketing functions such as promotions and distribution are carried out effectively, it is equally important to consider the strategic perspective. Doyle proposed an approach to marketing management based on internal and external networks. He argued that a marketing approach based on what he considered to be the core processes of innovation, operations and customer support is necessary for marketing to remain at the core of the business. It is easy for businesses to lose sight of the core policy of marketing and to concentrate on functions or particular aspects of the business. New technological developments, for example, may mesmerise, but firms should be careful to avoid falling into a situation where they cannot see the wood for the trees.

The Economist Intelligence Unit (1991) suggested that the main political, economic and social trends affecting marketing strategy in the years ahead would be globalisation, world peace and stability, demographic shifts, environmentalism, changing technologies, south-east Asia as an economic force, and Europe as a single market. These environmental trends are examined in more detail in chapter 3; suffice it to say here that these will all have implications for marketing strategies.

The management of marketing will change. The marketing policy will not change, however. Customers will still be at the centre of the business. The way in which those customers are served, the products or services they buy, how the firm may communicate or deliver to them may change. Marketers will therefore need to keep abreast of environmental developments. Technological change may be particularly important; the guiding principle, however, will remain the same.

MARKETING AND ENTERPRISE

The interface between marketing and entrepreneurship is significant. Marketing plays a crucial role in the creation and development of enterprise. All aspects of marketing practice have one common denominator: they are all part of the value-adding process, whereby firms add value to serve the needs of consumers.

This value-adding process essentially describes what the business does. It therefore includes the development of new and improved products, innovation, and entrepreneurship. Marketing practice also involves the creation and development of specialist marketing enterprises that service other firms, for example advertising agencies and market research companies. Marketing and marketing practice can therefore provide opportunities for new business ventures. (The critical role of marketing in enterprise development is further explored in chapter 2.)

THE NATURE OF MARKETING MANAGEMENT

Marketing management is concerned with how the different elements of marketing are organised, planned, and controlled. It describes what the businessperson or marketing personnel actually do. These activities can range from carrying out marketing research, developing communication campaigns and selling to the development of marketing strategies to take the firm successfully into the future.

This book introduces the principal elements of marketing in relation to the decisions the marketer has to make. These decisions are based on an understanding of the concepts underlying marketing, which ultimately revolve around understanding the customer. The marketer will therefore need to appreciate the forces at work in the marketing environment and understand the nature of consumer behaviour. Marketing research will be vital in doing this.

Decisions will be made on segmenting markets, on selecting particular segments, and on how best to position products. Marketing planning prepares the business for the challenges in the market. Management of the marketing mix, which includes four elements—the product, price, promotion, and place—is a significant aspect of the marketer's role. Marketing practice may need to be adapted to suit what the marketer is marketing. The nature of services marketing, business-to-business marketing, international marketing and marketing for non-profit organisations is also important.

In exploring the nature of marketing management it is useful to examine the relationships between marketing, customer service, and quality. The three are inter-related concepts, as fig. 1.2 demonstrates.

Fig. 1.2: The relationship between marketing, customer service, and quality

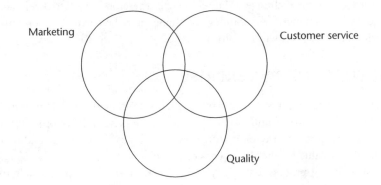

In the preceding sections we have examined the nature of marketing. We have seen how customer service is a strong aspect of the Superquinn approach to business. The importance of quality was also stressed. In the nineteen-eighties considerable emphasis was placed on a total quality approach to business.

Marketing, customer service and total quality management therefore have one crucial factor in common: understanding the needs of the customer. In the following section the broad nature of customer service and total quality management is described.

CUSTOMER SERVICE

Customer service has been defined as all the features, acts and information that augment the customer's ability to realise the potential value of a core product or service (Davidow and Uttal, 1989). Customer service is therefore a vital competitive tool that can be used to differentiate a business from its competitors. Davidow and Uttal considered that there were six important components of customer service: strategy, leadership, people policies, design, infrastructure, and measurement.

Customer service strategy implies matching customers' needs with the company's abilities. This requires segmentation of customers' service needs. In the case of airlines, for example, the service needs of frequent business travellers may be very different from those of the infrequent flier looking for special offers. The airline needs to determine the needs of each segment and match these needs with the required level of service.

Continuous leadership will be required. Managers are required to perform a leadership role, and this role will be facilitated if the culture of the company places a strong emphasis on customer service. Leadership must come from the top of the firm; managers must therefore understand the nature of customer service and lead by example.

We have seen that Superquinn believes that its customers want high levels of personal service, which can only be delivered through people. Organisational staff or customer service personnel will deliver customer service. They must understand customers' needs and be able to respond. The selection, training and development of customer service personnel will be important.

While many aspects of customer service can be delivered only through people, technology can also be used to deliver and augment customer service. If, for example, an airline customer requires only flight time information and no other services, this can easily be provided using the internet, talking timetables, or television-based information services such as Aertel.

The design of customer service implies understanding customer service requirements and translating these into operational procedures. Operating manuals, for example, will specify how service should be delivered and may detail how service personnel should carry out their task. Customer service infrastructure includes any equipment or facilities used to deliver customer service. These include dedicated telephone call centres and increasingly involve the use of information technology. We have already seen how AIB Bank began to provide an internet banking service; it is likely that many more marketers will use the internet as part of their customer service infrastructure.

Measurement of customer service implies a need to research, track and monitor customer service levels to determine whether they meet the needs of customers. If service levels fall short of requirements, causes should be identified and action taken.

The emphasis placed on defining the principal elements of service quality suggested by Davidow and Uttal were reinforced in research carried out by Zeithaml, Parasuraman, and Berry (1990). They carried out extensive qualitative research and developed a service quality model (chapter 11). Their subsequent research indicated that service performance gaps arose for a number of reasons, including role ambiguity of service personnel, role conflict, poor employee-job fit, poor technology-job fit, and inappropriate supervisory control systems, which lead to an inappropriate evaluation or payment system and a lack of teamwork.

TOTAL QUALITY MANAGEMENT

Total quality management (TQM) owes its origins to several researchers and writers on management, most notably Deming (1986), Juran (1989), and Ishikawa (1985). The Japanese led the way in the nineteen-seventies and eighties. Japanese products made huge inroads in many markets. Their main strategy was quality and price competition. Consumers certainly approved and in many product categories, from cameras to cars, responded with increased demand for Japanese products.

Many companies were unable to withstand the challenge, and the survivors realised that they would have to compete on quality. Total quality management grew from this need. It describes an approach to business that looks critically at the products and services a company produces in relation to the processes it takes to create them and the people who do the work to make certain that outputs fully satisfy agreed customer requirements (Bank, 1992).

Total quality management has at its core a focus on the customer. Customers are defined as

- the most important people in any business

- not dependent on the business—the business is dependent on them
- the purpose of everyone's work
- doing us a favour when they give us business
- a part of the business, not just outsiders
- not just statistics
- people with needs and wants
- deserving of the most courteous and attentive treatment we can give
- the lifeblood of any business.

TQM also demonstrates the importance of the *internal customer*. We are familiar with the external customer, the person in the market; internal customers are anyone who receives the work of another within the company. They are as important as the external customer, because they create a chain of quality that reaches out to the customer.

Core concepts of TQM

Total quality management therefore requires an understanding of the fundamental principle of marketing: the customer is at the centre of the business. A number of core concepts underlie TQM, as the following panel demonstrates.

CORE CONCEPTS OF TQM

1. Quality for profit
Profit can be made by improving the quality of products and services. Many companies have achieved additional profit by concentrating on quality, e.g. Ford ('Total quality excellence') and IBM ('Quality focus on the business process').

2. Get it right first time
Strive for perfection in work—*no* defects. Set up systems that prevent defects from happening.

3. Acceptable quality levels
There should be no such thing! For example, if you 'accept' a 99 per cent quality level, what about the 1 per cent? Unsafe drinking water for four days per year; no telephone service for nearly fifteen minutes every day; several thousand wrong prescriptions every year or incorrect surgical procedures carried out in hospitals …

4. Cost of quality
Include prevention costs, appraisal costs, internal failure costs, external failure costs, cost of lost opportunities. These are in effect the costs of poor quality; they can be avoided.

5. Competitive benchmarking
For example, the chief executive officer of Heinz Corporation, Tony O'Reilly, stated: 'While others use starch to thicken their tomato ketchup, Heinz only use tomatoes.' Heinz is attempting to be better than the best competitor in the business.

6. Everyone is involved
Everyone is a customer—the importance of the internal customer.

7. Synergy in teamwork
The sum of the total company is greater than the sum of the individuals who work there.

8. Ownership and elements of self-management
Everybody 'owns' the delivery of quality—not commercial ownership but psychological ownership. You own the problems, the processes, the solutions, the recognition, and the success. Individuals therefore have to engage in self-management—set goals and commitment but equally importantly be given the power required.

9. Managers as role models
Managers are role models for total quality. They have to lead by example.

10. Management feedback
Managers need to be able to get some idea of how they are doing as role models for quality—both from superiors and subordinates. They should not fear feedback.

11. Recognition and reward
Recognition and reward are required for the motivation of staff. They encourage positive attitudes to the concept of quality. Employees are also customers.

12. The quality delivery process
The firm should have an integrated process for delivering quality. This will start with the organisational mission and permeate all functions in the firm. It will describe how quality can be delivered.

Source: Bank, 1992.

Marketing, customer service, and quality: the implications for marketing management

Marketing, customer service and quality have a common theme: an understanding of the customer. In fig. 1.2 this is illustrated where the three sets intersect. In addition, marketing intersects with customer service, customer service with quality, and quality with marketing. Marketing managers need to appreciate these interfaces.

This brings us back to the concept of relationship marketing, which brings together all three elements (Christopher, Payne, and Ballantyne, 1992). Relationship marketing encompasses all the activities before, during and after the sale of the product. Customer service helps create bonds with customers and other markets or groups to ensure long-term relationships of mutual advantage. The provision of quality customer service involves the marketer understanding what the customer needs and determining how to serve that need with a value-added product.

In his book, Quinn (1991) emphasises the importance of listening to the customer—a fairly commonsense approach to understanding customers' needs but one that not every firm follows. He also considers it important to create more customer complaints, which may not at first glance appear to be an ideal tactic. However, customers' complaints provide an opportunity to learn. If the customer has taken the trouble to complain, it is in the business's interest to react; if they don't, or do so badly, the customer is unlikely to return. A complaint may ultimately turn into a dissatisfied customer only if you let it. It is therefore important that complaints are welcomed and acted upon. The potential for negative word-of-mouth reputation from customers who have complained and were treated badly, or indeed customers who did not complain because they felt it was pointless, is significant.

Another author (Daffy, 1996) also emphasised the importance of creating customers for life. He emphasised the concept of customer lifetime value. In other words, customers have a lifetime of purchasing ability; the more often they buy from you, the better. Consider the example of the tea market. The Irish are the highest per capita consumers of tea in the world, drinking on average four cups a day. It is this potential or lifetime value that the marketers of tea seek to serve and hold on to. In the tea market there was some concern about the potential of this lifetime value, as the following panel illustrates.

THE TEA MARKET IN IRELAND

In 1997 the Irish tea market was estimated to be worth £45 million. Two brands dominated the market: Lyons, with a 60 per cent share, and Barry's, with a 30 per cent share. Ninety per cent of tea volume sold was in the form of tea bags, though there were regional variations. In Dublin, for example, loose tea accounted for 5 per cent of volume, while in the west it accounted for 15 per cent.

At the end of the nineteen-nineties, tea marketers were a little concerned about the growth prospects in the market. In general, hot drinks were facing a serious challenge from the soft drinks sector. The 15–25 age group, which in previous generations graduated to tea and coffee, was tending to stay with carbonated soft drinks, mineral waters, and fruit juices. This was affecting growth and the attraction of new consumers.

Source: D. Sheeran, 'Tea in the twilight zone?', *Checkout Ireland*, December 1997.

Daffy also demonstrated the importance of getting feedback from the customer and of adopting customer care strategies, systems, and standards. This re-emphasises the core concepts of total quality and quality delivery.

It is important to note that good service for customers is not about surface-level or cosmetic issues: it must emanate from a core strategy. This must be supported internally in the firm, which demonstrates the need for integrated systems so that all departments are aware of and have access to the information required to deliver good service (Knutton, 1996).

JUMPING ON BANDWAGONS

One of the difficulties inherent in a discipline such as marketing, where new ideas and concepts are rapidly evolving, is determining the appropriateness of these for the company and its customers. There are dangers inherent in merely being a follower rather than assessing the relevance of particular actions for the company and its customers. In the rush to apply the principles of relationship marketing, for example, or to design customer loyalty schemes or develop a web site, companies should be careful not to lose sight of the customer's needs. Levitt (1975) warned of avoiding marketing mania, in other words becoming obsessively responsive to every passing whim of the customer.

Marketers need also to avoid alienating customers with reactive approaches to environmental changes. The development of the company-customer relationship needs to be carefully managed, and unwanted advances, for example in the name of relationship marketing, should be avoided (Griffith, 1998). Judgment should also be used in assessing new marketing tools or techniques. The pros and cons should be evaluated before decisions are made.

FURTHER READING

Carlson, J., *Moments of Truth*, Cambridge (Mass.): Ballinger 1987.
Daffy, C., *Once a Customer, Always a Customer,* Dublin: Oak Tree Press 1996.
Quinn, Feargal, *Crowning the Customer*, Dublin: O'Brien Press 1990.

DISCUSSION QUESTIONS

1. Explain why all organisations are not marketing-oriented. List examples of organisations you would consider to be very customer-oriented and some that are not.
2. The survey by the Marketing Institute (page 23) suggested that more importance should be given to marketing. State why you think marketing will become more important.
3. Is there an inherent conflict between the concepts of marketing and ethics? Were 'alcopops' or the computers-for-schools promotion unethical?
4. Why do you think total quality management became more important in the nineteen-eighties and nineties? Was it because firms were not marketing-oriented?
5. Do you think that an ability to accept and implement change is an important requirement for success in marketing? Give reasons for your answer.
6. Using fig. 1.2, list the possible interactions between marketing and quality, between marketing and customer service, and between quality and customer service.

REFERENCES

Bagozzi, R., 'Marketing as exchange', *Journal of Marketing*, vol. 39, October 1975.
Bank, J., *The Essence of Quality Management*, Englewood Cliffs (NJ): Prentice-Hall 1992.
Christopher, M., Payne, A., and Ballantyne, D., *Relationship Marketing: Bringing Quality, Customer Service and Marketing Together*, London: Butterworth-Heinemann 1992.
Condon, S., 'Marketing the key to growth', *Business and Finance*, November 1985.
Consultative Committee on Marketing, *Ireland and Marketing: Report of the Sectoral Development Committee*, Dublin: Stationery Office 1984.
Cook, T., 'What's wrong with Irish marketing practice?', *Irish Business*, October 1987.
Culliton, J., *The Culliton Report*, Dublin: Stationery Office 1992.
Cunningham, A., 'Where are our marketing samurai?' (presentation to Campus Ireland—Commerce and Industry), University College, Dublin, September 1987.

Daffy, C., *Once a Customer, Always a Customer*, Dublin: Oak Tree Press 1996.

Davidow, W., and Uttal, B., *Total Customer Service: The Ultimate Weapon*, Harper Perennial 1989.

Deming, W., *Out of the Crisis*, Cambridge: Cambridge University Press 1986.

Doyle, P., 'Marketing in the new millennium', *European Journal of Marketing*, vol. 29 (1995), no. 13.

Federation of Irish Industry, *Annual Report*, 1968.

Griffith, V., 'Knowing when to be of service', *Financial Times*, 12 February 1998.

Harrington, L., and Reed, G., 'E-commerce (finally) comes of age', *McKinsey Quarterly*, 1996, no. 2.

Ishikawa, K., *What is Total Quality Control?: The Japanese Way*, Englewood Cliffs (NJ): Prentice-Hall 1985.

Juran, J., *Leadership for Quality: An Executive Handbook*, New York: Free Press 1989.

Knutton, P., 'Customer strategy: start at the core, not at the edges', Works Management, July 1996.

Kotler, P., *Marketing Management: Analysis, Planning, and Control*, Englewood Cliffs (NJ): Prentice-Hall 1987.

Kotler, P., Armstrong, G., Saunders, J., and Wong, V., *Principles of Marketing* (European edition), Englewood Cliffs (NJ): Prentice-Hall 1996.

Kotler, P., and Levy, S., 'Broadening the concept of marketing', *Journal of Marketing*, 10–15 January 1969.

Lawther, S., Hastings, G., and Lowry, R., 'De-marketing: putting Kotler and Levy's ideas into practice', *Journal of Marketing Management*, May 1997.

Levitt, T., 'Marketing myopia', *Harvard Business Review*, July–August 1960.

Levitt, T., 'Marketing myopia: retrospective commentary', *Harvard Business Review*, September–October 1970.

Maslow, A., 'A theory of human motivation', *Psychological Review*, no. 50, 1943

Quinn, Feargal, *Crowning the Customer*, Dublin: O'Brien Press 1991.

Quinn, Feargal, 'Becoming a customer-driven organisation: three key questions', *Managing Service Quality*, vol. 6 (1996), no. 6.

Sectoral Committee Report on Industrial Organisation, Dublin: Stationery Office 1965.

Telesis Consultancy Group, *A Review of Irish Industrial Policy* (ESRI report no. 64), Dublin: Economic and Social Research Institute 1982.

Tierney, E., 'Lessons from the scandals', *Management*, January 1992.

Ward, J., 'Marketing myopia in industrial development', *Irish Marketing Review*, vol. 2 (1987).

Zeithaml, V., Parasuraman, A., and Berry, L., *Delivering Quality Customer Service: Balancing Customer Perceptions and Expectations*, New York: Free Press 1990.

Zwass, V., 'Electronic commerce: structures and issues', *International Journal of Electronic Commerce*, 1996.

2

Marketing and Enterprise Development

Chapter 1 drew attention to the importance of understanding customers' needs. Understanding needs is a fundamental starting-point for establishing a new business venture or developing an existing business. If a firm gets into difficulties, marketing will also play a role in the refocusing and turnaround efforts. Firms exist to serve needs, and an understanding of marketing is required if the firm is to understand these. The survival and development of a business will ultimately depend on its ability to serve market needs.

The formation and development of enterprises is important for Irish society, as it creates wealth and provides jobs. Historically, the establishment of new indigenous business ventures has not met the needs of society in job creation and economic development. As a result, state involvement and foreign direct investment have been significant. In the last two decades there is some evidence of change. Greater encouragement has been given to indigenous enterprise in the form of support services available from both the public and the private sector. Marketing will be fundamental in any attempts to increase the level of entrepreneurial activity in Ireland. Marketing can help identify unserved needs in both the domestic and the international market. It will play a role in researching those needs and developing, communicating and delivering the product to the market.

As the firm grows and develops, marketing will continue to be a vital feature. In subsequent chapters the principal elements of the firm's marketing management and practice are described and illustrated. Activities such as marketing research and the development of new products play an important role in continuing business success.

Marketing is also important if the business faces difficult circumstances, such as recession, declining sales, or performance difficulties. The firm may require a complete turnaround. In this chapter we explore the links between marketing and enterprise development and examine the role of marketing in achieving continued business success.

This chapter seeks to define the nature of entrepreneurship and intrapreneurship; to demonstrate the importance of entrepreneurship and intrapreneurship to Irish society; to evaluate the link between marketing and entrepreneurship and intrapreneurship; to describe the sources of new business ideas; to explain the role of marketing in enterprise development; and to analyse the role of marketing in corporate turnaround.

THE NATURE OF ENTREPRENEURSHIP AND INTRAPRENEURSHIP

Entrepreneurship is the fundamental principle underlying the establishment of most business and commercial activities. It is the process of organising, operating and assuming the risk of a business venture (Low and MacMillan, 1988). It typically characterises the start-up of small business operations. *Intrapreneurship* describes the initiation of ventures within a larger firm. The concepts and practice of marketing are inseparable from both entrepreneurship and intrapreneurship.

Both entrepreneurship and intrapreneurship are necessary for the creation, growth and development of business. In Ireland, economic commentators have considered that there is a weakness in entrepreneurship. This has largely been ascribed to cultural and historical factors, which it is felt discouraged or inhibited enterprise. Entrepreneurs apply marketing practice to research, develop and manage their enterprises. Marketing is a requirement for continuing success.

Intrapreneurs, while not assuming the risk of the business venture, will also apply marketing practices, such as research, product development, the generation of ideas, or innovative promotional and communication campaigns.

ENTREPRENEURSHIP AND IRISH SOCIETY

Successive economic commentaries on the Irish state since independence in 1922 have demonstrated the need for enterprise. Whether through direct state involvement or the encouragement of indigenous enterprise, the importance of the concept has long been recognised and has become a significant aspect of economic policy. In the nineteen-eighties the Telesis Report (1982) on industrial policy recommended that more support be given to indigenous enterprise. In the nineties the Culliton Report (1992) also recommended that more support be given to indigenous entrepreneurs. Entrepreneurship is encouraged because of the role that entrepreneurs play in society. This role can be broadly summarised under three headings: innovation, job creation, and linkages.

Innovation

Entrepreneurs and intrapreneurs foster innovation. They may create products and processes new to the world, or developments and improvements to existing ones. By using their ideas, skills and resources they are an engine for economic growth. Many products that we use every day as consumers or for our work—such as calculators, microwave ovens, and personal computers—were originally developed by entrepreneurial or intrapreneurial minds. Innovations and treatments in health care have contributed to a longer life expectancy; again, many of these were the result of entrepreneurial and intrapreneurial activities. The example of Iona Technologies illustrates how a successful business was established on the basis of innovation.

IONA TECHNOLOGIES

Iona Technologies, which specialises in the development of computer programs, developed from a 'campus company' formed in 1991 in Trinity College, Dublin, by a lecturer, Chris Horn. This status allowed Horn and his colleagues three years in which to reduce their day-to-day involvement in the university and take a proportionate reduction in salary. At the end of three years they had the option of leaving the university and going full-time. Horn and his colleagues decided to go with the business, and Iona moved from Trinity College to offices nearby in the city centre.

Iona was innovative not just in the products it developed but also in the way it marketed them. Direct contacts were established with target customers in person or through using e-mail and the internet. The approach paid dividends, and Iona now includes firms such as Ericsson, Nike, Boeing and Cable and Wireless among its customers. By 1997 Iona was employing 420 people. Seventy per cent of its business was in the United States, 10 per cent in Asia, and the remainder in Europe.

Source: *Sunday Business Post*, 26 October 1997.

Job creation

In general, smaller business and commercial ventures tend to create more jobs than larger ones. There are more small business and commercial firms than larger ones. With regard to state support and grants it is estimated that jobs can be generated in small businesses at a much lower cost per job than larger ones. Many smaller businesses operate in areas where large-scale job developments may be rare but where even a small number of jobs can prevent significant depopulation. Consider the example of small manufacturers in the food and beverage sector.

IRISH FOOD AND BEVERAGES

Since the nineteen-eighties a large number of small enterprises have been established in various parts of Ireland to manufacture food and beverages. Companies such as Lakeshore Mustard in County Tipperary, Folláin Jams and Preserves in County Cork, Cucina pastas and sauces in County Leitrim and Ferndale Quail in County Monaghan have sought to establish their products not just on the Irish market but internationally.

Many of these small enterprises are established in areas where there may not be significant job opportunities. Some are in rural areas where there has been some depopulation. All would be classified as SMEs, but collectively the sector provides a significant number of jobs. A common characteristic of all of them is the development of quality branded products, which typically compete in well-selected market niches.

Linkages

Many small business ventures establish linkages with larger firms, for example to supply raw materials, components or services that the larger undertaking may need, such as catering, transport, or security. Many channel members will be small businesses with linkages to larger manufacturers or service providers. These satellite businesses create jobs and contribute to the success of the larger firm; they are a source of information to larger businesses. They may have direct contact with customers, and any innovation they engage in will ultimately benefit the larger firm. The catering firm Campbell Bewley's was originally a sub-supply caterer, as the following panel shows.

CAMPBELL BEWLEY'S

Campbell Catering was founded in 1967. It expanded its catering operations in line with the number of factories that came with industrial development and ultimately stopped event catering and concentrated on contract catering for factories, hospitals, offices, and universities. In the late seventies the company began catering for the oil exploration industry, and operations began in Asia. In 1986 the company took over Bewley's Oriental Cafés, which had been established in 1843, and the company became Campbell Bewley's.

Campbell Bewley's expanded rapidly. Turnover in 1996 was £68 million, and by 1997 it had nineteen cafés in Ireland. The contract catering business had also expanded and included a contract to supply catering services at both ends of the Channel Tunnel. The company made an acquisition in the United States in 1997 with a chain of eleven cafés in Massachusetts costing £9.3 million. It planned to launch Bewley's branded coffee into these. By late 1997 the company was investigating the possibility of a stock market flotation to finance its international expansion.

Source: P. Campbell, 'Bringing the shareholder close to the customer', presentation to Marketing Institute and Institute of Directors, 29 March 1994; C. Murphy, 'Bewley's eyes flotation option to fund expansion', *Sunday Times*, 28 October 1997.

INTRAPRENEURSHIP

Intrapreneurs are enterprising individuals who work in successful organisations. This implies that, just as with entrepreneurs, there are enterprising traits and characteristics that the organisation can develop. The organisation has a role in the development of intrapreneurs in the form of support and encouragement.

Intrapreneurs share the traits of entrepreneurs and may indeed go on to establish their own business and become entrepreneurs. Intrapreneurs typically are people with good commercial insights. They are capable of understanding the forces at work in the business environment and are able to adapt to them. Intrapreneurs will spot opportunities and will usually possess innovative and creative abilities. They will have a capacity for analysis, implementation and control and will be good problem-solvers. It is likely that they will be good communicators and will have the ability to work with others.

Intrapreneurs will usually possess skills that suit them for marketing, communication and creative roles in the business. It is important for the firm to recognise the talents and intrapreneurial potential of individuals, as these can lead to mutually beneficial and profitable activities.

Intrapreneurship and society

Intrapreneurship will take place within the firm, but its results will ultimately benefit society to the extent that they lead to the development of new and better products, increased employment, and employee motivation and satisfaction. Intrapreneurship may also involve the creation of linkages. Fundamentally, intrapreneurship should benefit the firm in growth, profit, and employee commitment and motivation. In the case of Donnelly Mirrors, intrapreneurship led to the development of a new product and increased employment.

GLARE-FREE MIRRORS GENERATE NEW JOBS IN KILDARE

An innovation in rear-view car mirrors that cuts down night-time glare contributed to the creation of 190 new jobs at Donnelly Mirrors in Naas, County Kildare. The company developed and patented the glare-free technology for electrochromic mirrors. During night-time driving, electrochromic mirrors dim automatically to protect drivers from the glare generated by the headlights of following vehicles. The mirrors are produced in Ireland for Continental, American and Japanese car manufacturers.

The mirrors function by employing a thin film of an electrochemical compound that is situated behind the mirror. The compound works in a similar way to photochromatic spectacles, in that it senses the increasing light and decreases glare accordingly. Other models are being developed, such as one that can sense dusk and automatically activate the car lights, and another that can sense rain and turn on the windscreen wipers.

Source: *Sunday Business Post*, 8 June 1997.

Stimulating intrapreneurship

One of the issues that large companies have to contend with is the promotion of an enterprise culture. It can certainly be argued that an enterprise culture in a firm is necessary for the marketing policy to thrive also.

Entrepreneurs will have a personal interest in the success of the venture. This personal interest may be harder to generate in large companies. Internal marketing can certainly play a role in the creation and support of intrapreneurship. *Internal marketing* describes the application of the marketing policy within the firm. (This is discussed in more detail in chapter 3.) The desired result is that employees serve the customers' needs and provide high levels of customer satisfaction. Internal marketing will only be successful, however, to the extent that the firm values and encourages it.

Strategic orientation and organisational style will be significant determining factors in encouraging intrapreneurship (Pearson, 1989). *Strategy* describes what a firm does to achieve its objectives, while *organisational style* describes the way in which the firm operates. (These are considered in more detail in chapter 7.) Strategic orientation and organisational style have implications for organisational success. In addition, Drucker (1994) pointed out that success in the stimulation of enterprise within the firm must lead to strategies that work in the external market. This emphasises the importance of not losing sight of the customer in any entrepreneurial or intrapreneurial activities.

The conditions required for intrapreneurship to flourish in the firm have implications for procedures, structures, management development, performance appraisal, and job content (Jansen and van Wees, 1994). Burnside (1990) suggested that there were a number of stimulants that would improve the corporate climate for creativity and therefore of enterprise. There were also potential obstacles. The stimulants included the person's fellow-workers, the allocation of resources, and the nature of supervision Creating supports for creativity, an environment where challenges were encouraged and creative freedom were also significant stimulants. Obstacles to creativity included insufficient time, a desire to maintain the status quo, internal politics, and the ways in which creativity was evaluated.

Innovation—the process of identifying, creating and delivering new product or service values that did not exist before in the market—is another important factor in the stimulation of enterprise. Together with creativity, it will also be significant in the success of the firm's marketing efforts. Innovation is a prerequisite for enterprise creation and continued survival.

The *corporate culture* prevailing in the firm should therefore encourage creativity and innovation, in addition to an understanding of customers' needs. Corporate culture is the set of values that defines for members what an organisation stands for, how it operates, and what it considers important. The importance of corporate culture as a catalyst for intrapreneurship and a stimulus for a marketing orientation is well illustrated by the case of Southwest Airlines, one of the ten biggest airlines in the United States.

SOUTHWEST AIRLINES

Southwest Airlines was voted the best company to work for in America; it is also the most successful low-cost carrier in the United States. The company, which had sales revenues of £3,400 million in 1996, attributes its success to its culture, which involves teamwork, care, and how it treats people. Its culture is more relaxed than typical corporate America: uniformed employees wear shorts and golf-shirts, there is little bureaucracy and elitism, and it values individual differences and people's opinions.

The company places a lot of emphasis on attitude, recruiting people who have a positive outlook and who want to make a contribution to the company. In 1997 it had 140,000 applicants for 4,000 jobs. Prospective employees must demonstrate their good humour at the interview by cracking a joke or telling a funny story. Rates of pay are not especially attractive, but the company has a profit-sharing scheme, one of the oldest in the airline business, and there is significant potential for upward mobility. Several long-term employees from all levels have retired as millionaires.

Role models are an important aspect of company culture, none more so than Herb Kelleher, chief executive officer and a joint founder of the airline in 1967. He enjoys unrivalled popularity among employees, who are impressed by his approachability and his ability to recall first names.

Profit is promoted in the company as being the product of customer service: indeed the word 'profit' does not appear in the company's mission statement. Costs, however, are kept under tight control.

Source: D. Walsh, 'Ryanair's copycat role model: the best employer in America', *Sunday Business Post*, 12 April 1998.

Corporate culture will therefore play an important role not only in encouraging enterprise but also in instilling a marketing orientation.

THE LINK BETWEEN MARKETING, ENTREPRENEURSHIP, AND INTRAPRENEURSHIP

The link between marketing and both entrepreneurship and intrapreneurship exists at two broad levels: the philosophical and the practical. Marketing as a philosophy, or way of thinking, implies putting the customer at the centre of the business. Ultimately both the entrepreneur and the intrapreneur have to acknowledge that there must be customers for their products or ideas. Putting themselves in the position of the ultimate customer is therefore a prerequisite for success.

One research study concluded that both marketing and entrepreneurship are opportunity-driven, value-creating processes that can be applied in a wide variety of situations (Morris and Lewis, 1995). These would include any exchange relationship. Marketers, entrepreneurs and intrapreneurs, regardless of the nature of their firm, will look for opportunities to serve customers' needs.

At the practical level, the research, product development techniques, strategy, planning and management of the marketing mix will be used by both entrepreneurs and intrapreneurs. In the case of the entrepreneur the responsibility for marketing will rest completely with him or her as owner. In the case of the intrapreneur the responsibility for marketing will probably be corporate and will usually be taken over by the marketing department within the firm. Corporate intrapreneurship, however, is not the preserve of marketers or the marketing department; intrapreneurship should be encouraged among all employees.

There is evidence that, with regard to personality traits, marketing and entrepreneurship are linked. Entrepreneurship can also be linked to other management functions within the business (Foxall and Minkes, 1996). *Personality traits* are any relatively enduring ways in which one person differs from another (Guilford, 1959). Those associated with entrepreneurship include a desire for autonomy, social independence, a high tolerance of ambiguity, and a propensity for risk-taking (West and Farr, 1990). Researchers would also agree that traits such as a need for control and independence, achievement, persistence and a positive self-image are also significant. Generally, money is a means rather than an end.

It is possible to suggest that some of these traits may also be required to be a successful marketing practitioner. Research has established that marketing and entrepreneurship are correlated but that marketing can exist independently of the innovative, risk-taking climate of the entrepreneur (Miles and Arnold, 1991).

Innovation, new-product development, and enterprise

Innovation, according to Drucker (1994), is 'the specific tool of entrepreneurs, the means by which they exploit change as an opportunity for a different business or a different service. It is capable of being presented as a discipline, capable of being learned, and capable of being practised.'

Rosenfield and Servo (1990) considered that innovation consists of three essential elements:

$$innovation = conception + invention + exploitation$$

This implies that an idea must not only be conceived but must be translated into a product and successfully sold in the market. The starting-point is therefore the generation of ideas.

SOURCES OF IDEAS

Ideas for new enterprises or products, or for improvements to existing ones, can come form a number of sources. There is a strong relationship between the development process of a new product and the establishment of new enterprises. The new-product development process—whereby ideas are translated into successful products—is commonly used by both entrepreneurs and intrapreneurs. (This is considered in more detail in chapter 7.)

Typically, entrepreneurial ideas come from individual work experience, domestic experience, hobbies and leisure interests, competitors' offerings, market gap analysis, research and development activities, or import substitution. Intrapreneurial ideas may come from the same sources, though many companies devote considerable resources to research and development, such as Donnelly Mirrors. Intrapreneurial sources may also include competitor analysis and market gap analysis.

Individual work experience

As in the case of Iona Technologies, many ideas for new enterprises come from a person's work experience. In the work setting, opportunities may emerge for new products or services or for improvements to existing ones. In addition, the experience the person gains in the firm, in applied skills or management expertise, will be beneficial if they establish their own enterprise.

Opportunities may be spotted in the work environment. This was the case with the establishment of Careerline, as described in the following panel.

CORPORATE WEAR: A BUSINESS OPPORTUNITY

Careerline is Ireland's largest manufacturer of corporate wear. The company's managing director, Maura Ebbs, had worked in the personnel department of Bank of Ireland. She took an interest in the clothing that companies put their employees into and decided there was a business opportunity. She tendered for the Bank of Ireland contract and won it; after that other companies became customers, and a viable business was created. Within five years, customers included Bewley's, Gardner Merchant, ACC Bank, Irish Ferries, Super Valu, An Bord Gáis, and Iarnród Éireann.

The company supplies a complete package: it designs the corporate wear, chooses the manufacturer, supplies the clothing, and consults those who have to wear it. The company employs thirty people directly and contributes to the employment of five hundred others who act as suppliers.

Source: E. Oliver, 'Specialist clothing firm has designs on expansion', *Irish Times*, 20 February 1998.

Domestic experience

The home may be a source of ideas. We use many products and services in our homes, and many ideas for new products have come from people's domestic experience, as the next panel demonstrates.

LIR CHOCOLATES

Lir Chocolates is one of a number of successful hand-made chocolate companies. It was established by Mary White and Connie Doody. The idea came from experimenting with hand-made chocolates at home; the positive reaction from family and friends encouraged them to consider setting up a small business.

Lir competes in the high-priced segment of the hand-made chocolates market. Its main sales outlets are Brown Thomas, selected Tesco, Superquinn and Dunne's stores, and duty-free shops at Dublin Airport. Thirty-four per cent of output is exported.

Source: Richard Brophy, 'Behind bars', *Checkout Ireland*, July 1997; Lir Chocolates web site (www.lir.ie).

Hobbies and leisure interest

People's hobbies and leisure interests can yield ideas for new ventures, as happened with the Cavan and Leitrim Railway Company, which began operations in 1994, one of a number of railway restoration projects in different parts of the country.

THE CAVAN AND LEITRIM RAILWAY

The original Cavan and Leitrim Railway Company was established in 1887 to provide a narrow-gauge passenger and freight service on a line between Drumod, County Leitrim, and Belturbet, County Cavan, with a branch serving coal mines in Arigna. Eventually taken over by CIE, the lines were ultimately deemed to be uneconomic, and in 1959 they were closed.

In 1994 a group of railway enthusiasts decided to establish a museum and working railway at the Drumod end of the old line. The old company was re-incorporated as a limited liability company. The original station building was bought and restored, along with the engine shed, platforms and other buildings that had been abandoned in 1959. Track was relaid for about half a mile on the route of the former line, and the company began to offer trips using historic engines and carriages.

Finance for the venture was provided from the EU Interreg programme, the International Fund for Ireland, and private donations. The railway proved popular with tourists and school tours and was promoted as an interactive experience for visitors. This experience included a trip on a restored train and a guided tour of the company's workshops, where various items of rolling stock were in the process of being restored. Eventually the company hoped to fully restore the railway line to Mohill, approximately five miles away.

Source: *Cavan and Leitrim Railway Company Guidebook*, 1995.

Analysis of competitors

Observing competitors and analysing their product or service offerings can yield ideas for improvements or alternatives. Obviously, competitors' products cannot be directly copied, but they can provide ideas for variations. In many competitive markets firms will closely follow competitors' activities, and there may be scope for improving or building on what they have done.

ISOTONIC DRINKS

In 1988 Premier Dairies launched an isotonic drink (one that restores the body's pH balance after exercise) called Pocari, manufactured under licence from Japan. In 1989, however, Smith-Kline Beecham launched Lucozade Sport as an extension of its Lucozade brand; this was also an isotonic product and was supported with national advertising and promotion. It overtook Premier's product and established itself as brand leader in isotonic drinks. Ultimately the Pocari brand was discontinued, and Smith-Kline Beecham was left with the dominant position in the category.

Market gap analysis

Market gap analysis means examining the market for unserved segments or niches. It is a common method used by marketers to find opportunities either for new products or for existing products. The cook and entrepreneur Darina Allen considers that spotting a niche in the market for a cookery school was a precursor to her decision to establish an enterprise at Ballymaloe, County Cork.

BALLYMALOE COOKERY SCHOOL

Ballymaloe Cookery School has gained an international reputation since it began taking in students in 1982. The owner, Darina Allen, had completed a hotel and catering management course but was most interested in creative cookery. At the time the Irish food scene was rather limited: there were only five or six really good restaurants in the country, and Allen noticed that fresh food, herbs or the seasons rarely affected the menus offered.

The idea for the school came from an unserved niche in the market. To establish the business, Allen and her husband mortgaged their house and took out a loan to renovate the property to provide the facilities needed. Press and media interest generated some newspaper and magazine features, and in 1988 RTE approached them with a suggestion for a cookery programme, 'Simply Delicious', which eventually ran to eight series and eleven books.

Source: *Sunday Business Post*, 26 October 1997.

Research and development

Research and development may be a feature of both entrepreneurship and intrapreneurship. Companies may establish R&D departments or programmes to yield new ideas, as was the case with Donnelly Mirrors.

Import substitution

Imports may yield ideas for products that could be manufactured in Ireland. Consider the example of Fiacla toothpaste, as described in the next panel.

FIACLA TOOTHPASTE

Established in 1983, Fiacla toothpaste was the only wholly Irish-owned toothpaste manufacturer, employing between fifteen and twenty people. By the middle of the nineteen-nineties the company had achieved a share of approximately 15 per cent in a market that was catered for mainly by imported products. The Fiacla brand has been extended from toothpaste to mouthwash and related dental care products. The company also manufactures own-label products for some of the multiples.

As the company developed and sales reached a peak in the home market, export markets were investigated. The share of output for export increased and included Britain, France, Hong Kong, Nigeria, Dubai, and Saudi Arabia.

Sources: *Sunday Business Post*, 31 March 1991, 14 November 1993, 23 January 1994.

THE LIFE-CYCLE FOR ENTREPRENEURIAL FIRMS

The generation of ideas will be the first step in developing a successful enterprise. The examples given in previous sections illustrate where ideas came from and how they were translated into successful businesses. The new-product development process provides a framework for taking ideas, critically assessing them, and converting them into successful products.

The creation of a successful product will be the first stage in the entrepreneurial life-cycle of the firm. Just as products have a life-cycle—they are born, grow, and ultimately mature—so too have entrepreneurial firms. According to Siropolis (1990), the entrepreneurial firm goes through three distinct stages: *acceptance*, *breakthrough*, and *maturity*.

The acceptance stage is characterised by the firm struggling to break even and having low cash flows. The challenge is gaining acceptance for the product on the market. The product or service may have to be adjusted to suit market demands, and the essential communication objective is the creation of awareness. Little money may be available for marketing activities and promotion, and communication may be largely personal.

Breakthrough comes with rapid sales growth. This requires effective management of cash flow and an emphasis on improved production performance to meet the increased demand. Quality and delivery also become important, and the business needs to ensure that standards are not compromised with a larger body of customers. At this stage more funds may be available for marketing activities, and research will be required on product and market prospects.

The firm reaches maturity when there is stable, balanced growth. Management skills will need to be developed or fine-tuned. At this stage the firm may consider expansion options: for example, the successful fast-food chain Abrakebabra decided at an early stage to expand through franchising (see below). In so doing they created opportunities for others to set up new businesses. Other firms have expanded in different ways: for example, Iona Technologies expanded its activities to become a large-scale provider of computer programs, while Darina Allen of Ballymaloe expanded into publishing.

ABRAKEBABRA

The name Abrakebabra—a combination of 'kebab' and 'abracadabra'—was chosen by two brothers, Graham and Wyndham Beere, for their kebab restaurant, which they opened in the Dublin suburb of Rathmines in 1982. The brothers had seen the success of kebab outlets in London and decided to try it out in Dublin.

The concept proved equally popular in Dublin, and within a few years the brothers had opened several more outlets. They believed there was more potential and decided to use franchising as a means of expanding throughout the country. The franchise to run an individual restaurant could be bought for £10,000. It was estimated that the cost of providing a fully fitted new outlet was £90,000; if an existing fast-food outlet was being renovated this was reduced to £40,000. By 1997 there were fifty Abrakebabra outlets, nine of which were owned by the Beere brothers.

Sources: *Sunday Business Post*, 6 December 1992, 16 May 1993, 9 March 1997; *Examiner*, 23 December 1996; *Sunday Tribune*, 2 November 1997.

ENTREPRENEURIAL ROLES

Entrepreneurs perform a number of roles in the management and development of their business. They will have been the innovators, responsible for the initial establishment of the enterprise. In start-up ventures they will also have complete responsibility for marketing. They may have done all the initial research and development, and they will be responsible for the communication and promotion of their enterprise. It is not unusual, therefore, for entrepreneurs to work long hours developing prototypes and establishing the business. As the firm grows, the roles will change. The number of employees will grow, and tasks will be delegated; management skills will need to be further developed.

HORSEWEAR

The idea for specialist horse clothing came to a riding instructor, Tom McGuinness, from a frustration with the inadequacy of horse blankets on the market in the early nineteen-eighties. He conducted a survey of fifty people in the industry on their needs and priorities; he then bought a sewing-machine and worked for twelve weeks to develop a prototype. The blanket had an improved strapping system, so that it stayed on the horse properly, and was made of synthetic materials rather than the traditional woven jute.

Sales were very good, and production began in 1985. Ten years later the company was the largest manufacturer of horse blankets in Europe, employing eighty-five people in Dundalk and Cavan.

McGuinness attributes his success to good instincts about marketing and product development. As the business expanded, however, he realised he needed to develop his management skills, and he enrolled in two courses run by the Irish Management Institute: the effective marketing course and the business development course. These gave him the ability to analyse what was right in the business and to apply this so that it would keep on working.

The development of management and marketing skills was essential in the business, where 90 per cent of output was exported, mainly to the Continent and the United States. The company's policy has been to develop well-researched products in a range of colours and finishes to suit customers' needs.

Sources: *Sunday Business Post*, 29 May 1994, 31 March 1996; *Sunday Tribune*, 7 May 1995.

MARKETING WITHOUT MONEY

At the early stages in its life-cycle the entrepreneurial firm may have little money for marketing activities or for engaging marketing services. This is not necessarily a drawback, as there are many ways for the small business to market without significant amounts of money. Initial market research, whether primary or secondary, can be carried out by the entrepreneur: understanding the stages in the research process is the key.

Communication will be especially important. The entrepreneur should be able to explain clearly what the business is about, as there may be limited time to hold the attention of potential buyers or investors. Communication opportunities should be exploited. Local or national media may be interested in new business start-ups and may give coverage, as with the Ballymaloe Cookery School. Press statements can be prepared and sent to selected media, which may be interested in following up with a story.

Allied to the need for communication skills is the need for selling skills. The entrepreneur will have to convince buyers of the benefits of the product or service and be able to negotiate the sale.

Many catalogues, guides or brochures will give free listings or charge small amounts for a listing or profile. Specific publications, such as *Your Business*, published by the Small Firms Association, regularly feature items on small business and development. 'Networking' through business events, firms or social contacts is taken for granted in business and is a means of establishing contacts or following up leads. Advertising need not cost a lot: specific media, such as the Yellow Pages, may be quite affordable.

The internet provides an opportunity for the entrepreneur to communicate with a selected group of customers. Its interactive nature means that it can also be used for taking orders or for providing additional information to potential customers. There are certainly implications for other companies identifying such consumers. We have seen, for example, how Iona Technologies used the internet to good effect. One Australian study (Poon and Swatman, 1997) conducted among small businesses found that the perceived long-term benefits of use of the internet, such as business development, far outweighed the perceived short-term benefits, such as cost savings and communications efficiency. The internet, therefore, has significant short-term and long-term benefits. The costs associated with an internet site would obviously need to be assessed, and factors such as the cost of worldwide web site design and continuing site management will be important.

Concentrating on the smaller market means that the entrepreneur can be closer to customers and can build relationships with them. Close familiarisation with customers and their needs means that feedback and speed of reaction can be much faster than for larger firms. Smaller firms can therefore practise relationship marketing quite easily.

As the business expands and sales increase, more funds should become available for marketing, and the entrepreneur's responsibility for carrying out all the firm's marketing activities may then be reduced. It is also possible that, in addition to the availability of finance for enterprise development from state agencies, specific funds for marketing activities may also be available.

FINANCING FOR ENTERPRISE

One of the factors that many people have suggested contributed to the lower rate of new business start-ups in Ireland is the lack of funds. In particular, the lack of equity finance has been cited as a problem. In other words, businesses have been too small to finance growth from profits and not profitable enough to attract the attention of most venture capitalists.

The problem was recognised by the Government, with £33 million being provided for seed or venture capital under the Operational Programme for Industry, 1994–9. This was administered by Forbairt and was for investment in companies or projects that had good commercial prospects and from which a return was expected. A number of other venture capital funds were also created in the middle nineteen-nineties, as table 2.1 illustrates. As with other enterprise support, the nature of the product or service and its marketing potential will have a significant bearing on the venture capitalists' decision to invest.

Table 2.1: Venture capital funds

ICC Software Fund
A £10 million fund to be invested in profitable software-related companies
Smurfit Ventures Ltd
A £10 million fund aimed at small to medium-sized enterprises within a range of sectors
ACT Enterprise Fund
An £8 million fund for investment in start-ups, SMEs, and early-stage development companies
Bank of Ireland Entrepreneurs' Fund
A £10 million fund aimed at early-stage and high-potential start-up technology companies and the food sector; a particular emphasis is placed on establishing a presence in the American market
Dublin Seed Capital Fund
A £1 million fund aimed at start-up and first-stage expansion companies involved in manufacturing, international services, technology and innovation in the Dublin area; it is administered by the Dublin Business Innovation Centre (see below)
First Step
A £3 million fund administered by the First Step organisation (see below)
Trinity Venture Fund
A £12 million fund that will make investments in a cross-section of industry; the parties involved were AIB and Frank Reihill and Company
Guinness-Ulster Bank Equity Fund
A £6 million fund identifying start-ups and growth-oriented small and medium enterprises; sectors of particular interest included food, beverages, leisure or tourism, and textiles or apparel
Clona Food Venture Fund
A £1 million fund aimed at the food sector in Cork

Source: B. McCall, 'Filling the gap', *Enterprise and Innovation*, November 1997.

SUPPORT FOR ENTERPRISE

Considerable support is provided for entrepreneurs starting new businesses and for existing enterprises, in an effort to stimulate and encourage indigenous enterprise, and some of this support is specifically aimed at marketing development or initiatives. Support can come from the state sector, such as third-level colleges, Enterprise Ireland (formerly Forbairt, FÁS, and An Bord Tráchtála), and the county enterprise boards; from banks and financial institutions; and from voluntary bodies, such as the Small Firms Association, Plato, and First Step.

Specific marketing initiatives include the service development programme launched by Forbairt in 1997 and the support given by the county enterprise boards to specific research and marketing activities. Most support agencies will closely assess the entrepreneur's marketing plans, proposals, or assumptions. These should provide an indication of the thoroughness of the marketing research that has been carried out and the assumptions made in planning marketing strategy.

In 1998 the Government introduced a new support structure for enterprise development with the establishment of a new unified agency to provide support services to enterprise. This new body, Enterprise Ireland, was created to bring together the core company development, training and export development functions of Forbairt, FÁS, and An Bord Tráchtála. The idea is to achieve greater integration between these organisations and to streamline and refocus their activities.

The following section describes some of the main state and private-sector bodies that are involved in the support of enterprise and have a role in the development of marketing in Irish business. (The role of Enterprise Ireland in international marketing is further discussed in chapter 12.)

The county enterprise boards

Thirty-five county enterprise boards were established in 1993. Each board consists of representatives of business, industry, banking, and state agencies. Their remit is to assess projects within their geographical area, approve suitable projects, and provide them with funds. The boards were given a budget to 1999 and a target of creating 2,250 new jobs.

Applicants must be able to demonstrate that there is a market for their proposed product or service, that adequate finance is available, and that they have the necessary management or technical experience to implement the proposal. The board can decide to finance feasibility studies: these can be subsidised by up to 75 per cent, to a limit of £5,000. The maximum grant payable to an individual project is £50,000 or 50 per cent of the capital cost, whichever is the smaller.

The boards have assisted a broad range of projects, including services, tourism, crafts, general industry, food, and textiles.

Enterprise Ireland

Enterprise Ireland provides a range of support services and assistance to business. It has taken over the schemes formerly operated by Forbairt. For small businesses with fewer than fifty employees there are two main schemes: the small business programme and the enterprise development programme. Other schemes, such as the Mentor programme, which involves putting experienced managers into the business, and the management development programme, which provides assistance with the development of management skills, are also relevant.

Under the small business programme, capital grants of up to 25 per cent and employment grants of up to £5,000 per job are available. The enterprise development programme involves selecting fast-growth, high-risk projects, with Enterprise Ireland taking a 10 per cent equity stake in redeemable preference shares. Under this scheme, capital grants of up to 45 per cent and employment grants of up to £9,000 per job are available. Proposals are typically assessed according to the research the proposer has carried out, the proposed marketing mix, and the balance between fixed assets and working capital. In the past, Forbairt has assisted many firms to grow and develop, as the following example illustrates.

ATHLONE EXTRUSIONS

Athlone Extrusions became the first Irish company to originate from a receivership and secure a listing on the Dublin and London Stock Exchanges. Furthermore, all its employees with more than a year's service are shareholders in the company. An Italian company had set up a factory in Athlone to extrude polystyrene sheet to serve the British sanitary ware market but it went into receivership in 1983. Athlone Extrusions Ltd began trading later in 1983 and broadened both its products and its markets into areas such as point-of-sale display units and packaging.

A management buy-out was arranged in 1990, and the company began identifying new European markets. Forbairt supported a £6.9 million investment programme that included four new extrusion lines, and employment increased to 153, having started at about 40. The company went public in February 1998. Before the flotation the company set aside £750,000 from reserves to enable employees to buy shares. Each employee was entitled to 879 free shares per year of service; they were required to buy one share for every three free shares. Special bank loans were arranged for employees to enable them to do this. In total, £1.4 million was invested by employees in shares.

Source: Forbairt, Athlone; 'Extrusions goes public', *Enterprise and Innovation*, March 1998.

FÁS was the state employment and training agency involved in training and the development of human resources. It operated a wide variety of schemes, including programmes to develop marketing skills. These have been included in the remit of Enterprise Ireland.

An Bord Bia

An Bord Bia assists in the development and marketing of food and beverages. It can provide grants for marketing programmes and strategic marketing development. Other services include carrying out research and support for international trade shows. The board has a strong role in the development of export markets for food and beverages, as the following panel demonstrates

AN BORD BIA: FARMHOUSE CHEESES FOR SAINSBURY'S

In November 1997 An Bord Bia assisted five farmhouse cheese manufacturers in launching their products in Sainsbury's supermarkets in London, southern England, and Northern Ireland. The board had worked with Sainsbury's to secure listings for the Cashel Blue (County Tipperary), Gubbeen (County Cork), Doolin (County Waterford), St Killian (County Wexford) and Dubarra (County Dublin) brands.

An Bord Bia expected the initiative to generate sales of £250,000 in the first year, with the potential to double this within twelve to eighteen months.

Source: Bord Bia web site (www.bordbia.ie).

Business innovation centres

There are four business innovation centres: in Dublin, Cork, Limerick, and Galway. They are non-profit organisations, their main role being that of facilitator, providing advice, finance and support to projects in the medium to high-technology sector. The centres have a capital seed fund, which is provided by the state and the private sector. They can provide professional advisers on marketing, financial control, and strategy.

Plato

Plato is a small-business development network established by the Tallaght Partnership in 1993. It is primarily supported by the Local Urban and Rural Development Operational Programme, 1995–9. The network encourages co-operation between large companies and small to medium-sized companies. It involves large companies releasing senior managers to work in smaller firms as part of an arrangement lasting for two years. A report carried out by Goodbody Economic Consultants (1998) found that participating companies reported an increase in turnover of 22 per cent. Employment in the companies involved rose by 18 per cent. By 1998, eight networks had been established in different regions, and 932 companies were participating in the scheme. Companies that join must have been in business for at least three years and must have a significant potential for growth.

First Step

First Step was an initiative of the entrepreneur Norma Smurfit. It is a private, non-profit organisation financed by private companies and involves the provision of repayable loans, advice and support to start-up businesses. First Step is staffed by managers who have been seconded from industry. They continue to be paid by sponsoring companies.

INTERACTION BETWEEN EDUCATION AND ENTERPRISE

Universities and third-level colleges are involved not only in the research and teaching of business and enterprise courses but also in liaison with entrepreneurs and businesses. This may involve research, consultancy, training, or short-term courses.

One study (Clark and Carson, 1986) looked at how academic staff assisted in the development of marketing expertise in smaller enterprises. It examined the principles of *action learning*, which means learning by doing, and how these were useful in the development of approaches. It is important that colleges link with industry to keep abreast of developments and to provide graduates who can meet the needs of employers. We have seen how Iona Technologies grew from being a 'campus company' in Trinity College, Dublin, and most other third-level institutions have similar companies. Typically the colleges act as incubator units for the enterprise; generally companies that will be assisted are those that can demonstrate a need for linkage with the colleges. Ultimately, as with Iona Technologies, a decision has to be made to move on and to become a more independent concern.

EU funds

The EU is a significant provider of funds for supporting the development of small business. There are four broad areas of relevance: human resources, research and technological development, European structural fund initiatives, and subsidised loans. Under the Leonardo programme, for example, the design and development of training materials and human resource programmes, as well as short intensive courses that rely on industry and universities, could be subsidised. The Fourth Framework programme covered research on twenty specific areas and was administered by Forbairt.

There were thirteen separate structural fund initiatives. The most relevant in Ireland were the ADAPT programme, which aimed to make industry more competitive by facilitating adaptation to industrial change. The Interreg II programme was also significant: this related to cross-border co-operation and applied also in the north-east and south-east of the country.

Subsidised loans were administered by the European Investment Bank, with AIB and ICC co-ordinating the loan facilities in Ireland. Loans could be provided under the SME facility, which aimed to support the creation of employment in growing companies by subsidising capital investment in the industrial, agri-industrial, tourism and service sectors.

OVERVIEW OF SUPPORT FOR ENTERPRISE

This overview of the support available for enterprise from both the state and the private sector gives some indication of the supportive environment for enterprise in Ireland. A common factor is the importance placed on marketing research, plans, and proposals. This applies equally to start-up ventures and developing enterprises. An understanding of the fundamental principles underlying marketing and the role it plays in the business is essential.

MARKETING AND CONTINUED BUSINESS SUCCESS

Marketing plays a crucial role at the start-up and initial development of a business. It is also required to ensure continued business success. This implies a need to constantly review and evaluate the firm's marketing strategies and activities.

Environmental changes may require marketing changes. (In chapter 5 the role of the marketing audit—which provides a structure for a comprehensive review of the firm's marketing—is demonstrated.) The following panel illustrates the changes made by the multinational firm Proctor and Gamble. In this case the company reorganised itself in an attempt to become more responsive to market changes.

PROCTOR AND GAMBLE: RESPONDING MORE QUICKLY TO MARKET CHANGE

In 1998 Proctor and Gamble, the world's largest home products company, announced the appointment of a new chairman and its decision to split itself into seven business units based on product lines. This would replace its existing structure of four geographical units and was a reaction to the financial upheaval that had taken place in Russia and Asia. The rationale for the change given by the company was the need to become more efficient and innovative and to get to the market faster with new products.

Proctor and Gamble, whose brands include Ariel, Pampers, Tampax, Max Factor, and Fairy Liquid, had not been achieving its planned sales growth. It had planned to double global sales to $70,000 million by 2006, which required an annual sales growth of 7 per cent. Under the reorganisation, the new chairman planned to get more out of the firm's researchers, who include 1,250 scientists with a PhD. In spite of spending $1,500 million a year on research and development, most of the company's new products were improvements to existing lines, such as Crest toothpaste and Pantene hair spray. In some cases, such as the launch of the new product Febreze, which removed odours from fabrics, sales were originally confined to America, with the result that potential sales in other countries were lost.

The new global business units will divide the company into seven sections under the following titles: baby care, beauty care, fabric and home care, feminine protection, food and beverages, health care, and tissues and paper towels. The objective of the new plan will be to cut costs and make the company more responsive to the market. Though the company is being divided essentially along product lines, the global business units will be complemented by eight market development organisations that will work at regional and national levels to develop strategies for expanding business.

Source: G. Alexander, 'P&G gambles on shake-up to beat crisis', *Sunday Times*, 13 September 1998.

MARKETING AND TURNAROUND

The life-cycle for entrepreneurial firms illustrates the stages a business can go through as it seeks to become established. Once established, it will continue to face challenges. The changing needs of customer and environmental forces will have to be constantly monitored, and the firm may have to implement changes in response. The worst case is when the business gets into difficulties or collapses. The failure rate for new business ventures is quite high.

While many new and established businesses will get into difficulties and even disappear, there are also examples of firms that have been successfully turned around.

Marketing can play an important role in achieving this, as was the case with Waterford Stanley, an established business that went into receivership but was successfully taken over and rejuvenated.

WATERFORD STANLEY:
ACHIEVING A SUCCESSFUL TURNAROUND

In the early nineteen-eighties Waterford Foundry was in financial difficulties. A receiver had been appointed to the parent company, the TMG group, which sought to sell the business as a going concern. The company had a well-recognised brand— indeed Stanley cookers had been the dominant brand on the market. By the eighties, however, sales were declining. The company's market share had fallen to 50 per cent. Two competitors, Aga and Raeburn, had successfully eaten into its market share.

An offer was made for the company by two businessmen, Owen Conway and Frank Cruess-Callaghan. The offer was accepted, and they set about re-establishing the business. By the early nineties the company had an 89 per cent share of the market for multi-fuel cookers. The successful turnaround was achieved through improved research and development and successfully serving needs in both home and export markets. The company moved from being a manufacturer of one product for one market to multi-fuel products for both home and export markets.

Changes in environmental regulations and changing customers' needs were significant factors. In the Dublin market, for example, only smokeless fuels could be used. In addition, the kitchen range had been perceived as exclusively rural; new gas and oil-burning variants helped overcome this perception, and the company successfully directed its efforts towards estate agents, builders, architects and interior designers to strengthen its presence in the Dublin market. By the early nineties 40 per cent of its output was exported. Eleven new products were successfully launched within a period of six years.

New products were essential for the company's survival; they were also required because of environmental regulations. In the United States, for example, regulations on emissions from domestic fires led to 75 per cent of stove manufacturers getting out of the business. At the same time, Waterford's share of the American cast-iron stove market increased. It had entered into a joint venture with a Seattle company to develop a new type of pellet-burning stove, which met all the emission requirements.

By the late nineties Waterford Stanley's annual sales had reached £30 million. The company spent approximately 2 per cent of sales on research and development, which it considered was on a par with the rest of the industry. It also attributed its success to a well-planned marketing strategy. Research on customers' needs, quality marketing communications and a network of dealers capable of providing high levels of customer service were all significant factors.

Sources: 'Stanley makes a comeback', *Sunday Business Post*, 30 September 1990; 'Burning issue for Waterford Stanley is sales in Dublin', *Sunday Press*, 14 November 1993; 'Words of wisdom from Waterford Stanley boss', Sunday Business Post, 14 May 1995; 'Company's success is cast iron', *Sunday Business Post*, 11 October 1996.

Marketing contributed to the successful turnaround of Waterford Stanley. Having an identifiable brand and implementing an integrated marketing strategy were significant factors. The Waterford Stanley story illustrates the challenges faced by a company and how it reacted to them. Marketing does not guarantee success, but it is required for survival.

FURTHER READING

Burns, P., and Dewhurst, J., (eds.), *Small Business and Entrepreneurship* (second edition), London: Macmillan 1996.

Carson, D., Cromie, S., McGowan, P., and Hill, J., *Marketing and Entrepreneurship in SMEs*, Englewood Cliffs (NJ): Prentice-Hall 1995.

Garavan, T., Ó Cinnéide, B., and Fleming, P., *Entrepreneurship and Business Start-ups in Ireland*, Dublin: Oak Tree Press 1997.

O'Gorman, C., and Cunningham, J., *Enterprise in Action: An Introduction to Enterprise in an Irish Context*, Dublin: Oak Tree Press 1997.

DISCUSSION QUESTIONS

1. Analyse the pros and cons of running your own business. Have you got what it takes to be an entrepreneur?
2. Where do you think business opportunities will exist in Ireland in the future? Give reasons for your answer.
3. 'No business or organisation can exist without marketing.' Comment on this statement.
4. Explain the link between marketing, entrepreneurship, and intrapreneurship. Can they be mutually exclusive? Give examples.
5. The state devotes considerable resources to the encouragement of enterprise. Are there any disadvantages to this? Should the state have a more laissez-faire approach?
6. The Waterford Stanley case illustrates a successful turnaround. State the reasons why a firm may get into difficulties and how marketing can be used to correct the problem.

REFERENCES

Burnside, R., 'Improving the corporate climate for creativity' in West and Farr (eds.), *Innovation and Creativity at Work*.

Clark, W., and Carson, D., 'Marketing and the small business: a case history of education development', *Irish Marketing Review*, vol. 1 (1986).

Culliton, J., *The Culliton Report*, Dublin: Stationery Office 1992.

Drucker, P., *Innovation and Entrepreneurship* (third edition), London: Butterworth-Heinemann 1994.

Forbairt, 'New support structure for enterprise development', *Enterprise and Innovation*, March 1998.

Foxall, G., and Minkes, A., 'Beyond marketing: the diffusion of entrepreneurship in the modern corporation', *Journal of Strategic Marketing*, June 1996.

Guilford, J., *Personality*, New York: McGraw-Hill 1959.

Jansen, P., and van Wees, L., 'Conditions for internal entrepreneurship', *Journal of Management Development*, vol. 13 (1994), no. 9.

Low, M., and MacMillan, I., 'Entrepreneurship: past research and future challenges', *Journal of Management*, June 1988.

Miles, A., and Arnold, D., 'Marketing orientation and entrepreneurial orientation', *Entrepreneurship Theory and Practice*, summer 1991.

Morris, M., and Lewis, P., 'The determinants of entrepreneurial activity: implications for marketers', *European Journal of Marketing*, vol. 29 (1995), no. 7.

Pearson, G., 'Promoting entrepreneurship in large companies', *Long-Range Planning*, June 1989.

'Plato now heads for Belfast', *Sunday Business Post*, 12 April 1998.

Poon, S., and Swatman, P., 'Small business use of the internet: findings from Australian case studies', *International Marketing Review*, vol. 14 (1997), no. 5.

Siropolis, N., *Small Business Management: A Guide to Entrepreneurship*, New York: Houghton-Mifflin 1990.

Telesis Consulting Group, *Report on Irish Industrial Policy*, Dublin: Stationery Office 1982.

West, M., and Farr, J., *Innovation and Creativity at Work*, New York: Wiley 1990.

PART 2

The Market

3

The Forces in the Irish Marketing Environment

The *environment* refers to the forces external to the firm that affect its ability to develop and maintain successful transactions. The environment is composed of a number of elements that, individually or jointly, can determine success or failure for the business.

Environmental forces can represent threats to the firm, but they can also present opportunities. Environmental forces can change, and therefore marketers need to be flexible and able to adapt to these changes. The environment requires constant monitoring. Some changes may be well heralded in advance; others may take the firm by surprise. This chapter explores the main elements in the environment and examines some of the environmental influences that marketers need to take into account.

The environment can be divided into two main areas: the *micro-environment* and the *macro-environment* (fig 3.1). The micro-environment consists of forces that are closest to the firm, including the elements or functions within the firm itself, competitors, and customers. The macro-environment consists of broader social forces, such as demographics; these are further removed from the firm but are no less significant. In this chapter, these forces are examined mainly in the context of the Irish marketing environment.

THE MICRO-ENVIRONMENT

The micro-environment refers to a collection of forces that include the company itself, its suppliers, intermediaries, competitors, customers, and publics.

The company

Most companies and organisations are composed of individuals or groups of people working together to achieve a common purpose. This common purpose can be defined as serving the needs of the customer. The firm engages in a value-adding process: it takes inputs such as raw materials and, using its skills and resources, transforms them into products or services. If customers place enough value on the result of this process, they may buy the product or service. The firm must therefore be concerned about getting the value-adding process right. This will be based on understanding needs. If, for example, a coffee-producer obtains coffee beans from coffee plantations, processes them into instant coffee granules, gives them a brand name, and distributes them on the market, they have added value for the consumer. This value could be expressed in the form of such factors as convenience, taste, quality, and price.

Fig. 3.1: The forces in the marketing environment

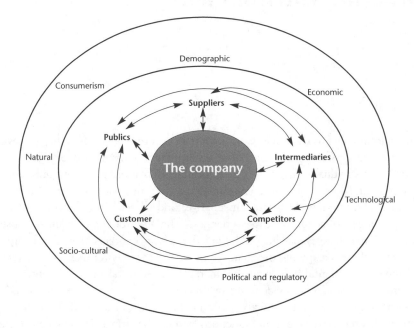

All organisations add value. When a theatre stages a play, for example, it is adding value in the form of enjoyment, creativity, or artistic merit.

In general, firms tend to be divided according to functional speciality and responsibility. Therefore there will usually be functional departments, such as marketing, finance, production or operations, and personnel or human resources. Each of these functions is involved in adding value.

The extent to which these functions are oriented towards serving customers' needs and are integrated is important. It is easy for functional specialists to concentrate on or become completely absorbed with their own specialism. Marketers, for example, will usually want to spend money to attract more customers; the finance department, however, may want to cut costs, leading to tension between the two. Functions will usually compete with each other for a greater share of internal resources. All of this may distract attention from the customer and an understanding of the customer's needs. Firms are myopic if they concentrate on internal rivalry at the expense of customers' needs. Serving the needs of customers should be an integrating force for all functions. The need for integration of functions emphasises the role of internal marketing.

Internal marketing

Internal marketing involves the application of the marketing policy within the firm. Expressed in simple terms, if the staff won't buy the product, then why should the customer? (Barnes, 1989). The objective of internal marketing is for all the firm's employees to be committed to the goal of ensuring the best possible treatment of customers. It complements the company's external marketing efforts, plays a role in customer satisfaction, and is directed at producing and maintaining a motivated and satisfied group of employees who will support the company's external marketing objectives.

Internal marketing is important because of the role it can play in focusing or refocusing the company's personnel on the importance of the customer. Firms can lose sight of the customer. Internal politics and the culture of the firm may mean that individual functions or departments spend more time competing for resources than attempting to achieve integration. Integration implies that all elements in the firm are working together with a common purpose. The customers' needs should be the means of achieving this integration.

Internal marketing therefore encompasses issues such as communication, discussion, corporate culture, quality standards, and change.

Suppliers

Most firms rely on suppliers to provide them with goods and services. Raw materials, equipment and transport are just some of the areas in which firms may rely on suppliers. Firms will also buy from marketing-related suppliers, such as advertising agencies, market research companies, and public relations consultants. Financial service suppliers, such as banks and insurance companies, are also important.

Business-to-business marketing covers the marketing activities of firms that supply other firms with goods and services that are incorporated into the value-adding process. It is important that the marketer is aware of the changes that may be taking place in the supplier environment. Factors such as scarcity of raw material or changes in technology may be experienced first by suppliers, but they have a knock-on effect on the firm and may cause increases in costs or require changes in the firm's value-adding process.

Intermediaries

Intermediaries include wholesalers, distributors, agents, and retailers. These are all elements of the *marketing channel*. (This is discussed in more detail in chapter 10.) A significant issue will be the development of relationships with intermediaries; *relationship marketing theory* (discussed in chapter 1) provides some insights on how to do this.

Relationship marketing with suppliers and intermediaries

Relationship marketing is important in managing the interaction between the firm and its suppliers and intermediaries. Relationship marketing simply involves the firm applying the marketing policy to those firms or individuals that it deals with. It involves treating them all as customers. It can therefore be applied to the supplier-marketer exchange and the marketer-intermediary exchange, and of course it is the basis of the marketer-customer exchange.

In relation to the supplier-marketer and the marketer-intermediary exchange, relationship marketing is based on the well-established business principle that co-operation between businesses should be mutually beneficial. Suppliers and intermediaries have an interest in ensuring that the firm prospers; similarly, the firm has an interest in ensuring that its suppliers and channel members prosper.

One study has examined how aquaculture went from being a cottage industry— fragmented, undercapitalised, with uneven product quality, and at the mercy of larger, foreign-owned distributors—to become the Irish Seafood Producers' Group, a successful, internationally competitive firm (Garvey and Torres, 1993). Significantly, relationship marketing approaches played an important part in the process. The company undertook a value chain analysis of its industry (see fig. 3.2). The value chain demonstrates how value is added in successive stages, from the obtaining of raw material to ultimate consumption by the consumer. This value chain analysis demonstrated a need for the producers' group to build co-operative relationships with producers, distributors, and retailers. The key to capturing value was considered to be getting to know the customer's customer (i.e. the retailer or caterer) and the customer's customer's customer (i.e. the consumer). One of the results of this approach was the ability of the group to negotiate promotions directly with large supermarket chains, which led to lower margins for the distributor but guaranteed higher volumes, which more than compensated for this.

Fig. 3.2: The aquabusiness chain

Commercialise

Produce ➜ Package ➜ Supply Sell Promote ➜ Distribute ➜ Retail ➜ Consume

If the firm and the members of the value chain have a strong relationship, this should help to ensure that needs are satisfied.

Customers

Central to any marketing is the customer. Customers can be classified as being *consumers*, *business-to-business*, or *international*. In this book, particular attention is paid to understanding consumers' behaviour (chapter 6), international marketing (chapter 12), and business-to-business markets (chapter 13). The role of marketing involves not just creating customers but also developing a relationship with those customers. Though marketers want to develop relationships with their suppliers and intermediaries, the fundamental relationship is between the marketer and the customer. The marketer needs to consider what the relationship means to the customer.

Barnes (1995) suggested viewing firm-customer relationships along a spectrum of intensity, from mere transactions to genuine relationships. Genuine relationships are characterised by the consumer experiencing a stronger sense of closeness to the marketer, which should contribute to a stronger desire to return to do business than if no relationship existed. The marketer therefore needs to fully understand customers' needs. Barnes suggested that this understanding could be facilitated with information on how pertinent dimensions or characteristics of the relationship are to the consumer, how the consumer views his or her interaction with the company, and how the consumer engages in that interaction.

Relationship marketing is therefore much more than retaining customers, developing customer data-bases, or locking customers into relationships that are difficult to get out of: it involves putting into practice the core principles of marketing, which require a more holistic view of the customer.

Customer care will be important in the maintenance of relationships. One model of customer care suggests that both quantitative and qualitative issues are involved (Carson and Gilmore, 1989). Quantitative issues include factors such as speed of delivery, while qualitative issues include factors such as courtesy. While rules and procedures are common for the former, in the qualitative or psychological areas it is the perceptions, attitudes and behaviour of customer contact personnel that are important. These are areas where marketing managers can have an impact or can implement improvements.

Competitors

Competition describes the rivalry that exists between firms in the market. Most markets are characterised by competition; and even where traditionally very little competition existed, rivalries are increasing. Greater integration in the European Union, for example, has meant more competition in many markets. In the health insurance market, for example, until 1996 there was one main provider in Ireland, the VHI. In that year the British health insurance company BUPA was established on the Irish market and recruited 36,000 members in its first twelve months of operation, using national advertising and promotion to establish itself. The VHI responded by increasing advertising expenditure and offering new services to members (*Sunday Business Post*, 23 November 1997).

Defining or identifying who competitors are may not always be easy. Some may be direct competitors, and these can usually be easily identified and will typically be the focus of most brand competition. In the lager market, for example, there are a number of direct competitors that compete for market share.

DIRECT COMPETITORS IN THE LAGER MARKET

It was estimated that almost 2 million hectolitres of lager were consumed in the Republic in 1996. Lager accounted for 42 per cent of total beer consumption, and the market had grown by $3^{1}/_{2}$ per cent since 1995. Consumers were very brand-conscious, and competition among brands was intense. In 1996 Heineken had the largest share, as the graph shows.

All the competitors supported their brands with extensive advertising, promotional and sponsorship campaigns. The 18–25 age group was the main target. Trade marketing activities in the channels were also extensive. Two broad channel types existed: the *on-trade*, which describes pubs, hotels, and bars, and the *off-trade*, which describes off-licences. Sales in the off-trade had grown in the nineteen-nineties as more people consumed beer at home. Heineken was brewed under licence by Murphy's brewery, while the other leading brands, Budweiser and Carlsberg, were brewed by Guinness, also under licence.

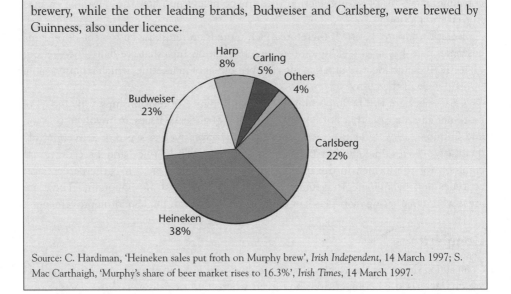

Source: C. Hardiman, 'Heineken sales put froth on Murphy brew', *Irish Independent*, 14 March 1997; S. Mac Carthaigh, 'Murphy's share of beer market rises to 16.3%', *Irish Times*, 14 March 1997.

Indirect competitors for a product or service may be quite diverse. In the case of lager, for example, the consumer may decide to go to the cinema rather than to the pub; in that case the cinema would be an indirect competitor. Obviously there can be many possible indirect competitors for most products and services, and the marketer may not be able to precisely determine them all. The important point is, who or what does the consumer perceive to be a competitor, and in what circumstances? Research into consumers' perceptions of competitors is therefore vital.

Competition can exist at different levels. Consider the example of the person who is hungry and decides to buy a snack (see fig. 3.3). *Generic competitors* are the broad range of products from which the consumer may choose. If the consumer decides to buy a bar of chocolate, they then move on to what *product form* they will buy. If the decision here is a toffee-centre product, they will have a number of *brand competitors* to choose from.

Fig. 3.3: Levels of competition

I am hungry
↓

What do I want to eat?   *Generic*
Crisps, fruit, chocolate ...   *competitors*
↓

What type of chocolate?   *Product form*
Biscuit, toffee-centre, plain ...   *competitors*
↓

What brand?   *Brand*
Cadbury's, Nestlé, Mars ...   *competitors*

Marketers, therefore, should not concentrate their attention only on brand competitors. It would be myopic for companies like Cadbury, Nestlé or Mars, for example, not to consider Tayto or Perri to be competitors. Consider the example of Irish Biscuits, which successfully developed a new product that took into account the nature of generic competition.

GENERIC COMPETITORS IN THE BISCUIT MARKET

The branded biscuit market in Ireland was valued at £125 million in 1997. Irish Biscuits had the dominant share, with 51 per cent; McVitie's was the other significant competitor, with 23 per cent. Within the market there were several categories: sweet biscuits (including mallows and rolls), countlines, chocolate packets, assortments, creams, and plain and savoury.

There had been some changes in consumers' perceptions of biscuit products in general. They increasingly regarded biscuits as part of an overall snacks market, where the choice could be a biscuit, yoghurt, crisps, ice cream, or a cake.

Irish Biscuits believed that in this situation it was important to develop products that bridged the gap between biscuit and snack. The development of the individually wrapped Chocolate Kimberley was a successful bridging product. It rapidly became a popular product, achieving sales of £4.76 million in its first year. It was positioned as a distinctive biscuit snack and supported by a £300,000 advertising campaign. In addition, extensive use was made of in-store displays. Its success prompted the company to investigate launches in the United States and Britain.

Source: *Checkout Ireland*, April 1996, November 1997.

Publics

In addition to the various forces described in the previous section, the firm will also interact at a microlevel with various publics. They may be other organisations, such as providers of financial services, Government departments, or the media, or they may be the general public. All these publics may influence the company very directly: for example, if the company is planning to go public, the views or opinions of leading stockbrokers or financial analysts may influence potential investors. News media coverage of the company or its products may influence perceptions or opinion.

THE MACRO-ENVIRONMENT

The *macro-environment* refers to a broad range of social forces, external to the business, that influence its activities. The following section describes some of the main forces in the macro-environment and their implications for marketers.

Demographics

Since the Great Famine of the eighteen-forties, the population of Ireland has exhibited a fairly steady decline. The rate of decline has varied as economic and social conditions have varied, but the underlying trend from 1900 to the nineteen-seventies has been downwards, as table 3.1 shows. By 1971 the decline had ceased, and by the 1981 census the total had exceeded what it had been at the turn of the century.

Table 3.1: Population (26 Counties)

1901	3.221 million
1911	3.139 million
1926	2.971 million
1936	2.968 million
1946	2.955 million
1951	2.960 million
1961	2.818 million
1971	2.978 million
1981	3.443 million
1991	3.525 million
1996	3.626 million

Source: Central Statistics Office.

Population decline could be attributed to two main causes: a declining birth rate, and emigration. The birth rate declined because of a combination of social factors, including late marriage. Migration patterns were dictated by economic conditions in Ireland as well as in emigrants' destinations.

Improved economic conditions in the nineties contributed to the increase in population recorded in 1996; emigration declined; and there was an increase in immigration. The 1996 census indicates that the population of the 26 Counties had increased by 3 per cent to just over 3.6 million (CSO, 1996). There was also a small increase in the birth rate, which was an additional contributory factor.

Table 3.2 shows the marriage, birth and death rates from 1950 to 1996. With the exception of 1996, when the birth rate increased slightly, the underlying trend in marriages, births and deaths has been downwards.

Table 3.2: Marriages, births, and deaths, 1950–96

	Marriages		Births		Deaths	
Year	Number	Rate*	Number	Rate*	Number	Rate*
1950	16,018	5.4	63,565	21.4	37,741	12.7
1960	15,465	5.5	60,735	21.5	34,243	12
1970	20,778	7.1	64,092	21.8	33,884	11.5
1980	21,792	6.4	74,388	21.9	32,980	9.7
1990	17,838	5.1	52,954	15.1	31,818	9.1

1991	17,441	4.9	52,718	15	31,305	8.9
1992	16,636	4.7	51,089	14.4	30,931	8.7
1993	16,824	4.7	49,456	13.8	31,656	8.9
1994	16,297	4.5	47,929	13.4	30,744	8.6
1995	15,623	4.4	48,530	13.5	31,494	8.8
1996	16,225	4.5	50,390	13.9	31,514	8.7

*per thousand of estimated population.
Source: Central Statistics Office.

The marriage rate has declined because of a combination of economic and social factors. Increasing affluence and job opportunities, for women in particular, mean that households may not have had to rely on the man to be the main earner, which was the tradition. Marriage was possibly being viewed less and less from an economic viewpoint.

Births outside marriage increased and in 1985 accounted for $8^1/2$ per cent of all births. By 1990 the figure was $14^1/2$ per cent, and by 1996 it had increased to almost 25 per cent.

Changes in the birth rate in 1997 were an interesting postscript to the 1996 census. The number of births in the third quarter of 1997 was the highest July–September figure for ten years. Births in that period were up for the fourth year in a row, with a 1 per cent increase over the corresponding period in 1996. The annual birth rate had been rising since 1994, after falling nearly 20 per cent since 1980.

The Economic and Social Research Institute considered that buoyancy in the economy was a factor in making families decide to have an extra child. Another factor was the 15,000 people who had migrated or returned to Ireland in the year to April 1997. Many of these were in the 23–35 age group, who are most likely to get married and have children. This inflow, up from around 8,000 in 1995/96 and nil in previous years, together with a natural increase of 19,000, meant a rise in population of about 34,000 in 1996. Most demographers believe that a sustained increase in the birth rate will depend on the longer-term economic situation (*Irish Times*, 3 February 1998).

A noteworthy aspect of the changes that have taken place in the population is the changing age profile. A declining birth rate and improvements in health and diet mean that the population is aging. Table 3.3 compares life expectancy for males and females between 1926 and 1991.

Table 3.3: Life expectancy, 1926 and 1991

At age	0	15	30	45	60	75	90
Males							
1926	57.4	50.7	38.4	26.5	15.8	7.7	3.3
1991	72.3	58.2	43.9	29.7	17	7.8	3
Females							
1926	57.9	50.5	38.6	27	16.4	8.4	3.7
1991	77.9	63.6	48.9	34.5	21.1	10.2	3.6

Source: Central Statistics Office.

The 1996 census showed that the majority of the population are aged twenty-five or older, as fig. 3.4 illustrates. The population is almost equally divided by sex, with only 25,623 more females than males. Increased life expectancy should see a continued increase in the older age groups. The main causes of death in the nineties were diseases of the circulatory system, cancer, and diseases of the respiratory system.

Fig. 3.4: Population of 26 Counties by age and sex, 1996

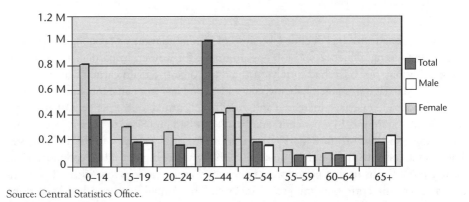

Source: Central Statistics Office.

As fig. 3.5 demonstrates, the geographical distribution of the population demonstrates a tendency towards increased urbanisation and increased concentration, with 52 per cent of the population of the 26 Counties living in Leinster, and almost 55 per cent of the population of Leinster living in Dublin. Towns in the vicinity of Dublin, such as Swords, Naas, and Maynooth, have seen their population increase since 1991 by 26 per cent, 26 per cent, and 42 per cent, respectively.

The internal migration from rural to urban areas has implications for marketers. The concentrated nature of urban areas means that transport, retailing and distribution can also be concentrated, which can lead to economies. Depopulated rural areas, however, may become less cost-effective. In many rural areas, concerns have been expressed about the negative consequences of depopulation in the form of reduced levels of infrastructure, public services, and employment.

While they are not necessarily an age-dependent category, marketers should also be aware of the needs of disabled consumers. Disability affects people of all ages, but it does not necessarily affect their ability to buy. People with disability and their carers are an important pressure group, and they are also an important market, not just for specialist products (Reed, 1997). Advertising or communication activities aimed at this market should not emphasise disability, and they certainly should not be patronising.

Fig. 3.5: Geographical distribution of population of 26 Counties

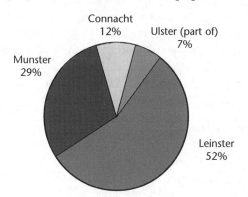

Connacht
12%

Ulster (part of)
7%

Munster
29%

Leinster
52%

Source: Central Statistics Office, 1998.

Implications for marketers

In general, the changing population profile presents both opportunities and challenges. A declining birth rate had meant a reduced market for products related to babies and children, but on the other hand the increased life expectancy means that consumers will remain in the market for longer, and the demand for products and services for the elderly will increase. Some have referred to this market as the 'golden years' or 'senior' market. One researcher noted that there was a danger of marketers stereotyping the senior market as lacking in spending power and innovation and being perceived as being difficult to segment (Turley, 1994). It was argued that there was an opportunity for marketers to direct their efforts at a segment that is active, engaged, and discerning.

A study in Britain suggested that the senior market could be segmented into four broad categories—'healthy indulgers', 'healthy hermits', 'ailing outgoers', and 'frail recluses'—and that marketing activities could be selected accordingly (Moschis and Mathur, 1997). Some manufacturers have undertaken research to assess the needs of older consumers, as the following panel demonstrates. There is certainly no doubt that the senior market is one that will present increased opportunities for marketers.

MARKETERS: IGNORE THE AGED AT YOUR PERIL

'Senior citizens' are a growing market force throughout Europe, and manufacturers of domestic appliances ignore this market at their peril. Not only is the proportion of people over fifty-five increasing in all European markets but this older generation of consumers needs labour-saving devices.

A survey by Electrolux showed that people over fifty-five have substantial purchasing power and increasingly discerning tastes. It showed that only two in five show brand loyalty when replacing white goods; so manufacturers must understand how these more mature consumers think.

Their cognitive age—how old they feel—is often ten or fifteen years less than their actual age. They think young and want to hold on to a life-style they enjoyed when they were younger. Older consumers tend to know what they want, but they are usually quite willing to experiment with new designs if there is a perceived benefit from the technology.

However, advancing years bring unavoidable changes, and manufacturers of consumer durables must make allowances for this.

- People grow shorter in stature after the age of forty, and women at a faster rate than men. Arthritis can limit mobility too; so a cooker with high-level controls or back-breakingly low shelves, for instance, is impractical.
- Eyesight deteriorates, so control panels should be clear and uncluttered. Labels should be in large type on non-reflective surfaces.
- Dexterity and the power to grip are diminished; so push-buttons and touch-pads should not be too small or too cramped.
- Clear and relevant instruction leaflets with household appliances are vital, with large type printed in black on a white background.

Youth culture has dominated marketing and advertising for at least four decades, and, relative to the rest of Europe, Ireland still has a young population; but demographic surveys carried out by Eurostat show that there will be well over 100 million Europeans in the over-55 category by the turn of the century. In Germany, for instance, they will make up nearly a third of the population, in Britain and Spain a quarter.

Source: M. Markey, 'Marketers, ignore the aged at your peril', *Sunday Business Post*, 6 October 1996.

At the other end of the spectrum, any increase in the birth rate will increase the market for associated products and services. In between the children's and older market are the teenage market, the singles market, the 'family formation' market, and a number of other age-related markets, all of which are catered for by an ever-expanding range of products and services. In youth marketing, the nineties witnessed 'generation X'— younger consumers who were more marketing-aware than previous generations and who appreciated direct and honest advertising (Dwek, 1997).

Another age-dependent category, the 45–55 age group, was described as the 'baby-boomers'. These tend to be rational buyers who base their brand loyalty on product and manufacturer integrity and prefer brands offering stability and longevity (Bond, 1997). To the extent that marketers segment or sub-segment their markets demographically, these individual age-dependent groups will be important.

The economic environment

Economic factors affect our purchasing power and spending patterns; and inflation, interest rates and tax will all have a bearing on the market. Inflation—which represents increases in the cost of living resulting from a sustained increase in the general price level—will have a direct effect on the consumer's purchasing power. If the rate of inflation is high and if incomes are not increasing, people may cut back on consumption, switch their purchases from expensive to cheaper items, or completely avoid certain purchases, such as luxury goods. In periods of low inflation the consumer's spending power is in effect increased. The consumer price index (CPI) gives an indication of the rate of inflation: this is calculated by taking the prices of a range of consumer products and services and measuring any price changes over time.

Interest rates, which represent the price of money, will also affect purchasing. When interest rates are high, consumers will be encouraged to save rather than to borrow; when they are low, the opposite is usually the case.

Rates of personal tax have a direct bearing on employees' take-home pay. High tax rates reduce disposable income and will therefore have an influence on the consumer's purchasing decisions. In Ireland the tax base is small: in 1997, for example, approximately a third of the population paid tax on their income (Revenue Commissioners, 1997); the remaining population are therefore considered to be dependent, giving a high dependence ratio. The Culliton Report in 1992 concluded that the tax system was in need of urgent reform and was a disincentive to enterprise; and tax reform subsequently became part of the programme of successive Governments.

Economic conditions at any given time will have a bearing on consumer and business confidence. If confidence levels are low, investment may be reduced and purchases postponed or re-evaluated. For most of the nineteen-nineties Ireland experienced a high rate of economic growth: between 1992 and 1996, for example, the average growth in gross domestic product was 6.4 per cent, while inflation averaged 2.2 per cent. Real GDP growth was well above the EU average. By 1998 the growth rate had reached 10 per cent, and consumers' spending increased as consumer confidence grew and low interest rates made borrowing attractive. A good indicator of consumer confidence has always been the sale of new cars, a significant purchase for most consumers. In 1997 sales of new cars in the Republic reached a record of 137,000, which was 14 per cent higher than the 1996 figure. Car dealers estimated that sales would slow down in 1998 but would still be between 100,000 and 110,000 (*Sunday Times*, 4 January 1998).

This sustained period of economic growth, coupled with low rates of inflation, resulted in economic buoyancy in most sectors of the economy. Some economists described this phenomenon as the 'Celtic tiger', as Ireland replicated the strong economic performance of some Asian countries. In 1998 the indications were that economic growth was set to continue.

The Culliton Report had concluded in 1992 that Ireland's industrial and economic performance since the mid-sixties had broadly matched and in some respects exceeded performance in EC countries generally. Culliton concluded that the main challenges facing Ireland in the nineties and beyond would be the reform of the EU common agricultural policy, European monetary union, the completion of the single European market, and an increasing awareness of environmental issues.

Reform of the common agricultural policy has seen significant reductions in the amount of agricultural produce placed in intervention. The single market was established in 1992, and the European Union was extended in 1996 to include Finland, Sweden, and Austria. Progress with EMU has been slower, with 1999 the target date for monetary union, though all member-states may not join at that time. It is planned that a new unit of currency, the euro, will be introduced as described in the following panel.

TIMETABLE TO THE EURO

1 January 1999
The value of the Irish pound is irrevocably fixed against the euro and against the currency of each of the other participating member-states. The euro is introduced as a unit of account.

1 January 2002 (at the latest)
The euro will be introduced as a cash-based currency. Euro coins and notes will be circulated in participating countries. The new and existing currencies will at first exist in tandem, with both euros and pounds being legal tender. The Central Bank will begin to withdraw pounds from circulation.

1 July 2002 (at the latest)
The pound will cease to be legal tender, and the euro will be the only currency valid in Ireland.

Source: European Information Centre.

The introduction of the euro will have implications for business. In addition to the euro becoming the unit of EU currency, each participating state will in effect be operating in the same economy. The central macro-issue for the Irish economy will be the rate at which the Irish pound enters monetary union. Another important consideration is that Britain, Ireland's largest trading partner, will not be participating in monetary union at the introductory stage; the rate at which the Irish pound entered EMU therefore determined the rate against sterling.

At a micro-level, companies' accounts procedures, invoices and receipts will be expressed in a new denomination. Cash registers, petrol pumps, public telephones and all other coin-operated machines will have to be adapted to take the new currency. IT systems that deal with accounts, billing, order processing, payroll and production systems will be particularly affected. At first retailers will have to introduce dual pricing, displaying the price of goods and services in both euros and pounds.

The increasing integration of the European Union presents both opportunities and threats for Ireland, with new markets opened up for Irish companies and equally the Irish market opened up to more competitors. The introduction of monetary union should result in a much larger market in which to invest and one in which currency fluctuation risks should cease to be an issue. It is expected that there will be increases in trade between member-states as a result. It may be possible for smaller businesses to exploit niche markets previously not viable; it is also probable that there will be an increase in direct selling, bypassing distributors. This may allow some existing exporters to rationalise their distribution channels on the Continent.

The Culliton Report made recommendations on reform of the tax system, on the provision of infrastructural needs, and on education, enterprise, and technology. In addition there were recommendations on direct support for industry, on institutional strengthening, and on specific aspects of the food industry. The Culliton recommendations, which to a large extent have formed the basis of successive

Governments' economic and industrial policy throughout the nineteen-nineties, are summarised in the following panel.

THE CULLITON RECOMMENDATIONS

Main recommendations on tax

A phased reform of the tax system, to include a broadening of the tax base through the reduction or abolition of many of the reliefs, exemptions, deductions, and expenditures.

The standard rate band to be extended to greatly reduce the numbers paying higher marginal rates, with special attention to the problem of single people on modest incomes.

No indication to be given of any continuation of the 10 per cent corporation tax rate beyond 2010.

Main recommendations on infrastructure

Increased investment in road improvements, changes in the ownership and institutional framework of ports, and greater competition in air services, telecommunications, and energy supply.

An active approach to the environment, the provision of safe disposal for hazardous industrial waste, and greater co-ordination and integration of planning and environmental protection.

The uses of European structural funds to be subjected to the strongest possible evaluation and to be allocated to priority development areas.

Main recommendations on education, enterprise, and technology

Education to de-emphasise the bias towards the liberal arts and traditional professions and to emphasise the need for productive enterprise and usable and marketable skills.

The development of a high-quality and respected stream of technical and vocational education, improved training for those at work, and an institutional reorganisation and redeployment of resources in the state training agency, FÁS.

The involvement of experienced industrialists in courses in advanced technology and higher education technology linkages and a greater emphasis on the acquisition of technology required to upgrade product quality and industrial competitiveness.

Main recommendations on direct support for industry

Reductions in grants to internationally mobile industry and a decisive shift from grants to the use of equity to meet gaps in financial markets for venture and seed capital.

Focusing the reduced grant budget towards industrial segments and niches of national competitive advantage.

Main recommendations on institutional strengthening

A redefinition of the role, functions and recruitment policy of the Department of Industry and Commerce.

One agency to be established from the IDA to look after the attracting of internationally mobile investment, and a new agency to be established to develop indigenous industry.

Main recommendations on the food industry

The performance of the beef industry to be improved; increased emphasis to be placed on the wholesome 'green' image of Irish food products; and specific product areas where Ireland has a marketing advantage to be identified.

Priority to be given to establishing the highest standards of safety and integrity in the food industry.

Export efforts to be concentrated on the British food market.

Source: Summarised from the Culliton Report, 1992.

Employment trends in Ireland have changed. The composition of employment has changed quite radically since the nineteen-seventies, reflecting the growing importance of services and a reduction in the significance of agriculture, as table 3.4 shows.

Table 3.4: Composition of employment, 1971–94

	1971	1984	1994	Change
Services	457,000	603,000	708,000	+55%
Industry	321,000	319,000	326,000	+2%
Agriculture	272,000	181,000	141,000	–49%

Source: Labour Force Survey (CSO).

The employment figures demonstrate quite vividly the decline in the importance of agriculture and the increased importance of services. The service economy has performed well, particularly financial services and tourism. Industrial employment has remained almost static since the seventies. While totals have remained largely the same, the composition has changed. Many manufacturing jobs in the seventies were in sectors such as textiles and motor vehicle assembly; by the nineties these had been replaced by sectors such as pharmaceuticals and computer manufacture and assembly.

Levels of unemployment are also significant, as those who are unemployed will have less purchasing power than the employed. Within the unemployment figures there are large numbers of long-term unemployed, who may not have the educational qualifications, training or skills to compete for jobs.

Table 3.5 gives details of the labour force for the years 1992–6. Unemployment figures contribute to the dependence ratio, but since 1993 there has been an annual reduction in the unemployment rate. In 1993 the rate was 16 per cent of the work force; by 1997 this had fallen to 10 per cent.

Table 3.5: Labour force (estimated)

	1992	1993	1994	1995	1996	1997
Agriculture, forestry, fishing	154,000	144,000	141,000	142,000	136,000	134,000
Mining, quarrying, turf production	6,000	5,000	5,000	5,000	5,000	6,000
Manufacturing	226,000	224,000	234,000	245,000	246,000	271,000
Building & construction	74,000	71,000	77,000	82,000	86,000	97,000
Electricity, gas, water	13,000	11,000	13,000	13,000	14,000	12,000
Commerce, insurance, finance	234,000	244,000	244,000	261,000	273,000	281,000
Transport, communication, storage	68,000	69,000	73,000	76,000	80,000	84,000
Public administration & defence	69,000	67,000	68,000	72,000	76,000	74,000
Other non-agricultural activity	300,000	313,000	326,000	343,000	369,000	379,000
Total at work	**1,143,000**	**1,148,000**	**1,182,000**	**1,239,000**	**1,285,000**	**1,338,000**
Total unemployment	217,000	230,000	218,000	191,000	190,000	179,000
Total labour force	**1,360,000**	**1,378,000**	**1,400,000**	**1,430,000**	**1,475,000**	**1,517,000**
Not in labour force	1,262,000	1,276,000	1,281,000	1,286,000	1,282,000	1,298,000

Source: Central Statistics Office.

Implications for marketers

The economic environment is fundamental in determining the consumer's spending power. In times of economic growth, as seen in Ireland in the middle to late nineties, the marketers of products and services ranging from new cars and new houses to hotels and restaurants experienced sales growth. The buoyant economy saw reductions in the unemployment rate and a significantly improved position in the Government's finances through increased revenues from income tax and VAT. In tougher economic times, such as during any form of economic recession, marketers can find it more difficult to achieve sales growth, as consumers' spending power decreases.

As with other environmental forces, the economic environment presents opportunities but can also provide threats. As we have seen, there was a direct relationship between purchases of new cars and economic well-being. Another product category that has grown significantly in the nineties is wine. As the following panel illustrates, a combination of social and economic factors contributed to this growth.

WINE CONSUMPTION IN IRELAND

In 1997 the sale of wine reached just over 3 million cases, or 37 million bottles. Approximately 50 per cent of adults were classified as regular wine-drinkers, up from 30 per cent in 1990. This growth has been attributed to a number of factors, including increased foreign travel; however, economic growth in the nineties meant that wine was no longer viewed as a luxury item. Life-style changes have also had an influence. According to the wine development board, between 1990 and 1996 there was a 49 per cent increase in wine consumption among women, a 45 per cent increase among those aged between and twenty-four, and a 59 per cent increase among the farming community.

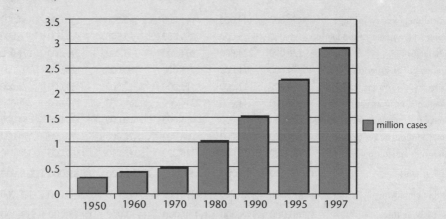

'New World' wines—from Chile, South Africa, Australia, and New Zealand—have sold very well: Australian wine is estimated to have 20 per cent of the Irish market. French wine, in comparison, has gone from 50 per cent to a 30 per cent share. A factor that is believed to have contributed to the growth in consumption of 'New World' wines was more understandable labelling, based on grape type rather than region. This helped demystify the world of wine for many consumers. Red wine has also become more popular, helped by publicity surrounding claims that it is healthier than white because it helps eliminate cholesterol from the bloodstream.

Source: E. Oliver, 'Irish turn to New World of wine in droves', *Irish Times*, 15 May 1998.

The technological environment

New technology creates opportunities, but it can also create a need for change. Technology can be a source of competitive advantage for firms that can use it to introduce or develop superior products or processes. It can also render existing products and processes obsolete and leave the unprepared firm behind.

Society is now experiencing a faster pace of technological change than ever before. In telecommunications, for example, there has been a rapid change from mechanical systems to computerised and cellular technology. This change, coupled with deregulation in telecommunications, has resulted in more choice for the consumer and more competition in the sector. Improvements in health technology have helped increase the average life-span, with surgical procedures such as transplants and heart bypasses becoming routine.

Technology has also had a very direct effect on marketers. In the retail sector, bar-code scanning has improved stock management techniques and can provide up-to-date information for marketers on stock levels or re-order quantities. Satellite television has increased the potential for global advertising campaigns, and the internet has just begun to have an impact on communication and the transfer of information. Digital television is also likely to become a significant development in the next century. Technological change can present challenges to firms in many ways. While changes in product and process technology will be significant for many, other environmental factors can be quite far-reaching. From the mid-nineties many firms have had to take action to deal with what came to be known as the 'year 2000 bug' or 'millennium bug'. The problem arises because certain widely used operating systems use only two digits to store information about a year, for example 98 to represent 1998; they cannot, therefore, handle dates after 1999. This could affect everything from the timer on household electrical appliances such as video recorders to the billing systems of organisations such as the ESB and Telecom Éireann. Retailers have had to ensure that their till receipts have the correct date.

A number of companies have already taken legal action against suppliers for selling software that was considered defective in this regard (*Sunday Business Post*, 8 February 1998). Other companies had to make significant budget allocations to resolve the problem, as the next panel shows.

DHL: SPENDING £25 MILLION TO BEAT YEAR 2000 BUG

This company has a budget of £25 million to ensure that its computer systems will be able to cope with the year 2000. It has identified the hardware that has to be replaced and hardware that can be upgraded. 'We have over 20 million lines of computer code in the company, and we also have 1,000 servers and 25,000 network users,' according to Derek Monahan, the IT manager at DHL. Along with Germany, Ireland was chosen as the site for the testing of DHL's year 2000 solutions.

Source: Charles Hogan, 'DHL spending £25m to beat Y2K', *Sunday Business Post*, 8 February 1998.

As the nineties closed, the year 2000 bug was not the only technological issue of concern to firms: significant attention was also being paid to the impact of electronic commerce.

ELECTRONIC COMMERCE

A number of definitions have been proposed for this increasingly important concept. Zwass (1996) described it as sharing business information, maintaining business relationships and conducting business transactions by means of telecommunications networks. It has also been defined by Andersen Consulting (1998) as part of a major research exercise on the use and perception of electronic commerce throughout Europe: they described it as an interchange of goods and services or property of any kind through an electronic medium.

Electronic commerce has grown in importance because of developments in electronic technology in areas such as telecommunications, networking, and data interchange. The technology has led to such developments as an increase in telephone transactions through call centres, the internet as a medium, and electronic data interchange (EDI), which has allowed firms to centralise purchasing and administrative functions. Andersen Consulting consider that electronic commerce can do a number of things for business, as the following panel illustrates.

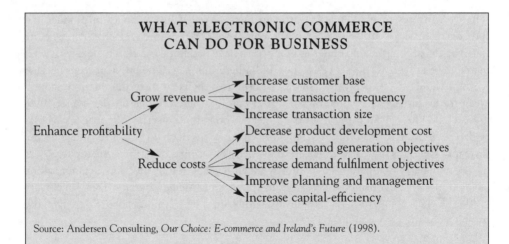

Source: Andersen Consulting, *Our Choice: E-commerce and Ireland's Future* (1998).

Andersen's European research showed that Irish companies believed that electronic commerce would have a major impact; it also showed that Irish companies tended to be the most enthusiastic about the opportunities, as table 3.6 shows. The research had been conducted among companies from a variety of industries in eight countries (Britain, France, Germany, Ireland, Italy, Netherlands, Spain, and Sweden).

Table 3.6: Companies' attitudes to electronic commerce

	Ireland	Average of eight countries
My company will be much more reliant on electronic commerce in five years	94%	82%
Electronic commerce will offer my company a competitive edge	77%	66%
Electronic commerce will provide a new channel for purchasing from suppliers	88%	81%
Electronic commerce will give customers more choice at better prices	83%	64%
Electronic commerce will open up new geographical markets	64%	52%

Implications for marketers

Technology is a source of competitive advantage for a firm. It leads to the development of new products and services and new processes; it is also an aid to marketers in their practice. Information technology, for example, has had a significant impact in areas such as marketing research, sales reporting, and budgeting and decision support systems.

The impact of new technology, especially in the area of electronic commerce, is likely to be a significant element in the environment of many firms. It is probable that the introduction of a single EU currency, the increasing penetration of cellular phones, digital television, increased internet usage and an increased use of EDI will hasten the process. The ability to link phones to computers, televisions to computers and computers to computers means that the ability of the marketer to interact with the customer will improve. This has obvious implications in areas such as marketing communication, customer service, product order and delivery, and payment.

The political and regulatory environment

Political stability is important for business. Instability causes uncertainty, which affects investment levels and trade. Ireland has a stable political environment and one that is generally supportive of investment and job creation.

The aspects of the political environment of most relevance to business are the laws enacted by the Oireachtas and the various Government agencies involved in the support and development of business and enterprise. The Companies Acts (1963 and 1986), the Sale of Goods and Supply of Services Act (1980) and the Consumer Information Act (1978) are all examples of legislation that has a direct influence on business and marketing practice. Increasingly, directives from the European Commission are having an influence on competition and on corporate governance and activities, as the example in the following panel shows. The Competition Act (1991), for example, required firms to ensure that their business and marketing strategies were in compliance with the law (Meade, 1993). The Act was based on the competition rules of the European Community contained in the Treaty of Rome (1957) and led to the introduction of comprehensive competition rules, established a competition authority, prohibited restrictive arrangements, and regulated the dominant positions that some firms enjoyed.

LOTTERY COMPETITION

In 1997 the European Commission ruled that foreign lotteries must be allowed to sell their lottery tickets in Ireland. Their sale had been prohibited by the Gaming and Lotteries Act (1956); the Commission stated that the prohibition was contrary to the rules of the single market, and the Government was given two months to change the legislation.

This change would allow more competition in a market dominated by the National Lottery, which had sales of £308 million a year. Rehab, the main competitor, was considering selling lottery tickets through its outlets for the British lottery promoter Camelot.

Source: *Irish Times*, 26 July 1997.

Statutory bodies, for example the ESB and Aer Lingus, are directly involved in providing goods and services. Other agencies provide services and support to business: for example, Enterprise Ireland has a central role in the development of indigenous enterprise and foreign markets. All statutory bodies and other Government agencies report to the relevant Government minister and department, and on occasion they may find they have to adapt or modify their activities to suit the political party in power, as Bord Fáilte found in 1997.

BORD FÁILTE AND THE SHAMROCK

In January 1997 Bord Fáilte, in conjunction with the Northern Ireland Tourist Board, adopted a new symbol, part of an initiative called 'Tourism Brand Ireland'. The original shamrock device, introduced in the nineteen-sixties, was replaced with a more abstract one depicting two people interacting; it also incorporated a shamrock but on a much reduced scale compared with the previous symbol. According to the two tourism bodies, the device represented what a holiday in Ireland was about: it put the shamrock in context. They began to use it in their advertising and promotional campaigns.

The new symbol was not greeted with complete approval. It also became a political issue when Fianna Fáil stated during the general election campaign that year that if elected they would change it.

Fianna Fáil became one of the parties in Government, and the symbol was duly changed to a new version of the shamrock in September. The issue was further complicated when the Northern Ireland Tourist board announced that it would not be changing and would continue to use the symbol adopted in January.

Source: *MII News*, January–February 1997; *Irish Times*, 26 September 1997.

Given the role that forces in the political environment can have, business interests will often seek to lobby or influence political decision-makers. Representative bodies, trade unions and individual organisations use lobbying to present their point of view, seek to have changes made, or emphasise particular issues. This lobbying may be conducted at local, national or EU level, as the account in the following panel shows.

THE REGULATION OF TOBACCO MARKETING

One of the most regulated areas of marketing practice is that of tobacco. By 1998 tobacco companies were not allowed to advertise on television, radio, or hoardings: advertising was allowed only in adult print media and in-store promotion. Advertising the act of smoking itself in any medium was prohibited: any image depicted had to be confined to the product and packaging. Health warnings had to be carried on packets and in advertising.

Sponsorship had not been as regulated. However, on 13 May 1998 the European Parliament voted to ban tobacco sponsorship completely. Immediately, the tobacco industry announced that they would be lobbying to have the decision reversed. Sponsorship, particularly of sports events, had become a significant aspect of tobacco companies' marketing.

Their chances of having the decision reversed could be slim, given the power of the anti-smoking lobby. Multi-million dollar court cases had been begun against tobacco companies in the United States in the nineties, and there was a general increase in smoking bans in public buildings, restaurants, and public transport.

The tobacco market in Ireland had experienced declining sales. In the cigarette market, for example, sales peaked in the seventies at 8,000 million cigarettes a year, which dropped to 5,800 million in the mid-eighties but had increased to 6,000 million by the late nineties. Gallaher were market leaders, with an estimated 47 per cent share, while John Player and P. J. Carroll were estimated to have 27 per cent and 26 per cent, respectively.

Significantly, tobacco generated large tax revenues for the state. In 1997, for example, the total market was valued at £893 million, and the total tax revenue by the state was £672 million of this.

Sources: *Checkout Ireland*, April 1998; *Irish Times*, 14 May 1998.

Implications for marketers

The political environment can be a source of rules and regulations that can have an impact on the marketer or on the way in which business is done. A central issue is the adapting of the business to change. But changes in laws or regulation can present opportunities: for example, the Galway company Thermo King reacted to a change in European regulation by developing a new product (Watson, 1993).

In 1989 the EC Transport Commission introduced legislation deregulating the length of trailers and regulated instead the total length of the trailer and tractor unit. The result was that no front-mounted refrigeration unit existed that could fit inside the dimensions prescribed in the new regulations. Thermo King developed a new refrigeration unit and in doing so was able to compress the design and development time usually required for developing such a product from between three and five years to eighteen months. This quick response showed how it was possible for a company to react quickly to an environmental threat.

Organisations may seek to lobby political decision-makers in an attempt to persuade them to reconsider plans or to modify them. In 1998, for example, Aer Rianta stepped up its lobbying of the European Union in an attempt to reverse the decision to abolish duty-free sales between member-states, scheduled for July 1999.

The socio-cultural environment

The socio-cultural environment involves forces that affect our values, beliefs, perceptions, and behaviour. Culture is a broad phenomenon and comprises a number of different elements, including material culture, social institutions, human culture, aesthetics, and language.

Material culture refers to a country's economic and technological profile and gives an indication of economic strength and technical advancement. Ireland is categorised as a developed country by the OECD. *Social institutions* are the educational and political systems that exist, both of which play a role in the encouragement, fostering and support of enterprise. In Ireland, levels of educational attainment are high in comparison with those of other EU countries.

Religion can be an important cultural determinant and influence. In Ireland the importance of religious institutions in determining culture was found to be above the European average in the nineteen-eighties (Turley, 1986); by the nineties there was some evidence of change. A survey conducted by the MRBI in 1998 showed a decline in attendance at Mass among Catholics. The survey of 1,000 adults, 922 of whom were Catholics, showed that 60 per cent attended mass weekly, whereas the corresponding figure for 1994 was 77 per cent. In 1983, 87 per cent attended weekly, while in 1973 the figure was 91 per cent (*Irish Times*, 4 February 1998).

Human culture refers to the values, beliefs and attitudes held by the population and is strongly influenced by factors such as family socialisation, religion, social class, and peers. The *aesthetic* aspects of culture are demonstrated in art, music and folklore and from the marketing viewpoint will often be used in national advertising and promotional campaigns. *Language* can also be significant, as seen in the launch of Teilifís na Gaeilge (now TG4) in 1997.

TEILIFÍS NA GAEILGE

Teilifís na Gaeilge was launched in 1997 to provide a television service in Irish. An important consideration was the ability of the station to attract advertisers and generate income. Advertisers awaited with interest the first viewership figures produced by the market research company A. C. Nielsen in June 1997. These showed that 500,000 people were watching weekly or more regularly and that 68 per cent of the national audience could receive the service.

Source: *Irish Times*, June 1997.

In the area of social changes, the nineties saw alterations in the law allowing for the wider sale of contraceptives, the decriminalisation of homosexuality, and the introduction of divorce. Social changes like these may present opportunities for marketers: for example, sales of contraceptives increased throughout the nineteen-nineties, particularly through vending machines, which were introduced in 1993. As the following panel demonstrates, marketers and advertisers also began to investigate the homosexual market.

IN SEARCH OF THE 'PINK POUND'

Estimates put the value of the disposable income of homosexuals at around £400 million annually. Marketers have not yet tapped in to this lucrative market by undertaking campaigns directly aimed at this market. There is certainly some evidence from other countries that homosexuals have higher than average disposable incomes and spend more on clothing, entertainment, grooming, financial services, drink, travel, music, and cards. An Australian travel survey found that homosexuals take 4.2 times as many trips by air and have 4.6 times more American Express gold cards than the national average. Almost 80 per cent of Britain's homosexual community take two or more overseas holidays a year. One washing-machine manufacturer decided to advertise between programmes that it knew homosexuals were watching after research told them that homosexuals changed their white goods more often than other people.

As for Irish marketers and advertisers, few have followed the approach of companies in Britain like Virgin and Smirnoff, which have actively aimed at the homosexual market. The reasons are probably the difficulties in quantifying the size of the market; and the fact that the homosexual community encompasses all professions and social classes may make it fragmented. It is also a fact that people consume regardless of their sexual orientation. Some advertisers may consider using the internet for focused campaigns, but it remains to be seen whether more marketers will develop specific campaigns or positioning strategies aimed at this market.

Sources: *Deadline*, June–July 1997; A. Pritchard and N. Morgan, 'The gay consumer: a meaningful market segmentation?', *Journal of Targeting, Measurement and Analysis for Marketing*, vol. 6 (1997), no. 1.

As a result of greater economic affluence and increased travel, tastes in food and drink have also changed. The consumption of products such as wine has increased, and some marketers have also found opportunities in the expanding 'ethnic' food market.

ETHNIC OPPORTUNITIES

Irish people are demonstrating an increased interest in foreign cuisine. Florian Ltd, a joint venture between Anwar Aziz and Genesis Equity, produces and markets the Shalimar brand of chilled Indian meals and the Chopsticks brand of Chinese meals. A variety of dishes is produced, which can be heated quickly and are aimed at consumers who have a busy life and who value convenience.

Aziz was the owner of a successful Indian restaurant in Dublin. Genesis is part of a venture capital company. Shalimar received help from Forbairt and opened a factory in County Monaghan in 1997. The products are stocked by multiples, including Dunne's Stores, Super Valu, and Spar. The company plans to expand its distribution in Ireland and to expand into the British market.

Changing tastes and life-styles mean that the market for chilled ready meals has increased. In 1997 it was estimated to be worth £220 million in Britain and £5 million in Ireland.

The meals are packed in modified atmospheric packaging (MAP). This nitrogen-filled packaging gives a chilled product a shelf life of between twelve and fourteen days, an important factor in convincing retailers to stock it. Bulk packages are also supplied to delicatessens.

Source: Iain Sebastian, 'Ethnic opportunities', *Enterprise and Innovation*, January 1998.

The fact that cultures vary from country to country has implications for international marketers. The same product or promotional campaign may not be suitable for all markets. Bord Fáilte, for example, varies the themes of its advertising and promotional campaigns in different markets. In markets like Italy it emphasises culture, nature, and scenery, while in the United States ancestry, music and history are the main themes.

Socio-cultural factors influence many product purchases. In Ireland, eighty per cent of homes are owner-occupied; this compares with an EU average of 56 per cent (*Irish Times*, 4 March 1998). This tendency can probably be explained by a combination of historical and cultural factors, which manifest themselves in the desire for ownership and security. Increased property prices in Dublin and the greater Dublin area in the middle and late nineteen-nineties, however, meant that many people could no longer afford to buy in those areas, and the market for property became buoyant in surrounding towns and counties and many people began to commute longer distances to work. This presented opportunities for transport providers: Iarnród Éireann, for example, operated daily commuter services from Dundalk, Longford, Athlone, Cork, Carlow, and Arklow. New services were introduced and stations opened on the lines from Kildare and Maynooth into the city, with a new brand, Arrow, developed for the purpose.

Implications for marketers

Cultural change provides opportunities for marketers. It can also be a threat for the marketer who cannot react or adapt. While the rate of cultural change can be quite slow—concepts such as tastes and values rarely change overnight—it is an important phenomenon. Cultural change may present opportunities for the development of new products or services.

A growth area in the publishing market in the nineteen-nineties was men's magazines, featuring articles on style, life-style, health, and fashion. The market was largely catered for by imported magazines, such as GQ, until 1998, when an Irish magazine, *Himself*, was launched (*Deadline*, March 1998). Cultural change may also mean that marketers have to re-evaluate the ways in which they segment the market and the development of positioning strategy.

The natural environment

In recent years there has been an increased awareness of the natural environment and its protection. The devastation of the rain forests of the Amazon, the effects of the Chernobyl nuclear leak in the nineteen-eighties, the effects of acid rain and the threat posed to rare or endangered flora and fauna have all received coverage. For some it was a call to action, as pressure groups were established and consumers began to seek out environmentally unharmful products.

Environmental protection took on added importance, and in the European Union many initiatives and directives were introduced. In some cases, such as the use of chlorofluorocarbon (CFC), which contributed to the depletion of the ozone layer, manufacturers began to produce aerosol products without this gas.

In addition to product development and support for environmental issues, firms often devote considerable resources to attempts to improve their environmental image. The Shell petroleum company, for example, planned to spend $200 million in 1998 on an international campaign aimed at improving its image in the aftermath of allegations about its environmental and human rights record. The company had been criticised by the environmental group Greenpeace over its plans for the disposal of the *Brent Spar* oil platform in the North Sea and for its failure to defend a writer and environmental campaigner from being put to death by the Nigerian government (*Marketing*, March 1998).

Many marketers were quick to jump on the environmental bandwagon in the nineteen-nineties. One study on cosmetic products, for example, found that of all competitors, the Body Shop came closest to openly explaining issues to consumers. While most competitors printed environmental information on their packaging, some of them made largely meaningless claims (Prothero, Peattie, and McDonagh, 1997). Consumers may be influenced by environmental information: for many it will be a factor used in evaluating a product. An Bord Glas, for example, which assists in the production, marketing and consumption of Irish fruit and vegetables, carried out a survey in 1997 that revealed that 25 per cent of consumers were buying some organic produce, compared with 23 per cent in 1995 (*Checkout Ireland*, December 1997). This indicated an increased awareness and concern among consumers about how fruit and vegetables were produced.

With regard to consumer behaviour patterns, many people began recycling household waste that previously they had dumped. A survey carried out in 1996 gave some indication of the importance people attached to recycling, as table 3. 7 illustrates. It also shows that there was a divergence between respondents' views on the importance of recycling and their actual behaviour. There was some disparity according to age groups and socio-economic backgrounds; this can partly be explained by the lack of means to recycle in some areas but also by the ability of respondents to say one thing and do another.

Table 3.7: Attitudes to recycling

Q. Do you think it is important or unimportant for products or items to be recycled?

	Total	14–34	35–54	55+	ABC1	C2DE	F
Very important	72%	72%	74%	70%	80%	67%	68%
Fairly important	22%	24%	22%	20%	15%	25%	28%
Neither important nor unimportant	5%	3%	4%	9%	1%	7%	4%
Fairly unimportant	1%	1%	1%	0%	0%	1%	0%
Very unimportant	0%	0%	0%	0%	0%	0%	0%

Q. Which items, if any, have you ever given to be recycled?

	Total	14–34	35–54	55+	ABC1	C2DE	F
Glass bottles	52%	53%	56%	46%	72%	46%	37%
Cans (aluminium)	33%	41%	33%	21%	45%	30%	22%
Paper products	20%	19%	23%	17%	37%	15%	3%
Clothes	13%	12%	17%	12%	23%	10%	6%

Plastic bottles	10%	11%	11%	6%	18%	6%	6%
Cardboard	9%	9%	9%	7%	20%	4%	1%
Christmas trees	6%	5%	9%	4%	11%	5%	1%
Plastic bags or refuse sacks	5%	6%	4%	5%	10%	3%	3%
None	32%	26%	29%	43%	14%	35%	52%

Base: all respondents.
Source: Taylor Nelson AGB, March 1996.

In January 1998 the European Union announced limits on the number of landfill dumping sites that will be allowed in Ireland by the year 2005. It is probable, therefore, that recycling will take on added significance in the future.

Many natural resources are non-renewable: for example, the Kinsale gas field operated by Marathon Petroleum, which supplies An Bord Gáis, will run out in 2001. The company has therefore been searching for alternative reserves and will be able to import gas from the North Sea by way of an interconnector between Ireland and Scotland. Marathon planned to build a gas-powered electricity generation station in the Dublin region to challenge the ESB's exclusive position (*Sunday Times*, 25 January 1998), but its plans will be dependent on getting a continued supply of gas.

Implications for marketers

Businesses exist within the natural environment and should therefore be sensitive to the preservation and protection of that environment. In many cases, regulations and controls must be complied with. There are, however, potentially more advantages for a marketer who takes the initiative rather than simply reacting. Many marketers, such as the Body Shop chain for example, have demonstrated that consumers are environmentally aware and will respond favourably to genuine environmentally unharmful products.

There will also be business opportunities in recycling. One company, Kerbside, began offering a weekly collection service for recyclable domestic rubbish in parts of Dublin. It is probable that such services will grow in other parts of the country. McDonagh and Prothero (1993) suggest that the basic requirement for marketers in relation to environmental marketing was a communication regime of integrity and clear-sightedness, both within companies and between companies and their relevant publics. They proposed a diagnostic tool that would allow the marketing manager to assess whether or not the company had a structure on which it could develop an environmental orientation. This involves an assessment of external communication on environmental issues, establishing who was responsible for environmental issues within the company, internal communication about the environment, and whether or not the firm had a written environmental policy.

CONSUMERISM

Consumerism is a force in the macro-environment designed to aid and protect the consumer by exerting moral, economic, political and legal pressures on business.

It may appear strange that consumers should need to be protected if the fundamental principle guiding the business is serving the customer's need. Consumerism as a force grew because of many cases of fraud, deceit, or misleading claims about products and services. But while contemporary consumerism has its origin in the nineteen-sixties, it is not a new phenomenon. From earliest times it was recognised that businesses or trades were in a stronger position relative to the customer. The customer needed to be protected from poor quality or fake products. The mediaeval guilds, for example, were established not just to regulate and control trades and professions but also to provide the customer with reassurance that when they bought from a member of the guild they were buying a genuine product. Goldsmiths and silversmiths, for example, had their products assayed and hallmarked.

Contemporary consumerism had its beginnings in the nineteen-sixties and was particularly strong in the United States. One of the leading proponents there was Ralph Nader, who came to national attention when he led a campaign to draw attention to design defects in a particular brand of car. The campaign gathered momentum because the manufacturer did nothing to rectify the defects, in spite of several accidents. This case, along with many others, demonstrated the need for consumer protection, and ultimately a Consumer Bill of Rights was introduced in 1969.

In Ireland the consumer movement has also grown. In 1966 the Consumers' Association of Ireland was founded to 'protect and promote the interests of the consumers of goods and services, and to enhance the quality of life for consumers.' The association is an independent, non-profit-making body and seeks to influence and lobby decision-makers on behalf of the consumer.

With greater European integration, consumer protection has become more standardised throughout EU member-states. A Department of Consumer Protection (DG XXIV) has been established by the European Union, with the power to propose new legislation, scrutinise draft directives, and financially support consumers' associations taking test cases in the courts. An ombudsman can receive and investigate complaints from a citizen of any EU country (Lansman, 1995).

The goals of consumerism

Consumerism and consumers' associations have a number of goals, which include:

- helping buyers cope with complexity
- protection from fraud
- representing consumers' interests
- protecting consumers' rights
- protecting the less well off.

The Consumers' Association of Ireland has been involved in identifying issues of concern to consumers, such as product safety. It has also sought to have consumer representation on state bodies. The association publishes a magazine, *Consumer Choice*, which reports on issues of interest to consumers and also publishes reports on product tests. These tests are based on market research, laboratory tests, or surveys of users, and they are independently and scientifically conducted.

PRODUCT TESTING BY THE CONSUMERS' ASSOCIATION

Comparative testing of products by independent organisations gives consumers unbiased information about the performance and characteristics of goods on the market. The Consumers' Association of Ireland is the only organisation in Ireland to carry out independent testing of goods and services. There are similar organisations in other European countries and in the United States, New Zealand, Australia, and other countries, each of which carries out similar tests and surveys.

A comparative test subjects different products designed for the same purpose to the same analyses and tests. The tests are conducted by expert testers in independent laboratories that specialise in the type of testing required. All products tested are bought anonymously in retail outlets, without manufacturers or suppliers being informed.

The test methods are scientific, repeatable, and transparent, with a relevant choice of criteria reflecting consumer usage. User trials are carried out by a selection of consumers, including those who are left-handed, those who are smaller or taller than average, and those with limiting disabilities. Men and women volunteers are used.

In some cases the association adapts tests reports from *Which?*, the magazine of the Consumers' Association in Britain; however, it reports only on products that are available in Ireland. International comparative tests are also conducted through International Research and Testing Ltd, a consortium of consumer firms from around the world.

Product tests aim to be representative and usually include the most widely available models. There are limits to the number of brands that can be tested, so the association will carry out research to establish which brands are most popular or widely available or have a particular feature worth investigating.

Source: *Consumer Choice*, May 1997.

The Consumer Bill of Rights in the United States (1969) established that consumers had the right to safety, the right to be informed, the right to choose, and the right to be heard. There is no similar legislation in Ireland; consumers are, however, protected by the provisions of various Acts. The main purpose of the Consumer Information Act (1978), for example, is to prevent false or misleading indications about goods, services or prices being given in the course of a business, trade, or profession. The scope of this particular Act is quite wide, covering descriptions of products and services, price indications, and advertising claims. The Act also established the Office of the Director of Consumer Affairs, who can receive and investigate complaints and has significant legal powers.

The Sale of Goods and Supply of Services Act (1980) amended and updated the law governing the relationship between consumers and suppliers of goods and services, while the Liability for Defective Products Act (1991) came about as the result of a directive of the EC. Under this Act the producers of a product are liable in tort for any damage caused wholly or partly by a defect in their product. Other Acts and regulations also apply.

These Acts do not confer rights on the consumer but are part of the criminal law. In relation to advertising, consumers can make complaints to the Advertising Standards Authority if they feel an advertisement has been misleading or is in breach of the code of standards. (A detailed discussion of the various Acts, regulations and standards that have implications for marketing practice is beyond the scope of this book. The reader should refer to the recommended reading at the end of the chapter.)

Reasons for the growth of consumerism

The consumer movement has grown in line with the growth in the availability of products on the market. As economies have grown, so too has the number of products and services. Many of these are technically advanced and complex, and consumers may not have the ability to understand or differentiate between them. Consumers may also have become sceptical about claims made in advertising or claims made by different competitors.

Increasingly, consumers are concerned about quality and safety controls, especially in cases where poor quality or safety have been demonstrated. The nineteen-nineties witnessed a greater interest among consumers in food additives and food safety and in environmental and health issues.

An examination of what consumers complain about also gives an indication of why the consumer movement has become a strong force. Complaints may include deceptive advertising, deceptive packaging, the exploitation of children, slow or inadequate servicing, misleading guarantees or warranties, poor product quality, and badly trained sales staff or the attitude of customer service staff. These complaints have one thing in common: a lack of understanding of the customer's needs.

Enlightened firms tend to view complaints as an opportunity to learn and to react quickly to solve the problem. It is important for firms to have an effective complaints handling procedure. Consumers are not unreasonable, and while mistakes should not happen, dissatisfaction may be considerably reduced by the way in which the firm deals with their complaint. Poor complaint handling serves to increase consumers' dissatisfaction and scepticism. It also leads to lost customers.

Implications for marketers

The consumer movement represents a threat to those firms that do not listen to their customers, that do not try to satisfy their needs, that provide misleading or scant information, or that have poor quality control—in other words, firms that are not marketing-oriented. If firms were truly marketing-oriented there would be no need for a consumer movement.

The objectives of marketers and the consumer movement are in fact the same. The consumer movement can be a source of information and ideas for marketers. It demonstrates what may be of concern to them; it may also alert the business to changes in the market. In 1998, for example, the Super Valu supermarket chain began buying beef from suppliers who used 'Enfer' testing (*Checkout*, January–February 1998). This test claims to establish whether the beef is free from BSE. Consumers had become increasingly concerned about this disease after a number of people developed a human variant from eating beef.

Marketers need to be familiar with the factors in the regulatory environment. In relation to product liability, for example, it is also advisable to investigate the desirability of taking out product liability insurance. While there may be rigorous quality control practices, it is possible for defective products to make it onto the market.

THE YEARS AHEAD

The analysis of the forces in the micro and macro-environment described in this chapter has given some indication of how environmental influences have affected firms in the past. Some ideas of probable future environmental trends have also been given.

What are the probable issues that will be faced in the years ahead? The Economist Intelligence Unit (1991) predicted that the main trends in the nineties would be increased globalisation, world peace and stability, demographic shifts, environmentalism, changing technologies, south-east Asia as an economic force, and Europe as a single market. The EIU has been proved correct, in that many of these trends were significant. Prediction, however, is an inexact science; and by the late nineties many countries of south-east Asia were experiencing economic turmoil and much of their economic progress had been considerably eroded.

It is nevertheless likely that the forces described by the EIU in 1991 will continue to be significant in the future. In the following section these trends are reviewed.

Globalisation

Globalisation describes a trend for companies to have a presence in more of the world, and, according to the EIU, this is stimulated by cheaper air travel, rising incomes, instant communication, the increased use of credit cards, the erosion of national barriers, financial deregulation, and shifting international cost structures. The trend towards globalisation seems set to continue. Andersen Consulting (1998) predicted, for example, that world internet use would grow from 100 million users in 1998 to 300 million in 2000 and 1,000 million by 2005. This would increase the potential use of the internet as a global business tool. Also in 1998 a new global alliance was announced in the airline industry, as the following panel illustrates.

ONEWORLD: GLOBAL ALLIANCE

In September 1998 British Airways, American Airlines, Canadian Airlines, Qantas and Cathay Pacific announced the creation of a global alliance called Oneworld. The alliance is primarily a marketing one. The five airlines will serve 632 destinations in 138 countries. Announcing the alliance, the chief executive of British Airways stated that response from customers showed a desire for airlines to work together to raise standards. The benefits to customers would include a seamless 'frequent flier' scheme.

Other airline alliances already existed, for example the Star alliance, involving Lufthansa, Thai, Varig, Air Canada, United Airlines, and SAS. The new alliance also prompted speculation that Europe's two remaining large unaligned carriers, Swissair and Air France, would form or join similar groups.

The Irish Government had given Aer Lingus approval to embark on the search for a strategic partner, and it was thought that a partnership with Oneworld was a strong possibility.

Source: Financial Times Service, 22 September 1998.

World peace and stability

The nineteen-nineties were characterised by a number of changes in the international scene. The Soviet Union disappeared as an entity and in its place was created a confederation of independent states. Similarly, countries of central and eastern Europe, such as Hungary and Poland, were no longer under Soviet influence. The result of these changes was the development of closer relationships between former protagonists and the end of what had been described as the Cold War. In South Africa the apartheid regime, which had virtually isolated the country from world trade because of sanctions, was replaced with a government democratically elected by all the people. South Africa's international trade increased dramatically as a result. In the Middle East and in Northern Ireland peace initiatives were also yielding results. In Northern Ireland, for example, peace brought boosts in investment and in the tourist industry.

Peace and stability are important if trade and investment are to flourish. Instability causes uncertainty and is bad for business. In the late nineties there were still potential threats to stability, and tensions still existed between states, for example between India and Pakistan and between north and south Korea. In Russia the late nineties were characterised by a currency crisis as the country grappled with economic reforms. Concerns were expressed about the country's ability to manage the crisis and maintain its newly established democratic system. These examples demonstrate how fragile the nature of peace and stability can be.

Demographic shifts

The nature of demographic changes in Ireland has already been described. Ireland has followed the trends of most industrialised countries, with a slowing down in the birth rate and an increase in the population over the age of fifty-five.

It is expected that there will be some changes in the populations of the main regions of the world, as table 3.8 illustrates. With regard to marketing opportunities, important markets will be Africa and Asia, though an important determinant of market growth will be income distribution and consumer spending power in these markets.

Table 3.8: Estimated population of major regions of the world, 2000–20

	2000	Proportion of total	2020	Proportion of total
Asia	3,698 million	59%	4,680 million	58%
Africa	872 million	14%	1,441 million	18%
Latin America	540 million	9%	719 million	9%
Europe	509 million	8%	514 million	6%
CIS	308 million	5%	343 million	4%
United States	266 million	4%	295 million	4%
Oceania	30 million	—	37 million	—

Source: Adapted from Eurostat.

Environmentalism

The EIU was correct in its view that environmental consciousness would increase in the nineteen-nineties. As evidenced in the previous section on the natural environment, this trend will continue. This means that issues such as *de-manufacturing* (which involves the disassembly of products into components that can be easily recycled), and recycling itself, will continue to be significant.

Changing technologies

It is likely that electronic commerce will be one of the most significant technological issues for businesses in the future. The nineteen-nineties saw significant advances in information technology and the beginnings of electronic commerce, and this development seems set to continue. According to Andersen Consulting (1998), electronic commerce is only part of a wider change in the economy. They consider that a new electronic economy (or 'e-economy') will develop. This economy will be characterised by electronically enabled enterprises (or 'e-enterprises'). As a result, they argue, markets and business relationships will change.

    The next century will see many technological changes for marketers, and the impact of some of these changes is considered in more detail in subsequent chapters. (The impact of the internet and digital television is considered in chapter 9, while the use of EDI is considered in chapter 10.)

South-east Asia as an economic force

In the early nineteen-nineties economic growth in south-east Asian countries was such that most observers felt the region would become a more significant economic force in world markets. By the end of the nineties this view had changed, as the region experienced a severe economic downturn.

The European single market

Efforts to complete the European single market continued throughout the nineties, though the speed of progress has been slow. In 1992 the single market became a reality. The introduction of the single currency in 1999 should continue the process of greater European integration and should help eliminate exchange rate uncertainty, though Britain, Denmark and Greece were not among the original members. As table 3.8 illustrated, as a proportion of world population the European population will decrease slightly, but this will continue to be one of the most affluent markets in the world and will continue to offer many opportunities for marketers.

Marketing in the years ahead

The analysis of the marketing environment has given some indication of the issues that are likely to be significant in the future and therefore provides some indication of how marketing may have to adapt. Doyle (1994) considered that while the fundamental principles of marketing would not change in the twenty-first century it was the pace of environmental change that would have most effect. Ten important environmental changes were described, and these, together with the appropriate marketing strategies and the organisational implications, are illustrated in the following panel.

THE CHANGING MARKETING ENVIRONMENT AND ITS IMPLICATIONS

Changing environment	Marketing strategy	Organising for marketing
Fashionisation	Speed	Breaking hierarchies
Micromarkets	Customisation	Small business units
Rising expectations	Quality	Self-managing teams
Technology	Information networks	Re-engineering
Competition	Core competence	Strategic alliances
Globalisation	Think global	Transnational companies
Commoditisation	Partnerships	Account management
Erosion of brands	Innovation	Expeditionary marketing
New constraints	Stakeholders	Role of the board

Source: Doyle, *Marketing Management and Strategy*.

Some of the issues raised by Doyle have already been discussed, and it is worth examining the additional issues raised. 'Fashionisation' refers to an increasing trend in many markets, ranging from cars to beer, for annual model changes, rapid obsolescence, and fickle demand. *Micro-markets* refers to smaller and more numerous market segments, while *rising expectations* refers to the increased expectation of the consumer in the areas of quality and service. *Commoditisation* is a feature of markets when products become obsolete or consumers become over-familiar with them, as a result of which prices go down and margins decline. Doyle argued that the position of many 'mega-brands', such as Coca-Cola, would be eroded by increases in micro-markets and competition from own-label products.

New constraints are forces ranging from changes in governments to economic and social changes. The strategic priorities as a result would concentrate on speed of response to these changes, the increased customisation of products and services to meet more sophisticated consumer needs, enhanced information networks, and the search for higher standards of quality.

FURTHER READING

Bird, T., *Consumer Law in Ireland*, Dublin: Round Hall Sweet and Maxwell 1999.

Clancy, P., Drudy, Sheelagh, Lynch, Kathleen, and O'Dowd, L., *Irish Society: Sociological Perspectives*, Dublin: Institute of Public Administration 1995.

Doolan, B., *Principles of Irish Law* (third edition), Dublin: Gill and Macmillan 1991.

Foley, E., *The Irish Market: A Profile*, Dublin: Marketing Institute 1996.

Lambkin, M., *The Irish Consumer Market*, Dublin: Marketing Society 1993.

Murphy, E., *Legal Framework for Irish ACCA Students*, Dublin: Gill and Macmillan 1997.

Whelan, Christopher (ed.), *Values and Social Change in Ireland*, Dublin: Gill and Macmillan 1994.

Central Statistics Office (www.cso.ie).

DISCUSSION QUESTIONS

1. Describe the micro and macro-forces likely to impinge on each of the following:
   (a) Goodfellas pizza
   (b) Durex condoms
   (c) Intel microprocessors
   (d) Dulux paint
   (e) Jury's hotels.
2. Explain why an understanding of the marketing environment is a prerequisite for successful marketing practice.
3. Comment on the role of internal marketing in the process of making firms customer-oriented.
4. Discuss the possible relationship dimensions for each of the following:
   (a) bank and customer
   (b) public transport provider and customer
   (c) manufacturer and road haulage contractor
   (d) airline and passenger
   (e) National Museum and visitor.
5. Describe how you feel each of the elements in the environment will change in the next five years.

REFERENCES

Andersen Consulting, *Our Choice: E-commerce and Ireland's Future*, Dublin: Andersen Consulting 1998.

Barnes, J., 'Internal marketing: if the staff won't buy it why should the customer?', *Irish Marketing Review*, vol. 4 (1989), no. 2.

Barnes, J., 'Establishing relationships: getting closer to the customer may be more difficult than you think', *Irish Marketing Review*, vol. 8 (1995).

Bond, C., 'Frightened and fifty: marketing to baby boomers', *Marketing*, 22 May 1997.

Carson, D., and Gilmore, A., 'Customer care: the neglected domain', *Irish Marketing Review*, vol. 4 (1989), no. 3.

Central Statistics Office, *Census of Population*, Dublin: Stationery Office 1996.

Doyle, P., *Marketing Management and Strategy*, Hemel Hempstead: Prentice-Hall International 1994.

Dwek, R., 'Cool customers', *Marketing Business*, February 1997.

Economist Intelligence Unit, *Marketing 2000: Critical Challenges for Corporate Survival*, London: EIU 1991.

Evans, J., and Laskin, R., 'The relationship marketing process: a conceptualisation and application', *Industrial Marketing Management*, vol. 23 (1994).

Garvey, S., and Torres, A., 'Winning success in aquaculture marketing', *Irish Marketing Review*, vol. 6 (1993).

Grönroos, C., 'Quo vadis marketing?: toward a relationship paradigm', *Journal of Marketing Management*, vol. 10 (1994).

Lansman, N., 'Consumer protection and the single market', *Company Secretary's Review*, 27 December 1995.

McDonagh, P., and Prothero, A., 'Environmental marketing: some practical guidelines for marketers', *Irish Marketing Review*, vol. 6 (1993).

Meade, J., 'The Competition Act: the implications for business', *Irish Marketing Review*, vol. 6 (1993).

Moschis, G., Lee, E., and Mathur, A., 'Targeting the mature market: opportunities and challenges', *Journal of Consumer Marketing*, vol. 14 (1997), no. 4.

Prothero, A., Peattie, K., and McDonagh, P., 'Communicating greener strategies: a study of on-pack communication', *Business Strategy and the Environment*, May 1997.

Reed, D., 'Disabled people: consumers able to buy', *Precision Marketing*, 12 May 1997.

Revenue Commissioners, *Annual Report*, Dublin: Stationery Office 1997.

Turley, D., 'Some perspectives on the Irish consumer', *Irish Marketing Review*, vol. 1 (1986).

Turley, D., 'The senior market: opportunity or oxymoron?', *Irish Marketing Review*, vol. 7 (1994).

Watson, M., 'Quick response as a competitive tool: Thermo King Europe's SMX', *Irish Marketing Review*, vol. 6 (1993).

Zwass, V., 'Electronic commerce: structures and issues', *International Journal of Electronic Commerce*, 1996.

4

Marketing Research

Marketers require information in order to make decisions about markets, customers, competitors, and the marketing mix. The changing marketing environment requires new information and requires existing information to be brought up to date.

Information can be gathered from a variety of sources. In particular, marketers need to be familiar with the theory and practice of market research. Research is vital to marketers, as it can provide them with information on the consumer's needs and wants. Market research plays an important role in developing effective marketing strategies and in understanding what is happening in the company's marketing environment. This chapter examines the sources of information available to marketers and the market research process, including the factors that must be taken into account in designing a research exercise.

THE NATURE OF RESEARCH

Research is the systematic collection and analysis of data that is relevant to the particular product or service. It is carried out in the context of political, economic and social influences, and it can apply to any aspect of the marketing process that requires investigation. Typically, research is conducted on markets, sales, products, advertising, promotion, distribution, and pricing. Within each of these, specialist research techniques and studies have developed: for example, the JNRR is a survey of the Irish public's readership patterns.

JNRR: OVER TWENTY-FIVE YEARS OF RELIABLE READERSHIP DATA

The Joint National Readership Research is an annual survey carried out for newspapers, magazines and cinemas by Lansdowne Market Research. The 1995/96 survey was the twenty-fifth conducted.

The primary objective is to measure average issue readership for newspapers and magazines. In addition, questions are included on the life-style of respondents, providing details on such matters as which bank services are used, how many respondents own cars, whether they have ever bought anything from a mail order catalogue, whether they drink wine or visit the theatre.

The research is based on a sample of five thousand respondents. Interviews are spread throughout the year, and there are 504 sample points throughout the country.

The benefits of the JNRR include helping publishers to sell advertising space and advertisers to buy space. In addition, it provides marketers with valuable information on the profile of readers, which is useful in making decisions about who to aim at in advertising campaigns.

The main purpose of research is to facilitate decision-making and to reduce risk. Managers need information to help them make decisions, and the more information they have and the more accurate and reliable that information is, the lower the risk will be in making those decisions. A manager considering the introduction of a new product to the market, for instance, will require information about the market, potential buyers, distribution channels and competitors to help them make that decision. Research will be used to determine whether a potential market exists, to profile potential buyers, and to help in the design of the marketing mix.

The JNRR not only gives the marketer information about respondents' readership of newspapers and magazines but also builds a life-style profile that can be used to make targeting and positioning decisions. The research is conducted each year, so the marketer can monitor changing trends.

The importance of listening to the customer

If the customer is at the centre of the business, it is important that the marketer listens to the customer. This is particularly so where the marketer does not come into regular face-to-face contact with the customer. Marketing research methods facilitate listening to the customer and finding out why the customer buys from the firm and identifying customers' attitudes, perceptions, opinions, and expectations of future needs. Customer research also provides first-hand information on how they perceive competitors. Customers may be quick to point out where improvements can be made.

INFORMATION TYPES

Information is the basis of all research. The research process involves the gathering, analysis, interpretation and presentation of information. Usually the information that marketers collect is broadly classified under three headings: *internal information, secondary information*, and *primary information*.

Internal information

Internal information is information that is available through the firm's own records and information system. Company accounts will provide information on sales and profits, which can be further analysed, for example, by product category, retail outlet, or market area. Accounts information will also yield cost and revenue budgets, which can be used in making decisions on such issues as the development of new products, communication campaigns, and marketing plans. Sales representatives' reports will give information on the sales of products within the geographical areas or retail outlets they are responsible for.

With the advent of new scanning technology and electronic data interchange, many marketers can get rapid information from retail outlets on the sales of particular products or product lines. As products are scanned at the check-out, an information data-base can be updated not only according to units sold but also to record stock levels.

All departments in the firm are providers of information: it is not purely a function of the marketing department. All companies and organisations have information available to them from internal sources, and marketers should be familiar with these sources and ensure that internal information is being regularly and reliably reported.

Secondary information

Secondary information is any published information that is available to the marketer, for example the census of population, industry reports, or published market research reports. It is information that already exists and has been compiled for a particular purpose. Typically, secondary information is useful for environmental monitoring, and it can be obtained from a variety of sources. The following panel lists some of the most commonly used secondary sources.

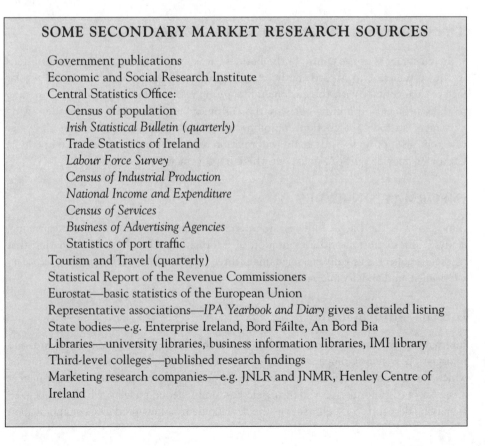

SOME SECONDARY MARKET RESEARCH SOURCES

Government publications
Economic and Social Research Institute
Central Statistics Office:
  Census of population
  Irish Statistical Bulletin (quarterly)
  Trade Statistics of Ireland
  Labour Force Survey
  Census of Industrial Production
  National Income and Expenditure
  Census of Services
  Business of Advertising Agencies
  Statistics of port traffic
Tourism and Travel (quarterly)
Statistical Report of the Revenue Commissioners
Eurostat—basic statistics of the European Union
Representative associations—*IPA Yearbook and Diary* gives a detailed listing
State bodies—e.g. Enterprise Ireland, Bord Fáilte, An Bord Bia
Libraries—university libraries, business information libraries, IMI library
Third-level colleges—published research findings
Marketing research companies—e.g. JNLR and JNMR, Henley Centre of Ireland

Primary information

Primary information is information that has to be generated at first hand, because no published sources are available or accessible, or where such information does not meet the information needs of the marketer. For instance, a company may wish to ascertain the attitudes or opinions of its own customers, and this information will not be available from secondary sources.

THE MARKET RESEARCH PROCESS

The *market research process* is the systematic way in which information is procured and provided in a usable form to the decision-maker. The process involves a series of stages. Fig. 4.1 outlines the stages commonly used in gathering market information from primary sources; each of these stages is then examined in turn.

Fig. 4.1: Stages in the market research process

Definition of research problem
↓
Select method of information collection (internal, secondary, primary)
↓
Use qualitative or quantitative research, or a combination of both
↓
Select population or sample to be surveyed
↓
Specify time and resources required
↓
Design of survey instrument
↓
Collection of data
↓
Analysis of data
↓
Report and presentation of data

Definition of research problem

This stage may prove the most difficult, as the marketer has to specify in advance what the research problem is. Sometimes it can be difficult to get agreement from the company or organisation on what the objectives of the research should be. It is vital, however, that the person carrying out the research has a clear and unambiguous brief.

The problem should not be defined too broadly or too narrowly. Too broad a definition can lead to unnecessary information being gathered, while too narrow a definition can result in important information being overlooked. A precise statement of the research problem is required, and this can then be translated into specific research objectives. Consider the following panel, where researchers had to design a research study for a proposed museum.

PIDGEON HOUSE POWER STATION: A NEW ROLE AS SCIENCE AND TECHNOLOGY MUSEUM?

Pidgeon House power station on the South Wall, Dublin, has been disused for several decades. A study group was established to determine whether the buildings could be converted into an interactive science and technology museum. In 1996 the group commissioned several research projects, one of which was to survey primary and secondary schools, which were considered to be an important potential visitor group. The research problem was that there was no information to help the researchers determine the likely level of interest among schools in such a museum. This problem was then translated into specific research objectives:

- to determine the number of schools that participate in field trips or study trips
- the factors considered important in selecting destinations for such trips
- the reaction of schools to the concept of an interactive science and technology museum
- the expectations schools would have of such a museum
- the price schools would expect to pay for admission
- what time of year schools are most likely to take study trips
- what modes of transport would normally be used.

Source: Tallaght RTC Student Research Project, 1996.

In many cases it may be difficult for the marketer to be specific, and some research will be *exploratory* in nature. This describes the assessment of general information to find relevant points to concentrate on: for example, a marketer wishing to expand into overseas markets may scan a number of markets before deciding which one to select. Other research projects will be *descriptive*, such as those dealing with the size of the market, the market share of the main competitors, or the attitudes and opinions of customers. *Causal* research describes research into cause-and-effect relationships: for instance, a company might be interested in finding out the effects, if any, an increase in price will have on sales of the product.

Method of information collection: internal, secondary, primary

The researcher needs to specify what methods of information collection will be used. In many cases companies will have information available to them internally from their own reporting system, and this may be enough to provide the marketer with the information needed. It is important that firms have an organised information reporting system, otherwise decision-makers may waste time and money because their system is not being properly used, or they may not realise the usefulness of internal information, because it is not being communicated or compiled in a meaningful way.

Secondary research is used frequently by decision-makers. It will usually be required in advance of meetings about the product or industry so that participants are informed about general background issues, or it may be required to build up specific knowledge of the industry or sector in which the business operates. Marketing practitioners need to keep themselves informed on developments in their business environment, and secondary research can be particularly useful in this regard.

In relation to the research problem itself, sometimes it can be wholly or partially solved using secondary sources of information. The difficulty for Irish marketers is that, in general, very little published research is available on specific markets or product categories: most research commissioned by marketers through market research companies is proprietary and is not generally published.

Primary research will be generated at first hand using one or a combination of research techniques. Primary research can be time-consuming and expensive, and the researcher therefore should be sure, before embarking on such a project, that all possible secondary sources have been examined. Primary research can involve a number of alternatives, as shown in the following panel.

METHODS OF PRIMARY RESEARCH

Observation: for example, observing the number of people selecting a particular product in a supermarket during a particular period.

Experiments: selecting subjects, giving them different treatments, controlling related factors, and measuring the results. A company wishing to test a new product before launch may experiment by using a test market or area. The product can be promoted in this area and stocked in a selected number of shops, and consumers' response can be measured. The test market should be representative of the total market, and this will give an indication of the probable success of the product.

Surveys: questioning people directly about their behaviour, attitudes, or opinions. The survey will usually involve the use of a questionnaire, which is a structured research instrument.

Qualitative and quantitative research

Qualitative research

Qualitative research involves attempting to gain insights into respondents' perceptions, attitudes, and motives. It is based on an understanding of psychology, and therefore the researcher should ideally have a background in psychology before attempting qualitative research. The main methods used by researchers are *depth interviews, focus groups,* and *projective techniques.*

In recent years there has been an increase in the use of qualitative research. One study reviewed some of the creative techniques used in qualitative research (O'Leary, 1993); it found that analysis was primarily based on psychological and sociological dimensions.

Depth interviews are usually conducted individually and are therefore ideal for dealing with sensitive subjects. The form of the interview is typically unstructured, so that the respondent is encouraged to open up to the researcher rather than simply answer a list of questions. The interviewer needs to be skilled at dealing with people, so that the respondent feels at ease and willing to answer the questions. Depth interviews are time-consuming and can also be expensive if several are needed.

Focus groups usually consist of eight to ten people, together with a moderator, who meet for a group discussion about a particular subject. Respondents are encouraged to discuss their attitudes, reactions, motives, life-styles, or feelings about the subject. They are recruited from specific groups: for example, a hotel interested in developing a new short holiday break for people over fifty-five might conduct a focus group comprising men and women over fifty-five. The new product could be explained to them and their opinions and ideas sought. The moderator will usually have a psychology background, as skill is required in the analysis of responses. The moderator will also have to ensure that the discussion does not become sidetracked or that no one person attempts to dominate the discussion.

Projective techniques will sometimes be used in both qualitative and quantitative research. Essentially these are attempts to understand the individual's underlying motives and feelings. Two of the main techniques used are *word association* and *sentence completion*; the following panel gives some examples of each.

PROJECTIVE TECHNIQUES

Word association involves asking interviewees to respond immediately to a word with the first word that comes to mind; respondents are therefore communicating their feelings indirectly. Asking the respondent for an immediate response is important, as it means they don't spend time searching for the answer they feel they should give. It is also usual to present a list of words, only some of which are actually of interest to the researcher; this disguises the purpose of the research when the researcher does not want the respondent to bias answers to later questions based on their earlier responses.

For example, a beer company interested in the perception of its brand might want to research spontaneous response to a number of brands:

Stimulus word	*Response*
Harp	....
Heineken	....
Budweiser	....
Foster's	....
Tennant's	....

Sentence completion requires the respondent to be a little bit more descriptive and forthcoming; for example:

People who drink Guinness are ....

....

....

Quantitative research

Quantitative research involves the analysis and manipulation of facts and figures—the collection of sufficient data to allow statistical analysis. Data for analysis may be available from secondary sources or it may have to be generated by primary means.

The techniques for the design, administration and analysis of questionnaires are particularly important in quantitative research, as in many research projects the questionnaire will usually be the means of obtaining the data for analysis. Questionnaires are structured research instruments and are used to measure behaviour, demographic characteristics, knowledge levels, attitudes, and opinions.

Sampling

The *sample* refers to those respondents selected for survey. They must be representative of the whole population of interest, and this implies a need to work out what will be a statistically valid sample. The researcher has therefore to decide who is to be surveyed, how many should be surveyed, and how respondents should be chosen.

It is rare that a census of the population of interest will be undertaken, unless it is physically and financially possible to do so. A census implies that the researcher will survey every member of a population, and there are cases where it may be possible to do so: for example, if Boeing were carrying out research on the needs of airlines in Ireland it would be quite feasible for them to survey all Irish airlines, as the total population is quite small. But in general, researchers will select a representative sample from the population of interest. In the JNRR research on page 96, for instance, it was seen that Lansdowne Market Research will survey five thousand adults per year. This sample would be structured to reflect the sex, age, class and geographical profile of the Irish population and therefore can be taken as representative of the adult population as a whole.

There are a number of different approaches to sampling.

Probability samples: Each element of a population from which the sample is drawn has a known chance (non-zero) of being selected. This is the only truly objective method of sampling. Its main drawback is that a *sampling frame* (a list of the population under survey) is necessary, and this is not always possible. An example of where it is possible would be Eircom conducting research among subscribers listed in a particular area's telephone directory.

Non-probability samples: This is a type of stratified sampling in which the selection of sampling units is within specified strata and is done non-randomly, usually controlled by quotas. In the JNRR example, Lansdowne Market Research would have a specified quota of respondents based on sex, age, class, and geographical region. Table 4.1 gives the adult population profile that was used as the basis for deciding how many respondents to interview from each category.

Table 4.1: Population profile used in JNRR research

Adult population (26 Counties) aged 15+ = 2,646,000.

Sex
Male	49%
Female	51%

Age
15–24	23%
25–34	19%
35–44	18%
45–54	14%
55–64	11%
65+	15%

Class
AB	10%
C1	20%
C2	25%
DE	30%
F50+	8%
F50–	7%

Region
Dublin	30%
Rest of Leinster	23%
Munster	29%
Connacht-Ulster	18%

Computing the size of the sample: Sample size depends on the basic characteristics of the population, the type of information required, and the costs entailed. In general the rule is the larger the sample size, the greater the reliability. When sample size is being computed the *non-response factor* should be borne in mind: in other words, there may be members of a particular population who will not consent to be surveyed. If the researcher carrying out a survey for Boeing, for example, approached all Irish airlines but only one agreed to participate, the response error would be quite high and would have to be reported in the research findings.

With *random sampling* the size of the sample can be computed mathematically in order to achieve a stated degree of precision. Random samples can be drawn where a complete list of the relevant population is available and each therefore has a calculable chance of being selected for survey. This involves the evaluation of a *confidence coefficient*, which indicates the specified degree of certainty with which a particular sample estimate can be accepted as a true estimator of the population being surveyed: for example, a level of confidence of 95 per cent would result in a 5 per cent level of significance. (For a detailed discussion of sampling the reader should consult the recommended reading given at the end of the chapter.)

Time and resources required

The time taken to complete the research, and the resources required, must be included in any research plan. Decision-makers will usually not have unlimited time or resources to complete the research; the time and resources available will, for instance, determine the extent of sampling that might be possible. In addition to the general costs of carrying out the research, such as the fees of a market research company, the marketer may also consider incentives to encourage a higher response rate, such as free products for participants or participation in a prize draw. Incentives should not, however, be such that they would bias the research findings.

Design of survey instrument

In most cases the survey instrument will be a questionnaire, the nature and design of which will vary according to the research being undertaken.

Questionnaires are structured survey instruments used by researchers to interact with interviewees. They are widely used by researchers conducting quantitative research. They can be of varying lengths and forms, but they should be kept short, simple, and easy to understand.

A number of questions should be borne in mind when a questionnaire is being designed, including:

- Exactly what information is required, and from whom?
- Will respondents be able to understand the questions, and will they be able to answer them?
- Are the words used in the questions clear and unambiguous?
- Are the words used likely to result in biased answers?
- Are the questions arranged in the correct sequence?
- Is the layout of the questionnaire clear and free from confusion?

The design of the survey instrument is a separate stage in the process, but it is important to note that it follows on from the research objectives. Researchers should ensure that the objectives have been clearly established before beginning the design of a questionnaire. The survey instrument will also determine the subsequent stages in the research process. Problems with the questionnaire will inevitably lead to difficulties in data collection and analysis. Poorly designed and structured questionnaires will probably yield low response rates or vague and unreliable data.

Questionnaires should always be tested among some representative respondents before the survey is undertaken. This should ensure that any potential difficulties are identified and can be dealt with before the survey takes place.

When the questionnaire is being designed, the method of analysis that will be used should also be borne in mind. If a statistical computer program is being used it must be possible for the researcher to code the answers into a form that is compatible with the program.

Question sequence

The following are some guidelines relating to the sequence of the questions:

1. Open the questionnaire with a few factual, easily answered questions.
2. Lead in to a small number of factual multiple-choice questions.
3. Follow with questions designed to gauge whether the interviewee has thought about or knows about the topic under review.
4. Move to a series of structured and semi-structured questions designed to cover very specific issues.
5. Introduce a selection of open-ended or wide-open questions so that the respondent can fully express himself or herself
6. Close with 'filter' questions—those designed to place the respondent according to the sampling frame

It is not unusual for the 'say/do' phenomenon to appear in market research. Respondents may give the answer they think they ought to give but will in fact engage in quite different behaviour. In new-product research, for example, the respondent may say that they will buy the product but will not. While it is very difficult—in most cases impossible—to monitor this, a well-designed questionnaire will have questions that verify the answers given by the respondent. In the case of new-product research, for example, the marketer could seek information on other new products the respondent has bought in order to determine their interest in new products in general.

Classification questions

Questionnaires will usually seek background information on respondents, such as their age, marital status, and social class. Usually, factors such as age will be presented on a scale, unless it is important to know the exact age.

Social class in Ireland is measured according to the respondent's occupation or the occupation of the head of household. This yields a number of groupings, commonly referred to as the ABC1 scale. The Central Statistics Office also produces socio-economic groupings, but the ABC1 scale is the most widely used in marketing. Researchers use a fairly comprehensive list of occupations for classifying people.

Rating scales

Questionnaires will often require respondents to *rate* something. There are three types of rating scale. The *Likert scale* and the *semantic differential* are the most commonly used; the

Stapel scale is probably used less frequently. The Likert scale asks the respondent to indicate agreement or disagreement with something.

THE LIKERT SCALE

Brand A contains more meaty chunks and less jelly than other cat foods.

Strongly agree	Agree	Neither agree nor disagree	Disagree	Strongly disagree
☐	☐	☐	☐	☐

The *semantic differential* presents bipolar adjectives on a scale, and respondents are asked to indicate on the scale the point that reflects their view.

THE SEMANTIC DIFFERENTIAL

Rise and Shine orange juice is:

good value for money ·· poor value for money
conveniently packaged ···································· inconveniently packaged

---

The *Stapel scale* consists of a single adjective in the middle of an even-numbered range of values.

THE STAPEL SCALE

Please indicate how accurately you think each of the following words describes our service:

+5	+4	+3	+2	+1	Fast	−1	−2	−3	−4	−5
+5	+4	+3	+2	+1	Slow	−1	−2	−3	−4	−5
+5	+4	+3	+2	+1	Reliable	−1	−2	−3	−4	−5
+5	+4	+3	+2	+1	Unreliable	−1	−2	−3	−4	−5

Fig. 4.2 illustrates a questionnaire used by Iarnród Éireann on its Inter-City routes. This was designed to elicit information on frequency of travel, purpose of journey, frequency of use of competing modes, ticket type bought, usage and opinions of catering services, and overall rating of the service. In addition, the questionnaire sought some basic background information. Respondents were asked to complete the questionnaires themselves, so appropriate instructions are included to ensure that they can progress through the questionnaire without difficulty. Also worth noting is the layout of the questionnaire, which includes number codes that would be used by the researcher when entering responses for analysis.

Fig. 4.2: Iarnród Éireann questionnaire

J.16246
(1 - 5)

OFFICE USE   QUESTIONNAIRE NO.

(6) (7)   (8) (9) (10) (11)

CARD 1 COL (12)

Dear Customer,
Irish Marketing Surveys, on behalf of Iarnród Eireann, are currently carrying out a series of surveys across all rail routes. Your views and opinions are very important and we would be grateful if you would complete this questionnaire.

Q.1 How often do you travel by train to the destination you are travelling to today?
PLEASE TICK ONE BOX ONLY

(13)
- Every day — 1
- 2 - 3 times per week — 2
- Once a week — 3
- Once a month — 4
- Once every 2-3 months — 5
- Once every 6 months — 6
- Less often than every 6 months — 7
- First time today — 8

Q.2 What is the main purpose of your journey today?
PLEASE TICK ONE BOX ONLY

(14)
- For work/on business — 1
- Visiting relations/friends — 2
- Shopping/leisure activity (e.g. concert/sports event) — 3
- Another reason ←Please write in & tick box — 4

Q.3 What other means of transport **could** you have taken for today's journey instead of the train?
PLEASE TICK ALL THAT APPLY

(15)
- By car, driving self — 1
- By car, passenger — 2
- By coach, Bus Eireann — 3
- By coach, Private Co. — 4
- ←Other means of transport Please write in & tick box — 5

Q.4 How often, do you travel to the destination you are travelling to today by each of the following means of transport? **PLEASE TICK ONE BOX ONLY FOR EACH: CAR, BUS EIREANN AND PRIVATE BUS.**

	CAR (PLEASE TICK ONE BOX ▾)	BUS EIREANN (PLEASE TICK ONE BOX ▾)	PRIVATE BUS (PLEASE TICK ONE BOX ▾)
	(16)	(17)	(18)
More than once a week	1	1	1
Once a month	2	2	2
Once every 2-3 months	3	3	3
Once every 6 months	4	4	4
Less often	5	5	5
Never use for this journey	6	6	6

Q.5 What type of ticket are you travelling on today?
PLEASE TICK ONE BOX ONLY

(19)
- Single — 1
- Day return — 2
- Midweek Return — 3
- Weekend Return — 4
- Monthly Ticket — 5
- Faircard — 6
- Family/Kid+ — 7
- Student/Travel Save Ticket — 8
- O.A.P. Pass — 9
- Contract Ticket — V
- Other ticket type ←Please write in — X

Q.6 Did you avail of any of the Irish Rail **catering** services today?
PLEASE TICK ONE BOX ONLY

(20)
- YES — 1
- NO — 2

↳If no, why did you not use any Irish Rail catering service today?
PLEASE TICK ONE BOX ONLY

(21)
- No catering service provided — 1
- Nothing to suit my taste — 2
- No need for meal/snack — 3
- Menu/variety of food not very inviting — 4
- Expensive — 5

↳If yes, which services did you use?
PLEASE TICK ALL THAT APPLY

(22)
- Trolley on train — 1
- Snack car on train — 2
- Full meal on train — 3
- Station Buffet - snack or meal — 4

Q.7 Please rate the catering service you have used today by ticking the appropriate box for each of the statements listed below. e.g. If you thought the **service** was "fair" tick the centre box on that line.
TICK ONE BOX ONLY ON EACH LINE

	VERY GOOD	GOOD	FAIR	POOR	VERY POOR	
VALUE FOR MONEY	1	2	3	4	5	(23)
QUALITY OF THE FOOD	1	2	3	4	5	(24)
SERVICE BY STAFF	1	2	3	4	5	(25)
VARIETY OF FOOD	1	2	3	4	5	(26)
PRESENTATION OF FOOD	1	2	3	4	5	(27)
HYGIENE	1	2	3	4	5	(28)

Q.8 We would like you to rate the service provided on this **train journey** today by ticking the appropriate box for each of the statements listed below. **TICK ONE BOX ONLY ON EACH LINE** e.g. If you felt that the "cleanliness" of the train was very good tick that box on that line.

	VERY GOOD	GOOD	FAIR	POOR	VERY POOR	
Cleanliness of the train	1	2	3	4	5	(29)
Comfort of the train	1	2	3	4	5	(30)
Toilet facilities on the train	1	2	3	4	5	(31)
Helpfulness of staff on the train	1	2	3	4	5	(32)
Overall value for money	1	2	3	4	5	(33)
Speed of journey	1	2	3	4	5	(34)
Reliability/punctuality of the service	1	2	3	4	5	(35)

BACKGROUND INFORMATION

Just to complete the interview we would appreciate if you would provide us with some general background details about yourself.

AGE: (38)
- Under 15 years — 1
- 15 - 18 years — 2
- 19 - 25 years — 3
- 26 - 34 years — 4
- 35 - 54 years — 5
- 55 - 65 years — 6
- 66+ years — 7

SEX: (39)
- Male — 1
- Female — 2

STATUS: (40)
- Single — 1
- Married — 2
- Other — 3

OCCUPATION: (41)
- Working full/part time — 1
- At school/full time education — 2
- Household duties — 3
- Retired — 4
- Looking for work — 5

THANK YOU FOR YOUR CO-OPERATION

Contact methods

If a structured questionnaire is being used, the main contact methods are personal interviews, telephone interviews, and postal interviews.

Personal interviews include interviewers stopping people on the street, giving out questionnaires on a train, or calling at people's homes. They are time-consuming and more expensive than the other two contact methods but are more flexible.

Telephone interviews have the advantage of being more cost-effective and less time-consuming, but they need to be highly structured, and the interviewer may not be able to verify the accuracy of data, for example the respondent's age.

Postal interviews are very cost-effective and can be highly structured but do not allow for respondents' questions and can have low response rates. If a more unstructured research approach is being adopted, depth interviews or focus groups will be more appropriate. Here the questionnaire will be a series of general questions or discussion points designed to prompt the interviewer or moderator.

A particular survey form that has grown in importance is 'mystery shopping' (*Sunday Business Post*, 12 April 1998). This involves trained assessors visiting retail outlets, presenting themselves as customers, and talking to sales staff. The purpose is to assess whether or not sales staff can explain the benefits of products and can answer questions; it therefore provides an assessment of the firm's sales and customer care training schemes.

Assessors usually complete a detailed questionnaire, which may cover such factors as initial greeting, general customer service, sales ability, and product knowledge. (See the extracts from a questionnaire used by UCI Cinemas in fig. 4.3.) The assessor or mystery shopper has to answer each of these questions with respect to the experience they had when they visited one of UCI's cinemas. In addition to the questions listed in fig. 4.3 the mystery UCI shopper also had to assess making a telephone booking, the external lobby, toilets, main foyer, and the quality of the food and beverages.

Fig. 4.3: UCI mystery visitor scheme

Site Location:
Date of Visit:
Show Time:
Film Seen:
Weather:

External Impressions

	Yes or No	Points Possible	Points Scored
Car Park neat, tidy and litter or weed free		3	
All lights on		1	
All signage clean and well illuminated		1	
Film display fully illuminated		1	
Film titles and certificates clearly on display		1	
All windows clean and free of smudges		1	
All film posters neatly presented		1	

Box Office
Number of Customers in the queue:
Number of kiosks open:
Number of staff members in the kiosks:
Time taken to receive tickets:
Name of person serving:

	Yes or No	Points Possible	Points Scored
Clear where tickets booked by phone could be collected		1	
All staff not smoking, chewing or eating		2	
Clear display of films, show times, certificates and prices		1	
Inside of the kiosk clean and tidy		1	
Tickets came directly from dispenser		3	
All staff neatly dressed in uniform and wearing name badge		4	
Greeted with eye contact or smile and all staff polite and courteous		6	
The box office appeared secure		2	

Concession Stand

All staff neat, tidy and in full uniform		4	
All food displays adequately stocked		2	
Straw and napkin dispensers adequately stocked		2	
Counter neat, tidy and free of spillages		2	
Staff member attempted to trade up order		10	
Correct Change tendered		2	
Greeted with eye contact or smile and all staff polite and courteous		6	
All displays fully illuminated		1	
All staff observing the no smoking or drinking or eating rule		2	

Auditorium

Queue well controlled or informed of show time		3	
Ticket Checked or Stub put into box		2	
If seat booked, shown or clearly directed to seat		1	
Seat clean and free of rips		3	
All floor areas clear of food or litter etc.		3	
Exit Signs illuminated		2	

Temperature Comfortable	4
Screen slides in focus or well presented	2
Film picture and sound quality good	5
Show started on time	3
Audience quiet and controlled by staff	5
All staff neatly dressed in uniform and wearing name badge	4
Greeted with eye contact or smile and all staff polite and courteous	6
Asked for ticket stub on return to cinema	5

Source: UCI.

The assessor can also present problems to members of the staff to see how they are dealt with or could complain about something and measure the reaction. Employees usually know that mystery shoppers are calling, but not when. Schemes will usually be spread over time, so that the performance of individual branches can be tracked. Usually, firms with several outlets or branches use the scores received by each outlet to make comparisons. An important aspect of this research is that employees should receive feedback, and the results can be used in training schemes. They can also be used to benchmark performance against that of competitors.

Collection of data

The method used will depend on the type of research being conducted. If a quantitative survey of consumers is being undertaken, this usually involves administering a questionnaire. The questionnaire is therefore the data collection instrument. If qualitative research is being undertaken the data will usually be collected through depth interviews or focus groups.

The period for the collection of data may need to be specified; for example, the Inter-City questionnaire (page 108) was administered over a week on each Inter-City route, on different trains at different times of day. This ensured that the research was not limited to particular days or to particular trains.

Analysis of data

If the information generated has been mostly qualitative in nature, the analysis will concentrate on the principal opinions, attitudes, or perceptions. This requires an objective analysis of respondents' opinions and viewpoints. Quantitative information will usually be subjected to various degrees of statistical analysis. As statistical analysis can be a laborious process, it will usually be done on computer, using a specialised statistical and research program. The analysis process involves the editing, coding and tabulation of data. Degrees of statistical analysis will depend on the complexity of the information collected. A number of statistical programs are available that can be used for the analysis of quantitative information, including SPSS, SAS, Systat, Minitab, and Microstat. These programs permit the tabulation and analysis of large quantities of information.

The statistical measures used will depend on the objectives of the research. At a basic level this will usually involve descriptions of averages, percentages, distributions, and measures of dispersion. Cross-tabulations that show the number of cases that have particular combinations of responses with two or more questions are useful for providing a more detailed analysis of information obtained. As shown in table 4.2, for example, Lansdowne Market Research has cross-tabulated those respondents who bought a new car in the previous three years with respondents' social class, and the result is a matrix that provides some interesting and helpful data for the marketers of new cars.

Table 4.2: New car purchases by class

	Total	AB (11%)	C1 (21%)	C2 (22%)	DE (20%)	F50+ (10%)	F50– (6%)
Ford	17%	11%	23%	16%	21%	8%	32%
Toyota	16%	13%	18%	17%	20%	16%	24%
Volkswagen	9%	8%	5%	5%	4%	32%	13%
Nissan	8%	7%	6%	14%	9%	9%	—
FIAT	5%	3%	5%	9%	6%	2%	—
Honda	4%	7%	5%	1%	—	2%	—
Renault	4%	6%	4%	2%	9%	3%	—

Source: Joint National Readership Research, 1995–6.

Cross-tabulations usually involve taking variables relating to the respondents, such as sex, age, or class, and cross-tabulating these with other variables, such as brands bought, quantity of the product bought, or opinions expressed. It is also usual to examine data for correlations, but care must be exercised, as a correlation indicates a degree of movement between two or more variables: it does not necessarily imply a causal relationship. For example, a research study on the consumption of household products might show that in particular households there was a correlation between the consumption of candles and the consumption of milk, but obviously there is no causal relationship between the two.

Report and presentation of data

The general guidelines for report-writing should be followed, in that the style should relate to the person who will receive it, clear language should be used, and diagrams and tables should be used for presenting quantitative information. The following panel gives a suggested framework for a research report.

SUGGESTED FORMAT FOR A RESEARCH REPORT

Title page
Table of contents
List of appendixes
Introduction
Main conclusions
Details of survey methods
Survey findings
Conclusions
Recommendations
List of tables
List of diagrams
References
Appendixes

The following panel gives some excerpts from a fictitious research report, which gives an indication of the style commonly used.

EXCERPTS FROM A SAMPLE RESEARCH REPORT

Introduction

The author was commissioned by O'Leary Foods to carry out a survey of people who buy freshly prepared meals from delicatessens. The survey sought information on their purchasing behaviour, specifically how often they bought prepared meals from delicatessens, the type of dishes bought, prices paid, and the shops used. In addition, the survey sought respondents' ratings for a number of leading delicatessens in Dublin, including O'Leary's outlets in Tallaght and Sutton.

The survey was carried out over one week, and the completed questionnaires were analysed using the SPSS statistical analysis program.

Main conclusions

There has been a marked increase in the number of prepared meals bought from delicatessens in the last three years. This increase has been evident in all areas of Dublin. People are buying more prepared meals, and they are also buying more frequently.

Prices vary considerably between different areas of the greater Dublin area, with shops in Howth, Sutton, Blackrock and Killiney being the most expensive. Shops in these areas can command higher prices for similar products; however, they tend to have a lower turnover than those in all other areas.

O'Leary's delicatessens in both Sutton and Tallaght were highly rated for quality, value for money, and customer service. However, the ratings for variety and presentation were considerably lower. McNamara's citywide chain of delicatessens received the strongest overall ratings of all competitors.

Details of survey methodology

A survey of five hundred householders was conducted in South County Dublin, Fingal, and Dún Laoghaire and Rathdown. The sample was drawn up according to the age and population breakdown in these areas, with a disproportionate number of housewives being chosen.

A self-administered questionnaire was chosen as the survey instrument. The questionnaire was tested on twenty respondents, representative of the population, and no changes or modifications were required. The survey was carried out between 10 a.m. and 8 p.m. from 6 to 12 January 1999.

Research findings

[This part of the report would give details of the research findings, which should be presented in a factual manner. Diagrams or tables could be used to help illustrate the findings.]

Conclusions

There has been an increase of 12 per cent in the number of prepared meals bought from delicatessens in the Dublin area. There has also been an increase of 8 per cent in purchasing frequency, reflecting changing meal patterns in households and an increase in the number of working wives and of one-person households.

Consumer tastes are changing. Many people are trying out more exotic dishes; however, more traditional dishes, such as quiche and lasagne, are still popular.

The prices charged for prepared meals can vary considerably in different parts of the greater Dublin area. Higher prices are commanded in Howth, Blackrock, and Killiney, but shops in these areas have a lower turnover (as much as 7 per cent lower) than those in the city.

O'Leary's delicatessens was rated highly for quality (86 per cent satisfaction rating), value for money (75 per cent satisfaction), and customer service (82 per cent satisfaction). In relation to variety and presentation, the ratings were considerably lower: 50 per cent and 57 per cent satisfaction, respectively. This should be a cause for concern.

O'Leary's delicatessens fared well generally in comparison with other delicatessens around the city. However, its main competitors received higher satisfaction ratings under all headings.

Recommendations

[If these are required they should follow logically from the 'Conclusions' section of the report. Recommendations should also specify courses of action.]

Things that can go wrong

Researchers are concerned to ensure that any research carried out is reliable and accurate; otherwise it is impossible to base decisions on research findings. There are a number of possible errors that researchers must be careful to avoid.

Sampling errors can occur where the sample taken is not representative of the population of interest. Care needs to be exercised in sample design.

Non-response error can occur when the researcher does not receive a response from the target sample. Possible reasons could be where the research topic is sensitive or embarrassing or where respondents are approached at an awkward or inconvenient time.

Data collection errors occur when respondents do not understand the questions asked. Researchers have to ensure that the wording used does not confuse the respondent.

Analysis errors happen when the researcher wrongly interprets research findings. Researchers need to view research findings objectively and should ensure that data has been accurately tabulated and analysed.

Report errors can occur if the researcher comes to the wrong conclusion or if the research findings are poorly communicated.

Needless to say, these sources of error should be avoided, and can be avoided with careful planning of the research project.

RESEARCH ETHICS

Ethics refers to moral rules, standards, codes or principles that provide guidelines for right and truthful behaviour in specific situations. Research practitioners are governed by codes of conduct and ethics that are designed to protect people from exploitation and ensure that research is conducted in an ethical manner. Researchers have responsibilities to their clients, to respondents, to the public, and to themselves. Researchers should honestly do what they purport to do: they should not manipulate research techniques to produce desired findings, and they should not undertake research assignments that are ethically unacceptable.

The code of research ethics developed by the Market Research Association in the United States is summarised in the following panel.

CODE OF PROFESSIONAL ETHICS AND PRACTICES

1. To maintain high standards of competence and integrity in survey design.
2. To maintain high levels of business and professional conduct.
3. To observe reasonable care and to be objective and accurate in the use of data.
4. To protect the anonymity of respondents.
5. To thoroughly instruct and supervise those responsible for carrying out the research.
6. To observe the rights of ownership of any materials received.
7. To make available to clients such details on the research methods and techniques used as may be reasonably required for proper interpretation of data.
8. To promote trust of the public for marketing and survey research activities.
9. To encourage observance of ethical practice among the research profession.

Source: Abstracted from text supplied by the Marketing Research Association, Inc., Chicago.

In general it can be taken that respondents have the right to choose whether or not to participate in the research, the right to have confidentiality protected, and the right to be informed about the nature of the research. A company cannot misrepresent a sales pitch as a research exercise; and research can only be conducted on minors with the consent of a parent or guardian.

The net result of unethical research practices would include the unwillingness of companies, organisations or the public to take part in research surveys, the distortion of policy-makers' and decision-makers' perceptions of issues, and a reduction in the public's ability to distinguish between valid and invalid research findings. Observance of the codes of ethical research practice ensures that respondents, clients and researchers are not compromised.

The following panel reproduces a leaflet given to participants in surveys by Lansdowne Market Research to explain the reasons why respondents were selected and the responsibilities the research company has to them.

STATEMENT TO RESPONDENTS

LANSDOWNE MARKET RESEARCH
12 Lower Hatch Street
Dublin 2

Thank you for helping with our survey by giving this interview.

Since its foundation in 1979, Lansdowne Market Research has grown to become Ireland's leading consumer research company.

In the course of a year, many thousands of people are interviewed by Lansdowne Market Research. However, those who help us do not always know why we ask so many questions or the uses to which we put the information. Here is a short explanation of what it is all about.

Q. Why were you chosen for interview?

A. On most surveys we have to interview a cross-section of the public, people from all walks of life and of all ages. The answers given by all the different types of people are analysed together to give an accurate picture of the country as a whole.

Q. Will someone try to sell me something?

A. No. You will not be approached by anyone selling anything as a result of this interview, and you will not be contacted again, unless
(a) the interview is one of a series in which you agree to take part,
(b) you stated your willingness for re-interview,
(c) as part of our 'Quality Control' procedure.

Q. Who commissioned this survey?

A. As stated earlier, market research is controlled by a strict code of standards. The person being interviewed does not know the name of the client, nor does the client know the names of the people who have been interviewed. This way we can guarantee that the information given to us is not biased by any preconceived ideas.

Q. How can I be sure that someone is a genuine market research interviewer?

A. (a) Ask to see an identity card. All our interviewers carry an identity card with their photo attached.
(b) Ring one of our telephone numbers and ask to speak to the field controller or manager.

Q. Why do you want my name, address, and telephone number?

A. It is possible that you might receive a letter or phone call from one of our supervisors. This letter or call will be to thank you once again for taking part in the survey and to find out if you were happy with the way the interview was carried out. You may also be asked a few questions about the survey itself to ensure that the answers you gave were recorded correctly. This forms part of our Quality Control Procedure, and your co-operation is greatly appreciated.

Q. How am I protected?

A. Market research is controlled by a strict code of standards, which guarantees anonymity both to the person who is interviewed and to the client for whom the research is being conducted. The interview you give is strictly confidential.

Unless your explicit permission has been obtained, the name and address of you or your family will not be disclosed to anyone.

Finally, we would like to thank you once again for agreeing to take part in this survey. We hope this leaflet will have helped to explain the background to market research. If you have any further questions, concerns or comments, please contact us at [telephone numbers].

MARKETING RESEARCH APPLICATIONS

Marketing research has several applications. It is used to measure and investigate aspects of consumers' behaviour, advertising and promotion effectiveness, new product or service ideas, package design, and price-sensitivity. Advertisers, for example, pay particular attention to the annual JNRR, JNLR, and JNMR. FMCG companies tend to buy continuous tracking research on their brands; this provides continuous information on the sales performance and market share of brands in the product category. Some researchers specialise in particular applications, and a significant body of knowledge has been built up in each. In general, regardless of the particular application, the research process includes the factors described in this chapter.

FURTHER READING

Malhotra, N., *Marketing Research: An Applied Orientation*, Englewood Cliffs (NJ): Prentice-Hall 1993.
Morris, Clare, *Quantitative Approaches in Business Studies* (third edition), London: Pitman 1993.
Moutinho, L., and Evans, M., *Applied Marketing Research*, London: Addison-Wesley 1992.

Weiers, Ronald, *Marketing Research*, Englewood Cliffs (NJ): Prentice-Hall 1988.
Whitehead, Geoffrey, *Statistics for Business* (second edition), London: Pitman 1992.

DISCUSSION QUESTIONS

1. Describe the steps in the research process you would adopt for each of the following projects:
   (*a*) A manufacturer wishes to research the market for a new fat-free ready-to-serve trifle.
   (*b*) A tour operator feels that the eighteen to thirty-year-old market is potentially lucrative and wishes to establish the type of holiday package (or packages) that would be most attractive.
   (*c*) A theatre group wants to discover how often people visit the theatre and the types of performances they prefer.
   In your answers you should clearly indicate how you would go about carrying out the research, specify your population of interest, and state what information you would require from them and how you would go about collecting it.
2. You have to chair a discussion in a focus group on people's attitudes to recycling domestic waste, such as glass and plastic. Prepare an outline of how you would select people for the group and the discussion points you feel should be covered.
3. A distributor of eggs wishes to find out about household use and consumption patterns in their area. Design a questionnaire that would elicit information on the size and composition of the household, how often eggs are bought, where they are bought, consumption rates, how eggs are cooked or prepared, and general classification of respondents' age and social class.
4. Comment on the issues that can affect the validity of marketing research.
5. Explain the importance of ethics in marketing research. Give some examples of unethical activities.

REFERENCES

O'Leary, P., 'Qualitative research: where it's at, where it's going', *Irish Marketing Review*, vol. 6 (1993).

5

Market Segmentation, Targeting, and Positioning

This chapter discusses the segmentation, targeting and positioning decisions that must be considered by marketers. Each is a step in the process of understanding the needs of the customer and attempting to match those needs with a marketing mix that the company can capably deliver. The process is part of the marketer's strategy: it enables the marketer to select the most profitable and viable customers to serve, to reach them with an offering that has a competitive advantage, and to communicate a position that is clearly perceived.

The importance of market segmentation, targeting and positioning is well illustrated in the attempt by British Airways to win back business passengers. The following panel illustrates the financial importance of the business travel segment of the airline market and shows how airlines direct product offerings at business travellers and position themselves with branded services.

COMPETING FOR THE LUCRATIVE BUSINESS TRAVELLER

British Airways was estimated to have lost £50 million in income because Club World passengers were abandoning it and flying with rival airlines for a better service. An internal survey of its Gold Card members, the most frequent British Airways fliers, revealed that 48 per cent of them preferred to fly with British Airways' business class competitors. The airline immediately scheduled its managers to fly in Club World in order to gather responses from customers during flights and to assess the service on board.

While Club World accounts for only 5 per cent of British Airways' passengers, it accounts for 25 per cent of income. It is therefore an important market segment. The £50 million drop in sales represented only a small fraction of Club World income in 1997, which was £2,000 million, but the company was worried by the numbers switching airlines.

Some competitors were reckoned to have more generous 'frequent flier' schemes than British Airways, an important incentive for many business travellers. In addition, airlines such as Virgin and Singapore Airlines had upgraded their Upper Class and Raffles Class, respectively, with high-technology seats, video entertainment, and limousine services to and from the airport. They concentrated on these benefits in selecting business travellers. The Club World service had been in existence since 1995, and British Airways decided to introduce a new, improved service in 1999.

Source: D. Parsley, 'Business passengers desert BA', *Sunday Times*, 20 September 1998.

MARKET SEGMENTATION

Market segmentation literally means the division of the market. It is based on the fact that most markets consist of buyers who have different needs and who cannot all be served with the same product offering. From a business point of view it is also based on the idea that by identifying buyers whose needs the firm can serve and by aiming a product at them, the marketer can be more effective and profitable. Segmentation is the first stage in the sequential process illustrated in fig. 5.1.

Fig. 5.1: The segmentation, targeting and positioning process

Market segmentation
(dividing the market)

↓

Target marketing
(deciding which segments to serve)

↓

Positioning
(establishing a distinct image for the product)

There are very few examples of products that are marketed in the same way to everyone. Marketers tend to divide up markets in an attempt to find the segment or segments they can best serve. Sometimes, when products are new to the market, they may be limited in their options or segments.

Market growth, however, may be dependent on producing variants and finding new segments. Few marketers attempt to be all things to all people, and many marketers engage in *product-differentiated marketing*, whereby two or more products with different features, benefits, options or sizes are offered. Consider the example of Intel, which began identifying niche markets in an attempt to increase sales.

INTEL GEARS NEW CHIPS TOWARDS NICHE MARKETS

Intel Corporation's new processors for high and low-end computer markets may help the firm stave off recent market losses. They also represent a more defined segmentation strategy for the company. The microchip giant released its 266 MHz Celeron processor and new 400 MHz Pentium II offerings in mid-April. The Celeron is aimed at the low-end consumer market, while the Pentium chips are geared for high-performance demand.

This niche-oriented approach is a new strategy for Intel. Rather than using older processors in cheaper machines, the company is now seeking to gear new products directly to the home user.

Source: J. Saunders, 'Intel gears new chips towards niche markets', *Computing Canada*, 4 May 1998.

Environmental changes can mean that markets become more segmented. For example, in addition to normal milk, consumers' health and dietary needs are catered for with low-fat milk, calcium and vitamin-enriched milk, and skimmed milk.

Markets in general are becoming more segmented. If there is only a small number of buyers it may be possible to customise the product for each buyer. For example, business-to-business marketers typically sell products to a small number of large customers, and their competitive advantage may be their ability to offer a customised product. For most other marketers, segmentation is a requirement, and in general, buyers will be grouped into broad categories with similar needs. There is no single basis on which to do this, and the marketer should consider all the alternative ways of dividing up the market.

Bases for segmentation

A number of different bases are used for market segmentation, and most marketers will use a combination of them, as no one base may be completely descriptive of the segments that exist. The most commonly used segmentation variables include *geographical area*, *demographics*, *behaviour*, and *psychographics*.

Geographical segmentation involves dividing the market by geographical area. This can be done by region, city, postal district, county, or any number of sub-divisions. Census data can be used to establish population numbers in particular areas. Population statistics provided by the Central Statistics Office, for example, divide the Irish population by province, county, age, sex, and other descriptors. These can be used by marketers to assess the size and profile of the market for their products.

In the Irish market, many products and services are available nationally. There are, however, many regional and local brands and in some cases national marketers with regional brands. In the bread and confectionery market, for example, a small number of large bakeries control the market, but there is also a larger number of smaller bakeries that serve local markets.

Guinness has one significant regional brand, Macardle's ale. This has a strong market presence in the north-east, the product having been brewed in Dundalk since the last century. Similarly, Beamish and Crawford's Beamish brand has a strong presence in Munster.

Geographical segmentation is also useful for international marketers. While the Irish market is quite small and homogeneous, the international markets that many companies compete in are much larger and more diverse, and this diversity can be more manifest in different geographical areas.

Consider the socio-economic and age profile of some of Ireland's tourism source markets in table 5.1. This shows the proportion of visitors who come from certain geographical areas; it also shows that, in general, visitors from Britain, Germany, France, Italy and the United States tend to come from the ABC1 socio-economic segment, which represents professional, managerial and white-collar workers. The age profile is somewhat different, with visitors from Britain and the United States tending to be older than those from Germany, France, and Italy. The tourism market therefore can be segmented by geographical area, by socio-economic background, and by age. It would also be possible to segment using other bases, such as reasons for visiting Ireland, length of visit, or type of accommodation used. Geographical segmentation can also be used by industrial marketers if their buyers are spread over different geographical areas.

Table 5.1: Socio-economic and age profile for selected tourism source markets, 1994

	Britain	Germany	France	Italy	United States
Proportion of all visitors	46%	9%	7%	3%	16%
Social class					
AB	36%	36%	38%	36%	45%
C1	35%	49%	51%	57%	43%
C2	22%	10%	8%	5%	10%
DE	7%	4%	3%	1%	2%
Age					
0–18	11%	11%	14%	10%	4%
19–24	9%	21%	18%	26%	10%
25–34	24%	31%	27%	37%	19%
35–44	22%	16%	20%	11%	14%
45+	34%	21%	20%	16%	52%

Source: Bord Fáilte Éireann.

Demographic segmentation involves dividing the market according to demographic factors, namely age, sex, and income. Table 5.2 shows the age and sex profile of respondents to a survey on snack foods. The result of this particular survey gives the marketers of such products an indication, by age and sex, of who is most likely to have bought these products. It would appear that the younger consumer, aged between fifteen and thirty, is most likely to have bought and consumed a snack product, and that women are more likely to snack than men.

Table 5.2: Age and sex profile of snack buyers

Q. Have you purchased to eat yourself any of these products in the last week?

	Total	15–30	35–54	55+	Male	Female
Crisps	36%	58%	28%	8%	32%	39%
Chocolates	35%	51%	29%	16%	33%	36%
Sweets	31%	45%	24%	18%	30%	32%
Individual ice cream	20%	28%	18%	11%	18%	23%
Individual chocolate biscuit	18%	21%	19%	12%	14%	22%
Individual one-serve cake	7%	8%	7%	5%	4%	9%
None	3%	2%	4%	4%	3%	3%
Don't know/can't remember	32%	15%	38%	53%	36%	28%

Source: Taylor Nelson AGB, May 1996.

Brands may be developed specifically for different age groups. Pioneer, the consumer electronics manufacturer, decided to develop a youth brand to rival the 'Freq' sub-brand launched by Sony (Elkin, 1998). The company planned to launch a range of portable CD and minidisc-players, car audio and home units.

Income is another possible demographic segmentation base. In general, income per capita will give an indication of the spending power of consumers in particular markets. This may be particularly relevant when examining international markets, as a low income per capita will indicate a poorer economy. Demographic segmentation may not be as useful to industrial marketers as they are to product or services marketers. Business-to-business marketers tend to sell to businesses or organisations rather than to individual consumers.

Behavioural segmentation is based on buyers' behaviour patterns. These can include the occasion when the buyer uses the product: for example, the business traveller may use a particular scheduled airline for normal business travel but when going on holiday may use a charter airline. Timing of use is also a basis on which the marketer can expand the use of the product. For instance, most consumers of Kellogg's corn flakes ate the product at breakfast, but the company mounted an advertising campaign to encourage consumers to use the product at other times of the day as a snack. Kellogg's hoped that this would open up a new segment for them. An Post produce St Patrick's Day cards every year to increase use of the postal service and in doing so have further segmented the greeting card market.

The *benefit* being sought by the consumer is another behavioural segmentation possibility. Consider the Swiss watch manufacturer Swatch, which has developed a range of watches suitable for casual, formal, sports or fashion wear.

The *rate* of use is another segmentation base. Some consumers consume more of the product than others: for example, a beer company might segment the market into heavy, medium and light users. The economist Pareto discovered a universal law that held that 80 per cent of anything can be attributed to 20 per cent of its causes. If this law were applied to usage rates of a product, the marketer might find that 20 per cent of buyers account for 80 per cent of sales. Heavy users of a product will therefore be a small but highly significant segment in the form of sales and profits. Most airlines place a considerable emphasis on business travellers, who, compared with air travellers in general, buy a disproportionate number of first-class and business-class seats (Clemens, 1997).

Research is increasingly being done on people's buying behaviour and motivations. One organisation, International Market Research Associates, carries out worldwide research on consumers' habits, life-styles, and opinions. Lansdowne Market Research carries out research on Irish consumers specifically for IMRA, and this is included in the international data. Altogether forty thousand interviews are carried out in forty-three countries, building a profile on buying styles. The following panel shows how the research is carried out and the results, which give an indication of Irish buying behaviour.

HOW WE BUY IN IRELAND

The IMRA research asks respondents to indicate agreement or disagreement with a series of statements, including:

'I am really satisfied with myself, even excited, when I get a really good deal.'
'I like to buy products with prestigious brand names.'
'I spend quite a lot of time researching brands before making a major purchase.'
'Once I find a brand that satisfies me, I usually don't experiment with new ones.'
'I always try to buy things on sale.'
'The most important thing about a brand is that it gives good value for money.'
'I generally prefer to buy exclusive, luxury brands.'
'I like to buy the newest or latest version of a product.'

The results give an indication of Irish buying motives and can be compared with the international average.

	Ireland	Global
Value for money	68%	60%
Look for a deal	61%	58%
Loyal to good brand	39%	38%
Buy on sale	30%	33%
Prestige names	26%	27%
Research first	24%	35%
Newest products	17%	19%
Luxury brands	9%	12%

Source: Lansdowne Market Research, 1995.

On the basis of this research, Lansdowne developed a number of statistical clusters, which yielded four distinct categories of buyer: 'deal-makers', 'price-seekers', 'brand loyalists', and 'luxury innovators'. These categories, which are presented in the next panel, could be used as a basis for market segmentation, not only in Ireland but internationally. They are broadly based segments that do give an indication of buyers' behaviour.

FOUR CATEGORIES OF BUYER

	Ireland	Europe	United States	Britain
Deal-makers	29%	26%	37%	26%
Price-seekers	24%	36%	36%	27%
Brand loyalists	24%	21%	11%	29%
Luxury innovators	23%	17%	17%	18%

Deal-makers

Deal-makers love the process of buying. They like to make bargains, and respond to price promotions. They also value quality. There is no sex differential, but there is a median age of thirty-two. They tend to have an average level of education.

Price-seekers

Price-seekers place more emphasis on price than on brand. Quality is rarely their first priority. They tend to be female, and the median age is forty. They are the least well educated of the four categories.

Brand loyalists

These are heavily influenced by brand values, and, while good value and a deal are important, finding the right brand is the priority. They tend to be slightly more conservative and traditional than other consumers. They are just as likely to be male as female, and they have a median age of thirty-six. They generally have a higher than average level of education.

Luxury innovators

Luxury innovators are highly brand-conscious and will focus on brand values and high-quality issues. They will pay a premium for the brand they want (unlike the brand loyalists). They are more likely to be male, with a younger average age, and have the highest level of education.

Source: Lansdowne Market Research, 1996.

Psychographics is essentially a technique for measuring people's life-style. (This is discussed in more detail in chapter 6.) As a segmentation variable it can be used to segment a market according to social class, life-style, personality, loyalty, or attitudes.

For marketing purposes, social class in Ireland is regarded as being derived from people's income. Table 5.3 gives the main grades used by marketers. These are sometimes used as a classification variable; however, they should be combined with other classification variables, as on their own they are of limited value.

Table 5.3: ABC1 social classification in Ireland

	Proportion of heads of household
AB (professional or managerial)	10%
C1 (white-collar)	20%
C2 (skilled working class)	25%
DE (unskilled working class)	30%
F1 (farmers with fifty or more acres)	8%
F2 (farmers with less than fifty acres)	7%

Source: Market Research Bureau of Ireland.

Life-style is probably a more meaningful basis for segmentation, as it builds up a broader profile of the buyer. It describes people's interests, activities, and opinions, and can be measured. An overview of some aspects of people's life-styles can be gleaned from the annual JNRR research, which specifically questions people about life-style factors. Table 5.4 presents some of the leisure activities engaged in by Irish adults.

Table 5.4: Leisure activities (monthly)

Listen to tapes, CDs, or records	59%
Play lotto	55%
Watch videos at home	50%
Sports reading	47%
Buy scratch card	38%
Buy takeaway food	37%
Eat in fast-food restaurant	30%
Eat Continental or oriental food	25%
Meal out in restaurant (social or business)	16%
Go to theatre or concert	6%
Go to horse racing or greyhound racing	3%

Base: all people aged fifteen or over.

Source: JNRR, 1993–4.

Life-style profiling can be used to segment a market and is used by many advertising agencies in developing campaigns suitable for particular segments. People's interest in various products is influenced by their life-style, and many of the products they consume are an expression of life-style.

Personality can also be used for segmentation purposes. Marketers attempt to endow their products with a personality so that the consumer can relate to them. Car manufacturers, for example, use advertising to give different brands a personality; common traits used include 'secure', 'dependable', 'strong', 'sporty', and 'sophisticated'.

Selected personalities will be suitable for the segments selected by the marketer: so marketers of children's products may use cartoon characters in their advertising to appeal to children.

Attitudes can also be used as a segmentation variable. A political party might segment its target voters according to their attitudes towards a particular candidate or particular political issue. Attitudes have a direct influence on people's behaviour, and knowing buyers' attitudes may help the marketer identify segments most likely to buy a particular product or service or to vote in a particular way.

The segmentation process

Applying the possible bases for market segmentation to the market gives the marketer a greater understanding of the needs and behavioural profile of buyers. The segmentation process describes how the organisation goes about segmenting its market. The stages in the process are illustrated in fig. 5.2.

Fig. 5.2: The segmentation process

Specify the market

↓

Describe who buys, what they buy, where they buy, and how they buy

↓

Build profile of individual segments, using any or all of the possible segmentation bases

↓

Determine the attractiveness of each segment

↓

Determine firm's ability to serve the most attractive segments

The process presents a sequential series of steps, the result of which should be a greater understanding of the profile of the segments in the market and the firm's ability to serve those segments profitably.

The process begins with the marketer specifying the market of interest and then attempting to outline specific aspects of buyers' behaviour, such as when, where and how they buy. Any one, or all, of the possible bases for segmentation could be used to give a greater insight into the needs of particular segments. Primary or secondary research, or both, may be conducted to profile the behaviour and classification of individual segments (recall tables 5.1 and 5.2, which give background information on the tourism and snack markets, respectively, obtained through primary research).

To determine the attractiveness of segments and the firm's ability to serve them, the marketer should consider the following points.

It should be possible to measure or quantify the segment. This implies a need for quantitative information on such aspects as the number of potential buyers in a particular segment, the quantity of the product they consume, or how often they consume. Quantifying the size and consumption profile of the segment enables marketers to determine whether they can meet demand levels or indeed whether the segment is large enough to be worth while.

Segments should be accessible to the marketer. Accessibility can refer to geographical location, the ability of the marketer to gain access to the distribution channels used by the segment, and the ability of the marketer to communicate with the segment. If buyers are dispersed across a wide geographical area, if it is difficult to convince the distribution channel to stock the product, or if communication is expensive or difficult, the segment becomes less attractive to the marketer.

Segments should yield a profit to the marketer. Quantification of the size of the segment will help the marketer to determine probable sales and profit levels. Small segments already well served by existing suppliers may not prove profitable. The profitability of individual segments will be determined by the cost of producing, delivering and communicating the product to the segment. It will also be influenced by the actions of competitors.

The business should be able to attract, serve and hold on to the segment. This aspect, referred to as actionability, requires the firm to assess its ability to deliver value to the segment on a continuous basis. There will be a strong link between the firm's general marketing strategy and segment actionability. The firm must identify segments within which it has a competitive advantage.

There are a number of benefits to a firm that uses the segmentation process, not least a greater understanding of its ability to match the needs of the market with its own capabilities. Not every firm can serve all possible segments, and the most attractive segments may not be the best for the firm if competitive or market conditions are unfavourable or if the firm has not got the marketing capabilities to deliver the desired benefit to the buyer.

TARGET MARKETING

Target marketing follows on from the initial segmentation decision. Once the firm has segmented its market, it must decide which segment (or segments) it wishes to serve. *Targeting* means selecting particular customers or customer groups at which to aim the firm's marketing mix. It may involve the development of different marketing mixes for different segments. A targeted segment will be one in which the firm can have a competitive advantage. There must be a demand for the firm's product, and it must be possible for the firm to compete effectively with its offering.

Many marketers have developed highly targeted marketing campaigns in response to the ever-increasing segmentation and sub-segmentation of markets. In broad terms, there are three approaches to target marketing: *undifferentiated marketing, differentiated marketing,* and *concentrated marketing.*

Undifferentiated marketing is essentially the mass marketing of the product. It is a suitable targeting approach where the needs of buyers are more or less the same and the market is not segmented. An example would be a campaign to encourage the population in general not to litter the countryside or to emphasise road safety to road-users. In both cases the campaign would be aimed at a broad national audience.

With regard to consumer products and services and industrial products, few firms engage in undifferentiated marketing. This is mainly because these markets tend to be highly segmented, with different groups of buyers who have different needs.

Differentiated marketing is a characteristic of many firms and involves the development of a separate marketing mix for each segment the firm serves. A manufacturer such as Cadbury seeks to serve a number of different segments in the chocolate and confectionery market: countline bars are aimed at the snack market, while boxed assortments are aimed at the gift or special occasion market, and drinking-chocolate is aimed at the beverage market. Each segment, which has a different need profile, is catered for with a distinct product offering. Segments may differ in age or background characteristics, or there may be many similarities; however, the need in each case will be different. Thus the person looking for a gift is very different from the person seeking to replenish their supply of drinking-chocolate; the same firm, however, can direct a particular product at each of these buyers.

Differentiated marketing is a feature of product, service and industrial firms. In the detergent market, for example, Lever Brothers market the brand leader in the category, Persil. They also market the Surf brand, which is cheaper than Persil and aimed at the value-for-money segment (*Checkout Ireland*, April 1997).

Concentrated marketing means that even though there are a number of segments in the market, the marketer decides to concentrate on a particular one. Though there are several segments in the car market, for example, companies like Porsche and Ferrari tend to concentrate on high-value, prestige sports cars. There can be dangers inherent in relying on a concentrated approach: for example, in recessionary times the sales of high-value prestige products tend to decline.

Sometimes marketers may decide to enlarge their market coverage by identifying new niches. In 1997 Mercedes-Benz launched the small A140 model in the European market, aimed at a niche that was still prepared to pay for Mercedes quality (Klebnikov, 1997). A concentrated approach can work very well for start-up ventures or newer companies that may not have the resources to serve a variety of segments and that can build up a loyal customer base by concentrating on a particular segment, whose needs they can serve. It may also be applicable to specialist industrial marketers that concentrate on serving a specific segment with their product, for example a manufacturer of packaging machinery for the dairy industry.

In many markets, consumer demand in different specialist segments requires the marketer to be able to keep up with the latest requirements. Consider the case of Magee, where change and adaptation were required to hold on to the niche in the market they served.

MAGEE: CUTTING ITS CLOTH FOR NEW MARKETS

Walk into the Donegal premises of Magee, Ireland's premier tweed manufacturer, and there are echoes of another, more genteel era. A tweed jacket thick enough to be worn walking through a hedge hangs in a display case. Rolls of tweed from cottage industry producers in various parts of County Donegal are piled on the floor.

But behind the traditional exterior at Magee there is a different world. Philip Carder runs Magee's weaving plant. He stands among rolls of cloth ready for export. 'Cloth manufactured here might be destined for a suit to be sold in one of the top US outlets,' he explains. 'We might be a small company in an obscure part of Europe, but nonetheless the global market is very real for us. Our orders come in and out via computer. We are contemplating a site on the internet. Clothing is one of the world's oldest industries; we have to marry it to the most modern manufacturing and marketing methods. If we don't adapt we won't survive.'

Magee is privately owned and has been run by the Temple family since the beginning of the century. The firm has been producing its distinctive speckled Donegal tweed for more than 120 years; yet tweed is only a small part of its business, accounting for about 5 per cent of total sales in Ireland and Britain. Magee uses a wide range of other fabrics. 'We realised that we could not survive on tweed alone,' says Lynn Temple, chairman at Magee. 'The hallmark of our products used to be hardiness—making a suit that lasted a lifetime. People are not so interested in durability any more. Now there is a very different marketing approach. The most important thing is satisfying the whims of fashion. We sell on design more than cloth. Even a small company like ours has to be on its toes all the time trying to anticipate next season's styles.'

Magee has a weaving division and clothing factories in Donegal and in Ballymena, County Antrim, employing 600 in total. In 1996 clothing sales were £15 million and the weaving plant had a turnover of £3 million. While other small textile manufacturers have been swallowed up by the big chains or disappeared in the face of low-cost competition from overseas, Magee has successfully kept its niche near the top of the market. 'We are not in the volume business,' says Temple. 'Our aim is to sell highly designed, high-quality natural fabrics and offer customers variety. We are not producing row upon row of identical suits.'

Each day Magee produces about four hundred suits in various cloths, colours, and designs. It markets a wide range of styles—from morning-coats sold to shops such as Moss Brothers to pin-stripe suits and clothes with a more rugged, country look. Organising such a varied output is a logistical nightmare but it has paid dividends. Magee now exports 15 per cent of its clothing. In 1995 the company started making women's jackets and skirts; women's wear now accounts for 40 per cent of export sales.

One successful marketing strategy has been a 'stocks special' scheme, through which a customer can walk into a Magee stockist in Düsseldorf or Derby, select a cloth, and be guaranteed delivery within four weeks. Orders are sent back to Donegal, where suits, jackets and skirts are made and despatched. 'We want to bring the customer waiting time down to fifteen days,' says Temple. 'That means streamlining our production still further. The land is poor in Donegal, and over the years people have been forced to develop various crafts. Our work force is highly skilled and dedicated. Despite that, we have to keep investing in new equipment. We are about to put in a new £250,000 computer system for processing orders. For a small company like ours that represents a big investment.'

Many of the smaller, more 'up-market' suit and jacket retailers in Britain and elsewhere in Europe have traditionally relied on German cloth manufacturers. 'The cost of labour is so high in German factories that now they are outsourcing increasing amounts of their cloth from eastern Europe,' says Temple. 'Quality is suffering as a result. People also want a bit more flair in their clothes and have become tired of the rather predictable German look.'

Keeping up with the latest design trends is crucial. Magee's designers attend the big fairs and monitor changing tastes. 'We put a lot of resources into working with the Italian market. Italy is still the final arbiter in much of the clothing industry. If you can sell to the Italians you can sell to anyone.'

Source: K. Cooke, 'Cutting its cloth for new markets', *Financial Times*, 16 July 1997.

PRODUCT POSITIONING

Product positioning is the third stage in the process. It involves establishing a unique position for the product in the mind of the consumer. Product positioning is strongly related to perception and image. Marketers hope that the buyer will perceive their product to be unique and that they will have a distinctive image of the product and its benefits. The difficulty for buyers is that they are constantly being bombarded with advertising and promotions, all of which are attempts to distinctively position products. Marketers trying to find a distinct position must therefore compete for attention with all other competitors.

GUINNESS AND THE BIG PINT

In 1996 Guinness unveiled a £12 million marketing campaign aimed at younger consumers. The campaign was based on the 'big pint' and used television, radio and press advertising. A series of humorous advertisements was designed to appeal to younger drinkers, particularly those in the 18–25 age group. They included television commercials featuring three 'wise men'—a Chinese man, an Indian, and a native American—who are seen pondering on how the big pint can fit in a human hand. In the end each gives up and decides, 'Don't ponder it, just drink it.'

Guinness has been aiming advertising campaigns at younger drinkers in an effort to capture a bigger share of the growing beer market. The company believed that it could not afford to become complacent; it could not assume that just because previous generations drank Guinness, younger drinkers will automatically follow. The company continually reviewed its communication strategy to make sure it was contemporary in style and relevant to younger drinkers.

Source: S. Creaton, 'Guinness's big pint aims to collar younger heads', *Irish Times*, 22 October 1996.

The product's positioning will be based on the value the marketing mix can deliver to the consumer. This value may be expressed in a number of ways, including product benefits, features, style, value for money, uniqueness, and sophistication. A number of broad positioning approaches are used by marketers; but whichever is used, the marketing mix must live up to the consumer's expectations: the position adopted must be realistic. Positioning decisions will be made in the context of general marketing and product strategies. Companies desire a distinct position not just for their products but for the company as well.

Positioning strategies

There are a number of product positioning strategies, and which one the marketer selects will depend on the nature of the buyer's needs. Positioning may be based on the features of the product, the benefits of the product, the occasion on which the product is used, the type of user, or the competitive conditions in the market.

Product features will be emphasised by some marketers to differentiate their products. Consider the advertisement for Premier Europe (fig. 5.3). Aer Lingus specifies the benefits of premier service by describing in detail the features of the product, such as seat size and in-flight service, in an attempt to position this service in the business traveller segment.

Fig. 5.3: Premier Europe

Benefit positioning involves the marketer concentrating on the perceived benefits of the product. Benefits emphasised typically include value for money, quality, uniqueness, time and labour savings, and lifetime guarantees. Consider the advertisement for the Nordic Track aerobic exerciser (fig. 5.4), in which the manufacturers list the benefits of using their product.

Fig. 5.4: Nordic Track exerciser

Absolutely Fabulous Abdominals

If you are looking to show off a flat and toned midriff on the beach this summer, then look no further. Abworks by Nordictrack makes it easier, more effective and more enjoyable than ever before, to achieve the firm and attractive waistline you desire. Its unique design means that it works better than any roller can. AbWorks is the ONLY abdominal exerciser to offer:

- *Crunch and reverse crunch design*
- *Targeting of upper abs, lower abs and obliques*
- *Full back and neck support*
- *15 different exercises*
- *Fully adjustable resistance*
- *Gin Miller 20 minute workout video included*
- *NordicTrack quality guarantee*

Abworks
'THE ULTIMATE ABDOMINAL CONDITIONER'

3 TIMES AS EFFECTIVE

Most abdominal exercisers only target your upper abs. AbWork's unique patented leg bar is designed to help you target those hard-to-reach lower abs, crucial for that washboard stomach you desire. And if this were not enough already, AbWorks also targets those 'love handles' on the side (technically called obliques).

Better than ANY roller

Normal ab rollers offer :

- *NO reverse crunch design*
- *NO full back support*
- *NO adjustable resistance*
- *NO cushioned support to get you off the floor*
- *NO targeting of lower abs*
- *LIMITED exercise combinations*

FULL NECK AND BACK SUPPORT

The exclusive 'Travelling Support System' cushions you from head to hip, effectively supporting your head, neck and back through every ab exercise. At last you can have the ultimate abs you've always wanted without undue stress to your neck or back.

ONLY 15 MINUTES A WEEK

The padded back support moves with you, correctly positioning you to get the most from each repetition, so it takes fewer reps to get noticeable results. AbWorks is so effective, it takes just 5 minutes 3 times a week for tighter, firmer abs – fast !

THE WORLD'S FINEST

AbWorks is not a gimmick. It is a serious exerciser designed and built by NordicTrack, manufacturers of the world's finest in-home fitness equipment. As with all our products, AbWorks comes to you with a Lifetime of Customer Service. You will also receive Gin Miller's exercise video and a nutrition guide to help get the most of your new exerciser.

AFFORDABLE FITNESS

Priced at £99 (plus £10 delivery), payable in two monthly instalments of £59.50 and £49.50, Abworks is the best value abdominal exerciser around. After all, you can buy an ab exerciser for less, but will it achieve the results you desire? Will it support the vulnerable neck and back areas? Will it target the lower abs and obliques as well as the upper abs? One thing's certain - without the peace of mind that goes with the NordicTrack name, you can't know for sure. So if you're really serious about trimming and toning your waistline, get a serious exerciser - Abworks from NordicTrack.

WHY SETTLE FOR ANYTHING LESS?
For more details on the Ultimate Abdominal Exerciser call

0800 616179

IT COSTS NOTHING TO FIND OUT MORE
Call free 24 hours a day, 7 days a week.
PLEASE QUOTE REFERENCE ST3E8
Or send your name, address and telephone number to :
NordicTrack (UK) Ltd. Dept ST3E8. FREEPOST CV2617. Warwick CV34 6BR.
No stamp is required. Or fax your details to us on 01926 470811.

Abworks
'THE ULTIMATE ABDOMINAL CONDITIONER'
by **NordicTrack**

Benefits will typically be emphasised by industrial marketers. For example, Nutrasweet AG positions itself by concentrating on the partnership it would like to develop with food and beverage manufacturers.

Positioning on the basis of *usage occasion* is another possibility. Irish Distillers, producers of a range of whiskeys and alcoholic drinks, emphasise the service their customer care department can deliver to their trade customers.

Other examples of usage occasion would include a fast-food restaurant emphasising the speed and convenience of its service for people in a hurry; an insurance company that promises to deal with a particular emergency when the occasion arises; and the VHI's positioning in fig. 5.5.

Fig. 5.5: VHI

The *type of user* can also be used as a positioning strategy. Heavy users can be encouraged to continue using the product, while medium and light users can be encouraged to increase their use. Guinness, for instance, was traditionally positioned as a male product; in the nineteen-eighties and nineties, however, it aimed at the female market, who were either light or non-users. The type of user can also refer to the personality used in the positioning: consider the Breitling watch (fig. 5.6), where the company associates its products with skilled pilots.

Fig. 5.6: Breitling watches

BREITLING
1884

CHRONOMAT

The rugged and compact CHRONOMAT was designed and developed in cooperation with the crack pilots of Italy's elite *Frecce Tricolori* flying team.

Probably the world's favorite up-market selfwinding chronograph, its crisply technical good looks and straight profile are designed for total functional convenience. The BREITLING CHRONOMAT: mastering time with the ease and efficiency of the *Concorde's* sleek flowing lines.

Mechanical chronograph

Designed for service in the demanding, split-second world of fighter aircraft, the CHRONOMAT is easy to handle and operate, measuring times from ⅕th second to 12 hours and providing intermediate and cumulative flying times when needed. Its rotating bezel with rider tabs can be used to set a time reference or deadline.

Available in steel, steel and gold or 18K yellow or white gold. Leather strap; PILOT or ROULEAUX bracelet.

AVAILABLE FROM SELECTED JEWELLERS THROUGHOUT GREAT BRITAIN AND IRELAND.
FOR YOUR NEAREST STOCKIST TELEPHONE 0171 637 5167

INSTRUMENTS   FOR   PROFESSIONALS

Competitive positioning is an extremely important aspect of a firm's marketing strategy. The competitive nature of most markets requires that firms differentiate their product offerings. Positioning can be used to demonstrate the advantages of one particular product over another, to reinforce what one competitor can do, or to motivate or reassure buyers.

Competitive positioning is in many ways the cutting edge of marketing practice. Firms may do battle with each other through their positioning: they may imitate each other, anticipate what their competitors are going to do, adapt their position as competitive conditions dictate, or use positioning in an effort to defend their market share. In general, firms use advertising as their main positioning tool.

Positioning needs to be flexible to changes not only in the competitive environment but also in the general business environment. Buyers' needs change and segment profiles change, so marketers may have to adapt or update their positioning accordingly.

In some cases, competitors position themselves directly against other competitors, usually in relation to differences in price or quality. As a positioning strategy this will only work if there is a difference and if the difference is perceived by the buyer. In the early nineteen-eighties, for example, British Airways sought to differentiate itself with the statement 'We'll take more care of you.' One of its rivals, British Caledonian, responded with 'We'll take less fare of you.' On the other hand, many marketers will not use positioning to take on competitors directly: instead they will concentrate on establishing a position that emphasises the value of their own product or service.

Positioning tends to evolve as markets and brands evolve. It is therefore a dynamic process. Firms need to be careful not to let their position become stereotyped or outdated. Johnson and Johnson, for instance, have successfully managed to position its baby care products, such as shampoo and soap, at adults; while the Lucozade brand, which traditionally was positioned as a product for people recovering from illness, has been repositioned as an energy-giving drink for active people. In both cases the firms were reacting to changes in the market and were seeking more profitable market segments to serve.

Positioning and product image are closely connected. On occasion, marketers may attempt to change the positioning if they feel the image needs to be changed, as Showerings, the cider producers, did in the mid-nineties.

A NEW IMAGE FOR CIDER

In 1990 Showerings decided they needed to change the image of cider. The popular image was of a product associated with under-age drinking and not a drink to be seen with socially; some supermarkets were refusing to stock it. The company, which had an 85 per cent share of the cider market, became the principal force behind the establishment of the Cider Industry Council. The council began to lobby politicians and the media with information and videos on the product and the significance of the market. It also became involved in sponsoring efforts to combat under-age drinking.

Research showed that cider was not in fact the favourite drink of under-age drinkers, who were just as likely to consume other alcoholic drinks. The teenage 'cider party' image was strong, however, and Showerings decided that it needed to specifically promote its Bulmer's brand. An advertising and promotional budget of £2 million a year was established, most of which was spent on television advertising, supported by cinema, poster and radio campaigns. The advertising reflected the quality of the product and was aimed at the 18 to 34-year-old market. Long-neck bottles were launched in the pub trade to compete with higher-priced bottled lagers. The cider range was expanded in 1994 with the launch of the Coopers brand, which, unlike other ciders, has a head when poured, giving it a lager-like appearance.

The efforts of the Cider Industry Council and Showerings have seen the image of cider transformed. By 1995 the cider market was growing by 20 per cent per year, and Showerings' turnover had doubled to £70 million a year, 95 per cent of which was in the cider area.

Source: *Irish Times*, 30 June 1995; *Sunday Business Post*, 10 September 1995.

Positioning is strongly linked to product and corporate image. Marketers such as Cadbury (fig. 5.7) and Kellogg (fig. 5.8) emphasise their strengths and the dominance of their brands. In the case of Cadbury, the positioning statement for its Dairy Milk brand is self-explanatory, while Kellogg's positioning statement contains an important competitive message in relation to their corn flake brand.

In some cases marketers have to consider repositioning their products or brands. This usually happens as the result of declining sales, declining relevance of the product to buyers, or a need to update the product's image. The identification of new needs or new segments may also mean that the product or service has to be changed or reformulated and subsequently repositioned. It is important to note that if the product does not meet buyers' needs, a repositioning on its own will not work: the product's features or physical characteristics may need to be changed in a particular way.

Positioning maps

Positioning maps are a useful tool for marketers, especially in relation to competitive positioning decisions. Positioning maps are based on people's perception of particular products or services. They are useful when the marketer is examining the positions that competing products occupy in the consumer's mind and when attempting to find new positions that are unserved or poorly served by existing competitors.

Positioning maps can be constructed using information gathered from market research. Consider the example in the following panel, which demonstrates how the research in positioning might be carried out and how a positioning map is constructed.

The positioning map is a useful analytical tool for marketers. Any number of variables can be used for the axes on the map, and positions can be mapped on the basis of research into buyers' perceptions. The map can also be used to identify unserved positions in the market that may become new segments.

POSITIONING RESEARCH AND THE POSITIONING MAP

The marketer of a brand of orange juice (brand A) wishes to research how its brand is perceived relative to competitors. There are six brands in the market: A, B, C, D, E, and F. The marketer carries out market research to determine how consumers perceive the different brands according to factors such as taste, value for money, nutrition, and package convenience. Respondents are asked a series of questions to establish their perceptions.

In relation to the following brands of orange juice, please indicate on the scale your ratings in relation to the statements presented.

Brand A
The carton is easy to open and reseal.

Strongly agree   ☐   ☐   ☐   ☐   ☐   Strongly disagree

This brand is good value for money.

Strongly agree   ☐   ☐   ☐   ☐   ☐   Strongly disagree

This would be repeated for all other brands. The results would then be tabulated and the researcher would be in a position to develop a positioning map. Suppose a hundred consumers of orange juice were surveyed and the researcher decided to map all six brands according to these consumers' perceptions of ease of use of the carton and value for money. The results might look something like the following positioning map. One axis represents the scale value for money, while the other represents the ease of use of the carton. The position of each brand is mapped according to respondents' ratings. The map also indicates where the marketer of brand A might consider repositioning the brand; the A2 position could be reached if the carton was redesigned to improve ease of use and if buyers perceived this to be so. The A2 position would give brand A a positioning advantage over brand B, which is perceived to be better with regard to both value and ease of use. The marketer for brand A could thus investigate the cost of a package redesign to improve market position.

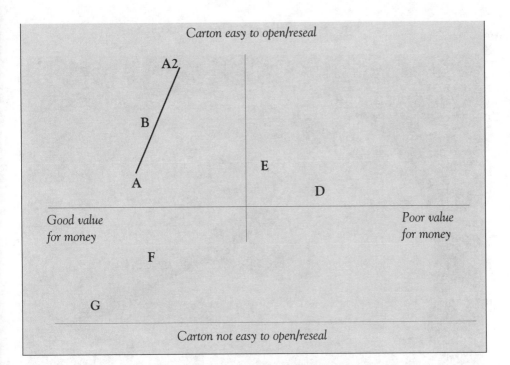

Fig. 5.7: Cadbury's Dairy Milk

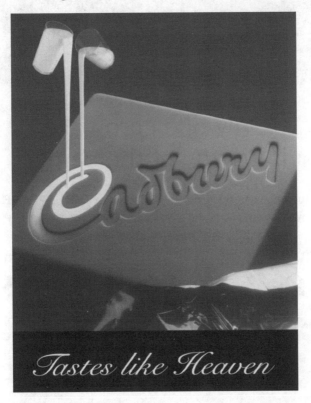

Fig. 5.8: Kellogg's Corn Flakes

Only one corn flake is worthy of the name.

Only the finest sun-ripened corn goes to make Kellogg's Corn Flakes.
That's what makes us Ireland's No.1 sunshine breakfast, with 700,000
servings eaten every day.
Well you wouldn't expect us to put our name to anything but the best.

Kellogg's **CORN FLAKES**

THE ORIGINAL AND BEST

FURTHER READING

McDonald, M., and Dunbar, I., *Market Segmentation*, London: Macmillan 1995.

DISCUSSION QUESTIONS

1. Pick a consumer product, a service and an industrial product and describe the possible bases that a marketer could use to segment the market for each. Use secondary research sources, if available, to help you in your task.
2. Evaluate the pros and cons of using undifferentiated, differentiated and concentrated target marketing campaigns. Select examples of products or services that use each of the approaches.
3. Describe the positioning approaches used by the marketers of baby foods, lager, rock concerts, and photocopiers.
4. Prepare an outline of how you would research and prepare a positioning map based on consumers' perceptions of the following:
   (*a*) a visit to the theatre
   (*b*) brands of cat food
   (*c*) suppliers of computer programs.
   In your answer you should use any number of variables you feel are appropriate for the particular cases given.
5. List some products or services that you feel could be repositioned. Give reasons for each one you choose.

REFERENCES

Clemens, J., 'Business flyers make profits soar', *Marketing Week*, 7 August 1997.
Elkin, T., 'Pioneer eyes tie-ins for youth shift', *Brandweek*, 27 April 1998.
Klebnikov, P., 'Mercedes-Benz's bold niche strategy', *Forbes*, 8 September 1997.

6

Understanding Buyer Behaviour

Marketing requires an understanding of the needs and wants of buyers. To achieve this, marketers must attempt to gain insights into buyers' behaviour. Understanding the reasons why people behave as they do in relation to the marketer's offering, or how they might behave in the future, helps the marketer make decisions.

Behaviour is not always predictable, and gaining an appreciation and understanding of buyers' behaviour can be interesting, complex, and puzzling. It can never be taken for granted that buyers will behave in a particular way, as behaviour is determined by both personal and social factors.

Behaviour always has a reason, even though it may appear illogical or irrational. The key to understanding behaviour is avoiding judgment on what may appear irrational and identifying the factors that determine behaviour in the market. Marketing strategies will be developed on the basis of behavioural determinants. Consider the changes that have taken place in the bread market, for example. Here, changes in buyers' tastes and behaviour presented an opportunity for Cuisine de France to develop a range of products that competed with the more traditional types of bread.

CUISINE DE FRANCE

The consumption of bread in Ireland is high—66 kg per person per year—but within that figure is an increasing variety of types of bread. The bread market has witnessed changes in consumers' tastes and buying behaviour; and these provided an opportunity for the Cuisine de France company, which was established in the early nineteen-nineties.

The total bread market was valued at £200 million by the Breadbakers' Association in 1996. There had been significant structural change in the market. A combination of factors, including improvements in baking technology and own-label competition in the multiples, led to the closure or amalgamation of many bakeries. By the mid-nineties there were three main competitors: Brennan's, Irish Pride, and Pat the Baker. These operated large-scale bakeries and enjoyed significant economies of scale. Brennan's was estimated to be the market leader, with a 25 per cent market share.

Of products, 70 per cent were in the white bread category, and white sliced pans were bought by 75 per cent of households; brown sliced pans were bought by 42 per cent of households. Soda bread or wholemeal and small rolls or baps were bought by 21 per cent and 19 per cent of households, respectively.

While these traditional product categories accounted for the bulk of the market, significant growth was achieved in the frozen bread business, and by 1996 it was estimated to be worth £35 million. The force behind this had been Cuisine de France, which pioneered the introduction of frozen partially baked bread from France. Ovens were sold to supermarkets and retailers around the country, and the staff were trained to use them. Partly baking the bread first gave the yeast a chance to activate, prove, and stabilise. The bread is baked to just below browning point and then frozen, so all the retailer has to do is bake it for six or seven minutes to brown it. Bread is delivered at least three times a week to retailers.

The frozen bread could be baked as required by the retailer in the shop; freshly baked loaves could therefore be provided several times a day if necessary. Consumers responded very favourably, and the number of retailers investing in ovens increased significantly.

Taste was an important factor. The partly baked bread had to be imported from France, because people wanted the distinctive taste of French bread, which cannot be achieved with Irish flour, though the company hoped it would be possible to identify an Irish mill that could produce flour to French specifications.

The company expanded its range to include different types of bread. In addition, other bakery products, such as croissants, scones and muffins were added. In 1997 the agri-business group IAWS paid £51 million for the Cuisine de France business, and the company planned to use the business to expand the brand to the Continent.

Sources: R. Crowley, 'Bon appetit', *Examiner*, 12 April 1995; feature on the bread market, *Sunday Business Post*, 17 March 1996; K. Barrington, 'More bread for Cuisine shareholders', *Sunday Business Post*, 14 December 1997.

The Cuisine de France example demonstrates a change in consumers' behaviour patterns in the bread market. Consumers were looking for products that were essentially different from more traditional forms. This provided an opportunity for the company to cater for consumers' needs with a new product range.

THE NATURE OF BUYER BEHAVIOUR

The study of buyer behaviour gives the marketer an insight into how buyers establish a need for the product, how they identify and evaluate options, and the factors that influence their decision-making and ultimate choice. 'Consumer behaviour' has been defined as the behaviour consumers display in searching for, buying, using, evaluating and disposing of products and services that they expect will satisfy their needs (Schiffman and Kanuk, 1994). It involves a study of the behaviour of individual consumers and also the behaviour of firms as consumers.

Much of the theory that underlies buyer behaviour derives from the disciplines of psychology and sociology. Psychology is the study of human and animal behaviour, while sociology is the study of the collective behaviour of people in groups. In addition to these two disciplines, economics, geography and history have also contributed to the understanding of why we behave as we do.

Buyer behaviour is a process of which the physical purchase of the product is only one stage. Many underlying influences, both internal and external, influence the buyer's decision. Market research can be used to assist the marketer in the process of understanding buyers' behaviour: research techniques can be used to assess and measure aspects of buyers' behaviour such as motivation, perception, and attitude. Consider the example in fig. 6.1, which could be used to measure respondents' attitudes to flying with an airline. The results of research exercises such as this give the marketer an overview of how buyers evaluate the product; they also help explain why buyers engage in different behaviour patterns.

Fig. 6.1: Evaluative scale for measuring attitudes towards an airline

Compared with other airlines, flying with airline A is:

Good value	[1]	[2]	[3]	[4]	[5]	Poor value
Convenient	[1]	[2]	[3]	[4]	[5]	Inconvenient
Stressful	[1]	[2]	[3]	[4]	[5]	Relaxing
Pleasant	[1]	[2]	[3]	[4]	[5]	Unpleasant

CONSUMER SOVEREIGNTY

One of the fundamentals of marketing is that the consumer is sovereign. This implies that the consumer will ultimately make up his or her own mind about the purchase of a product. As we have seen in chapter 1, this decision will be needs-based. The marketer can attempt to influence the consumer's decision-making process with a product offering, but ultimately the decision is made by the consumer. This is an important principle: buyers are not unthinking beings that can be easily led or can be dictated to by marketers.

The consumer will not act in a way contradictory to his or her own goals or motives, though motivation and behaviour can undoubtedly be influenced by the activities of marketers. The consumer will consider the alternatives presented by the marketer but will ultimately make up his or her own mind about whether or not to buy.

In making up their own mind, consumers can exhibit varying degrees of involvement.

Involvement

Involvement refers to the perceived importance of an object or event to the person. In general, people will become more involved in decision-making regarding products that have high personal relevance and involve high risk, for example cars, computers, or clothes. Other product decisions will have low levels of involvement, for example products such as light-bulbs, matches, or toilet rolls. Where consumers are making a high-involvement decision they will generally search for more alternatives, carry out more evaluation, and look for advice.

For low-involvement decisions, consumer are less likely to engage in extensive search and evaluation. In many instances they will buy products essentially on grounds of convenience. A consumer may prefer a particular brand of milk, for example, if given a choice; but if they visit their local shop to buy milk and find that it does not stock the preferred brand, they are unlikely to leave to search for the preferred brand elsewhere.

In industrial buying situations it can be argued that employees are in fact being paid to make involved decisions, for example an analysis of different tenders from possible suppliers. In this situation the employee uses professional skills to make a decision that may involve high or low levels of involvement, depending on the product in question.

The level of consumer involvement is determined by a combination of personal and situational factors. It will depend on the importance of the decision to the consumer and the context in which the decision is being made.

Consumer involvement is particularly important in understanding the power of branding. Consumers may use the brand as a strategy for risk avoidance. They may become brand-loyal as a means of reducing tension and avoiding having to make involved decisions. Marketers may use their brand advertising to inform the consumer how their brand can take the risk out of potentially involved decisions. One brand that has been particularly successful and that positions itself as the best product in an appearance-conscious market is Gillette. As the following panel demonstrates, Gillette paid particular attention to researching buyers' behaviour, creating a powerful brand, and the development of new products.

GILLETTE: A CUT ABOVE THE REST

For the international toiletries giant Gillette, the success of the Sensor razor posed a problem. The razor might indeed be 'the best a man can get'—as people were constantly reminded in television advertising—but wasn't the hapless shaver entitled to equally mould-breaking toiletries to add style to his bathroom shelf? What could be done to make it more exciting?

Gillette dominates the wet shave market, with an estimated share of 60 per cent of worldwide sales. Gillette earned this dominant position through large investments in research and development and through careful consumer research. Every day about ten thousand men carefully record the results of their shaves for Gillette. Five hundred of these men shave in special cubicles under carefully controlled and monitored conditions, including observation through one-way glass and video cameras. Shavers record the precise number of nicks and cuts. In certain cases researchers even collect sheared whiskers to weigh and measure. As a result, Gillette scientists know that an average man's beard grows 0.4 mm a day. During an average lifetime a man will spend 3,350 hours scraping $27^{1}/_{2}$ feet of whiskers from his face. Gillette even uses electron microscopes to study blade surfaces and miniature cameras to analyse the actual shaving process.

Gillette maintains that it has never been concerned with the low end of the market: status-seeking men, it believes, will always buy a 'classy' product. Most men, it considers, see shaving as a serious business and their appearance as a matter of importance. It also believes that men will pay more for a superior shaving product.

Since the safety razor was patented by Gillette in 1904, the company has always been innovative in product development. The safety razor changed shaving from being a tedious, difficult, time-consuming and often bloody task that was endured at most twice a week. Only the rich could afford to have a barber shave them daily. The safety razor gained wide acceptance during the First World War, when a free razor was given to every American soldier. In this manner millions of men just entering shaving age were introduced to the daily self-shaving habit.

Gillette was the first to develop the double-blade razor in 1971, the first with swivel-head razors in 1977 (the Contour), and in 1985 the first with the Contour Plus, which incorporated a lubricating strip for a smoother shave. The Sensor, launched in the late nineteen-eighties, was a development of the Contour and was designed with a more advanced lubricating strip and swivel head. The Sensor and a subsequent development, the Sensor Excel, were very successful, and Gillette increased its share to 71 per cent of the North American and European markets. The company's sales grew from $3,000 million in 1986 to $66,100 million in 1997.

Gillette was not the first to introduce disposable razors: this was done by Bic in Europe in 1975. Gillette introduced the first disposable in the United States the following year.

The morning shaving ritual continues to occupy a special place in most men's lives: it affirms their masculinity, and the first shave remains a rite of passage into manhood. A survey by New York psychologists reported that though men complain about the bother of shaving, 97 per cent of the sample would not want a cream that would permanently rid them of facial hair.

Though shaving may require less skill and danger than it once did, many men still want the razors they use to reflect their beliefs that shaving remains a serious business. A typical man regards his razor as an important personal tool, a kind of extension of self, like an expensive pen or set of golf clubs.

In 1991 the company launched a new range of shaving foams, gels, after-shave moisturiser, deodorants, and anti-perspirants, known as the Gillette Series. Gillette had already been a producer of shaving foams, but the new range was designed to be a complete revamp of pre-shaving and post-shaving products, as well as an entry for Gillette to the lucrative men's toiletries market. The award-winning containers made sparkling use of bare metal in their silver-and-blue colour scheme to suggest steel and water. Fresh thinking was given to the plastic actuator and cap to give a different look from the general run of aerosols. Futuristic graphics were used, and the products were advertised using strong life-style imagery as 'the best a man can get.' Almost all the products in the range have achieved number 1 or number 2 market share in their various categories.

In 1998, after spending $1,000 million in research and development, Gillette launched the Mach 3, a razor with three blades, each of which is 10 per cent thinner than previous blades and is made from a combination of steel and diamond-like carbon. The company planned to spend $300 million marketing the new product. The selling price was 35 per cent more than the existing Sensor Excel, and it was expected that the Mach 3 would ultimately eat into the sales of the Sensor Excel.

Sources: R. Cobb, 'Gillette: a cut above the rest', *Marketing*, 30 September 1993; T. McEnaney, 'Spending $1 billion to be a cut above the rest', *Sunday Tribune*, 19 April 1998; 'Gillette sharpens up', *Sunday Business Post*, 17 May 1998.

Consider also the advertisement for Dulux paint (fig. 6.2), which offers a colour card and colour solutions booklet to help customers make up their mind. This is designed to reduce the risk in what can be an involved decision.

Fig. 6.2: ICI Dulux Colour Solutions

Source: HGW Paints.

The level of involvement will play a role in determining the amount of time and effort the consumer devotes to the buying process. This process can be explained and illustrated using a model of consumer behaviour.

A MODEL OF CONSUMER BEHAVIOUR

The basic model of buyer behaviour was developed by Howard and Sheth (1969) and is illustrated in fig. 6.3. This is a stimulus-response model: it proposes that the buyer is stimulated by marketing and other environmental factors and makes a response. The 'black box' describes all the psychological and decision factors specific to the buyer. These are a combination of personal traits and characteristics and the way in which the buyer makes decisions.

Fig. 6.3: 'Black box' model of buyer behaviour

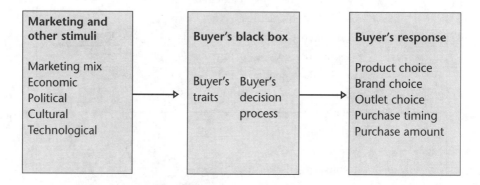

This basic model of buyer behaviour is a useful introduction to the process of understanding how we make decisions, the influences that may come into play, and the possible responses the buyer may make. The model shows that buyers do not make their decisions in a vacuum: most people will be influenced by a variety of sources. Even when consumers have made up their mind about what to buy, factors can intervene to change that decision. They may have seen the advertisements for a particular brand, may have processed the information received, and may have a positive intention to buy, but they may not end up buying the product. Other factors can intervene so that intention does not translate into purchase. For example, when the consumer reaches the supermarket they discover that a competing brand is on special promotion, and they opt for it instead.

The model, therefore, will not be a perfect predictor of behaviour, but it does give marketers a basic structure for understanding how buyers make their decisions and the factors that influence them. The 'black box' model is not the most comprehensive model of buyer behaviour, and other models have been developed; for the purposes of this introductory text, however, it provides an introduction to concepts underlying buyer behaviour. The rest of the chapter expands on the components of the black box model.

Marketing and other stimuli

The primary stimulant to buyers will be the firm's marketing mix—the bundle of benefits and added values that the marketer hopes will stimulate the buyer into action. (The components of the marketing mix—product, price, promotion, and place—are dealt with in chapters 7–10.) Suffice it to say that the marketing mix should be capable of meeting the buyer's needs if it is to have a chance of consideration.

In chapter 3 the factors in the marketer's environment were discussed. These environmental forces affect the firm's ability to meet the customer's needs. Changes and developments in the economic, demographic, technological, political, legal or natural environments can influence buyers' decision-making.

Environmental factors that influence consumers' behaviour

As the 'black box' model illustrates, a number of factors influence and can stimulate the consumer.

Cultural factors

Human behaviour is learnt. We learn our basic sets of values, perceptions, beliefs and attitudes from our family, but also from the culture of our country. *Culture* describes the way of life or personality of a society. It exists to serve the needs of society and has an influence on consumers' behaviour within that society.

Culture has an influence on defining values. In one research study dealing with values, Ireland emerged as exceptional and idiosyncratic (Turley, 1995).

There are a number of different aspects to culture. These include:

• material culture: economics, technology
• social institutions: religion, education, politics
• human culture: values, beliefs, attitudes
• aesthetics: music, folklore, tradition.

Cultural analysis is relevant for marketers, not just in their home market but also in international markets, where different influences may affect how the product is marketed. Culture is dynamic in nature, though change tends to be a slow process and is heavily influenced by other cultures, by travel, and by the media.

In Ireland, as in other industrialised countries, cultural changes have taken place, and these can be reflected in our buying behaviour. Consider table 6.1, which shows the consumption of beer, wine and spirits in a number of European countries. There are obvious differences in consumption patterns between different countries, though of particular interest is the fact that beer consumption in Ireland and in Germany is almost equal, while wine consumption is very low in Ireland. While culture is not the only influence on the consumption of these products, it undoubtedly plays an important part.

Table 6.1: Consumption of beer, wine and spirits per capita, 1994

	Beer	*Wine*	*Spirits*
Germany	137.5 litres	24.6 litres	7.4 units
Ireland	**137.2 litres**	**6 litres**	**4.3 units**
Austria	129.3 litres	33.9 litres	3.5 units
Belgium	116.3 litres	28.4 litres	3.7 units
Denmark	115.3 litres	26.1 litres	2.7 units
Britain	101 litres	14.5 litres	3.9 units
Finland	81.4 litres	10.8 litres	4.7 units
Spain	69.5 litres	38.2 litres	7.3 units
France	24.7 litres	47.2 litres	3.2 units
Italy	23.5 litres	53.5 litres	2.6 units

Source: Euromonitor, 1994.

Not all products can be marketed in the same way in different markets or cultures. Behavioural determinants must be considered. In the European confectionery market, for example, Danish, Irish and British consumers have the highest consumption of chocolate and sweets (17 kg, 14 kg and 13 kg per person per year, respectively), which displays some similarities in buyers' behaviour in these markets. This behaviour is not, however, mirrored in other European markets, where consumption is much lower (*Times*, 8 January 1996).

The Henley Centre of Ireland produced some research findings in 1992 that indicated that the Irish adult population could be divided into five distinct groups, based on identity (Henley Centre, 1992). The research is specific to Ireland, and the identities are linked to cultural factors.

IRISH IDENTITIES IN THE NINETEEN-NINETIES

Young Irelanders (26 per cent)
Generally young people who are optimistic about the future in Ireland and believe that products made in Ireland are usually better than those from other countries. They have above average ability in the Irish language, which they believe will become more significant in the future.

Envious neighbours (26 per cent)
Also mainly young people. They believe that life in other European countries is more stylish and glamorous than in Ireland, and only a minority see themselves as having a future in Ireland. They do not think that Irish will become more important in the future.

Anglo-Hibernians (21 per cent)
The most affluent group, strongly based in Leinster, with a higher proportion of males than females. They are very confident about their future, are not envious of other

European countries, and also think that Irish will increase in importance in the years ahead.

Future pessimists (18 per cent)
These see themselves as having no future in Ireland, and do not believe that Irish will become more important in the future.

Old romantics (9 per cent)
These show many of the characteristics of the 'Young Irelander' group but are older and more certain of the superiority of Irish goods. They are convinced of the increasing importance of Irish, but virtually none are capable of speaking or reading it.

Source: Henley Centre of Ireland, 1992.

The Henley Centre research presents some interesting points for marketers. For example, the groups could potentially be used as a basis for segmentation. The perception of Irish-made products undoubtedly influences their purchasing, and their views on Irish could possibly be of significance with regard to communication strategies or the media they may consume, for example TG4.

Social factors

Social factors are any influences that groups of which one is a member, or that one comes in contact with, have on the consumer's behaviour. People interact with other people in domestic, work and social settings, and these interactions have an influence on our behaviour. A group that serves as a point of comparison for the individual and influences buyers' behaviour is known as a *reference group*.

There are both primary and secondary reference groups. *Primary reference groups* have most influence and include the person's family, friends, neighbours, and fellow-workers or fellow-students. *Secondary reference groups* usually have less influence and typically include churches, professional associations, and trade unions. It is also possible to have *aspirational reference groups*, which are groups of which the person is not actually a member but would like to be, for example a professional institute. The individual may engage in behaviour in an effort to join, for example by pursuing a course of study.

Opinion-leaders are referents who are the first to buy new products or to accept new ideas and whose opinion is sought by others. They play an important role in the adoption process for new products because of the influence they can have over other consumers, who, because of perceived risk, may be *opinion-seekers*.

The family is one of the most important reference groups, because it is within the family that people become socialised. The family, as a group, is also a significant purchasing unit, with many products being specifically marketed to families: consider 'family pack' products in the supermarket, or family holidays. The term *family* can also be interpreted quite widely.

IARNRÓD ÉIREANN—REDFINING THE IRISH FAMILY?

For many years Iarnród Éireann defined a family, for the purpose of selling family rail tickets, as 'a husband and/or wife and up to four of their children under the age of sixteen'. Falling sales of family tickets, however, convinced it that it should re-examine this definition, so in 1991 it changed it to 'two adults and up to four children under the age of sixteen'.

Source: Iarnród Éireann.

Whatever its composition, the different members of the family can have varying amounts of influence on purchasing decisions. Some decisions will be husband-dominant, some will be wife-dominant, and some will be joint. One research study (Mohan, 1995) examined husbands' and wives' perceptions of their roles in the purchase of six chosen consumer products or services. It found that some decisions were more husband-dominant (lawnmower, car, and television), while the wife's influence was stronger for sitting-room suite and washing machine. There was a high level of joint decision-making for mortgage choice.

Increasingly, however, the distinctions between the roles of family members are becoming blurred, as shown by the results of a survey carried out in 1995 on the division of household tasks (table 6.2).

Table 6.2: Division of household tasks

| | Actual allocation Task shared equally | | |
Age	15–34	35–54	55+
Washing and drying dishes (weekdays)	45%	42%	30
Organising bills and household money	43%	44%	36
Feeding young children*	37%	41%	13
Gardening	33%	27%	24
Vacuum-cleaning	31%	26%	24
Weekly shopping	23%	19%	16
Preparing main meal (weekdays)	23%	20%	15
Ironing clothes	16%	11%	5
Cleaning bathroom or toilet	16%	15%	12

Base: all households with males and females.
*Households with children.

Source: Taylor Nelson AGB, 1995.

It would appear that the younger man is more likely to be sharing the tasks equally. Probable reasons for this would include a change in traditional roles brought about by

Ireland's changing employment profile. There are more women in the work force or returning to work, and more women who are the sole breadwinner in the family. It is also probable that changing life-styles and changing attitudes about the role of women are starting to have an effect.

Where there are children in the family they will also influence family decisions. Many advertisements for food products, entertainment, toys and holidays are specifically aimed at children, who can be quite a sceptical audience. A research study in 1988 drew some conclusions on how sceptical children are of the claims advanced in television commercials. It argued that successful campaigns are contingent on advertisers understanding the stages in the child's cognitive growth (Turley and Gallagher, 1988).

In the nineteen-sixties Walls, which marketed ice cream in Britain, segmented the children's market into three groups: 'adventurers', 'hungry Horaces', and 'little madams' ('Washes Whiter', Channel 4, 1991). They had found that the product type bought by the child was influenced by personality. 'Adventurers' liked shaped ice cream products, such as space rockets or characters, while 'hungry Horaces' were price-sensitive and wanted as much ice cream as possible for their money. 'Little madams' were girls who could relate to slightly more sophisticated products. Walls developed and aimed particular products at each of these segments.

The buyer's decision-making process

The central component of the model of buyer behaviour is the black box. Understanding the components of the black box involves examining the buyer's decision-making process and the personal and psychological forces that have an impact.

In trying to understand the buyer's decision-making process, it is useful to examine the 'hierarchy of effects' model, which proposes that people go through a number of sequential stages in making decisions (Dewey, 1910). The sequence can vary, depending on the level of involvement. Fig. 6.4 illustrates the hierarchy of effects decision-making model.

Fig. 6.4: 'Hierarchy of effects' decision-making model

problem recognition
↓
search for information
↓
alternative evaluation
↓
choice
↓
outcomes

Problem recognition

Problem recognition can be stimulated in many ways. The consumer may feel hungry and want something to eat; they go to the fridge and find it is empty, and then decide to visit a local delicatessen. Problem recognition can also be stimulated by advertising and promotions, by social trends, or by sight, smell, or other stimuli.

Problem recognition will occur when the consumer notices that the present state of affairs is not the ideal or desired state. Because of this they will be motivated to do something about it. Depending on the importance of the problem to the person, a certain level of involvement will also be activated.

Search for information

The amount of searching the consumer engages in will depend on the degree of risk involved. For routine purchases of staple products, this process will be limited and will depend more on factors such as availability. For purchases of consumer durables or high-involvement products in general, the search process may be quite extensive.

Evaluation of alternatives

The consumer will evaluate alternatives using three main criteria:

(a) the specifications the consumer sets;
(b) the standards the consumer sets;
(c) the expectations the consumer has.

These criteria will be heavily influenced by social factors and by advertising. Evaluative criteria will be based on beliefs. The consumer's beliefs will shape their attitude to the product, which can be positive or negative. Attitudes play an important part in the determination of purchasing intention; positive attitudes towards a particular product make it more likely that the consumer will buy it.

Choice

The consumer chooses not only what product to buy but also where to buy it. Choice involves evaluating alternative actions or behaviour and forming a behavioural intention or plan to engage in the selected behaviour. The consumer may use a number of choice criteria, for example price, features, quality, or guarantees.

Outcome

The outcome of the consumer's decision will either be satisfaction, which may lead to repeat purchases and positive word-of-mouth communication, or dissatisfaction, which will usually not result in repeat purchases and may lead to negative word-of-mouth communication. Marketers need to be just as concerned about the evaluation the consumer makes after the purchase as they are about the evaluation made when alternatives were being considered before purchase.

High involvement v. low involvement

Generally, for high-involvement decisions the consumer will follow the five stages described in fig. 6.4 above. The model can, however, be modified for low-involvement decisions, as fig. 6.5 demonstrates.

Fig. 6.5: Hierarchy of effects for low-involvement decisions

In the case of low-involvement decisions, problem recognition is typically non-complex. If, for example, the consumer runs out of milk, alternative evaluation may involve quite a limited search, and choice may depend more on factors such as availability or convenience than on more complex factors, such as choice of retail outlet.

Personal factors and psychological factors

The second component of the black box is the characteristics of the individual. These can be broadly described as personal and psychological.

Personal factors

Age: Consumers' tastes and behaviour will vary with age. For example, breakfast cereals aimed at children, such as Kellogg's Frosties or Coco Krispies, are sweet-tasting and use cartoon characters to communicate the benefits of the product. Cereals aimed at adults, such as Kellogg's All Bran, stress the importance of dietary fibre. Consider the example of usage of male toiletries by age (table 6.3). It can be seen from this that younger men have the highest level of consumption of toiletries among all the product categories. This may not be surprising, perhaps, given the development of new ranges by companies such as Gillette (page 145).

Table 6.3: Male usage of toiletry products by age

	Total	*15–35*	*35–54*	*55+*
Deodorant	69%	89%	68%	35%
After-shave lotion	65%	74%	66%	50%
Bath or shower gel	55%	75%	50%	27%
Body spray or eau de Cologne	28%	44%	24%	9%

	Total	15–35	35–54	55+
Hair gel, tonic, spray, cream	28%	42%	20%	12%
Moisturiser or skin cream	9%	15%	4%	4%
None	12%	0%	11%	33%

Source: Taylor Nelson AGB, March 1996.

It is not just humans whose needs vary with age: dog and cat owners can buy different pet foods formulated for young, growing or mature animals.

Fig. 6.6: 'Catisfaction'

Occupation: In Ireland the ABC1 socio-economic classification, which is used predominantly by marketers, is based on the occupation of the head of the household (see page 126). There are two other scales derived by the Central Statistics Office from the census of population, but these are rarely used. Market segmentation may be based on occupation, and products may be developed for specific occupations. For example, advertising campaigns for cellular phones stress the benefits to people whose jobs may require them to travel or to work at different sites. Many computer programs have been developed with specific occupations in mind, for example accountants. Care has to be exercised in using social classification as a means of segmentation. The marketer should not stereotype buyers on grounds of social class. Also, many products are consumed by all classes.

Life-style: This refers to the person's pattern of living in the world, expressed in their activities, interests, and opinions. It is influenced by culture, values, demographics, social class, reference groups, and family, as well as by individual psychological characteristics. The concept is widely used by marketers in segmentation and positioning decisions.

Life-styles are identified using the AIO (activities, interests, opinions) framework. Typical components used in AIO analysis are given in table 6.4. These can be used as the basis for measuring life-style, and researchers can build a profile of buyers on the basis of their activities, interests, and opinions. This can be used by marketers when making positioning decisions.

Life-style is particularly used in marketing communications, in the belief that people will identify with obvious life-style settings used in advertising, for instance. In theory, if a person identifies with the life-style portrayed in the advertising, it increases the probability that they will buy the product.

Table 6.4: Typical AIO life-style components

Activities	Interests	Opinions
work	family	themselves
hobbies	fashion	social issues
entertainment	food	education
sports	home	future
holidays	community	politics
shopping	achievement	culture

In the Joint National Readership Research, which provides annual readership details for newspapers and magazines, a number of questions are asked about life-style. The research divides the population into six clusters according to special interests and life-style, as described in the following panel. These clusters are not based on class, age or living conditions but rather on attitudes to life and probable behaviour patterns.

IRISH LIFE-STYLE CLUSTERS

'**Extroverts**' (17 per cent) tend to be very style-oriented and fashion-conscious and like to stand out in a crowd. They could be classified as early adopters as far as their purchasing habits are concerned and are inclined to refer to newspapers to keep themselves informed.

'**Non-conformists**' (12 per cent) are somewhat aimless. They tend to be incautious or indifferent in their approach to product reliability, advertising, and health. Reflecting a younger profile, they are not home-oriented and express the most rebellious attitudes.

'**Cultured**' people (17 per cent) like to stay away from crowds, are environmentally conscious, and enjoy places of cultural interest. They are relatively averse to risk, and are discerning shoppers of branded goods.

'**Homely**' people (19 per cent) are very home-oriented and enjoy gardening, home improvement, and staying at home. They also tend to be brand-led and conservative in their outlook.

'**Ambitious**' people (21 per cent) are a younger group, fairly idealistic and career-oriented, believing that career is more important than money. They are not averse to risk, particularly in financial areas, and are not in any way home birds.

'**Conventional**' people (14 per cent) care very little for style or fashion. They do not seek out new products or information, preferring a traditional, conservative life-style.

Source: JNRR, 1995–6.

Personality: This refers to a person's distinguishing psychological characteristics, which lead to relatively consistent and enduring responses to his or her environment. Every person has a unique personality, which manifests itself in traits such as dominance, self-confidence, innovativeness, or autonomy.

Marketers attempt to endow products with personalities in the belief that people will identify with particular personality traits. Personality is particularly associated with brands. The following panel, for example, lists some of the brand personalities that one commentator suggests are a feature of some leading British brands, many of which are available in Ireland. Some of these 'personalities' have been built up over several decades as part of concerted positioning campaigns. The personality derives from how the brand is communicated and perceived. It also demonstrates the difficulty that marketers can have if the personality of the brand does not change as times change: for example, according to this commentator, Barclay's Bank still had a nineteen-seventies personality.

BRAND PERSONALITIES

Barclay's Bank	Seventies-style High Street banking
Cadbury	Small purple pleasures; world of chocolate
Coca-Cola	America for everyone
Levi's	Classic style, authenticity
Mars	Countlines
Marks and Spencer	Editorial ability, innovative luxury
Nescafé	Suburban niceness, familiar product brand
Nike	Just do it (youth and attitude)
Persil	Caring household cleaning
Sainsbury's	Middle-class quartermaster
Sony	Innovative design in gizmos
Virgin	David v. Goliath

Source: Peter Wallis (SRU Management Consultancy), 'Elastic brands', *Sunday Times*, 3 November 1996.

One research study in the United States suggested that there were five brand personality dimensions: sincerity, excitement, competence, sophistication, and ruggedness (Aaker, 1997). The research had been conducted among a representative sample of the American population based on these five demographic characteristics. It is certainly possible to relate various well-known brands to these dimensions.

Psychological factors

Motivation exists when a need is sufficiently pressing to direct a person to seek satisfaction of that need. It is a force that impels us into action. People feel tension if a need exists; to reduce this tension we will take action. Our behaviour will be goal-oriented: we are motivated to achieve particular goals.

Marketers are interested in motivation because consumers' needs and goals will be determinants of the products and brands they consider to be relevant to them as a means of achieving their goals. Some of these goals are generic (for example, if a person is hungry they will be motivated to do something about it), while some goals will be brand-specific or product-specific (so the person who is hungry might decide to buy a specific product, such as a packet of Tayto crisps).

There are several theories of motivation, but this chapter will limit its discussion to one, Maslow's hierarchy of needs. Maslow (1943) proposed that people were driven by needs that can be arranged in a hierarchy (fig. 6.7). The needs ascend; as needs at the bottom of the hierarchy are satisfied, the person moves on to the next level. As soon as the needs on one level have been satisfied, the needs on the next level will come into play. This is relevant to marketers, as various products and services can be seen as possible satisfiers of particular types of needs. An insurance company sells products on the basis of safety needs, while the motives for buying an expensive car may have more to do with prestige and esteem than with transport. Maslow's hierarchy is particularly useful when considering positioning and communication strategies.

Fig. 6.7: Maslow's hierarchy of needs

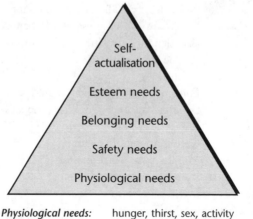

Physiological needs:	hunger, thirst, sex, activity
Safety needs:	security, order, stability
Belonging needs:	love, affection, affiliation, identification
Esteem needs:	prestige, success, self-respect
Self-actualisation:	self-fulfilment

Consumers' motives will be a strong influence on the products or type of products they buy. In the boxed chocolate assortment market, for example, different sets of motives can apply to different brands.

MILK TRAY: SATISFYING A NEED SINCE THE NINETEEN-THIRTIES

Cadbury, the manufacturer of two leading assortments, Milk Tray and Roses, considers that different motives come into play for each of the brands.

A person who buys a box of Milk Tray as a gift has a different set of motives from someone who buys Roses. According to the brand manager, 'Roses are a gesture. There are no symbolic purchasing reasons attached to buying a box of Roses. With Milk Tray, though, you are talking about a different set of standards. It could be love. It could be sincerity. It could be emotive reasons.'

The brand was launched in Ireland in the nineteen-thirties, and over time the appearance has changed. In 1997, for example, the company devised a new, curved shape for the box. This was the third change to the box during the nineteen-nineties, though the distinctive purple-and-gold colouring has always been retained. New chocolates have been added and the selection changed to suit changing tastes.

Cadbury typically spends £500,000 a year in marketing the brand. Its original television advertising campaign was inspired by the James Bond era, 'where the guy would go to any length to get the lady a box of Milk Tray.' In the sixties and seventies this appeal was appropriate because there was a clear role distinction between men and women. The role of women has changed since then: women have become more powerful, and the advertising has changed to reflect this. The catch-line 'and all because the lady loves Milk Tray' has, however, been retained. Not surprisingly, women eat more Milk Tray than men. In the broader chocolate market, sales are split equally by sex: in the formal chocolate gift market, women account for 65 per cent of purchases.

Source: A. O'Toole, 'Most chocaholics are women', *Sunday Business Post*, 21 December 1997.

PERCEPTION

A motivated person is ready to act; how they do so is influenced by their perception of the situation. *Perception* is the process by which a person selects, organises and interprets stimuli to create a meaningful picture of the world. Perception is therefore important in the product evaluation process with regard to the buyer's perception both of the marketing mix and its ability to satisfy needs.

Perception is a physiological process, because it involves the use of sensory receptors such as the eyes and ears, which send impulses to the brain through the central nervous system.

The lowest level at which a person can perceive a stimulus is called the *absolute threshold*. The minimum difference that can be perceived between two stimuli is called the *just noticeable difference*. These are important concepts with regard to communication and product or pricing changes. An advertisement has to reach the absolute threshold to register in the person's mind. A chocolate manufacturer faced with rising cocoa costs might decide to reduce the amount of cocoa in each bar rather than increase the price of the product. If the consumer noticed the change this would be above the just noticeable difference; if not, it would be below. Similarly, if the price of a product was changed and was above the just noticeable difference, the consumer might decide to reconsider their choice.

People generally select stimuli according to interest, expectations, and motives. They are therefore selective in what they perceive. With regard to advertising, we will be more likely to perceive advertisements for products that we are interested in. Selective perception can manifest itself in a number of ways.

Selective exposure: People will only notice certain stimuli. For example, if we are hungry we are more likely to notice the smell coming from a coffee shop, or advertisements for food products. This caused one company in Britain to investigate using 'sensory' advertising.

Selective distortion: People can distort the stimuli to suit themselves, so as to support rather than challenge their preconceptions. Advertising campaigns may demonstrate the dangers of smoking to people's health, but people may distort the message by convincing themselves that it will never happen to them.

Selective retention: People retain only a certain amount of information, usually what is of most interest. Marketers cannot expect the individual to remember everything, so in many advertising campaigns the same short message is repeated many times.

Perception and company or product image are strongly related. In general, marketers attempt to create and maintain a positive image for their company and products through their communication activities. Retailers pay particular attention to shop design and image, whether in supermarkets, where the first sensory experience is the smell from the in-store bakery or the display of fresh fruit and vegetables, or a fashion retailer, where garments are displayed using creative and innovative window dressing.

ASSAULTS ON THE SENSES AT BUS STOPS

In 1996 the advertising agency Young and Rubicam in Britain devised a promotional campaign for the Batik range of soft drinks marketed by Del Monte. Ten bus shelters were selected for the promotion and were specially adapted so that a citrus fragrance was released automatically by means of an infra-red device when someone came within range. The advertising panels on the shelter featured the Batik range.

Del Monte hoped the fragrance would add an extra dimension to their advertising and act as a stimulus to perception. As people waiting at a bus stop were unlikely to associate a citrus fragrance with the experience, the chances were they would notice.

Source: *Irish Times*, 31 August 1996.

LEARNING

Learning involves changes in people's behaviour arising from experience. It is of interest to marketers because consumers learn about concepts, products, and brands. There are two broad schools of thought about learning: the behavioural theories and the cognitive theories.

Behavioural theories view learning as observable responses to stimuli. The two main theorists were Pavlov (1927) and Skinner (1938). Pavlov showed in his experiments with animals that *conditioned learning* occurs when a stimulus that is paired with another stimulus that elicits a known response serves to produce the same response when used alone. By combining the sound of a bell with giving a dog food, he showed that eventually the dog will associate the sound of the bell with the food and will salivate merely on hearing the bell. This is known as *classical conditioning*. Its relevance for marketers derives from association and repetition. For example, many advertisers have used pieces of classical music or invented jingles in their advertising. If this is repeated often enough, the person may come to associate the music with the product.

Instrumental conditioning was demonstrated by Skinner, again using animals. Here learning occurs by a process of trial and error, in which rewards result in repeat behaviour. Every time the animal engaged in the desired behaviour it was rewarded. Laboratory animals therefore associated particular behaviour with rewards and would repeat the behaviour to obtain the reward.

With regard to human behaviour, instrumental conditioning theory suggests that the buyer will associate particular behaviour with a reward and will engage in purchasing behaviour to obtain that reward. Consider the example of supermarkets rewarding loyalty, as described below. Members of these 'loyalty clubs' learnt that engaging in purchasing behaviour with participating firms was instrumental in their receiving rewards.

The examples in the panel below are indicative of the increased prevalence of loyalty schemes in the nineteen-nineties. Airlines and petrol retailers had in many cases led the way with such schemes. From a psychological viewpoint, three main effects determine whether a loyalty scheme will alter consumers' behaviour. Loyalty can be measured directly, whether to the brand or indirectly to the scheme itself. The value the consumer places on the reward will also be a determinant, as will the timing or the time allowed for the scheme (Dowling and Uncles, 1997). Generally, marketers consider that loyalty schemes encourage loyal customers to pass on recommendations to others and to offer advice and feedback to the marketer on the scheme. Loyalty schemes are usually designed to ensure that they maximise the buyers' motivation to make further purchases.

REWARDING LOYALTY

Superclub was the first supermarket loyalty scheme, launched in 1993 by the Superquinn chain. It also involved a number of partner firms, ranging from Texaco service stations to UCI cinemas. These pay a fee for the service and buy points that they distribute to their own customers. Consumers could join the club and were given a membership card with a bar-coded membership number. Every pound spent with any participating company earned points, which could be redeemed for a range of gifts, including electrical goods, household items, and flights to a number of destinations. The scheme was run by a company called Superclub Target Marketing.

By 1998 Superclub had over 350,000 members, and Superquinn had franchised the system to a chain of Brazilian shops. They had also carried out consultancy work for companies in Scandinavia and Portugal. The company had calculated that average expenditure per customer had increased since the scheme was launched. Many participating firms give bonus points from time to time on selected items and services, so the careful shopper has the chance to considerably increase the total number of points.

Other supermarkets watched with interest, but it was 1997 before Dunne's Stores and Quinnsworth (Tesco Ireland) launched their Value Card and Tesco Club Card, respectively. Dunne's Value Card concept was different from Superclub, in that points were converted into cash vouchers that could be used to pay for purchases. The Tesco Club Card also involved the consumer receiving vouchers, redeemable when making purchases in the shop.

In 1998 the Spar chain launched a scheme involving itself and the phone card company Switchcom. They produced branded pre-paid phone cards that could be used from any phone, including mobiles. Consumers could collect points and redeem them for phone cards.

The appeal of these cards was in the fact that points could be accumulated quite quickly. Many consumers were members of more than one scheme. For retailers it provided a data-base of club members and allowed them to monitor customer loyalty. If items with bonus points could be shown to sell faster than items without, manufacturers could be encouraged to give price reductions or incentives.

The general reaction of customers to loyalty cards has been positive. Lansdowne Market Research carried out some research on consumers' attitudes to loyalty schemes in 1997, and the results were published in the trade magazine *Checkout* in September 1997. A number of questions were asked, including questions about what shoppers thought of loyalty schemes and why they participated.

Are loyalty schemes a good or a bad idea?

Very good	26%
Good	45%
Neither good nor bad	17%
Bad	9%
Very bad	3%

Reasons for participation:

To receive goods on offer	38%
I'm shopping, so I might as well	36%
To save money or receive discounts	22%
Other reasons	4%

Shoppers were also asked if they would switch shops as a result of loyalty schemes. The majority would not, as the following figures indicate. This suggests that loyalty cards have an important role in reinforcing loyal behaviour.

Likelihood of switching shops because of loyalty schemes

Very likely	9%
Likely	17%
Neither likely nor unlikely	17%
Unlikely	22%
Very unlikely	35%

Sources: *Sunday Tribune*, 3 November 1996; *Irish Times*, 27 June 1997; 'New loyalists in the Republic', *Checkout Ireland*, September 1997; Christine Doherty, 'Changing face of loyalty schemes', *Sunday Business Post*, 17 May 1998.

Cognitive learning theory

Cognitive learning theory holds that the kind of learning most characteristic of humans is problem-solving. The individual processes information, stores it, retains it, and retrieves it. Memory is therefore important in the process. For memory to function, the information must be rehearsed, encoded, stored, and retrieved.

People are most likely to memorise advertisements that they find interesting or of relevance to them and that are repeated often enough. The individual may see and hear many advertisements, but only some will be committed to memory. These will have been rehearsed and encoded. When the need arises, they can be retrieved from memory.

While cognitive learning theory is probably the most relevant theory with regard to understanding human learning, classical and instrumental learning are also relevant with regard to learning associated with advertising and promotion. The repeated use of the same message or of free gifts with the product that reinforce the consumer's decision are examples of this. In the area of branding, brand extensions demonstrate that consumers can generalise. Pavlov showed in his experiments that dogs would react in the same way to the sound of jingling keys as to the sound of the bell. This is known as *stimulus generalisation*. Marketers such as Cadbury have used this concept in extending their brand from chocolate bars to cakes, biscuits, desserts, and cream liqueurs. All these products are branded with the Cadbury name, and the familiar purple colour appears on many of them. Cadbury hope that the consumer will generalise and consider any Cadbury product to be a good choice.

ATTITUDES

Attitudes are learnt predispositions to respond in a consistently favourable or unfavourable way with respect to product, brand, person, idea, or organisation.

Attitudes consist of three components:

- **cognitive**—the consumer's beliefs about the object
- **affective**—the consumer's emotions or feeling about the product
- **conative**—the likelihood that the consumer will act in a particular manner.

These three components are related. If the consumer believes that the product is good they will have a positive feeling about the product and will be more likely to buy it. Attitudes are therefore important determinants of behaviour. Attitudes can be measured using *attitude scales* (see fig. 6.8), which are quite common in research questionnaires. The results from questions like those in the following questionnaire can be numerically tabulated, giving a quantifiable indication of attitude.

Marketers may attempt to change or influence attitudes by trying to influence one or other of the attitude components. It can be difficult to get people to change their beliefs about something; the marketer may therefore have to encourage a re-evaluation or attempt to change the image of the attitude object. Advertising campaigns to encourage consumers to switch from spreads to butter or to revert to using sugar are examples of this.

INFLUENCERS ON THE BUYING DECISION

The consumer will usually go through a decision-making process that may or may not involve outside influencers. As stated in the definition of buyer behaviour, the physical purchase is only one part of the process. There are a number of roles in the decision process, and these can be performed by different people. The essential roles are:

(1) *initiator*—the person who first suggests the idea to buy;
(2) *influencer*—whose views carry weight in the final decision;
(3) *decider*—who ultimately decides what to buy, in what quantity, and where to buy;
(4) *buyer*—who actually makes the purchase;
(5) *user*—who actually uses the product.

Fig. 6.8: Attitude scales

Semantic differential scale—measures attitudes by getting the respondent to rate the attitude object using bipolar adjectives; for example:

We would like you to tell us what you think about our shop. Please tick the point in the scale that reflects your feelings.

Modern	☐	☐	☐	☐	☐	Old-fashioned
Low prices	☐	☐	☐	☐	☐	High prices
Good service	☐	☐	☐	☐	☐	Poor service
Convenient	☐	☐	☐	☐	☐	Inconvenient

Likert scale—consists of a number of evaluative statements, which the respondent is asked to agree or disagree with; for example:

	Strongly agree	Agree	Neutral	Disagree	Strongly disagree
This shop offers a wide product range	☐	☐	☐	☐	☐
This shop has an easy-to-follow layout	☐	☐	☐	☐	☐

These roles can be particularly pronounced in family buying and in industrial buying situations. In most families, different family members may take on different roles, which may vary depending on the product. For example, children may be an influence on the holiday the family takes but may not be an influence on the power tools the family buys. In the industrial buying situation it may be a particular person's job to perform one of the roles: for example, the buyer might be the purchasing manager. Understanding that there are different buyer roles is important, as the marketer may want to select particular role members. Most in-store promotions, for instance, are aimed at the buyer, as they are being asked to make a decision about the promoted item there and then.

Buyer's response

The third element of the black box model is the buyer's response. Marketers typically measure response in sales of the product; however, the timing of the response, the retail outlet chosen and the amount bought are other possible responses. The consumer may see an advertisement for a new model of car and may be quite impressed. They may commit the advertisement to memory and retrieve it when they are actually changing their car or buying their first car at some later time. Responses, therefore, are not always immediate. Buyers also make decisions about the outlets they will use. Outlets that are perceived to be inconvenient or offering poor choice may not be considered. Buyers may

Fig. 6.9: Brown Thomas

DISHWASHER   MODEL'S   OWN

KITCHEN   ESSENTIALS   BY

PRANDELLI   BODUM   VILLEROY & BOCH

CIRCULON   BODA NOVA   CROSONO

KITCHEN HEAVEN 2ND FLOOR

BROWN THOMAS
Dublin · Cork

go to outlets that they feel are consistent with their life-style: consider, for example, the Brown Thomas advertisement shown in fig. 6.9.

The timing of the buyer's response is also important. Many airlines and travel companies attempt to fill spare capacity in the winter months by offering special deals; but consumers who cannot take holidays at that time of year may not be able to respond. The amount that buyers buy is also a response variable; this is especially a factor in sales promotions, where banded offers, special price offers and promotional packs may encourage the buyer to buy more.

It is important to note that it is possible for marketers to have an influence at the response stage. Advertising and promotion can be used to attract undecided buyers or consumers who are willing to switch brands.

REPEAT PURCHASE AND BRAND LOYALTY

A desirable behavioural response is repeat purchase and brand loyalty. Consumers tend to continuously buy products and brands that they like and that meet their needs.

Loyalty cannot be taken for granted. Changing needs, competitive product offerings and sales promotions aim to tempt buyers away. Loyalty schemes, such as those described above, are an attempt to secure consumer loyalty. Loyalty, however, is much more than simple repeat purchase: there can be different dimensions to loyalty. One study examined the nature of loyalty and suggested a matrix with four dimensions, as fig. 6.10 illustrates. This demonstrates the importance of the relationship between customer attitude and loyal behaviour.

Fig. 6.10: Dimensions of customer loyalty

		Repeat patronage	
		High	Low
Relative attitude	High	**Loyalty**	**Latent loyalty**
	Low	**Sporadic**	**No loyalty**

Source: A. Dick and K. Basu, 'Customer loyalty: towards an integrated conceptual framework', *Journal of the Academy of Marketing Science*, vol. 22 (1994), no. 2.

Marketers, therefore, need to follow changing trends and where necessary adapt products or develop new offerings to keep pace with changing market conditions. Advertising can be used to encourage the customer to be loyal, not only by reminding the customer that the product is still there but also by helping to reinforce the buyer's decision.

Holding on to loyal customers is a core principle of marketing. It generally costs a lot more to create new customers than to hold on to existing ones. Customers can of course switch to other products or service providers; marketers, however, can influence these defection rates in an attempt to keep them low. Banks, for example, will aim their advertising at students, many of whom open an account for the first time when they go to university.

One study measured defection rates from financial service institutions among students (Colgate, Stewart, and Kinsella, 1996), which found that the defection rate was 18 per cent. Banks have certainly realised the importance of holding on to student customers. They have also provided inducements to students to stay, such as minimised bank charges, good customer service, access to overdrafts, and accessibility.

Airlines have 'frequent flier' schemes to reward loyal users, while Superclub members can receive rewards by remaining loyal to a range of firms. In competitive markets, brand loyalty will come under pressure, and understanding the nature of buyer behaviour with regard to the influences and the personal and psychological forces that are at work can help the marketer in the process of maintaining brand loyalty.

FURTHER READING

MacDonagh, J., and Weldridge, R., *Behavioural Science for Marketing and Business Students*, Dublin: Gill and Macmillan 1994.

Peter, J., and Olsen, J., *Understanding Consumer Behaviour*, Homewood (Ill.): Irwin 1994.

Schiffman, L., and Kanuk, L., *Consumer Behaviour* (fifth edition), Englewood Cliffs (NJ): Prentice-Hall 1994.

DISCUSSION QUESTIONS

1. Using the 'black box' model presented in this chapter, comment on the behavioural factors that would be of interest to the marketers of the following products:

   (a) a new brand of toothpaste;
   (b) an Irish-made detergent;
   (c) an inclusive tour operator selling sun holidays;
   (d) a packaging machine.

   In your answer you should describe all the factors from the black box structure that would be relevant.

2. Explain how marketers can attempt to influence buyer behaviour at different stages in the decision-making process.

3. Comment on the usefulness of buyer behaviour in the segmentation process.

4. Select an advertisement for any product or service. Using Maslow's hierarchy of needs, identify the needs or motives it seeks to address.

5. Explain how you would develop a customer loyalty scheme for each of the following:

   (a) a pub or night club;
   (b) An Post;

(c) Bus Éireann;

(d) Jury's Hotels.

Is it possible for all firms to have such loyalty schemes?

REFERENCES

Aaker, J., 'Dimensions of brand personality', *Journal of Marketing Research*, August 1997.

Colgate, M., Stewart, K., and Kinsella, R., 'Customer defection: a study of the student market in Ireland', *International Journal of Bank Marketing*, March 1996.

Dewey, J., *How We Think*, New York: Heath 1910.

Dowling, G., and Uncles, Mark, 'Do customer loyalty programs really work?', *Sloan Management Review*, summer 1997.

Henley Centre of Ireland, *Planning for Social Change*, Dublin: Henley Centre of Ireland 1992.

Howard, J., and Sheth, J., *The Theory of Buyer Behaviour*, New York: Wiley 1969.

Maslow, A., 'A theory of human motivation', *Psychological Review*, vol. 50, 1943.

Mohan, Mark, 'The influence of marital roles in consumer decision-making', *Irish Marketing Review*, vol. 8 (1995).

Pavlov, I., *Conditioned Reflexes*, London: Oxford University Press 1927.

Schiffman, L., and Kanuk, L., *Consumer Behaviour* (fifth edition), Englewood Cliffs (NJ): Prentice-Hall 1994.

Skinner, B., *The Behaviour of Organisms*, New York: Appleton-Century-Crofts 1938.

Turley, D., 'The Irish consumer through Irish eyes: European values survey, 1990', *Irish Marketing Review*, vol. 8 (1995).

Turley, D., and Gallagher, H., 'Children and television advertising: a cognitive development perspective', *Irish Marketing Review*, vol. 3 (1988).

CASE STUDIES

TESCO IRELAND

On 12 May 1997 Tesco Ireland formally acquired the retail interests of Associated British Foods in Ireland. The £630 million deal included the purchase of all the Quinnsworth, Crazy Prices and Bloomfield outlets in the Republic and Stewarts, Crazy Prices and West Side Stores in Northern Ireland. In effect Tesco purchased the market leaders in both areas; under the old ABF regime the operations north and south were split. Tesco PLC decided to maintain that approach, setting up Tesco Ireland in the Republic and handling the Northern Ireland operation from Britain. With regard to image, market research showed that Quinnsworth held the middle ground. Dunne's Stores, on the other hand, was strongly associated with value and lower prices, whereas Superquinn was perceived as offering quality, friendly staff and good service. The Super Valu chain was associated with convenience. Quinnsworth's position had always proved a challenge, as it never had a very clear identity or USP.

Quinnsworth

Quinnsworth's strengths included its range and quality of produce and the layout and cleanliness of its stores. Crazy Prices held similar strengths, although performing better on value and prices, bringing it closer to Dunnes' positioning. The main challenges facing Quinnsworth at the time of the takeover were perceptions of customer care and the shopping experience (store atmosphere and modernity). In addition, Dunne's Stores were starting to improve their image, raising perceptions of the quality of product offered, of service, and of understanding of shoppers' needs. For Crazy Prices the challenge was to create a point of differentiation, as it lacked a distinctive image. In the previous years its price-competitive image had been eroded by forces in the market. The price profile of the big supermarkets converged somewhat, leading to an erosion in the competitive strength of Crazy Prices.

Dunne's Stores

Apart from value, prices, and convenience, the image of Dunne's Stores was weak. The main issues it needed to address were quality, range and freshness of produce, level of service, and store atmosphere. At the time of Tesco's entry into Ireland, Dunne's was well on the way to addressing many of these issues.

Super Valu

Super Valu's positioning revolved around opening hours, convenience, and friendliness. Its association with the attributes of range, freshness, service and understanding shoppers' needs was weak.

Superquinn

Superquinn consistently surpassed all competition in quality, range, store atmosphere, and service. However, as the competition started to improve their standards, Superquinn's challenge was to maintain this point of differentiation.

Changes in perceptions since Tesco's arrival

Immediately after the takeover, Tesco Ireland set about a programme of rebranding the stores it had acquired to streamline systems and introduce new standards of customer service to the market. As part of the package for the move to 'Tescoisation' of stores, the company introduced the highly successful British Clubcard scheme for customers, as well as an increased range of own-label products that were obtained both in local and foreign markets.

Within the first year a total of thirty-two stores were rebranded to Tesco, and market share was maintained. The first of these stores was the new Tesco Ireland in Athlone, which was quickly followed by rebranded openings in Dundalk, Dublin, Galway, Limerick, Cork, and Longford, among others. The customers in each store were consulted on the changes they wanted and were invited back after the reopening to comment on their new stores, reinforcing the Tesco Ireland commitment to listening to customers. Many improvements were made in layout and cleanliness, quality of fresh food, friendliness of staff, range of store labels, and value for money.

The perception that prices had gone up over the year was offset by that of a rise in quality, resulting in a positive shift in value perceptions for Tesco Ireland. Pricing remained a big issue for all competitors in the early and middle part of 1998, as sterling continued to fluctuate wildly, affecting first imports and then home-produced products. For many customers the obvious source of blame for price increases was the arrival of Tesco.

Throughout 1998 Tesco Ireland continued to bring a range of services and promotions to customers, building on the strengths of the Quinnsworth offering and taking the best of the British offering, adapting it to the Irish environment. By the end of 1998 there were three Clubcard strategic partners: Esso, Lifestyle Sports, and Budget Travel. Clubcard customers were able to avail of special offers through their Clubcard mailings and in-store promotions, such as Clubcard winter flight breaks. Baby Club was launched as a sub-club of Clubcard, with many stores holding special evenings for customers throughout the year. Clubcard customers were invited to take part in store gourmet evenings and Clubcard nights.

Value was strengthened by keen price offers every week. Promotions were more than price-based, with customers given the chance to participate in 'Computers for Schools' and many national and local competitions throughout the year. With regard to product range, perceptions of Tesco range of store labels improved dramatically in quality and choice, though store labels remained an important strength for Dunne's. Throughout

1998 Dunne's continued to be fierce competitors and at times were seen to upstage Tesco Ireland by launching Babyclub and Shell as a Valueclub partner before the Tesco initiatives were introduced. At times Dunne's ran Valueclub triple and double points promotions throughout their stores.

Despite these improvements, Tesco Ireland remained comparatively weak in the areas of support for local Irish suppliers and customer service, low prices and value, store atmosphere, and quality of produce. In the next eighteen months the main competitors, Dunne's and Super Valu, made even greater strides in improving their offering.

With the perception that Tesco Ireland's prices had increased, Dunne's became even more strongly associated with low prices, despite parity between the two competitors in hundreds of grocery lines. Dunne's appeared to be concentrating on the areas of staff and the range and quality of produce. However, their service was still seen as an important weakness.

Super Valu made steady and consistent strides in improving its offering. Grocery shoppers' perceptions improved significantly, particularly in the areas of quality and range of produce, friendliness of staff, and shop atmosphere. While it was expected that Super Valu would continue to improve its standards, its lack of scanning data and central control proved a challenge. During 1998 Super Valu acquired the supermarket wing of Roche's Stores, giving the company retail space in some important locations throughout the country at a time when the Government was putting a cap on the size of new superstores.

Superquinn's image appeared to have suffered in most areas, as all the principal competitors were making significant progress in improving their overall offering, and Superquinn's previous point of differentiation was therefore eroded. However, they retained the overall quality halo that had been built up over many years.

Most encouragingly, customers' perceptions of Tesco Ireland in the renamed stores well outperformed that of customers from the stores yet to be renamed. However, despite the many improvements customers perceivd Tesco Ireland to have made over the eighteen months, it could be argued that Tesco Ireland's strengths were still quite clinical such as store layout, range and cleanliness. In positioning terms, Tesco Ireland continued to dominate the central ground and it did have the advantage of having a broader appeal than some of its competitors.

In summary, while customers perceived Tesco to have made significant improvements in the eighteen months after the takeover, so did the competition, and the consumer was becoming increasingly demanding. The current central positioning of Tesco Ireland has the advantage of a broad appeal. However, the issues of store atmosphere, shopping experience and competitive offer need to be addressed. In going forward, an important issue will be how to differentiate Tesco Ireland from the competition.

DISCUSSION QUESTIONS

1. Evaluate the impact of Tesco's arrival on Irish grocery retailing.
2. Comment on the use of the Clubcard loyalty scheme in the company's operation. What are the benefits of the scheme to customers and to the company?
3. Develop a positioning strategy for Tesco Ireland that will help differentiate it from the competition.

THE IRISH SUN CARE MARKET

In the nineteen-nineties the world sun care market increased in significance. Increased awareness of the harmful effects of over-exposure to the sun's rays meant an increase in sales of sun care products. In spite of this, it was estimated that there was still an opportunity for significant growth in the Irish market. It was thought that consumers were more inclined to buy such products for foreign holidays, for example, and were less likely to use them when at home. As a result, competitors considered commissioning some market research to investigate Irish buyers' behaviour.

Main trends in the sun care market

A number of significant trends characterised the market.
1. The sun tan continued to have an appeal as a physical attribute and as a symbol of health, associated with success, travel, and a healthy outdoor life.
2. Medical warnings about the danger of excessive exposure to the sun had benefited the market. Consumers were more aware of the dangers of melanoma and more informed about the sun care products available.
3. In addition to the protection given by sun screen products, consumers were also aware of the benefits of using after-sun products.
4. Products with a higher sun protection factor were increasing in popularity.
5. Sales were strongly related to climate.
6. The increasing practice of taking two or more holidays a year helped increase year-round sales.

Product segments

There were three distinct product segments.
1. Sun tan products: these included oil, creams, lotions, and milk formulations. An important buying criterion was the level of protection afforded (sun protection factor).
2. After-sun products: a range of gels, lotions, and creams. These were also manufactured by sun care producers and in many cases marketed along with sun tan products to provide a complete range.
3. Artificial sun tan products: these were less popular than the other types and were primarily cosmetic products.

The nature of protection

The sun's rays are made up of several different types of radiation, the rays that cause most damage to skin being the ultra-violet rays. These in turn are divided into UVA, which causes aging, UVB, which causes burning, and UVC, which can cause skin cancer and eye damage.

Manufacturers had innovated over the years and produced products that provided higher levels of protection and were waterproof and stainproof.

Sun care products were graded according to the degree of protection claimed, and this grade was printed on the packaging. The higher the number, the higher the protection afforded; grades ranged from 2 to 30, which provided sun block protection. In general, doctors tended to recommend a grade above 15.

Buyer behaviour

The sun care market was paradoxical in nature. This led to behavioural changes, so that sunbathing changed from being a carefree activity to one where more care and caution was involved. In spite of this, many GPs regularly reported cases of severe sunburning, especially in any hot summer weather. It was as if some people did not think the sun was as strong in Ireland as on a holiday beach in Spain, according to one.

All manufacturers of sun care products had been emphasising the dangers of melanoma in their promotional campaigns. Packaging also contained extensive information on the dangers of over-exposure. Manufacturers felt that many people who worked outdoors or engaged in sports or other outdoor pursuits did not always consider using sun protection. They also felt there might still be confusion among consumers about the numbering system used to grade protection on packages.

Brands

There were several brands of sun care products on the market; the main ones were Ambre Solaire, Clinique, Hawaiian Tropic, Johnson and Johnson, Nivea, and Piz Buin. In addition, the arrival of the British pharmacy chain Boots in the Irish market increased the share of own-label products sold.

Purchasing outlets

The main purchasing outlets were supermarkets, pharmacies, department stores, and, to a lesser extent, duty-free shops.

Research

Sun care manufacturers felt there was a need to find out more about the Irish market. In particular, they were interested in people's sunbathing habits, as well as the amount of time they spent outdoors for work or leisure, and they were keen to determine whether people's usage patterns corresponded to this. Another critical factor was respondents' understanding of the numbering system used to indicate protection levels. Manufacturers felt there was a need to measure frequency of purchase, place of purchase, brand awareness, brand purchase, level of protection sought, and the use of the product both at home and when abroad.

Your services have been engaged to prepare a detailed research proposal that will achieve the manufacturers' objectives. As part of your proposal you should design a questionnaire to be used in the research.

PART 3

The Marketing Mix

7

The Product

Marketers tend to use the term *product* in a very broad sense. Kotler and Armstrong (1994) defined a product as anything that can be offered to a market for attention, acquisition, use or consumption that might satisfy a want or need. It includes physical objects, services, people, places, organisations, and ideas. This chapter examines the nature of the product and the marketing decisions required in the creation and development of product strategy.

Firms devote considerable skills and resources to the management and development of their products. Products should meet the needs of the market. The creation and development of products to meet these needs, and sustaining products or brands that have developed strong relationships in the market, will be vital. Branding, for example, is one dimension of the product that requires careful management and that can yield significant benefits, as the following panel illustrates.

BRANDS BECOME THE BIGGEST ASSETS OF ALL

In late 1998 British Sky Broadcasting made a bid of £623 million for Manchester United Football Club. The bid emphasised a continued interest in value that could be placed on brands. Brands are important because they can create trust among consumers, and trust is a precondition of loyalty. They are also important because of their value to shareholders. An analysis conducted by Interbrand and Citibank on the stock market performance of heavily brand-dependent companies showed how they outperformed the rest of the companies in the British FTSE 350 index by between 15 and 20 per cent over a period of fifteen years.

The difficulty for most companies has been in putting a cash value on the brand. The value of brands can be readily seen in what companies are prepared to pay for them and in the extent to which the market capitalisation of branded-goods companies exceeds their tangible asset value. In the case of companies like Coca-Cola, for example, this value can be as high as 4,000 per cent.

Companies have built and developed their brands in different ways. Manchester United was considered to have built its reputation by decades of word of mouth, industry reputation, and quality heritage. Other brands have been built in the market through powerful advertising. Diageo's range, which includes Guinness, Smirnoff, Häagen-Dazs, Bailey, and Burger King, represents a group of brands built in large part

---

through consistent high-quality marketing and advertising. The company places a value of £18,000 million on these brands; this represents five times the value of the tangible assets.

Source: L. Butterfield, 'Brands become the biggest assets of all', *Sunday Times*, 20 September 1998.

This account shows that the dimensions of the product are wide and make a significant contribution to the general success of the company. In this chapter these dimensions are considered in more detail.

PRODUCT LEVELS

Products can be considered as having different *levels* or *dimensions*. The *core level* is what the consumer is really buying: for example, the National Lottery considers that when consumers buy a lotto ticket they are buying a dream. The core dimensions of the product should meet the core needs of the buyer.

The next product level is the tangible aspects of the product, including the product's features, quality level, styling, design, branding, and packaging. Tangible aspects can be readily perceived by the consumer and will often be used by marketers in positioning the product.

The *augmented product level* is the guarantee or warranty that may come with the product, delivery, credit, installation, customer service, and after-sales service. The augmented aspects of products will differ: electrical retailers will usually provide many aspects of augmented service, a TSN may not. The augmented level of the product should not necessarily be viewed as an extra. Customers may expect high levels of service and will expect difficulties or product failures to be sorted out.

The *potential product* refers to the level the product may reach or be developed towards. Arguably, all products can be developed by means of new benefits or added values. The potential product level describes how products might compete in the future.

AVANTI FROM DUREX

In September 1997 the Avanti brand was launched by the condom manufacturers Durex. Avanti was the result of ten years of research and cost the manufacturers £15 million to develop. The product was transparent, odourless, and half the thickness of traditional latex condoms. The manufacturers claimed it increased sensitivity without reducing safety and began advertising in *Vogue*, *GQ*, and the national press.

Research had revealed that many young people had not considered using condoms as a contraceptive, or had abandoned them because they dulled their sensations. Avanti cost twice the price of rival products and was to be launched in the United States and throughout Europe.

Source: *Sunday Times*, 28 October 1997.

THE PRODUCT MIX

The product mix is the set of all products the marketer makes available to the seller. For an individual company this is a complete description of its range: for example, for a company such as Guinness it would include its stouts, ales, and lagers. These can be further sub-divided. For example, in the ale category there are three brands: Smithwick's, Kilkenny, and Macardle's. Each of these brands is retailed in draught, bottled and canned form. Smithwick's and Kilkenny are national brands, while the Macardle's brand is strong in the north-east.

The product mix can therefore be considered as having width, length, and depth. The width refers to the number of different product lines offered. The length refers to the number of items in the product mix. The depth describes the number of variations of each product that is offered. Ale represents one product line for Guinness; length is determined by the number of ales (three) and depth by the number of variations of each, for example different bottle or can sizes.

In general, firms will seek to achieve consistency among the products in the mix. Obviously for Guinness there is consistency in the production, packaging and distribution of stouts, ales, and lagers. Similar plant and machinery may be used for all three. There is also consistency in distribution, in that all the products in the mix are sold in pubs and off-licences, and they can be transported and delivered to outlets in the same delivery. Strategically, Guinness maintains three brands of ale to maximise its presence in the channels of distribution. The Macardle's brand is maintained because of its historically strong position in the region.

Branding can also be used to achieve marketing consistency among products. For example, the Golden Vale brand appears on a range of dairy and meat products, and the Tayto brand appears on a range of crisps and extruded snacks.

PRODUCT CLASSIFICATION

Products can be classified in a number of ways. *Non-durable goods* are products that are consumed in one or a few uses. These include most foods and drinks. *Durable goods* are designed to last longer and include such products as household electrical items, cooking utensils, personal computers, and sports wear.

Convenience goods are goods that are bought frequently and with a minimum of effort. In recent years the convenience market has grown in importance. It includes products such as soft drinks and snacks, chilled ready meals, and fast-food restaurants. All are designed to minimise the consumer's efforts in preparation and search. Consumer staples such as milk, bread and newspapers are largely classified as convenience goods, as are most impulse purchases.

Shopping goods are goods that the consumer spends some time considering before purchasing. These typically represent high-involvement purchases for the consumer, who may go to considerable lengths to analyse and evaluate the different products on offer. *Speciality goods* usually have a high involvement also; these are goods with unique characteristics for which the consumer will make a special purchasing effort, for example an expensive brand of clothing, or products related to a specialist hobby.

The classification of the product will be a determinant of distribution policy. Convenience and impulse products tend to be widely available and distributed in a variety of retail outlets and by other means, including vending machines. Shopping and speciality goods are more selectively distributed; for some speciality goods only a small number of outlets in the country may stock the product.

PRODUCT MANAGEMENT

In small, single-product firms there may be few variations in the width, depth or length of the product mix. In larger, multi-product companies there may be more variation. An examination of the top hundred grocery brands in Ireland, for example, reveals that within many product categories, and among categories, many brands are owned by a single parent firm. Multinationals such as Proctor and Gamble, which owns seven of the top brands, and Van den Bergh Foods, which owns ten, have a presence in several product categories.

Product management also applies in services and in business-to-business markets. Again, an individual manager could be assigned to specific products or services. In the nineteen-sixties the concept of product management was first introduced by Proctor and Gamble. Product managers were given responsibility for a brand or a number of brands, the idea being that they would become, in effect, small-scale marketing managers. Product managers concentrate their efforts on the products or brands assigned to them, and they are responsible for the research, promotion and advertising of the brands, reporting to a marketing manager or marketing director.

According to Lysanski (1985), the product manager performs a 'boundary role' in the firm. This is illustrated in fig. 7.1.

Fig. 7.1: The product manager's boundary role

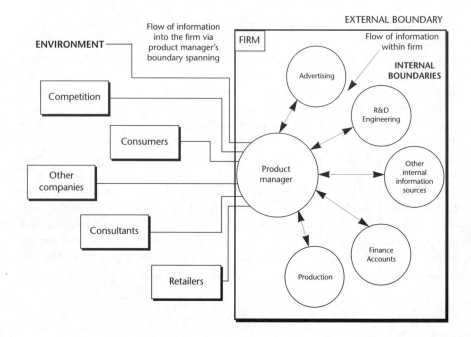

The concept of product management gained popularity, especially in large multi-product companies. In many cases, within brands there could be quite extensive variations in packet sizes or varieties. Similarly, product managers were often given responsibility for *product lines*. These are groups of products that are closely related because they function in a similar manner, are sold to the same groups of customers, are marketed through the same outlets, or fall within given price ranges. In the case of Proctor and Gamble, three of the top brands are detergents: Ariel, Bold, and Daz. These constitute a product line. Another one of its brands is Fairy Liquid; this would belong to a separate product line.

BRANDING

Brands have been used for many years to distinguish products. In the last hundred years or so there has been a significant growth in branding activities. This growth can be ascribed to the industrial revolution and the development of marketing practice. More products and services are produced, more means of communication and promotion are available, and there is greater competition for the consumer's attention.

A brand is a name, sign, symbol or design, or a combination of these, intended to identify the goods or services of one seller and to distinguish them from those of competitors. A brand has been defined by de Chernatony and McDonald (1993) as an identifiable product, service, person or place augmented in such a way that the buyer or user perceives relevant unique added values that match their needs most closely. Furthermore, its success results from being able to sustain these added values in the face of competition.

Branding helps to differentiate products and is a powerful competitive tool. Inanimate objects can be given an identity and image to enable them to compete in the market, and the brand owner can create a valuable company asset. Branding has been described as the DNA of the business (Macrae, Parkinson, and Sheerman, 1995). DNA contains the unique inherited codes that determine the shape, form and function of an organism; branding may be viewed analogously as a business process that determines the particular combination of product quality, innovation, technology, trade partnerships, logistics and other factors crucial to a firm's sustainable competitive advantage.

Branding can be viewed as a system, as illustrated in fig. 7.2. The degree of branding affects the buyer's perceptions, attitudes and behaviour and the brand's financial performance, which thereby affects brand strategy (McDowell et al., 1997).

Fig. 7.2: The branding system

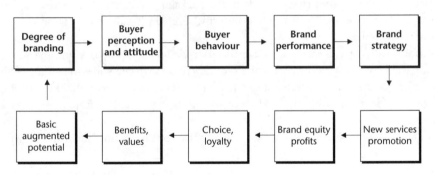

Brand names give the owner proprietorial rights, which can be legally protected. Many brands have been on the market for generations, such as Guinness; some brands have disappeared, such as Phoenix ale and Halpin's tea, which were significant brands in the nineteen-fifties and sixties. Other brands have been revived, as the following panel shows.

REVIVING EIGHTEENTH-CENTURY WHISKEY BRANDS

In 1987 Cooley Distillery PLC was founded by two businessmen, John Teeling and Dónal Kinsella. The company acquired the assets of John Locke and Company, which in 1757 had received the world's first licence to operate a distillery, at Kilbeggan, County Westmeath. The production of whiskey had ceased at Locke's in the nineteen-fifties. Cooley Distillery renovated and reopened the plant and set about reviving the brand.

In 1994 the company relaunched Locke's Irish Whiskey, a quality blended whiskey containing 40 per cent malt. Another Locke's brand, Kilbeggan Irish Whiskey, a standard blend, originally introduced in the late nineteenth century, was also relaunched. A third brand, Tyrconnell, was relaunched to compete in the single-malt segment of the market. This brand had been introduced by Watt's distillery in Derry in 1762.

Brands were essential for Cooley if it was to compete in the brand-conscious national and international whiskey market. The brands it revived had considerable heritage and historical associations. By 1997 the Kilbeggan brand had captured 32 per cent of the sales of Irish whiskey in the German market, and the company claimed a 15 to 20 per cent share of the Irish whiskey market in France and Britain.

Sources: *Sunday Tribune*, 25 May 1997; *Irish Times*, 11 June 1997; *Sunday Business Post*, 16 June 1997.

The benefits of brands to the buyer

Brands can communicate the product's benefits and tell the buyer something about the product. Brands such as the Wash 'n' Go range of hair care products or Shake 'n' Vac carpet freshener suggest something of the products' benefits and how they can be used.

Branding is an aid to recognition. The colours, shapes and names used make it easier for the consumer to identify products in the shop. The brand can also be used to draw attention to new and beneficial products or services. The chocolate and confectionery manufacturer Cadbury tends to use purple in the packaging of its range of products. The Cadbury name appears in its distinctive lettering, and the result is packaging that is instantly recognisable.

Psychologically, brands may satisfy identification and security needs. Consumers may feel comfortable or reassured when a brand provides them with the value they want. The purchaser of designer-label clothing or of a particular brand of car may be looking to the brand to provide them with the added benefit of being socially acceptable or well recognised.

Brand loyalty may be rewarded not just with continued satisfaction but also with gifts or added benefits, such as the rewards frequent travellers can obtain from some airlines or that the regular shopper can obtain from the multiple supermarkets as part of their loyalty schemes.

The benefits of brands to the company

Brands can represent significant assets to the business. In 1996 the multinational FMCG company Unilever paid £73.125 million for a 75 per cent stake in Lyon's tea. This represented several times the asset value of the company. Unilever wanted to add the brand leader in the Irish tea market to its range.

UNILEVER AND THE IRISH TEA MARKET

In July 1996 Unilever bought 75 per cent of Lyon's tea from Allied Domecq. Lyon's had a dominant position in the Irish tea market, with an estimated 60 per cent share. It also had high profit margins. This was not Unilever's first attempt to gain a position in the Irish tea market. In 1993 the company had launched the Lipton's brand. Supported by a £2 million advertising campaign, the brand achieved a share of 9 per cent. However, this was not sustained, and the share ultimately fell to 2 per cent.

Source: *Sunday Times*, 17 November 1996.

Brand equity is the power and value the brand holds in the market. Some of this power is financial, in the form of market share or profitability; the rest is more psychological, in the form of recognition and attractiveness to buyers. Generally, brands with high equity have high levels of brand loyalty and name-awareness. There are usually strong brand associations and other assets, such as patents or strong trade relationships. In 1995, for example, the British holiday company First Choice paid £5.3 million for the sun holiday business of the Irish operator JWT (*Irish Times*, 19 August 1997). First Choice was buying a well-established and well-recognised Irish brand name.

Brand names and trade marks can be registered and legally protected. A trade mark is a word or device used to distinguish the goods of one enterprise from those of another and can include labels, individual brand names, signatures, and shape. It therefore has two functions: an identification for the owner, and a quality guarantee for the customer. Trade marks are a means of legally protecting the goodwill of the business.

Trade marks can be registered in any country. This is important, as in some countries an unregistered trade mark confers no rights on the owner.

Marketers have frequently gone to court in an attempt to protect their brands, as the following case demonstrates. Following the successful introduction of own-label products, many supermarkets began to produce imitations of branded products. A number of legal cases have been taken, which emphasise the need for manufacturers to register not just the brand name but also the packaging and labelling styles as trade marks. In one case in Britain, taken by United Biscuits against ASDA supermarkets, the supermarket chain was found guilty of passing off, because of the great similarities between its own label, Puffin biscuits, and United Biscuits' well-known Penguin brand (Benson, 1997).

BRAND PROTECTION

In 1996 the footwear manufacturer Doc Marten applied for an interlocutory injunction to restrain Dunne's Stores from continuing to sell a range of shoes closely resembling Doc Marten's. The High Court did not grant an injunction, the judge ruling that the retailer had bought the shoes in good faith from two manufacturers in Britain and Italy.

Source: *Irish Times*, 26 September 1996.

Brands aid the sale of the product. The image, personality and identity given to the brand become associated with the product. The brand can be used as the centrepiece in advertising and promotional campaigns and is part of the total communication package. Loyal and profitable users can be attracted with focused brand positioning, and many marketers will use brands as a base for segmentation, as Showerings did in the drinks market.

RITZ

Showerings of Clonmel maintains a number of brands in its range, all of which have unique characteristics and user profiles. One brand that has performed well is Ritz, a cider-based product aimed at the twenties market, introduced in 1984.

Ritz had its packaging and promotion changed in 1997, when the long-neck bottle was completely wrapped in a matt black material and given a frosted neck. A new advertisement for the product was developed that had no scenes of anyone drinking, as research had shown that people in their twenties were put off by people drinking in advertisements. The advertisement depicts a group of young people on a night out, with Ritz branding intercut throughout. The company also signed a sponsorship deal with a dance club owned by the band U2.

Source: *Sunday Business Post*, 25 May 1997.

Brands help the marketer deliver meaning to the buyer and the market. The brand name itself may convey attributes of the product: for example, Duracell suggests something about the long life of the product, and Tayto is a play on the word 'potato'.

Functional and emotional benefits can be linked to the brand through advertising and promotion. Panafluke emphasises the functional nature of liver-fluke eradication, while CK One, the fragrance for men and women from Calvin Klein, has a more emotive proposition.

Marketers may attempt to link the brand with certain consumer or social values. Low Low, the sunflower spread from the Kerry Group, is linked with diet and health, while the charitable organisation Alone emphasises the importance of visiting or keeping in touch with the elderly.

Successful brands can be further extended by increasing sales and market share. Lucozade was launched as a drink for convalescents in 1927. In the eighties, with sport and life-style becoming ever more significant, Smith-Kline Beecham developed Lucozade Sport. Mars has extended its business into ice cream; and the Virgin brand covers air and rail travel, music, financial services, and computers.

Brand personality

Advertisers have considerable scope for giving brands a personality, which does not have to involve humans. Brands can be endowed with personality traits so that people can better relate to them. The Andrex brand of toilet roll and Dulux paint have consistently used dogs in their advertising. Cartoon or animated characters can also be developed, as the food company Batchelor did with the characters Beany and Barney, used for many years to promote the company's range of canned products. An Bord Gáis has used animated teddy bears in its advertising and promotion.

Brand personality reflects the nature of the product and the target market. Banks and financial institutions tend to emphasise traits such as security, service, dependability, and friendliness. Drink brands may emphasise sociability, trendiness, and attractiveness, while many chocolate brands have been given strong sex-role traits, as with Cadbury's Flake and Nestlé's Yorkie, which have been endowed with female and male personalities, respectively.

Irish grocery brands

Table 7.1 presents a list of the top hundred grocery brands in Ireland according to estimated retail sales. This gives some indication of which products were doing well in the grocery sector; it also shows the value individual brands can have. Over time, changes in relative position will no doubt occur.

While the top one hundred were dominated by foreign-owned brands, it is interesting to note that a number of Irish brands also performed well. Donegal Catch and Goodfellas Pizza, both owned by Green Isle Foods, were launched in 1989 and 1993, respectively. The Irish Biscuits brand extension Chocolate Kimberley, launched in 1996, also performed extremely well. The Kerrygold butter brand made something of a come-back, having lost out considerably to dairy spreads since the mid-eighties. The sales value of brands in confectionery, snack foods and ice cream also tends to confirm that the Irish are a nation of snackers.

Table 7.1: The top hundred grocery brands in Ireland, 1996

Sales figures are at RSP

	Sales (£M)		Sales (£M)
1. Coca-Cola	47.54	51. Kellogg's Rice Krispies	7.04
2. 7-Up	28.43	52. Snickers	7.02
3. Lyon's tea	26.75	53. Batchelor's peas	7.01
4. Tayto crisps	24.6	54. Quality Street	7

Sales figures are at RSP

	Sales (£M)		Sales (£M)
5. Pampers	23	55. Galtee cheese	6.81
6. Kerrygold	22	56. Rolo	6.8
7. Dairygold	21	57. Daz	6.75
8. Siúcra	20.1	58. Pringles	6.56
9. Yoplait yoghurt	20	59. Bird's Eye peas	6.55
10. Donegal Catch	19	60. Lynx	6.54
11. Club soft drinks	18.04	61. Cadbury's Milk Tray	6.53
12. Goodfellas pizza	17.5	62. Hunky Dorys	6.52
13. Pedigree Chum	17.03	63. Galtee Snap Packs	6.5
14. Kellogg's corn flakes	17	64. Calvita cheese	6.4
15. HB Hazelbrook Farm	16.6	65. Gillette Sensor, Excel	6.15
16. Lucozade	14.94	66. Galaxy	6.1
17. Denny GM sausages	13.8	67. Yorkie	6
18. Gateaux	13.5	68. Capri Sun	5.9
19. Barry's tea	13.25	69. Magnum	5.89
20. Cadbury's Roses	13.24	70. HB Cornetto	5.705
21. Kit-Kat	13.2	71. Denny Waifos	5.7
22. Persil	12.8	72. Always	5.6
23. Perri crisps	12.5	73. Inversoft	5.55
24. Mars	12	74. Ballygowan	5.45
25. Galtee rashers	11.5	75. Fairy Liquid	5.44
26. Maxwell House	11.4	76. Kittensoft	5.4
27. Cadbury's Snack	11.2	77. Fanta	5.39
28. Ariel	10.4	78. Surf	5.33
29. Sqeez	10	79. Domestos	5.32
30. Cadbury's Dairy Milk	9.6	80. Sno yoghurt	5.3
31. Batchelor's beans	9.5	81. Erin packet soup	5.25
32. Mitchelstown cheese	9.4	82. Comfort	5.2
33. Colgate	9.3	83. Hellmann's mayonnaise	5.18
34. Denny sliced meats	9.2	84. Zip firelighters	5.15
35. Mr Kipling cakes	9.1	85. John West tuna	5.1
36. Twix	9	86. Robinson's drinks	4.91
37. Time Out	8.9	87. Maltesers	4.9
38. Nescafé Gold Blend	8.4	88. Bisto	4.81
39. King Crisps	7.88	89. Andrex	4.8
40. Low Low	7.8	90. Chocolate Kimberley	4.76
41. Flora margarine	7.7	91. Huggies	4.59
42. Whiskas	7.6	92. Bird's Eye potato waffles	4.586
43. Petit Filous	7.52	93. HB choc ice	4.57
44. Bird's Eye fish fingers	7.51	94. Bird's Eye frozen chips	4.56
45. Aero	7.5	95. Penguin multipacks	4.54

46. Pepsi	7.44	96. Club Milk	4.53
47. TK	7.29	97. Dolmio pasta sauce	4.52
48. Bold	7.21	98. Kellogg's Frosties	4.5
49. Weetabix	7.19	99. Tropicana	4.49
50. Knorr packet soup	7.1	100. Gino Ginelli	4.25

Source: *Checkout Ireland*, April 1997.

Brand extensions

A brand extension is any attempt to extend a successful brand name to cover new or related products or services. In psychology this is known as the 'halo' effect, which has been defined as a judgment or perception made on the basis of one characteristic (MacDonagh and Weldridge, 1994). In other words, consumers may make a judgment on a new product or a modified product on the basis of the brand name they are already familiar with. If they have a positive disposition towards the brand, this may transfer to other brand offerings.

The concept has been used by marketers to extend their brand coverage and to build market share. The Avonmore brand, for example, has been extended from its original base, which was whole milk, into low-fat and calcium-enriched milk. Cheese and dairy spreads were added, and in the early nineties a range of fresh soup, Avonmore Country Ladle, was launched. The range was further extended in the nineties with dessert products, and in 1997 a range of fresh cooking sauces, Avonmore Art of Sauce, was introduced.

Brand extensions may prolong the life of the brand and reduce the risks involved in the launch of new products, but it is not always a successful strategy. Avonmore Afters, a dessert product launched by Avonmore in the late eighties, did not succeed in capturing a satisfactory market share for the company and was withdrawn in the mid-nineties.

Many global marketers, such as Hoover and Black and Decker, have used brand extension strategies in international markets, and their names appear on a wide variety of related electrical products. In 1998 R. and A. Bailey began testing 'The Whiskey', a new whiskey brand that it planned to aim at 25 to 35-year-olds. The company had spent over £500,000 on research and development and had tested the product in outlets in Dublin before a regional launch in the rest of the country in June 1998 and a European launch in January 1999 (*Marketing*, March 1998). Another drinks company, Showerings, extended its successful Ritz brand with Ritz TQ.

RITZ TQ

Drinks companies have long been aware of the important role design plays in the promotion of a product, particularly when it comes to attracting the younger consumer. Having identified a niche in the ready-to-drink spirit sector, Showerings launched Ritz TQ in July 1997, competing directly with the likes of Smirnoff Mule and Bacardi Breezer.

The design brief was highly specific. 'Products like these are growing steadily,' the

Ritz TQ brand manager, P. J. Brigdale, explained. 'The market is predominantly 18 to 24-year-olds, with a slight female bias. There is also a degree of trading up from the alcopops sector involved, which is perceived by them as a more juvenile choice.'

Ritz TQ is a tequila-based drink with orange and lime juices. The Ritz name was kept because of the strength of the brand. 'We wanted to signal to the consumer that they already knew and understood the name but this gives them an alternative. We wanted the bottle to have a strong club appeal with cutting-edge packaging, superior to competitors.' In the end Ritz TQ made its debut on the pub shelves in a very distinctive metallic, heat-shrunk sleeve, the printing of which took months to perfect.

'Taste is the key,' according to Brigdale. 'If a product is rejected on taste grounds the consumer just won't go back to it. Livery design, however, is different. If a bottle is shy and doesn't bring notice to itself on the shelf, it is going to make it more difficult for the product to be called for. If a packaging is downright embarrassing, if the girl or guy has a problem with my drinking it, it is in trouble. While taste is the key, packaging is, if you like, the call to action.'

Showerings therefore engaged the services of packaging designers as part of the product development process. The size, shape, labelling and colours used were all extensively researched. Consumer tests before launch indicated that it was perceived as 'something that cool people drink.' Initial sales figures for the product have been healthy, and Showerings feel it has unleashed another successful brand.

Source: Based on a feature in the *Sunday Business Post*, 26 October 1997.

Brand extensions can sometimes be quite improbable. A fashion success in the nineties has been the Caterpillar range of footwear, clothing, and fashion accessories, an extension of a brand of earth-moving and construction equipment.

Brand repositioning

Consumer needs, market conditions or the activities of competitors may require the updating or repositioning of the brand. Repositioning can make the life of the brand potentially infinite.

Irish Distillers have several whiskey brands in their range, each of which has an individual image and identity. In the mid-eighties they concentrated considerable marketing effort on Power's Gold Label, which proved to be the most difficult and elusive to position. Power's was the best-selling Irish whiskey, yet its product image was the most diffuse. The majority of the brand's drinkers were over fifty, and it was largely consumed outside Dublin. The company's research confirmed that the brand was generally perceived as long-established and traditional, with a distinctive flavour. The company developed a communication theme and an advertising campaign that integrated the brand's existing qualities of tradition and 'earthiness' into a product image that sought to woo a target audience of men and women from their mid-twenties upwards (Cummins, 1986).

Keeping up with trends or changing social conditions may be necessary for the survival of a brand. Marketers will therefore update advertising, logos, packaging design and promotional activities. HB adopted a new logo for its ice cream in 1997 (*Checkout Ireland*, November 1997). Research had shown that the existing logo, adopted in 1973, had become outdated. The new design was a heart-shaped symbol in yellow and red with the letters *HB* underneath in blue.

In February 1998 Bird's Eye launched a new Captain Birdseye character (*Irish Times*, 13 February 1998). The original Captain Birdseye had been created in the seventies in commercials for the company's fish fingers. The actor who played the part in the television commercials was retiring, and a new, much younger character was created and featured in the company's advertising as well as on packaging. Bird's Eye hoped that the younger character would appeal to younger women shoppers.

Occasionally marketers will change brand names. Mars changed the name on one of its British and Irish countline bars, Marathon, to Snickers, which was the brand name used on the product in the United States. In 1998 another of the company's leading brands, Opal Fruits, was changed to Star Burst (*Sunday Business Post*, 12 April 1998). Extreme care is needed in considering such a change if consumers are not be confused. Mars chose to change the names because it wanted a single brand name to be used in all markets. It did not make the change for Opal Fruits overnight. The packaging was first changed to incorporate 'Opal Fruits—internationally known as Star Burst.' This was followed some months later by 'Star Burst—formerly known as Opal Fruits.' The company estimated that it would take customers six months to get used to the change.

The own-label challenge

Retailers' own-label brands have steadily increased their share in many markets. In 1994 it was estimated that they accounted for 15 per cent of the total Irish grocery market (Pratt, 1994). The challenge from these brands has been felt by both national and international manufacturers. Retailers have used own-label brands to create and enhance their image and to give them more power in distribution channels.

The challenge in the Irish market began principally with staple products, such as bread and milk, but has gradually been extended. In the grocery sector all the major multiples and retail groups have developed ranges of own-label products. The fundamental reasons why retailers have developed own-label brands are:

- to give them more control in the distribution channel;
- to improve the margin they can earn from products;
- to maximise control on the use of shelf space;
- to enhance their reputation for quality and value.

Retailers argue that they bring quality own-label products to the consumer at reduced prices. But the own-label challenge has not been without criticism. Many manufacturers argue that the quality of products can suffer in the search for lower costs, and that many of the retailer's own brands are in effect 'copycat' products. It is also argued that smaller manufacturers that devote a large proportion of their production to own-label products become tied into a highly controlled relationship.

In the nineties there was considerable debate about the future of brands. Discounting and the proliferation of supermarket own-brand products convinced some that branding was in peril. The debate did help to illustrate two alternative theories of branding, as the next panel shows. Some argued that the 'crisis' in branding had occurred because of the accelerating power of retailers and the sophistication of retailer brands. It was also argued that increased awareness among consumers impaired the power of the traditional mass media, and this was exacerbated by the weakness of marketing departments in major companies (Fanning, 1995).

THE BRANDING RETHINK

In the recessionary nineties in Britain, brands got a rough ride, and retail discounting got the upper hand. On the one hand proponents of the strong theory of branding argued that recognised brand names were separable assets, with value that was separate from the value of the manufacturing company. The source of this value is the fact that branding is instrumental in building a strong positive image for the goods (or shop), which then has a positive effect on purchasing (or patronage). To build and protect brand value it is necessary to invest in the brand and to add value (long-term survival dictates this), however hard or costly this might be in a recession.

Discounters, on the other hand, are not seen as investors in brands. They make minimum use of advertising support, slash prices, and drive down their costs. In a recession this is relatively easy to achieve—indeed short-term survival may dictate it. The crunch question is, can the recognised brands sit out the hard times while the discounters blossom in the short run?

The weak theory of branding is more low-key. Recognised brands are seen as providing some order, simplicity and assurance in a crowded world. Recognised brands add to the 'comfort' level of consumers, but they are not all-powerful. Brands are largely inseparable (for example, it makes little sense to think of Heinz baked beans without its factories, distribution system, and so forth). Branding can only support sales. In conjunction with other factors, the brand name can have an impact on purchasing (or patronage) but not in the powerful sense of strong or exclusive brand loyalty by the final customer.

In most markets, competitors are selling something pretty similar, and customers know this. The implications of this are that there will be big brands and small brands, which are unlikely to be bought by consumers in a strictly loyal way, but the branding will reassure consumers. It is therefore possible for a cost-driven discounter to have market presence and, in its own way, to offer order, simplicity and reassurance to its customers.

Source: Mark Uncles, 'The branding rethink', *Marketing*, 22 July 1993.

The debate on brands demonstrates the importance of market research and of senior managers taking responsibility for their brands. The growth in distributors' own brands led to intense competition with and between manufacturers' brands. It was argued that imitation and passing off by copycat retailer products would lead manufacturers to accelerate their innovation and R&D (Romeo, 1995). In most cases, retailers introduced own-label products in well-proven product categories. By being more innovative in their product offerings, manufacturers could successfully differentiate themselves from the retailers' brands.

Increased price competition among retailers is likely to be good for manufacturers' brands, as is the development of new modes of shopping, such as home shopping by means of multimedia technology.

The brand name

In many cases, companies have put considerable effort into the creation of brand names. Names have been created by word association, word play, and the development of new words. Attempts will be made to come up with words that describe the product or service. Some companies simply use their own trade name or company name.

The process of successfully selecting brand names can be based on seven essential steps, as fig. 7.3 illustrates. This demonstrates the seven-step selection process that was used in selecting the Finches brand name for a range of soft drinks. The expert use of market research in choosing a final brand name is of critical importance.

Fig. 7.3: Selecting a brand name

1. Defining the product and the market
2. Selecting branding objectives
3. Selecting a branding strategy
4. Choosing a type of commercial name
5. Name generation
6. Assessing and selecting brand names
7. The brand name in action

Source: D. McLoughlin and F. Feely, 'Successful brand name selection: Finches soft drinks', *Irish Marketing Review*, vol. 9 (1996).

Another study suggests that there are five different types of brand name: *generic, descriptive, suggestive, arbitrary*, and *coined* (Kohli and Thakor, 1997). Generic names include most company trade names, for example Avonmore and Cadbury. Descriptive names describe the product, for example Night Saver or Powerscreen. Suggestive would include Premium Choice and First Trust; while arbitrary names would include such names as Kodak. Coined names usually represent a play on words , for example Weetabix, Tayto, or Waifos.

PACKAGING

Packaging adds value to products. It is a means of differentiation and can be a source of competitive advantage. Many products are instantly recognisable because of the shape or design of the packaging, some of which are patented and legally protected, such as the traditional Coca-Cola bottle and the Perrier bottle.

Packaging and product are in many cases synonymous, as for example the packaging used for the correction fluid Tippex; in other cases there may be no packaging, as for example with shovels in a hardware shop.

Innovative or novel packaging can gain attention, as with the Pringle brand of potato crisps, packed in a cylindrical container. This differentiates it significantly from most of its competitors. For most products, packaging is an inherent part of the product, serving a number of functions.

Protection

The packaging may protect the product during storage and handling. In addition, it may protect the product from contamination and maintain the contents in a fit state for consumption or use, as with food, drink, pharmaceuticals, cosmetics, and petroleum products. The biscuit manufacturer Jacob introduced resealable tubs for its range of mallow biscuits, Kimberley, Mikado, and Coconut Creams, in 1997. These were designed to keep the product fresher for longer and were reusable (*Checkout Ireland*, November 1997).

Convenience

Packaging is convenient for the consumer if it facilitates use or storage. Ready-to-serve food products, microwavable containers and built-in measures make products more convenient to use.

Convenience is also important for channel members involved in distribution, transport, and storage. How the package is to be transported and how much handling or stacking is required may influence the materials used and the design of the packaging. Many packaging innovations have come about in an attempt to make products more convenient and attractive to consumers.

SHERIDAN'S: CREATING A CONVENIENT POUR

In October 1992 Gilbey, the manufacturer of Bailey's Irish Cream, launched the Sheridan's liqueur brand, a unique product development combining two separate liquids: a coffee-chocolate liqueur and a vanilla cream liqueur. When poured, the vanilla cream settles on the top, giving the product a Guinness-like appearance.

Sheridan's was the result of a £1 million research and development programme. The product would not have been possible without the design of the distinctive package, a bottle divided in two to contain the separate liquids. At first a screw-on top was provided for each part of the bottle, and the consumer poured first from one part, then the other. This proved inconvenient for consumers, and research showed that they wanted a quicker, easier way to pour the product. Gilbey began a research programme, the result of which was a new integrated pouring mechanism, which they described as their 'perfect-pour cap'. This gave the consumer a perfectly layered serving of one-third vanilla cream and two-thirds coffee chocolate in one pour.

The innovation increased the appeal of the brand by making the product easier to serve. In 1995 it became the best-selling liqueur in Ireland after Bailey's Irish Cream.

Sources: *Irish Independent*, 2 December 1993; *Sunday Business Post*, 5 March 1995.

Economy

Packaging makes products economical to buy and use. Generally, the larger the package the lower the cost of the individual serving or measure will be. In the case of many household products, such as detergent or breakfast cereal, a variety of packet sizes is available. For other products, such as raw materials or components, packet sizes also vary. It is more economical for manufacturers to buy in bulk, and therefore packaging will be designed to suit their requirements.

Promotion

Packaging plays an important part in communicating and promoting the product. The colours used and the shape, design, illustrations, labels and information on the packet may attract attention and be used by the consumer to make comparisons. On-pack promotions, such as competitions, discount coupons, and special offers, play an important part in sales promotion.

Information

Packaging not only identifies and promotes the product but also provides information, some of which may be legally required, such as ingredients on food products or health warnings on tobacco products. Other labelling requirements include the country of origin and country of manufacture.

Increasingly, EU packaging regulations are having an influence. The packaging directive issued in 1996, for example, aims at a 25 per cent reduction in packaging waste by 2001. More emphasis is being placed on the recycling of packaging materials, with a common symbol to show that the packet is recyclable.

Instructions on how to use or assemble the product may be given on the packaging. Many products have a bar-code printed on the packet, which allows the product to be scanned, facilitating pricing and stock control. Manufacturers who have received quality approval by associations or Government bodies may also indicate this on their packaging: in Ireland the Q mark of the Irish Quality Association or the ISO 9000 designation appear on many packets, as does the Guaranteed Irish symbol. Guaranteed Irish is a limited company that has as its objective increasing the awareness of, and demand for, Irish products and services. Manufacturers and service providers can become registered users of the Guaranteed Irish mark, provided their products and services originate in Ireland and they comply with the company's regulations. The mark can be used on packaging and also in advertising and point-of-sale and promotional materials.

Other marks or symbols that can appear on packaging include the royal warrants that some manufacturers are granted for supplying members of European royal families. This applies to a large number of British products, ranging from Barbour outdoor clothing to Gordon's gin. Other European examples include the Danish beer Carlsberg. In Britain, royal warrants are granted to companies that have regularly supplied goods or services for a minimum of five years to any of the four senior members of the royal family. They are normally granted for ten years, and there are rules to ensure that high standards are maintained. A number of Irish companies hold warrants, including Ulster Weavers, which produces linen tea-towels, calendar towels, table napkins, and other kitchen co-ordinates (Gunin, 1998). In some cases, such as the Smirnoff vodka brand, the coat of arms of the Russian imperial family is still used on the label, indicating something of the brand's heritage. To some extent these marks were an early form of quality approval, with royal warrants in England dating from the time of King Henry VIII. (Source: http://www.royal.gov.uk/faq/warrant.htm.)

Consumer attitudes to packaging

In research carried out by Lansdowne Market Research in 1997 there were some interesting findings in relation to consumers' attitudes to different forms of packaging, as table 7.2 shows. The same study indicated that 88 per cent of respondents agreed that packaging materials should be recyclable. It is interesting to note that while glass bottles were viewed as being the best individual form of packaging for keeping food fresh and for hygiene, it was not the packaging that respondents felt they would like to see used more often for grocery products.

Table 7.2: Consumer attitudes to packaging

	Cans	Cellophane bags	Box	Tin	Plastic bottle	Glass bottle
Keeps food fresh for longer	14	25	7	18	5	31
Very hygienic	10	23	5	14	7	41
Most convenient form of pack	8	44	17	11	7	13
Protects my groceries best	9	35	23	11	5	17
Would like more groceries packed this way	6	39	29	8	5	15

Base: grocery shoppers.
Source: *Checkout Ireland* and *Shopper Focus* (Lansdowne Market Research), May 1997

Packaging design

Given the functions the packaging has to perform, packaging design needs to be carefully planned. Typically, marketers use the services of design consultants to create or modify packaging. Designers consider the nature and positioning of the product and the needs of the marketer. Materials, colours, illustrations, typefaces and shapes will all be co-ordinated to get the message across. Sometimes packaging re-design is necessary as part of a product revamp. Allied Domecq, the owner of the Harvey's Bristol Cream brand of sherry, redesigned its bottle in cobalt blue as part of its repositioning of sherry from a sweet drink consumed only at Christmas to something dry and exclusive (*Marketing*, 28 November 1998).

PACKAGING DESIGN

Bailey's Irish Cream: The bottle shape was originally designed to reflect an old Irish whiskey crock. The Bailey's symbol was inspired by the age of master-craftsmen, and the rural scene depicted on the label was commissioned to convey the Irishness of the drink.

Smirnoff Mule: The product is a cocktail of vodka, ginger beer, and lime, invented in Hollywood in the nineteen-forties, where it was served in copper mugs. Copper was chosen as the colour for the bottle when it was launched in 1996.

Premier Milk: Premier was the first dairy to produce milk in cardboard cartons, in 1962; previously, milk was supplied only in glass bottles. In 1993 Premier introduced the snap-pack resealable carton, designed to be easier for the consumer to use.

Chocolate Kimberley: Black packaging was used for this extension of the Kimberley brand. Few competing products used black, especially for countline products. Part of Irish Biscuits' strategy was to establish the single-serve product in the countline market.

Source: *Checkout Ireland*, August 1997

THE PRODUCT LIFE-CYCLE

The sales potential and profitability of a product change over time. Product life-cycle theory is an attempt to recognise distinct stages in the sales and profit history of the product. It is based on a biological analogy, whereby products are introduced, grow, mature, and ultimately decline. Unlike many biological examples, however, many products may have potentially infinite lives if they are changed and adapted. Many brands have been around for hundreds of years and continue to prosper.

Life-cycle theory has four basic assertions: products have a limited life, product sales pass through distinct stages over time, profits rise and fall at different stages, and products require different management strategies at each stage in the cycle.

There are four distinct stages in the life-cycle: introduction, growth, maturity, and decline, as illustrated in fig. 7.4.

Fig. 7.4: The product life-cycle

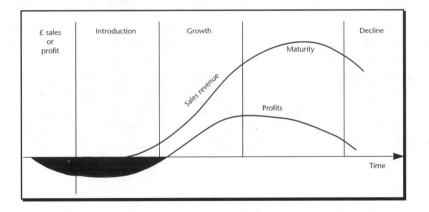

Introduction

At the introductory stage, the principal marketing consideration is creating awareness among channel members and potential consumers. New products usually have to be marketed to channel members first, so that they can place orders and have the product in stock when consumer advertising or communication begins. The creation of consumer awareness should be followed by encouragement to try the product. Marketers may therefore have to consider using sampling, couponing or other forms of promotion to facilitate trial.

Growth

The growth phase is characterised by an acceptance of the product in the market and a consequent growth in sales. The business must therefore have the production, marketing and management ability to meet the increased demand. This can pose particular problems where the product has gained a rapid acceptance in the market: if the marketer cannot supply the demand, there is a shortage, and prices go up. If demand continues to increase, competitors will be attracted to the market. If, however, demand is somewhat transient, or it is just a fad, the delay in supply may result in lost sales.

Competitors generally closely monitor the introduction and early growth stages of new products, and this may determine whether they enter the market, or how quickly they will follow. They will have had the advantage of observing how the product has performed at the early stages and can learn from any mistakes made. The marketer must therefore be ready to make changes to fend off attack by competitors. Factors such as design, which would have been vital in the initial development of the product, will also be important throughout the product life-cycle.

The successful mineral water brand Ballygowan, launched in the mid-eighties, was followed by several other Irish spring water brands. This showed the need for the company to reconsider the package design, as consumers were finding it difficult to differentiate between the many imitation products. Ballygowan moved to a complete re-design to deal with this and also to produce a design that would be suitable in overseas markets, where it hoped to achieve sales growth. In overseas markets the packaging needed to be a little more sophisticated. A design company's services were engaged, and a new range of bottles was designed (Mortell, 1993).

Maturity

The maturity phase is characterised by a slowing down in sales as the product reaches market saturation. Maturity is a critical point for many products and brands; without development or extension the product may go into decline. The principal issue for the marketer is extending maturity and determining how the product or brand can best be developed. The product may not have to be changed: additional sales may be achieved in new segments or markets, for example overseas markets. In many cases, however, mature products will need to have marketing resources devoted to them. Possibilities include repositioning, adding extensions, and new variations.

Decline

The decline phase is apparent when sales and profits begin to fall. The difficulty for the marketer is in determining whether the decline is terminal or whether the product can be saved. If the marketer does not react, the decline may occur more quickly. It is necessary to determine whether marketing resources should be devoted to a declining product or brand. In many cases products or brands do indeed disappear from the market, though they may reappear again, as happened with the Cooley Distillery whiskey brands (see page 184). In the clothing market, fashions or styles can also be resurrected and reintroduced.

For other products, decline ultimately means the end. This demonstrates the importance of the marketer reacting in time by changing, innovating, or developing alternatives to the declining product.

Determinants of the product life-cycle

The product life-cycle is measured over time. For some products and brands the life-cycle can be measured in weeks or months, for others it is years. It is important that marketers do not consider it to be a self-fulfilling prophecy: in other words, a product or brand may not necessarily have to decline or disappear.

Several factors can explain the shape and length of the product's life-cycle: the product's characteristics, the marketing strategies employed, external environmental factors, and market-related factors (Meenaghan and O'Sullivan, 1986). The shape is determined not only by analysing these factors but also by the interaction between them. The product's life-cycle, therefore, is not necessarily time-dependent. The management will have a critical strategic role in effecting changes over the life-cycle of the product.

Diffusion of innovations

Diffusion refers to how products spread in the market. It has been defined as the process whereby an innovation is communicated through certain channels over time among members of a social system (Rogers, 1983). Marketers have been interested in the topic because of the regular launch of new products and a desire to ensure that they are effective.

Marketers want to guide and control the diffusion process by adjusting the marketing mix to elicit the desired response from the market. The diffusion process is related to the product life-cycle but different in that it refers to the proportion of potential adopters within a social system, whereas the product life-cycle is based on absolute sales over time.

CATEGORIES OF ADOPTERS

Rogers, in his research on the adoption of new products, concluded that the adoption process could be illustrated as a normal distribution and that, depending on the time of adoption, there were five broad categories of adopters, as illustrated in fig. 7.5.

Fig. 7.5: Categories of adopters

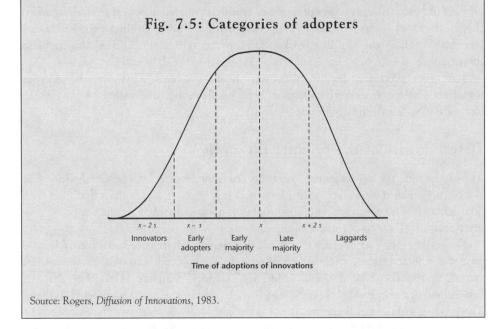

Time of adoptions of innovations

Source: Rogers, *Diffusion of Innovations*, 1983.

Innovators: Innovators represent the first $2\frac{1}{2}$ per cent of adopters. They are venturesome, willing to take risks, and quite outward-looking. They are communicative and are involved in many networks of people. Given that they are the first buyers of new products that may be expensive, they will usually have above-average income. They tend to be well educated, open-minded, and cosmopolitan. The first people to adopt mobile cellular phones, for example, displayed these characteristics (Rogan, 1988).

Early adopters: Representing the next $13\frac{1}{2}$ per cent of adopters, this group enjoy the prestige and respect that early purchasing brings. They tend to be opinion-leaders, who influence others. Like the innovators, they have higher-than-average incomes. One study on the adoption of direct banking services, for example, found that the early adopters exerted a higher degree of opinion-leadership and had a more favourable attitude to change (Lockett and Littler, 1997). It also found that they were more involved in related product categories, for example in buying products over the phone.

Early majority: The early majority represent a significant 34 per cent of potential adopters. They tend to have status within their social class. They are communicative and attentive to sources of information. They tend to be deliberate and to interact frequently with their peers.

Late majority: Also accounting for 34 per cent of adopters, the late majority differ from the early majority in being less cosmopolitan and less well off. They tend also to be older. They will be sceptical about new products, cautious, and subject to economic necessity.

Laggards: Laggards represent the last group of adopters. They are price-conscious, and suspicious of novelty and change. They tend to be conservative in behaviour and have lower levels of income. They tend to be traditional and to have a local view of the world.

These categories of adopter can be used by marketers as a means of segmenting the market for new products. It is important at the outset to select the innovators and early adopters. Communications may need to be tailored to them: for example, advertising may depict people with similar traits or life-styles. As the product diffuses, communication may be adapted to cater for broader buyer characteristics. Caution is required, however. There is a danger inherent in early communication. If the product is portrayed in too narrow a way, this may inhibit subsequent adopters.

The rate of adoption of innovations can be explained by a number of factors, and the characteristics of the product itself will have a bearing. Five characteristics in particular are important (Rogers, 1983). The *relative advantage* of using the product is the degree to which the innovation is perceived as better than the product or idea it supersedes. The *compatibility* of the innovation with the consumer's existing values, past experiences and needs will be important. The degree of *complexity* refers to the degree to which the innovation is perceived as being difficult to understand; and the degree of *trialability* refers to how easy it is for the consumer to try out the innovation. *Observability* refers to the extent to which the product stimulates word-of-mouth comment or conversation.

Product diffusion will also be influenced by other factors, including competition, pricing, and economic conditions, as the next panel illustrates.

GROWTH IN THE MOBILE PHONE MARKET

The first mobile phones were introduced in Ireland by Telecom Éireann in the mid-eighties. The consumer paid approximately £2,000 for an instrument and connection to the Eircell network. The market grew slowly, and by 1996 it was estimated that 8 per cent of the population were using mobile phones. More rapid growth came with the licensing of a competitor, Esat Digiphone. In 1997 the number of users had increased to 12 per cent of the population, though this was still far behind the 37 per cent penetration in some Scandinavian countries.

The move to mobiles was spurred by a combination of factors, including a booming economy, lower prices, and intense competition between Eircell and Esat for new subscribers. Prices had been reduced considerably from their mid-eighties level and included an offer from Telecom Éireann of a single payment of £99 for a 'ready-to-go' model. This did not require line rental or equipment rental and could be operated with special cards that the consumer could buy to top up their credit.

Sources: Dónal Rogan, 'A Profile of the Early Customer for the Mobile Cellular Telephone in Ireland', MBS thesis, University College, Dublin, 1988; Eircell, 'Ready-to-go' advertising campaign, 1997–8; B. O'Keeffe, 'Ireland fourth for mobile growth', *Irish Times*, 12 December 1998.

The adoption and diffusion of industrial products

With regard to the adoption and diffusion of new industrial products, it has been suggested that the process is influenced by behavioural variables generically categorised as organisational traits, environmental aspects, and individual factors (Kennedy, 1983). Organisational traits include such factors as the structure, size and climate prevailing in the firm. The environmental aspects include both the micro and macro-forces that impinge on the firm. The individual factors refer to the individual's characteristics and traits that they will bring with them into the firm.

The *new-product development process* describes how firms or individuals find new ideas for products or services and convert them into commercial successes. It is based essentially on the principle that consumers or firms want new goods and services and that the development of these helps a business to achieve growth and profitability. The new-product development process precedes the introduction phase of the product life-cycle. It is also required to extend the life of the product or to replace it with something else.

What is a new product?

The term *new* in a business or marketing context is rather broad. A new product or service is one that is essentially different from those already marketed by the firm. Products can be technically new, such as a personal CD-player, or they may be a new consumer concept, for example designer sunglasses. A packaging change, such as an aerosol deodorant, may also constitute newness. New products can be classified in two ways: from the consumer's viewpoint, and from the firm's viewpoint.

Classification of new products from the consumer's viewpoint

In determining newness from the consumer's viewpoint, the central issue is the effect of the product on the consumer—in other words, the disruptive influence the use of the product has on established consumption patterns. *Continuous innovations* are continuing changes that may take place: for example, every few years car manufacturers may update their models by adding new features. In some instances the manufacturer may also change the brand name, as when Ford revealed its replacement for the Escort, the Focus, in 1998.

FORD DROPS ESCORT AS IT WHEELS ON THE FOCUS

The Escort brand was used for thirty years, and 18 million were sold throughout the world—2$\frac{1}{2}$ million more than the Model T. The new name was launched at the Geneva Motor Show in March 1998. The name was not the only one considered; Ford had come quite close to using the name Fusion. The introduction of the Focus was speeded up because of increased competition, especially from the General Motors Astra.

The first Escort was a rear-wheel-drive model. Its success was boosted in 1970 when it won the London-to-Mexico Rally; it had been consistently successful since then and was runner-up in the World Rally championship in 1997.

The first front-wheel-drive model was produced in 1980. The sporty XR3i version was a favourite of nineteen-eighties 'boy racers'. A facelift in 1990 was regarded as a failure, and the car was comprehensively revised five years later. By then Ford was already working on a replacement.

The search for new names becomes progressively more difficult. Ford is said to have spent £500,000 on researching the name Mondeo.

Sources: John Jay and Andrew Lorenz, 'Escort gives way to Ford Fusion', *Sunday Times*, 15 February 1998; Alan Copps, 'Ford drops Escort as it wheels in the Focus', *Times*, 3 March 1998.

Consider how continuous innovation contributed to the growth of the ice cream market in Ireland. In the clothing industry, changes in fashion or style would usually be considered continuous.

CONTINUOUS INNOVATION IN THE ICE CREAM MARKET

The Irish have the second-highest level of consumption of ice cream in Europe. The market for ice cream grew rapidly from the nineteen-eighties, not least because of continuous product innovation. The largest manufacturer, HB, estimated that in 1983 the market was worth £26 million; by 1997 it was estimated at £100 million. The three main competitors were HB, Mars, and Nestlé. Most of the innovation has been in the form and texture of the product, with manufacturers competing to produce new combinations or re-textured products. In the children's market, water ices in various shapes and forms were popular.

Consumption per capita (litres)

Sweden	13.6
Ireland	**10.67**
Denmark	10.27
Italy	9.10
Belgium	8.56
Britain	8.16
Netherlands	8.15
Germany	8.11
Switzerland	7.13
Austria	7.13
France	6.91
Greece	4.47
Portugal	3.88
Spain	0.54

Ice cream is predominantly an impulse purchase: it is estimated that up to 70 per cent is bought on impulse. As a result, manufacturers are keen to promote and distribute their products widely and, as HB demonstrated, to protect their distribution channels.

In the nineties a conscious effort was made to sell to the adult market, and in 1991 HB launched the Magnum brand, a higher-priced, high-quality product that proved extremely successful. The product and its subsequent variations were essentially combinations of ice cream and chocolate on a stick. The American company Häagen-Dazs entered the Irish market in 1992, supplying its product directly in refrigerated containers. This was similar to Magnum and was also aimed at the adult market, with an advertising campaign that sought to establish a connection between ice cream and sensuality. Both Magnum and Häagen-Dazs extended their ranges with different chocolate coverings and, in the case of Häagen-Dazs, with a Bailey's and a Malibu-flavoured product.

The confectionery manufacturers Mars and Nestlé entered the market, Mars in 1990 and Nestlé in 1995. Both companies introduced ice cream versions of familiar confectionery brands, such as Mars and Aero. The innovation here was in the production process, with both companies investing in new plant to manufacture ice cream variants of their products.

Sources: *Irish Independent*, 7 August 1995; *Examiner*, 1 May 1997; *Sunday Business Post*, 4 May 1997.

Dynamically continuous innovations include products such as electric knives and cellular phones. The innovative aspect of these products is the way in which they are used. Products such as the Sony Walkman, introduced in 1979, could be included in this category. Other dynamically continuous innovations include the first disposable cameras, introduced by Fuji in 1985, and the first disposable contact lenses, which appeared on the market in 1987.

Discontinuous innovations are essentially products that are new to the world, such as personal computers and electronic calculators. In this case the product is radically different from anything that went before. Many products and services we take for granted were originally discontinuous innovations. The first television was demonstrated by John Logie Baird in 1926, and penicillin was discovered by Alexander Fleming in 1928.

Classification of new products from the firm's viewpoint

The firm can assess newness in technological or market terms. This yields a number of possibilities, as fig. 7.6 demonstrates. It is apparent, therefore, that product life-cycles can be extended in technological and market terms. This helps explain why so many products have lasted for so long; it also indicates to the marketer that the marketing or the technological dimensions of the product can usually be developed.

Fig. 7.6: Dimensions of technological and market newness

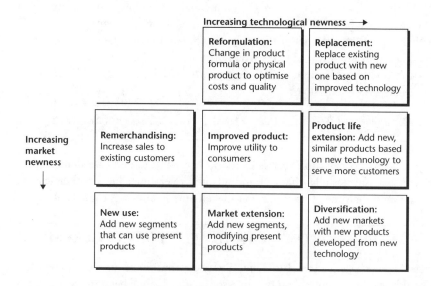

The development, successful launch and subsequent improvement of a new product is well illustrated by the case of Fairy Liquid. Over time, the product was reformulated and improved, and new segments were added.

THE MAKING OF A MEGA-BRAND

In 1960 Proctor and Gamble launched Fairy Liquid on the British market. The launch involved distributing 15 million trial bottles to 85 per cent of the country's homes. The launch had been preceded by extensive research, though the washing-up market was still in its infancy, with only 17 per cent of households using a liquid and the rest using soap powder or soap.

In 1980 the production of Fairy Liquid reached 10 million gallons a year. In 1981 Fairy's market share was 27 per cent, and the actor Nanette Newman was introduced to endorse the product. In 1984–5 the company introduced a lemon variant, and market share increased to 32 per cent. By 1987 this had increased to 34 per cent, with the lemon variant accounting for one-third of sales. In 1988 a new formulation offered '15 per cent extra mileage,' together with better handling of grease.

In 1992 Fairy Liquid was replaced with Fairy Excel, which was '50 per cent better at dealing with grease.' Market share increased to 50 per cent. In 1993 Fairy Excel Plus was launched, with the slogan 'The power of four for the price of one'—claiming that one bottle of Excel Plus would last as long as four bottles of ordinary liquid. Excel Plus was launched simultaneously in Britain, Ireland, Germany, Denmark, Belgium, the Netherlands, Sweden, and Finland.

Consistent themes in the advertising of the product since 1960 have been the mildness of the product, its extra 'mileage', and an unashamed admission that it is dearer but that it is the better-value option. Various interpretations of the mother-and-child theme have also been used. Commercials have concentrated on a 'feel-good' theme, with soft and homely imagery being used—including one in 1994 that used a father instead of a mother at the sink. The jingle used for the commercials has been modified only slightly and is essentially the same as the first one produced in 1960. Proctor and Gamble has consistantly supported the brand with advertising and some below-the-line promotion.

Source: Alan Mitchell, 'P&G comes clean on brand-new Fairy', *Marketing*, 14 October 1993.

Marketers do need to exercise caution. The Fairy Liquid case demonstrates how a product was successfully changed and adapted over time; but another leading brand, Persil, found that one of its continuous-development strategies came badly unstuck.

PERSIL POWER TAKES ITS TOLL ON PERSIL

Persil Power was launched in May 1993 as a continuous product innovation. The Persil brand had been around for quite some time, having been introduced in Ireland, for example, in 1909. Persil Power was a new formulation, which promised the consumer an improved cleaning ability. However, tests conducted by the Consumers' Association in Britain showed that the product could damage clothes. The company was forced to admit that launching the product was a mistake and that it would be reformulated.

The immediate impact of the negative publicity was a loss in market share for the brand and a reduction in the parent company's share price. In Britain the brand's market share dropped from 27 per cent before the launch in May to 24 per cent in July and August. In Ireland the brand lost its number 1 position in the market, and it took two years to recover this.

Sources: 'Persil Power takes toll on Persil', *Marketing*, 29 September 1994; *Checkout Ireland*, April 1997.

Reasons for developing a new product

The development of new products has at its core the satisfaction of customers' needs. Consumers' preferences change, and environmental influences may mean that current products no longer meet consumer specifications. In the food and beverage sector, manufacturers have developed low-fat, low-salt, sugar-free, high-fibre and low-cholesterol products, and other variations of existing products, to meet the needs of an increasingly health-conscious consumer.

In the music industry, where needs may be largely intangible and where there are always opportunities, Polygram felt there was a gap for a new band aimed at the youth market. It advertised for would-be pop stars, and in 1994 it created the group Boyzone, which went on to become an international success. The Polygram strategy was also pursued by a number of others, and groups such as the Spice Girls and OTT emerged in a similar way.

Development also meets a number of organisational needs, including sales and profit growth, adding value, the creation of competitive advantage, responding to competitive pressure, and extending the product life-cycle. HB ice cream in creating the Magnum brand achieved growth in sales and market share; it also prepared the company for increased competition.

New-product development may be a stimulant to business growth, resulting in improved sales, cash flow, and profits. Firms may not be able to expand into new segments or markets without a new product, for example into export markets. In existing segments and markets the firm may wish to use new products to extend its range.

New-product development is part of the value-adding process. Existing products may have more features and benefits added to them. Products that are new to the world may be the result of research and development efforts within the firm, whereby company personnel have added value. The resourcefulness and creativity of company personnel is an important part of the process.

New products are a possible source of competitive advantage. If the firm can bring a superior product or service to the market that has advantages over competitors, it can use this to differentiate itself. Being first on the market certainly has advantages, though competitive advantage will be eroded as competitors enter offering similar or superior products.

Not everyone can be the first on the market with a new product; many firms will be followers and will need to develop new products to do so. Responding to competitors with new products may be necessary to protect the firm's own market position.

New-product development is a necessary part of the product life-cycle; it is the process that creates and that can ultimately extend the life of the product. Many new products are a reaction to declining sales of existing products, which may be replaced or modified to prolong their life.

The new-product development process

The new-product development process involves a number of distinct stages, from the original idea to the successful commercialisation of the product. The stages provide a guideline for marketers and indicate the resource and skill requirements necessary for the process.

The idea stage

Ideas can come from a variety of sources. They may come from personnel within the firm, or they may come from the consumer. *Intrapreneurs*—enterprising individuals within the company—may be the source of ideas: they may be marketing, operations, production or R&D managers or workers. Marketing channel members may also provide ideas. All firms will keep abreast of competitors' activities in the market. While this may involve the firm essentially following competitors, it may also provide the catalyst for it to develop its own unique product or service variation.

Consumers may be the source of ideas for new products. Consumer research may emphasise aspects of the product or service that the consumer is dissatisfied with, or may suggest changes to a product and ways in which it can be improved.

Not all ideas will be suitable. Ideas should be screened so that those that are inconsistent with the firm's goals and objectives are eliminated. In general, a number of criteria should be applied when ideas are being screened, including

- the relationship of the idea to the firm's existing products or services;
- the effect the proposed product or service may have on existing sales;
- the resource requirements necessary to produce and market the new product;
- the segments or markets it will be capable of attracting;
- the value-adding that will take place;
- the ability of the management to successfully develop and commercialise the product.

These criteria should enable the management to assess the firm's ability to develop the idea. They may point to deficiencies in skills or resources and give the firm an indication of what will be required for it to successfully develop the idea.

Revenue and cost analysis

Revenue and cost analysis will examine the financial implications of the idea. Costs can be estimated, and potential sales income forecast. The analysis will assess the ability of the product or service to achieve the return on investment that may be required. Break-even analysis will be useful in exploring the relationship between sales and fixed and variable costs. The aircraft manufacturer Airbus had plans to develop a long-range, high-capacity aircraft called the A3XX, which would seat up to eight hundred people, twice the capacity of its largest existing aircraft. The expected development costs were estimated to be $9,000 million (*Sunday Times*, 15 February 1998).

Costs will also be incurred if a marketer is considering a change in product or packaging. In 1995 Murphy's brewery introduced draught technology into bottled stout; before this it was available only in cans. In conjunction with its parent company, Heineken, and its British distributor, Whitbread, the company spent £8 million on developing a plastic device inserted in the bottle during the filling process (*Checkout Ireland*, August 1997).

The development process

The development process refers to how the firm takes the idea and develops it into a more tangible product concept that can be assessed and tested. The objective of the development stage is to produce a product that meets consumers' needs, is safe, and can be produced by the firm. Regulations regarding copyright, patents, product safety and consumer law will have to be adhered to.

There are four essential stages in the development process: concept testing, product design, preference testing, and the selection of a brand name.

STAGES IN THE PRODUCT DEVELOPMENT PROCESS

Concept testing typically involves the use of focus groups of target customers who will be asked to give their views and opinions on the proposed product or service. The researcher may use descriptions, mock-ups, drawings or illustrations to explain what the product will be or how it will look. Respondents will be asked for their assessment. The researcher will also seek information on consumers' decision-making processes in relation to the product or the general type of product.

Product design follows from concept testing. At this stage designers will prepare detailed designs for manufacture or, in the case of services, outlines of what the service will comprise. They will refer to the research carried out on the concept. Issues such as ease of use, attractiveness, materials used and ergonomic design may be some of the specific issues to be dealt with at this stage.

Preference testing involves testing consumers' preferences for different levels of product quality or features. Conjoint analysis can be used at this stage, which involves experiments with different price and attribute levels to determine how the consumer differentiates between them.

Selecting a brand name is important not just from the marketing viewpoint but also in ensuring that the name selected is not already in use or that it does not bear too close a similarity to one already in use.

Test-marketing or market simulation

The risk of a new product failing in the market is reduced if market testing is carried out. Test-marketing involves testing the product under typical market conditions. While it may not be possible to completely replicate all factors in the market, for example the response of competitors, it usually gives a good indication of the product's potential.

Test-marketing involves making the product available in selected distribution outlets, supported by marketing communication. Consider the new lager launched by Guinness in 1998.

A NEW LAGER FROM GUINNESS

Guinness began test-marketing a new brand of lager in 1998, its first Irish branded lager since the launch of Harp almost forty years ago. The product was called Breó and was classified as a white lager-style beer. This was closer to lager than ale, with a distinctive taste. The product took eighteen months to research and develop. Guinness was anxious to develop a new brand in the growing lager market; in 1997 the consumption of lager was up by $6\frac{1}{2}$ per cent. Test-marketing was concentrated at first in selected pubs in Dublin, before a national launch. The brand was aimed at younger drinkers. The product was served slightly colder than other draught beers, at 3° Celsius.

Guinness had consulted a brand name agency when selecting the name. It did not like the ideas, however, and decided to come up with its own suggestions. Breó, based on the Irish word *breo*, 'firebrand', was finally settled on.

Guinness was budgeting £5 million for advertising and marketing the new brand. At first outdoor, press, pub posters and point-of-sale material were the main media used.

Sources: Paul O'Kane, 'Guinness launches a new lager', *Sunday Tribune*, 19 April 1998; E. Moloney, 'New blond brew proves a fiery mix', *Irish Independent*, 23 April 1998; Christine Doherty, '£5 million blizzard of publicity for Guinness white beer', *Sunday Business Post*, 26 April 1998.

Consumers' response to the new product can be measured, though competitors can intervene and attempt to distort the results by discounting their products or running promotion campaigns. It also gives competitors the chance to see the product or service and start the process of developing their own alternative. If they can replicate the product or service quite quickly they may be able to seize the advantage.

Market simulation involves the establishment of a laboratory test market. This is an artificial means of testing a product, and one that can be expensive. Simulation involves exposing a sample of consumers to advertisements for the new product; they are then given samples of the product to take home and use. Interviews are then held to determine levels of satisfaction and purchasing intention. Repeat purchase levels are measured by offering the consumer the chance to buy the product again. On the results of the simulation, potential sales would be predicted. The main problem with simulated testing is that real market conditions are not replicated; however, it is a good means of testing products where, for competitive reasons, secrecy is important.

Test-marketing and simulation can be used for many products. They may not, however, be easy to implement with some services or industrial products. It would be difficult for a holiday company to test-market a new resort without bringing customers to it. In the case of large industrial purchases, such as ships, the shipbuilder would have to complete the vessel before it would be possible to test it.

In general, test-marketing or simulation can be used to assess how the product is likely to perform in the market. It is a form of research, and it is therefore important to ensure that the product is tested with a sufficiently large sample and that the results are carefully interpreted. There may be a tendency for consumers to express positive opinions about something new, which may not necessarily translate into repeat sales.

Commercialisation

Commercialisation typically involves the full-scale launch of the product on the market. This includes persuading the marketing channel to accept and stock the product and persuading customers to buy the product for the first time. Timing is therefore important. The product will generally have to be in the channel before any form of consumer marketing communication can be engaged in.

Timing is critically important for product launches. The product must be ready for the market, the channel must be able to obtain it easily, and the buyer must be able to get information. Critical factors in the launch include ensuring that the trade press and other appropriate media are aware of the launch, that launch events are well planned, and that communication opportunities are maximised. On occasion, product launches may be accompanied by elaborate hospitality or entertainment, usually directed at the trade and media.

The important issue in a launch is ensuring that the audience you want to communicate with is present. This provides an opportunity to explain the new product and the marketing campaign that would accompany it; it also provides an opportunity for questions and feedback. Obviously, large firms may have the budget for large-scale launches; for smaller firms, the launch may have more to do with meeting the trade, providing them with the necessary information, and getting any possible publicity.

Sometimes firms will use the services of event managers or public relations companies to assist in the launch.

Success of failure?

Success means that the new product is adopted by a sufficiently large number of consumers, and a proportion of these will become regular users of the product. It is to be expected that some consumers may try the new product once or twice but then revert to their former brand or switch to competitors' offerings, and this has to be allowed for by the marketer. Success is maintained by the marketer staying close to the customer and the marketing channels, communicating with them, ensuring product quality, and ultimately developing the product to its full potential.

Not all new products or services will be commercial successes. In 1978 Guinness launched a new product called Guinness Light, a light stout aimed principally at women. It did not achieve the desired level of sales, and it was withdrawn from the market after a few months. Perhaps it was a little ahead of its time. The B&I Line launched a high-speed jetfoil service on the Irish Sea in 1985. The vessel, built by the aircraft manufacturer Boeing, was capable of faster speeds than conventional car ferries. It could only operate successfully, however, in calm seas; when the sea was rough it proved too uncomfortable for passengers. The Irish Sea proved to be unsuitable for successful operation, services were frequently disrupted, and the company ultimately decided to withdraw it. Ten years later high-speed catamaran ferries were being used on the Irish Sea, and these did not experience the same problems as the jetfoil, because of improved technology. Bailey launched a chocolate peppermint cream liqueur, Penny Royal, in 1989. It was more expensive than its existing product and not sufficiently different to guarantee repeat purchases, and it was ultimately phased out. The subsequent launch of Sheridan's liqueur was more successful, the product being significantly different from Bailey's Irish Cream.

Products fail for a variety of reasons. The company may have carried out inadequate market research and analysis, or research results may have been based on an unrepresentative sample, and a sufficient number of consumers may not actually adopt the product. On occasion, new products with defects may make their way onto the market. These may not work properly and may have to be recalled by the manufacturer, inconveniencing the customer and adding to the manufacturer's costs.

Sometimes the costs of developing new products may be higher than expected, and this pushes up the price, which may become unattractive to the buyer. Poor timing can also be a problem: for example, in markets where seasonality is an issue, such as clothing and toys, there is usually a critical period in which anything new must be launched to make sure it reaches the retailer, and ultimately the consumer, in time.

Competitors will certainly play a large part in the failure of many new products. They may be able to produce their own version of the product quickly, or they may use price promotions on their existing products to tempt the consumer away.

The importance of new-product development in the firm

The new-product development process is an important part of the value-adding process in any firm. It implies that the firm keeps its existing product or service range and market developments under review.

The firm should have a procedure for periodically reviewing its new-product development activities. Some have specific research and development departments; others may rely on intrapreneurs to come up with ideas; while in start-up enterprises the process is inseparable from the role of the entrepreneur. The new-product development process demonstrates the importance of market information and research. Formal research exercises may probe specific aspects of the opinions, attitudes or behaviour of consumers or channels. More informal information, such as feedback from channel members or comments, questions or complaints from consumers, may also be the source of ideas.

The new-product development process demonstrates the need for the firm to keep its product range under review. There should be a product development plan for each of the firm's products. This will outline possible development scenarios for the product. If few exist, this may be an indication that the firm should be looking for alternatives to develop. For example, Newbridge Cutlery decided to launch a range of silver jewellery in 1996. This provided a product that could be aimed at new distribution channels in addition to some of its existing outlets.

New-product development may not always come from within the firm. Companies can consider licensing arrangements, mergers or acquisitions as possible sources of new-product development.

Timing market entry

Research has shown that the first firms to develop markets for a new product, known as *market pioneers*, tend to enjoy a long-term competitive advantage over later entrants, reflected in a higher level of market share and profitability. What is not so well understood is whether there is much variation in the experience of later market entrants; in other words, is it better to be an early follower of a pioneer in a still-growing market than to be a late entrant in a mature market? A study by Lambkin (1989) used samples from the PIMS (Profit Impact of Market Strategies) data-base; the results showed that there were substantial differences both within and between the categories of pioneers, early followers and late entrants with regard to their competitive strategies and performance. From the point of view of later entrants, the evidence suggests that it is better to be early than late into a new market, though the effects of timing are moderated by the choice of competitive strategy. The most successful early followers appeared to be those who manage to leap-frog the market by entering on a larger scale than existing firms and by offering a superior product.

FURTHER READING

de Chernatony, L., and McDonald, M., *Creating Powerful Brands*, London: Butterworth Heinemann 1993.

Hart, S., and Murphy, J., *Brands: The New Wealth Creators*, London: Macmillan 1998.

Urban, G., and Hauser, J., *The Design and Marketing of New Products* (second edition), Englewood Cliffs (NJ): Prentice-Hall 1993.

DISCUSSION QUESTIONS

1. Analyse the different product levels for each of the following:
   * An Post
   * Fiacla toothpaste
   * Bank of Ireland
   * Ballygowan
   * *Irish Farmers' Journal.*
2. Comment on how you feel branding will develop in the future. Will there be more or fewer brands around?
3. Select some appropriate brand names for each of the following:
   * a new range of sun-care products
   * a home delivery service for special-occasion cakes
   * a pet shop
   * a canning machine
   * a new detergent.
4. Discuss the implications of an increased environmental awareness among consumers on the packaging decision. Do you think marketers will be forced to use less packaging?
5. Describe the stages in the new-product development process for
   * a new cat food with added vitamins and minerals
   * a plant care service for offices, specialising in exotic plants
   * an activity pack for children travelling on long journeys
   * a Spanish Armada theme park on the west coast.

REFERENCES

Benson, C., 'Puffin and Penguin: a step forward for brand owners', *Journal of Brand Management*, June 1997.

Cummins, M., 'Brand positioning: a case history of an Irish whiskey', *Irish Marketing Review*, vol. 1 (1986).

de Chernatony, L., and McDonald, M., *Creating Powerful Brands*, London: Butterworth Heinemann 1993.

Fanning, J., 'Branding: regaining the initiative', *Irish Marketing Review*, vol. 8 (1995).

Gunin, J., 'Ulster linen brings a touch of Ireland', *Home Textiles Today*, 11 May 1998.

Kennedy, A., 'The adoption and diffusion of new industrial products: a literature review', *European Journal of Marketing*, vol. 17 (1983), no. 3.

Kohli, C., and Thakor, M., 'Branding consumer goods: insights from theory and practice', *Journal of Consumer Marketing*, vol. 14 (1997), no. 3.

Kotler, P., and Armstrong, G., *Principles of Marketing* (sixth edition), Englewood Cliffs (NJ): Prentice-Hall 1994.

Lambkin, Mary, 'Timing market entry: a key to competitive success', *Irish Marketing Review*, vol. 4 (1989), no. 2.

Lockett, A., and Littler, D., 'The adoption of direct banking services', *Journal of Marketing Management*, vol. 13, no. 8, November 1997.

Lysanski, S., 'A boundary theory investigation of the product manager's role', *Journal of Marketing*, vol. 49 (1985), no. 1.

McDowell Mudambi, S., Doyle, P., and Wong, V., 'An exploration of branding in industrial markets', *Industrial Marketing Management*, vol. 26 (1997).

Macrae, C., Parkinson, S., and Sheerman, J., 'Managing marketing's DNA: the role of branding', *Irish Marketing Review*, vol. 8 (1995).

Meenaghan, J., and O'Sullivan, P., 'The shape and length of the product lifecycle', *Irish Marketing Review*, vol. 1 (1986).

Mortell, M., 'Design in the product lifecycle: Ballygowan spring water', *Irish Marketing Review*, vol. 6 (1993).

Pratt, Maurice, Proceedings of the National Marketing Conference, MII, October 1994.

Rogan, Dónal, 'A Profile of the Early Customer for the Mobile Cellular Telephone in Ireland', MBS thesis, University College, Dublin, 1988.

Rogers, E., *Diffusion of Innovations* (third edition), New York: Free Press 1983.

Romeo, A., 'Brands and competitive strategy', *Irish Marketing Review*, vol. 8 (1995).

8

Pricing Decisions

Typically, marketers will be concerned with decisions on setting a price for the product or service and with decisions on the role of price in the firm's competitive strategy. In these decisions, factors such as demand, the nature of the product, the profile of the market and the profile of consumers and their price-sensitivity will all be considered. Competitors' prices and their pricing strategies will usually have a significant influence.

A number of different approaches are used in calculating price, all of which require an estimate of the costs that will be incurred. The price must produce a satisfactory level of profit for the firm. Price will often form a significant part of promotional campaigns and may become a central aspect of the firm's strategy; for example, Ryanair described itself as 'the low-cost airline'.

Pricing involves putting a value on a product or service. This means that buyers know what they have to pay, and sellers know what they can expect to receive.

PRICING POLICY

Pricing policy acts to guide the business in its pricing decisions. Pricing policy will depend on a number of factors, including the position of the product in its life-cycle, the competitiveness of the industry in which the business operates, and the general strategic thrust of the business.

Pricing policy will also be determined by the other elements in the marketing mix. The price should be consistent with the other elements; a high-value product, for example, communicated with an 'exclusive' image and selectively distributed, will be priced accordingly.

If a new product is being introduced, the company may decide to adopt a *price-skimming* approach, which involves charging the highest price that buyers who most desire the product will pay. If the company wishes to build market share it will typically use a penetration approach, which involves penetrating the market with a low price. This has consistently been the pricing strategy pursued by Ryanair since it entered the airline market in 1984. Pricing was a central aspect of strategy for the other low-cost airlines that were established in Europe in the nineteen-nineties, as the following panel illustrates.

LOW-COST AIRLINES

The liberalisation of the European air travel market has led to an increase in air travel and the introduction of a new breed of airline: the low-cost carrier. Some of Europe's oldest airlines also entered the fray, with British Airways establishing the low-cost airline Go in 1998. Other low-cost airlines included Ryanair, Air One, Easyjet, Debonair, and Virgin Express.

All these carriers had one strategy in common: price competition. This translates into low fares and tight control on costs. As a result, complimentary in-flight service or 'frequent-flier' schemes, used by other airlines as a means of differentiation, were not a feature.

In many cases the low-cost carriers used 'secondary' airports, such as Luton or Stanstead in London, as opposed to Heathrow. Landing and service charges were usually lower in these airports; it was also easier to secure landing and take-off slots. The use of these airports did lead to some consumer scepticism, and it also became a competitive issue, with other airlines emphasising that they served more central airports. Ryanair, for example, hosted trips for journalists to the airports they served in attempts to prove that they were not isolated or remote.

The experience in Europe has been different from that in the United States, where airport capacity and risk capital were more readily available. Improvements in Europe's rail networks also mean growing competition. Many of the low-cost carriers have found the going tough and have signed code-shares with larger partners, operated franchises for larger carriers, entered fares agreements, taken government subsidies, and otherwise sought protection.

The idea of pan-European low-fare competition among scheduled airlines was one in which few had faith, as many of the low-cost carriers were too small and undercapitalised.

Sources: J. Feldman, 'Lovers, not fighters', *Air Transport World*, May 1998; S. Binchy, 'Ryanair aims for landmark on three new Euro routes', *Sunday Business Post*, 17 May 1998.

A company with a mature product may find itself forced to offer price incentives to hold its position in the market. If the product is in decline there may be no alternative but to accept a gradual reduction in price. The business may also have policies in relation to discriminatory pricing, special-event pricing, discounting, and other factors that affect the final price.

In general, the marketer will find it necessary to change or adapt price as demand and competitive conditions dictate.

THE DYNAMICS OF PRICING

Pricing plays a fundamental role in marketing strategy. It is used as a competitive tool in the market and may be emphasised in advertising, as fig. 8.1 indicates.

How the marketer reacts to price changes in the market will be a significant aspect of marketing strategy. Some price changes may be the result of competitors' actions; others may be the result of economic influences, such as shortages or shifts in the price of substitute products. Other factors that could influence price changes include regulatory changes: for example, in 1998 Aer Rianta, which was running a campaign for the retention of duty-free sales, stated that the loss of duty-free income in 1999 could lead to increases in landing charges for airlines using their airports. The organisation was asserting that if it lost sales in one area of its business it would have to raise prices in another area to maintain income.

Fig. 8.1: A price-competition advertisement

From February 9th to February 22nd inclusive,
you can visit family and friends anywhere
in the country with
Bus Eireann's Just-for-Fun ticket fare
of £8 return on any route.
Now you can't say fairer than that.

For travel information contact: Central Bus Station (Busaras), Store St., Dublin 1 (01) 8366111;
Parnell Place Bus Station, Cork (021) 508188; Colbert Station, Limerick (061) 313333; Ceannt
Station, Galway (091) 562000; Plunkett Station, Waterford (051) 879000; Casement Station,
Tralee, (066) 23566 or your local Bus Eireann office, Tourist Office or Travel Agent.

Tickets purchased on or before February 22nd are valid up to 30 days for the return journey.

Internet: http://www.buseireann.ie
email: info@buseireann.ie

Consumers' perception of price is important, as they may use it to compare competitors' offerings. This applies to many products and especially to services, where intangibility may mean that the consumer uses the price as an indication of the quality of service.

Price promotions may become a significant part of the firm's marketing communication activities. Discounts, rebates and other price promotions will affect the price the consumer pays. Marketers need to use price promotions strategically: they should not be used as a substitute for advertising or product development but as part of an integrated marketing strategy. They can have a particular role in protecting brands in competitive battles. Price-value promotions, for example, can involve giving extra products at no extra cost, or premiums, such as gifts. There is evidence that these can be used to enhance brand appeal and can help neutralise the competitive effects of retailers' own-label or regional brands (Everett, 1998).

Price will also be used to motivate and give an incentive to marketing channel members. Discounts may be given especially where the channel member increases volumes.

If the marketer is introducing new products to the market, the price charged will be an important influence on the rate of the product's diffusion. It may also determine how quickly the marketer will recoup the costs of developing and introducing the new product. In many new-product introductions the initial price will be high and will be lowered as competitors enter the market.

Price changes may be subject to political or legal sanction. The standard fares charged on public transport services operated by the subsidiary companies of CIE can be changed only by ministerial order. Government approval is usually required for some other price changes, such as television licence fees and electricity charges. Pricing practices often come in for public and official scrutiny, as in 1997, when comparisons were drawn between the price charged for a pint of stout in different parts of the country, and a ministerial order was issued reversing a price increase.

THE PRICE OF A PINT

In 1997 considerable attention was focused on the price charged for a pint of stout in different parts of Ireland. The issue came to a head when, early in the year, publicans outside Dublin increased the price by 5p. Prices in urban areas, especially Dublin, differed considerably from those in rural areas. Dublin publicans argued that the costs of buying and running a pub in Dublin were much higher than anywhere else and that therefore they had to charge higher prices.

The 5p increase by many publicans outside Dublin was, however, considered unjustified, and in February publicans were warned by the relevant minister of state that a ministerial order would be issued, fixing the price at the November 1996 level. The publicans refused to reverse the price increase, and in April the minister issued the Retail Prices (Intoxicating Liquor) Order (1997), which had the effect of fixing the price at the level of 4 November 1996.

Later in the year the Competition Authority began an investigation into pricing practices among publicans.

Sources: *Irish Times*, 19 February 1997 and 29 April 1997; *Irish Independent*, 13 December 1997.

With the introduction of the euro, consumers may need some time to get used to the new currency, as with decimalisation in 1971. When making decisions about purchases, customers will often have acceptable price ranges in mind, within which they evaluate particular products. The introduction of the euro means they would have to convert their existing acceptable price ranges into a new denomination.

PRICE COMPETITION

Price competition will inevitably be a factor in most companies' competitive environment. In addition, consumers will very often use price as the basis for comparing competitors' offerings. Price competition occasionally becomes more intense, when it is usually known as a price war.

Price wars are usually a feature of highly competitive markets; they have included sporadic encounters between the large supermarkets and between airlines. The effect of these battles tends to reverberate in the channels. A research study conducted in 1983, when Dunne's Stores entered the Northern Ireland grocery market and began a price war with the long-established market leader, Stewart's, demonstrated a number of effects (Bell and Brown, 1986). The prices on many FMCGs were cut, and the battle lasted for about six weeks. Every member of the channel felt the effects, and while consumers enjoyed a spell of very low prices, they also suffered from the side effects of overcrowded shops, long check-out queues, and frequent shortages. The only beneficiaries, the research concluded, were the media, especially the *Belfast Telegraph*, which enjoyed a dramatic increase in advertising income.

By the end of the eighties there was evidence of change (McGoldrick, 1993). Multiple grocers in Britain and Ireland were recording higher profits, had significant power over manufacturers, and were investing in new supermarkets. Their strategy had switched from intense price competition to one of desensitising consumers to price and shifting attention to new types of shops, wider product ranges, and new services.

Price wars can be quite destructive. They can lead to problems in the channels of distribution, and channel members may not like the uncertainty that can result. In extreme cases there can be a shake-out in the market, with some competitors leaving. This happened on the Dublin–London air route in the early nineties. British Airways was one of the leading airlines on the route, but under extreme competitive pressure the company decided to withdraw, such were the low levels of profit available.

This experience illustrates the worst case for the marketer. It also emphasises the danger of price-based competitive strategies. Low prices need to be accompanied by a low cost base. Ryanair managed to keep its costs low during the eighties and nineties by buying second-hand aircraft and providing a 'no-frills' service. Marketers with high cost structures will find intense price competition difficult to sustain.

PRICING AND THE OBJECTIVES OF THE BUSINESS

Businesses exist to make a profit, and their performance will ultimately be evaluated on profitability. Some organisations are non-profit-making but still may be expected to generate income to cover some or all of their costs. Price is therefore the marketing tool that will generate a profit for the business or will generate the income needed to cover costs or to make a contribution towards them. The price charged must generate a profit, and for most businesses this is the primary objective.

All firms incur costs, such as costs of production, staffing, and administration. Marketing activities, such as product development, research or promotional campaigns, can represent significant costs. The price is the means of recovering costs and generating a profit and is therefore the only element of the marketing mix that actually generates income for the firm.

While the maximisation of income and profit will be the most significant pricing objective, price will also play a role in other aspects of the firm's marketing. Establishing the pricing objectives can be considered the first stage in the pricing process, as fig. 8.2 demonstrates.

Fig. 8.2: Stages in the pricing process

1.   Establish pricing objectives
2.   Determine demand levels
3.   Calculate costs
4.   Analyse competitors' prices and pricing strategies
5.   Select a method of calculating price
6.   Consider influencing factors that may determine the final price

ESTABLISHING PRICING OBJECTIVES

Firms will seek to establish the price that maximises sales income and profit. Specific sales and profit targets will usually be established as part of the sales or revenue budgets. In multi-product firms, targets may vary by product category or brand and will take into account such factors as the stage of the product in the life-cycle, promotional campaigns, and competitive market conditions. Oxenfeldt (1973) suggested a number of potential pricing objectives, as illustrated in fig. 8.3.

Fig. 8.3: Potential pricing objectives

1. Maximise long-term profits
2. Maximise short-term profits
3. Growth
4. Stabilise market
5. Desensitise customers to price
6. Maintain price leadership arrangement
7. Discourage entrants
8. Speed the exit of marginal firms

9. Avoid government investigation and control

10. Maintain loyalty of middlemen and get their sales support

11. Avoid demands for 'more' from suppliers—labour in particular

12. Enhance the image of the firm and its offerings

13. Be regarded as 'fair' by customers (ultimate)

14. Create interest and excitement about the item

15. Be considered trustworthy and reliable by rivals

16. Help in the sale of weak items in the line

17. Discourage others from cutting prices

18. Make a product 'visible'

19. 'Spoil' the market to obtain high price for sale of business

20. Build traffic

Source: A. Oxenfeldt, 'A decision-making structure for price decisions', *Journal of Marketing*, vol. 37, January 1973.

Price is an integral part of the marketing mix and will be used to achieve particular objectives. If a business is aiming for a significant increase in market share it may decide to charge a lower price than competitors to attract more buyers, the increased number of buyers making up for the lower profits that the lower price will yield.

Competitive market conditions may force the firm to reduce prices, which can cause particular problems if the firm has a high cost structure. If costs cannot be reduced, profits will be. To avoid this profit reduction, promotional campaigns or special offers could be considered in an attempt to maintain income and profitability. In general, marketers will monitor competitive pricing conditions closely.

Some businesses will seek to charge high prices to maximise their present gain. This approach may be adopted for new products where there are few if any competitors and where the firm seeks to recoup the costs of development and market launch. Inevitably, as competitors enter the market, prices will be forced down.

The marketer must have clear pricing objectives and must establish how these relate to the firm's marketing environment.

DETERMINING DEMAND LEVELS

Economics provides a basis for understanding product demand. The principles of supply and demand and an understanding of price elasticity are fundamental to the pricing decision.

Economic theory provides the general rule of supply and demand. This states that luxury goods that are in short supply will command a higher price than they are perhaps really worth, simply because more people want them than can be supplied. On the other hand, where goods are plentiful, prices will be lower, because people will not pay the higher prices for them. Consider the demand for tickets for the all-Ireland hurling or football finals, and contrast this with the demand for tickets for a local football or hurling match.

The price elasticity of demand gives an indication of the consumer's sensitivity to changes in price. If the price of a product or service goes up or down, demand for it may be affected. Price elasticity gives an indication of how demand will be affected.

Price elasticity can be calculated using the following equation. If the price elasticity of demand equals 1, this implies that demand rises or falls by the same percentage by which the price rises or falls. If the price elasticity of demand is greater than 1, demand rises or falls at a greater rate than that of price change. A price elasticity of demand less than 1 indicates that demand rises or falls at a lower rate than the rate of price change.

$$price\ elasticity\ of\ demand = \frac{percentage\ change\ in\ quantity\ demanded}{percentage\ change\ in\ price}$$

Demand is considered to be elastic if a small change in price changes the quantity demanded; it is inelastic if a small change in price hardly changes the quantity demanded. Price elasticity for the same product may not be the same for an increase and a decrease. Consumer price elasticity must also be assessed in the context of market prices; it will be influenced by how much the price diverges from the average market price. Demand will typically be elastic for products that have close competitors, for example a litre of Avonmore milk as against a litre of Premier milk. Inelasticity may be exhibited in the price paid for a service such as a hairdresser or beautician, where the consumer is more conscious of appearance or the result than of the price they have to pay.

The calculation of price elasticity and research on factors such as consumer sensitivity to special price promotions is of relevance to marketers. One research study in Britain calculated the price elasticities of the five leading brands in a hundred product categories by regression analysis (Hamilton, East, and Kalafatis, 1997). Elasticities were found to be widely spread among product categories, with 19 per cent of them positive. The study also revealed greater price elasticity for new brands and no difference in elasticities between growing and declining brands. Brand leaders were slightly less sensitive to price changes than other brands; and higher advertising expenditure was associated with lower price-sensitivity. These results, while they cannot be considered to provide a general rule, do illustrate the links between price-sensitivity and such issues as whether or not the product is a brand leader, and the relationship between advertising expenditure and price-sensitivity.

Another study, conducted in the United States, used scanner data from a supermarket to investigate the effect of promotional factors on price elasticities in various product categories (Walter and Bommer, 1996). It found that factors specific to the product, such as the brand and its market position, were more significant in affecting elasticities in product categories than promotional factors, such as the frequency and magnitude of the price offer. Promotions on brands with significant market share within a category could therefore have a disproportionate effect.

Marketers need to understand how price-sensitive their consumers actually are. If demand for the product is highly elastic, there may be little scope for increasing the price.

Instead the marketer may have to concentrate on ways of reducing the cost or improving the general product offering to maintain profit levels. Generally, companies assess price elasticity on the basis of past experience. This poses a difficulty for marketers who have had little experience of price changes and their consequent effect on demand.

Price elasticity can vary with time. For example, it can be shown to vary over the stages of the product life-cycle. In the beginning it is usually the least price-sensitive consumers, the innovators and early adopters, who adopt new products or innovations; the most price-sensitive consumers tend to be the late majority and the laggards.

CALCULATING COSTS

Costs can be classified as *variable* or *fixed*. Variable costs vary as output or sales vary and typically include raw materials and labour; examples of variable marketing costs include coupon and rebate redemptions. While several thousand coupons may be inserted in magazines or direct-mailed, the cost to the business will depend on the number of coupons or rebates that are redeemed by the consumer. Fixed costs, on the other hand, remain fixed, regardless of output or sales: an example would be the rent the company pays on its premises. An example of a fixed marketing cost would be the salary paid to a marketing manager.

The sum of fixed and variable costs equals total cost. Average cost is total cost divided by the number of units produced. Once the average cost is known, the business can use this as a basis for deciding what the selling price should be and what profit it will make per unit. Broadly speaking, it is the average cost plus the desired profit margin that determines the price per unit that will be charged.

An important consideration is that costs can increase because of inflation. Prices must therefore increase in line with inflation if the business is to maintain its real profits.

ANALYSIS OF COMPETITORS' PRICES AND PRICING STRATEGY

Monitoring competitors' prices and pricing strategies is a continuous activity. In very price-competitive markets, prices and strategies may change regularly; the marketer will need to keep abreast of these changes. Price is used by many firms as their main competitive tool. Competitively, it is flexible, as it can be varied, typically with some form of price promotion. This can be an advantage if there are environmental changes that require a quick response.

In markets with several competitors offering broadly similar products, prices will usually be competitive. The tendency will be for individual competitors to reduce prices to achieve an increase in market share.

The business must also be able to react to changes that competitors may make in their prices. It is wise to carry out some research to determine how buyers perceive price. In perceptual terms, it is a truism that the higher the price the higher the perceived quality of the product, and the lower the price the lower the perceived quality.

Price is a powerful positioning tool. Some firms emphasise quality and service levels and place less emphasis on price. This may be appropriate where buyers are less price-sensitive; in other cases, firms may emphasise price or value for money. For example, Dunne's Stores used the slogan 'Dunne's Stores—better value beats them all' for many years. The company's advertising emphasised this fact.

Firms that pursue strategies based strongly on price competition need to be careful that, in the search for a highly competitive price, the other elements of the marketing mix do not end up turning consumers away from the product. When own-label grocery products were launched on the Irish market, many of the supermarkets concentrated on low prices and neglected quality. The consumer did indeed respond to low prices but was not happy with the quality received. Quinnsworth, for example, introduced its first own-label range in 1977. Approximately fifty imported products were introduced, but consumers perceived the quality to be too low. The company had to change strategy and develop a home-produced range of products, in partnership with Irish manufacturers and distributors (Pratt, 1994). Consumers were used to the quality levels of national brands, and this is what they used in making comparisons.

SELECTING A METHOD FOR CALCULATING PRICES

A number of pricing methods are available to the business, and the method selected can depend on such considerations as the industry in which the firm operates and the type of product or service the company produces. Four main methods can be used: cost-plus, perceived value, break-even and target profit, and going rate.

Cost-plus pricing involves adding a standard mark-up to the cost of the product, for example taking the average cost of the product and adding a 25 per cent mark-up. Cost-based approaches to pricing are based on the assumption that costs can be identified and calculated. This is a common approach in the retail sector, where products are bought from manufacturers or middlemen and a mark-up is added. The mark-up must take into account the costs the retailer incurs in selling the product and a satisfactory profit margin.

The formula for calculating the mark-up price is:

$$mark\text{-}up\ price = \frac{unit\ costs}{1 - desired\ return\ on\ sales}$$

Consider a clothing retailer who buys men's suits from a wholesaler. Each suit costs £100, and it is estimated that the cost of selling each suit, including rent, wages, and administration, is £20 per suit. If the desired return on sales is 25 per cent, the mark-up price would be:

$$mark\text{-}up\ price = \frac{100 + 20}{1 - 0.25} = £160\ per\ suit$$

As a pricing method, the cost-plus approach is simple to calculate, and it can be varied to suit different product categories. The mark-up on frozen food, for example, might be higher than the mark-up on canned food, because of the higher costs of refrigeration.

The difficulty with cost-based approaches to pricing, however, is that they may not be able to take into account the demand for a product at different price levels. In the example above, what would happen if the retailer discovered that a close competitor was offering similar suits at £139? A reduction in price will drive down profit, unless costs can be cut. Cost-based methods may not take the demand elasticity of particular segments or competitive conditions into account; they are unlikely therefore to lead to maximisation of profit.

Perceived-value pricing is based on the perception of the buyer, which may need to be researched by the marketer. The research would seek to determine what perceived value the product or service has for the consumer, and how they translate that value into monetary terms. Perceived-value pricing is often used by the marketers of services where the nature of the service is more intangible.

Perceived-value approaches do take market and demand conditions into account. Many airlines, for example, charge different prices according to the time the person wants to travel, the flexibility they require, and how far in advance they book their journey. From experience, airlines know that they can fill a certain proportion of seats with travellers who booked fourteen days in advance with APEX, a certain proportion with business travellers who require maximum flexibility on booking and travel times, and a certain proportion with stand-by passengers who turn up on the day. Prices are therefore tailored to suit the demand elasticities of each of these segments and their perception of the value of the fare they receive.

Break-even and target profit pricing involves calculating a price based on a relationship between cost and volume of sales. The break-even point is the point where income and costs are equal. Below this point, costs exceed income, and a loss is incurred; above this point, income exceeds costs, and a profit is earned. Break-even analysis involves estimating how much income is needed to cover the fixed costs of producing a product and at the same time to cover the variable costs.

This pricing technique is particularly useful for pricing new products. Using the relationship between fixed costs, variable costs, price, sales income, and target profit, the marketer can calculate the sales volume required to break even or to achieve a planned level of profit.

Consider the case of an entrepreneur who wishes to establish a small business making jams and marmalades. The fixed costs are estimated at £50,000 per year. The estimated variable costs per unit are 50p per jar, and the selling price is to be £1 per jar. How many jars must be sold to break even?

The break-even point in units can be calculated using the formula

$$\text{break-even units} = \frac{\text{total fixed costs}}{\text{unit contribution to fixed cost}}$$

$$\text{break-even units} = \frac{50,000}{1 - 0.50} = 100,000 \text{ jars}$$

Therefore, 100,000 jars must be sold to break even. Obviously, the entrepreneur will require a profit. Assuming this is a profit of £20,000 a year, how many units must be sold to achieve this?

This can be calculated by adding the required profit to the formula:

$$\text{target profit units} = \frac{\text{total fixed costs} + \text{desired profit}}{\text{unit contribution to fixed cost}}$$

$$\text{target profit units} = \frac{50,000 + 20,000}{1 - 0.50} = 140,000 \text{ jars}$$

The entrepreneur therefore knows what will have to be sold at this particular price and cost structure to achieve the desired level of profit.

Break-even analysis can be used to test assumptions, for example whether the sales needed to earn the required profit can be realistically achieved, given the size of the market or competitive conditions. On researching the market for jam and marmalade, the entrepreneur may decide that a higher price can be charged. An examination of costs may reveal that obtaining raw materials from a cheaper supplier can reduce variable costs. Consider how the target profit units would change if the price were £1.10 per jar, the variable costs were 40p per jar, and the required profit remained the same. The revised break-even and target profit is then calculated:

$$\text{target profit units} = \frac{50,000 + 20,000}{1.10 - 0.40} = 100,000 \text{ jars}$$

In this case a considerably reduced number of units can be sold to make the same amount of profit.

These examples show the benefits of analysing the relationship between price, costs, and sales volume. The marketer should also use experience of the market and market information to supplement this analysis.

Going-rate pricing means pricing according to what competitors in the industry are charging. Industrial marketers, such as steel manufacturers and petroleum producers, often use this approach. In many world commodity markets a going rate is established, though this can change as a result of oversupply or shortages. It is also a fairly common approach in the financial services sector, where interest rates offered or charged tend not to vary very much between different banks or lending institutions.

Going-rate pricing tends to preserve harmony in a particular industry or market. That harmony may be disrupted if some competitors change the rate. It can also be argued that going-rate pricing may be a form of cartel arrangement, whereby manufacturers or service providers have implicitly agreed prices and the consumer ends up with little choice. Such arrangements usually encourage inefficiency.

Selecting the final price

A number of factors can be taken into account before the final price is chosen.

Pricing points are specific points at which products are sold: for example, the price of a litre of milk or of a countline bar are usually standard among most retailers. Any new product coming onto the market has to take this into account. When Irish Biscuits launched Chocolate Kimberly, it was priced in comparison with other countline bars. In the case of many FMCG products, pricing points will vary according to packet size.

Psychological dimensions of the price may be important. Consumers' perceptions of price will be an important determinant in the product evaluation process. Many consumers will use the price as an indication of the quality of the product; they will perceive a direct relationship between the quality of the product and the price charged. Psychologically, prices ending in odd numbers also have significance, as consumers have a tendency to round down prices in their minds. Thus a product that costs £9.99 may be perceived as costing approximately £9, rather than approximately £10.

Discounted prices are a feature of many price promotions; they may also be a feature where the consumer pays in cash or buys large quantities of a product. The marketer must remember that a discount is a cost and so should try to strike a balance between a discount the buyer considers to be worth while and one that does not incur an unacceptable cost for the marketer. Regular customers may expect discounts, and it becomes an incentive in encouraging repeat business.

Loss leaders will occasionally be offered by retailers to encourage shoppers to do their shopping in the particular shop. A number of leading brands may be chosen and promoted at a loss to entice consumers to shop there. The cost of doing this is considered to be a promotional expense for the business.

Special-event pricing typically includes the January sales and other special sale events. Retailers frequently use these as part of their promotional strategy. Under the Consumer Information Act (1978) a product must have been available for at least twenty-eight consecutive days at a higher price before the price can be described as a 'sale' price.

Discriminatory pricing involves offering discounts to specific segments of the market, such as students, unemployed people, or pensioners. Service providers who are anxious to stimulate demand at off-peak times often do this. It takes into account the fact that some groups are more price-sensitive than others and may therefore be willing to be more flexible with regard to time. Discriminatory pricing is widely practised by transport operators, cinemas and theatres, restaurants, and hairdressers.

Discriminatory pricing can also be selectively practised by using promotional campaigns. The marketer may wish to attract consumers in one area or segment without offering the discount to everyone. Discount coupons can therefore be aimed directly at particular areas or segments, which can be redeemed when a purchase is made. In this way the marketer does not end up discounting all sales.

TAXES

In calculating the price to the consumer, the marketer must also consider such costs as value-added tax and any excise duty that may be added on. Going back to the example of the price of a pint of stout (page 218), the national average price for a pint of draught Guinness in April 1998 was £2.05 (*Irish Times*, 17 April 1998), with prices varying from £1.83 to £2.65. Of the average price the brewery received 49.9p, the publican 82p, and the state 73.1p (37.1p excise duty and 36p VAT).

DEALING WITH PRICE CHANGES

Inevitably marketers will have to change prices. Price reductions do not tend to cause the same difficulties for marketers as price increases, which will rarely be popular with consumers. Competitive pressures will also be influential. Marketers therefore need to carefully examine the options open to them if they need to change prices.

The price-sensitivity of segments will be an important factor. Some segments may be less resistant to price increases, and it may be possible to charge them proportionately more than other price-sensitive ones. Additional services or augmented aspects of the product may be charged for where previously there was no charge. Minimum order sizes may be increased, or charges may be introduced for additional services, such as repair or servicing. In some cases the marketer may have no option but to make fundamental changes to the product, such as making it smaller or reducing the quality of raw materials.

PRICING AND THE PRODUCT LIFE-CYCLE

The stage the product is at in the life-cycle will affect the price. At the introductory stage, if the product is unique or new to the world, the price charged will typically be high. This will help recover the costs of development and launching. If a business has developed a new product or if a product is protected by patent, a high price will usually be set so as to 'skim' the market. This recognises that the company has incurred costs in bringing the new product to the market and it needs to recover those costs as quickly as possible before competitors enter the market with similar products or close substitutes and force prices down. The first electronic calculator and the first instant camera were launched on the market at high prices, which were subsequently lowered as more competitors launched competing products. If the product is being launched into a market where competitors already exist, the ability to charge higher prices will depend on the product's unique selling points.

As the product moves through the life-cycle, the price will inevitably be forced downwards. This downward pressure will begin to become apparent in the growth phase; competitors will enter the market, substitutes may be developed, and the marketer will face increasing price competition. Pressure on price will require the cost structure of the product to be examined, especially when profits begin to decline. At the mature stage in the life-cycle, price promotions will frequently be used as the marketer seeks to maximise sales volume. Decline may see prices further reduced as the product is phased out of the market.

PRICING STRATEGIES

Pricing strategies will be determined by the firm's pricing policies and objectives, which are determined by general company strategy. Porter's (1980) generic strategies, for example, each yield a different pricing strategy. Cost leadership will be based on penetration pricing approaches. Costs will be kept tightly controlled, so the company can compete on price. Differentiation, where the emphasis is more on quality and added value, may yield more higher-priced pricing strategies. With the third strategy, focus, prices will be tailored to the demand levels and market profiles of the chosen segments.

Tellis (1986) suggested a taxonomy of pricing strategies, as illustrated in fig. 8.4. This proposes three broad objectives for the firm and three broad characteristics of customers.

Fig. 8.4: Tellis's taxonomy of pricing strategies

Objectives of firm			
Characteristics of consumers	Vary prices among segments	Exploit competitive position	Balance price over product line
Some have high search costs	Random discounts	Price signalling	Image pricing
Some have low reservation price	Periodic discounts	Penetration pricing Experience curve pricing	Price bundling Premium pricing
All have special transaction costs	Second-market discounting	Geographical pricing	Complementary pricing

The three broad characteristics of customers refer to those who have high search costs. These customers do not know exactly which firm sells the product they want, and they have to search for it. To some the opportunity cost of time exceeds the benefit of a search, so they will be willing to buy without full information. Those with a low reservation price are price-sensitive customers. The third category suggests that all consumers have certain transaction costs, other than search costs, such as travelling costs, risk, or the cost of money.

The pricing strategies suggested by Tellis can be briefly summarised. Where prices are varied between segments, *random discounts* imply maintaining a high cost normally but randomly discounting. Uninformed consumers will therefore be more likely to buy at the high price, while informed consumers will look around or will wait until they can buy at the low price. *Periodic discounts* could apply for transport products: for example, travellers expect to pay higher prices in the peak demand period but can get lower prices if they wait for off-peak times. *Second-market discounting* involves charging lower prices in some segments or markets. The rationale is that as long as the sale generates a price over the variable cost, this will make a contribution to the continuing business. Companies may therefore charge lower prices to students or to pensioners, who may not be in the primary market.

Pricing strategies that are used to exploit competitive position include *price signalling*. This refers to charging a high price for a low-quality product on the grounds that the consumer will perceive the product to be of high quality because of the price. This strategy may not encourage repeat business. *Penetration pricing* involves charging low prices to build market share; while *experience-curve* pricing means that prices can be lowered later in the product's life-cycle as the marketer gains the benefits of the economies of experience. *Geographical pricing* involves charging different prices in different geographical markets.

Product-line pricing strategies are relevant when a firm has a set of related products. *Image pricing* involves the firm bringing out an identical version of its current product with a different name and a higher price; the idea is to suggest quality to uninformed consumers. *Price bundling* involves maximising price yield among a number of products. *Premium pricing* involves charging high prices for quality products, while *complementary pricing* applies in situations where products may require accessories, for example charging a low price for a razor but a relatively higher price for blades.

The anatomy of the relationship between price and quality levels also yields a number of possible pricing strategies, as illustrated in fig. 8.5. There is certainly a strong link between price and perceived quality.

Fig. 8.5: Nine marketing mix strategies on price v. quality

		PRICE		
		High	**Medium**	**Low**
	High	Premium	High value	Superb value
QUALITY	*Medium*	Overcharging	Medium value	Good value
	Low	Rip-off	False economy	Economy

Source: P. Kotler and G. Armstrong, *Marketing: An Introduction*, Englewood Cliffs (NJ): Prentice-Hall 1993.

Consumer perception of the price-quality relationship is significant. If consumers feel that they are being cheated or over-charged they will take action. Such strategies can hardly be considered to be good ethical practice. In other cases, such strategies as offering high value or superb value may be very popular with the consumer but may not yield an adequate return for the marketer.

CONSUMER PERCEPTION AND PRICE

How the consumer perceives price will be critically important for the marketer. This emphasises the need for research on consumers' perceptions. One study demonstrated that price had very little influence over consumer choice (Ehrenberg, Scriven, and Barnard, 1997). It argued that price promotions had a minimal, short-term effect on brand sales and that these generally appealed to a small proportion of existing brand users rather than attracting new customers. It also suggested that these were usually a loss-making endeavour in the long run. The study suggested that consumers had habitual acceptable price ranges for brands they found salient and that price increases of habitual brands lose very few customers, as they generally remain within this acceptable price range. It also noted that price elasticities differed very little between similar brands. In general, it was argued that marketers should concentrate on advertising to build brand saliency and should avoid head-on price competition and price promotions as unprofitable.

This particular study is of interest in that it demonstrates how price is linked to the other elements of the marketing mix. Consumers obviously don't always make their decisions on price criteria alone: their perceptions of brand saliency and the price range that is acceptable to them are also important factors. Marketers could therefore avoid expensive price battles and price-promotional campaigns by concentrating instead on brand salience—in other words, positioning away from price.

Consumers' perception of price is also important in the context of the adoption of new products. The new-product adopter categories can be characterised according to their sensitivity to the price of the new product, with those consumers who adopt the product at earlier stages tending to be less price-sensitive than those who enter the market later.

FURTHER READING

Clarke, P., *Accounting Information for Managers*, Dublin: Oak Tree Press 1995.
Dodge, R., and Hanna, N., *Pricing: Policies and Procedures*, London: Macmillan 1995.
Nagle, T., and Holden, R., *Strategy and Tactics of Pricing* (second edition), Englewood Cliffs (NJ): Prentice-Hall 1995.

DISCUSSION QUESTIONS

1. Select a number of products or services that exhibit elastic and inelastic demand. Explain your choices.
2. Explain why an airline can charge different prices to different customers for the same flight.
3. Can all marketers use discriminatory pricing techniques? Why, or why not?
4. Comment on the relationship between pricing and brand loyalty. Are loyal consumers likely to be impervious to price changes?
5. Explain why pricing decisions must be made in the context of the other elements of the marketing mix.

References

Bell, Jim, and Brown, Stephen, 'Anatomy of a supermarket price war', *Irish Marketing Review*, vol. 1 (1986).

Ehrenberg, A., Scriven, J., and Barnard, N., 'Advertising and price', *Journal of Advertising Research*, May–June 1997.

Everett, F., 'Price promos can protect brand equity', *Brand Week*, 4 May 1998.

Hamilton, W., East, R., and Kalafatis, S., 'Brand price elasticities', *Journal of Marketing Management*, vol. 13, no. 4, May 1997.

McGoldrick, P., 'Grocery pricing in the 1990s: war or peace?', *Irish Marketing Review*, vol. 6 (1993).

Porter, M., *Competitive Strategy*, New York: Free Press 1980.

Pratt, Maurice, 'Own Brands: The Benefits' (conference paper, National Marketing Conference), *Business and Finance*, October 1994.

Tellis, G., 'Beyond the many faces of price: an integration of pricing strategies', *Journal of Marketing*, vol. 50, October 1986.

Walter, R., and Bommer, W., 'Measuring the impact of product and promotion-related factors on product category price elasticities', *Journal of Business Research*, July 1996.

9

Marketing Communication

Marketers must communicate with their customers. In the competitive market there will usually be many firms seeking to differentiate their offerings through communication and promotional techniques. Marketers seek to gain attention for their products, to remind buyers of the value they can deliver, to promote special offers, and to position their products in the minds of consumers. Different methods of communication, such as advertising, sales promotions, and public relations, are used to achieve this. This chapter explores the nature of communication and the methods of communication used by marketers.

Just as the nature of the product is a broad concept in marketing, so too is the concept of communication. All firms use different media to get their message across. In some cases, as with the Surf detergent brand, getting the message across helped restore the brand's fortunes.

THE ROLE OF COMMUNICATION
IN MAINTAINING POSITION

Surf was launched by Lever Brothers in 1952 with the slogan 'Boils spotless—spotless whites,' relaunched as 'Square Deal Surf' in 1962, and redefined with the slogan 'Great cleaning at a great price—Lever guarantees it.' Surf has benefited greatly from a consumer trend towards effective, value-for-money brands. Primarily a value brand, it was the fastest-growing detergent brand in Ireland between 1993 and 1997 and captured 9 per cent of the market. This success was helped, according to Lever Brothers, by a television advertising campaign featuring Mary McEvoy from the popular television serial 'Glenroe'. In the campaign she promised viewers: 'If you're not happy, Lever Brothers will give you your money back.'

Source: *Checkout Ireland*, April 1997.

THE COMMUNICATIONS MODEL

Communication broadly describes the transmission of a message from a sender to a receiver. The communications model (fig. 9.1) is a good basis for explaining the process. As marketers and firms need to communicate to potential and existing buyers and to various publics, an appreciation of the model is a requirement. There are a number of elements in the model, each of which is described.

Fig. 9.1: The communications model

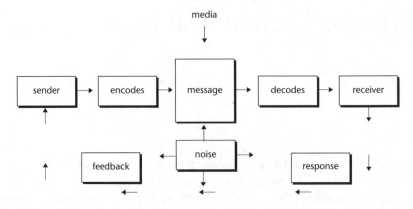

The *sender* is the person or firm sending the message. This could include the marketer of a brand, a charity, or a political party. It is important that the sender is clearly identified so that the receiver is not confused.

Encoding describes the process of putting the message into symbolic form. The sender will use words, pictures, music, images, or any combination of these, to convey the message. The marketer will encode symbols that describe and enhance the product and that convey the desired image. These symbols will relate to the position the marketer would like the product to occupy in the buyer's mind.

The *message* is the actual symbols that the sender transmits. Consider the advertisement for Bailey's Irish Cream (fig. 9.2): the symbols used are the illustration of the bottle, the liqueur being poured into the glass of ice, the background colours, Bailey's logo, and the advertising copy, 'Pure magic on ice.' In this particular case the message suggests a way of consuming the product and transmits an image of strong brand identity.

The message can be transmitted through a variety of *media*, that is, the possible channels the sender can use. These channels can be person-to-person, such as a sales representative, or can involve the use of press, radio, television, poster sites, events, or other non-personal media. The Bailey's Irish Cream example in fig. 9.2 appeared in a variety of press and poster sites.

Noise is anything that can interrupt or disturb the communication process. It can include physical factors that may prevent receivers seeing or hearing the message, the actions of competitors that confuse or cause the message to be ignored, distractions, or other factors in the receiver's environment that impinge on the transmission of the message. Noise can also affect the response and feedback aspects of communication: for example, a buyer may see an advertisement for the marketer's product, decide to buy it, and go to the supermarket; when they are shopping they notice an in-store promotion for a competing brand, which, though it is not their preferred brand, they decide to buy. In this situation the receiver received the message, had a positive evaluation of the message, and did intend to buy, but factors intervened that prevented them doing so. On their next visit to the supermarket they may indeed buy the marketer's brand, but on this occasion the feedback the marketer gets is largely negative.

Large numbers of messages are directed at consumers every day, and this volume of messages can be a source of noise. Receivers cannot pay attention to everything, so some messages will not be noticed. People will generally notice or be receptive to communications about things that are of interest to them; they may remember only small parts of messages, and they can distort messages to suit themselves if they do not like the contents of the message. All these noise factors provide a challenge to the marketer to design messages and use media that will be noticed and that will get the message through.

Fig. 9.2: Bailey's Irish Cream

Decoding refers to the mental process of interpretation and assigning meaning to the symbols transmitted by the sender. It takes place largely in the brain: we see, hear, touch, taste or smell stimuli, an impulse is sent through the central nervous system to the brain, and it interprets and assigns a meaning to the information received. Obviously it is important that clear stimuli are transmitted, so the receiver does not experience difficulty interpreting. Stimuli that are confusing or difficult to interpret can be ignored or misinterpreted.

The *receiver* is the person or group who receives the message. This could be an individual consumer, a segment of the market, a firm, or any other public. The sender needs to ensure that the message is aimed at an appropriate receiver: for example, if communicating with a firm, it is important to reach the decision-makers or those who influence the decision.

The *response* refers to the receiver's reaction to the message. The response is a rather broad concept, in that it does not necessarily imply immediacy. Consider an advertisement for a fitted kitchen. The receiver may be impressed with the advertisement and decide that they would like to have one, but they may not buy until some time in the future.

Feedback is the part of the response that is actually communicated back to the sender: thus, if the receiver, having seen an advertisement, decides to buy a product, the marketer receives feedback through an increase in sales. As with the response, feedback is also a broad concept. Sales can certainly be used as a measure of feedback, but there are other possibilities. In the example of the fitted kitchen, the response may be communicated only at some future time, perhaps several years away. Some communications attempt to make the receiver more aware of a particular issue, such as environmental awareness; and some may involve several responses, such as road safety.

STEPS IN THE COMMUNICATION PROCESS

Seven essential steps are involved in the marketing communication process, as illustrated in fig. 9.3. These provide a structure for the marketer's communication activities; they emphasise the different stages involved in developing a co-ordinated communication campaign.

Fig. 9.3: Steps in the marketing communication process

Identification of audience
↓
Determination of communication objectives
↓
Design of message
↓
Selection of communication channel
↓
Setting and allocation of communication budget
↓

↓

Selection of promotional mix

↓

Evaluation of results

Identifying the audience

As with the segmentation decision, marketers do not necessarily want to communicate to everyone. Messages will be aimed at the audience most likely to be receptive and those who are of most interest to the marketer.

Fundamentally, marketers should understand the needs of the target audience. They will therefore specify the characteristics of the target audience according to its background profile, location, interests, attitudes, and opinions. A profile of the target audience will enable the marketer to make decisions about how the message should be structured and how to reach the audience.

Communication objectives

One of the best ways of considering possible objectives is to specify the response that the sender seeks. Responses can be broadly cognitive, affective, behavioural, or a combination of all three.

A *cognitive* response involves putting something in the receiver's mind, for example getting the receiver to consider the benefits of the product or to consider using the product. *Affective* responses refer to positive or negative emotions about the content of the message. The receiver will develop a positive attitude towards the product if they like or are interested in the content of the message, and a negative attitude if they don't. The *behavioural* response involves the receiver engaging in some form of behaviour as a result of the message. In theory, if the receiver considers the message and likes the content, they will be more likely to engage in favourable behaviour.

The AIDA ('attention, interest, desire, action') model (fig. 9.4) is often used to illustrate the objectives of the marketing communication process. Gaining attention is the cognitive stage of the model; stimulating interest and desire is affective; and taking action is behavioural.

Fig. 9.4: The AIDA model

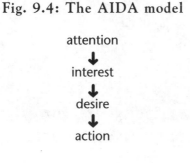

The four stages in the AIDA model are sequential, the idea being that the marketer's communications should attract attention, stimulate interest and desire, and obtain action. The AIDA model is a useful basis for any communication activities such as personal selling or advertising.

The message

The challenge to the sender is to design a message that will successfully get through the channels and result in a positive response. The sender must decide which symbols to combine into a message; this will largely depend on the nature of the product and on the characteristics of the intended audience. The sender will decide on the appeal of the product. Some products have a strong rational appeal, such as the money or time the buyer will save by using a particular brand. Consider the advertisement for the ESB (fig. 9.5), where the message advances a number of rational reasons for buying the brand.

Fig. 9.5: ESB

Special offers only available while stocks last at ESB shops and participating stores nationwide.
Offers only available from Sunday 20th to Saturday 26th September inclusive.
www.esb.ie

Other appeals will be more subjective and will attempt to stimulate the receiver's emotions. Consider the advertisement for Pantene Pro-V from Procter and Gamble (fig. 9.6), which uses quite emotive symbolism in a message about a range of hair care products.

Fig. 9.6:

Don't go it alone. Pantene formulated its shampoo and conditioner to work together for the ultimate in healthy looking hair. First, Pantene Shampoo delivers pro-vitamins to the source of

new hair to build strength from the time it's born, then Vitalising Conditioner moisturises and protects that hair for life. Used in harmony, there's no better care for beautiful hair.

love your hair

www.pantene.com

Some messages will have a strong moral appeal and will seek to stimulate a sense of right or duty, for example the advertising used by the Drinks Industry Group (fig. 9.7), which highlights the issue of sensible drinking.

Fig. 9.7: Drinks Industry Group

In general, designing the message requires the sender to consider a number of structural factors, such as what wording to use and the type of illustrations, colours, characters, background, theme and personalities that might be appropriate. Usually these aspects of design will be taken into account by the creative department in an advertising agency. Marketers will usually require that logos, colours, text, characters and other factors that have come to be associated with a brand will be maintained but that new themes or situations will be developed. The design of messages that are being sent by interpersonal means, such as through a sales representative, will involve factors such as arguments to be advanced during presentation and what to include in the sales presenter.

Message design will be strongly influenced by the marketing strategy being pursued by the marketer. The launch of a new product will require a message emphasising such aspects as innovativeness or benefits. Some messages will be informative, such as a special promotion or sale, while others will be image-building.

The marketer may want to aim at a particular audience with a specific message. Consider the example of the National Lottery (fig. 9.8), where the message seeks to justify a price increase and is aimed at the national market.

Fig. 9.8: National Lottery

BECAUSE DREAMS COST A LOTTO MORE, THERE'S A LOTTO MORE TO PLAY FOR.

	WAS	NOW
MINIMUM JACKPOT	£500,000	£1 MILLION
MATCH 5 + BONUS	£5,000	£7,500
MATCH 5	£560*	£840*
MATCH 4 + BONUS	NEW!	£100
MATCH 4	£23*	£35*
MATCH 3 + BONUS	£10	£15

*Average - actual prize amounts vary depending on the number of winners in any given Lotto draw.

Whatever your dreams, you can be sure they cost more today than they did ten years ago when the Lottery first started. So, from Saturday September 26th we're doubling the Lotto Jackpot to a guaranteed £1 million pounds. We're also increasing other prizes by 50% and adding a new prize for 4 + Bonus Number. To make this possible, we're increasing the cost of playing from 50p to 75p per panel - a little more to pay but a Lotto more to play for.

GUARANTEED AT LEAST £1,000,000 EVERY DRAW

Message design can give the sender or the creative department tremendous scope for design and creativity. Themes can be amusing, serious, off-beat, evocative, or informative. Consumers in Ireland are accustomed to well-produced, creative and high-quality advertising campaigns on television and radio, in print, and on posters. Messages that cannot compete in this environment may not be noticed.

Symbolism can be very important. *Semiotics* is the study of the meanings that people attach specifically to non-verbal symbols. Perceptually, pictures are usually considered to be more powerful than words, and marketers are interested in how consumers perceive the symbols they use. Consider the following examples:

teddy bear—tamed aggression
penguin—coolness, refreshment, friendliness
tiger—strong and fearless.

(Source: R. Alsop, 'Agencies scrutinise their ads for psychological symbolism', *Wall Street Journal*, 11 June 1987.)

These symbols have been used in various advertising and communication campaigns: for example, An Bord Gáis has used a teddy bear in its advertising, McVitie uses penguins in its advertisements for the Penguin brand of chocolate biscuits, and Esso has used a tiger in advertising its fuels.

Some invented symbols have become internationally recognised, as the following panel illustrates.

BIBENDUM: CELEBRATING A HUNDRED YEARS

As Édouard Michelin walked through the entrance of the Universal and Colonial Exhibition in Lyon with his brother in 1898 he noticed a pile of tyres of different diameters near his own stand. Inspired, he proclaimed: 'With arms and legs it would be a man.' So it was that in April 1898 that first sketch of a man made of tyres left the drawing-board to appear on posters throughout France.

A series of posters showed him drinking nails and broken bottles and saying in Latin, '*Nunc est bibendum*,' meaning 'Now is the time to drink.' This represents the idea that Michelin tyres drink any obstacle in their way; it was soon to become a slogan for the group, and within a few months the little figure was named Bibendum. Now that warm and cuddly pile of tyres is celebrating his hundredth birthday. As a present, Michelin will be giving its old friend a new shape and will launch numerous souvenirs and festivities in his honour.

Michelin enjoyed worldwide fame and fortune in the early years of the twentieth century, when it was the first company to fit pneumatic tyres to motor vehicles. People could relate easily to Bibendum, as his stature strongly resembled the drivers of the time, who wrapped themselves in layers of clothing to stay warm in their open cars.

Source: *Irish Marketing Journal*, February 1998.

Occasionally a credible source may be used by the sender. Celebrities, sports stars, entertainers or company personnel may be used to deliver the message and thereby endorse the product or service. The actor Mary McEvoy endorsed the Surf brand of detergent for Lever Brothers, and the chief executive of GM-Opel in Ireland, Arnold O'Byrne, appeared in advertisements for the Opel range of cars.

The use of company personnel in advertising has become more common, as the next panel demonstrates. Companies may use their senior personnel in an attempt to create an image of authority and to put a human face on the firm. If actors are used instead, the credibility factor may be much lower. In many instances the personnel used have become advertising institutions and are easily recognisable. This has been referred to as the Pygmalion principle: in other words, an unknown talent is transformed into a celebrity (Meenaghan, 1988). The principle has had applications in entertainment and sport but also in the professions and the academic world.

POWER IN THE PERSONAL TOUCH

Maurice Pratt, group marketing manager of Power supermarkets, first appeared in advertisements for Quinnsworth in 1983 on the launch of its 'yellow pack' range. The idea had come from Canada, where many chief executives promoted their company in advertising. In 1986 Arnold O'Byrne, the managing director of GM-Opel, appeared in his first commercial, which was an attempt by the company to put an Irish face on the brand. In financial services, Adrian Taheny, the general manager of the Educational Building Society, appeared in 1993, to be followed by Garry Hynes of Church and General and Richard Sheridan of First Call Direct. In 1998 Esat Digifone began using its chief executive, Denis O'Brien, in its television advertisement.

Sources: Gabi Thesing, 'Power in personal touch', *Sunday Business Post*, 4 June 1996; Esat Digifone advertisement, March 1998.

In using any personality, the marketer has to ensure that the celebrity does not overwhelm the message. The receiver can become confused or may remember only that they have seen the person but may not remember the product. It is also possible for confusion to exist if the personality endorses a number of brands: for example, the pop group Spice Girls endorsed a brand of chocolate and a brand of anti-perspirant.

Some messages will be very specific in stating the benefits of the product, describing features, or informing the receiver of special characteristics or offers. Other messages may be more subtle and may concentrate more on visual image than on text. Such messages are usually more effective for well-established brands such as Guinness, where consumers are already familiar with features and benefits.

SELECTING THE COMMUNICATION CHANNEL

There are two choices: using personal channels or non-personal channels. Personal channels include company salespeople, experts, personal influence, and trade fairs or similar events. The firm's sales personnel will spend much of their time communicating about the product to potential buyers, distributors, or retailers. The selling process itself involves presentation and communication, and salespeople will also be involved in customer service and building relationships with customers, all of which involve interpersonal communication.

Experts will occasionally be used to communicate about particular products on behalf of the firm. For example, a dentist might communicate the benefits of a particular brand of toothbrush, or a vet might communicate about the nutritional benefit of a brand of dog food. Sometimes professional bodies or associations will endorse particular products or services; usually, however, such bodies have strict policies on endorsement and will do so only if they believe it will be of benefit to their members or to the wider public.

Personal influence can be a feature of the relationship between a salesperson and a buyer, between an expert and an audience, or between a company manager and decision-makers. It is therefore a broad base for communication. Potentially any sender can have influence over a receiver if the receiver can be influenced. Typically, receivers are more influenced when they have not got the information they need to make decisions, when they have difficult or risky decisions to make, or when they are not experts on the particular subject.

Trade fairs can be used by many marketers as an opportunity for communicating with quite focused audiences. They are particularly useful for industrial marketers: usually the people who attend come from particular industries, and it is therefore an opportunity to communicate directly with potential buyers or decision-makers.

Events are another opportunity for interpersonal communication. Launches of a product to the trade, sponsored events and corporate entertainment are all opportunities for communication.

Non-personal communication channels usually involve using the media. This can be the mass media, such as the national press, radio, or television, or it can be more selective, such as local press and trade or specialist publications. In these channels the message is communicated using symbols, which are broadcast in a non-personal way. The difficulty for marketers in using non-personal channels is that they may not be suitable for complicated products; the receiver is not able to ask questions, and the marketer may not be able to ascertain immediately whether they understood the message. Personal channels, on the other hand, facilitate questions, and the sender is in a better position to determine whether the receiver understands the message.

Most marketers will use a combination of personal and non-personal channels; which one or which combination they select will be determined by their communication objectives, the nature of the product and the message they wish to communicate, and competitive considerations. If competitors are using extensive advertising campaigns to support and position their brands, the marketer may need to do likewise.

There are no hard and fast rules on the use of channels. Some companies have used extensive mass media advertising to build their brands; others use other channels or combinations of channels to reach the target audience. In addition to advertising, Hugo Boss devoted significant resources to the sponsorship of formula 1 racing, while the Body Shop has engaged in social activism, espousing a number of environmental and animal rights issues (Joachimsthaler and Aaker, 1997).

SETTING AND ALLOCATING THE COMMUNICATION BUDGET

Budgets will usually be a limiting factor in the methods and means of communication. Four main approaches are used to determine resources for marketing communication; many marketers use a combination of approaches.

The *affordable approach* is based on what the firm can afford, after other costs and expenses have been met. This is typical of many smaller firms and business start-ups, where spending on communication may be based on what is left over after other expenditure has been taken into account. The problem with this approach is that communication is relegated to a residual position, and objectives may not be met, because the budget is incapable of achieving them.

The *objective and task* approach has more to recommend it. This involves determining what needs to be done and allocating resources accordingly. Specific communication objectives are detailed, and the tasks that need to be carried out are specified. The communicator is forced to specify in detail what it is required to achieve, and this can then be costed and the expense justified.

Sometimes firms base their communication budget on *competitive parity*, which uses competitors' spending and communication activities as the yardstick for their communication budget. They need to be careful, however: if competitors are not spending much on communication, this does not mean that the marketer should follow. In many cases the fact that competitors spend little on their communication activities may be an opportunity for the marketer to emphasise and position their product using a communication campaign.

The *percentage-of-sales* method involves relating communications to a unit of activity, namely sales in money terms. This is used by many firms, which spend an annual amount on communication based on their sales. The method is an attempt to link the effects of communication on sales. There are difficulties with the approach for firms that need to communicate but that do not sell anything, for example many non-profit marketers. Care also has to be exercised so that the policy is not applied too rigidly. If sales are falling, this may not mean that communication expenditure as a percentage should also fall.

Factors influencing spending on communication

A firm's communication needs will vary according to the particular situation. New firms or organisations marketing new products may establish awareness as a central communication objective, while another firm operating in a highly competitive environment may need to keep up with the communication activities of competitors. Communication will play an important part in the firm's positioning decision. Establishing a distinctive image in people's minds may be achieved largely through communication activities. Changes in the firm's environment may give rise to the need for a communication campaign, as could changes in role or circumstances.

The problem that many smaller firms can have in making decisions about their marketing communication budget is that financial resources may be limited. However, not all communication has to be bought in. While communication through non-personal channels, such as the use of advertising, may involve direct outlays, other channels may not. Firms should remember that their staff, physical resources and time are also communication resources. Company personnel can communicate to target audiences in a variety of settings; in-house layout of publications may be more cost-effective than obtaining this service from printers; and events and contacts provide an opportunity for the firm to communicate with receivers.

In deciding on the marketing communication budget, the firm should seek to maximise value. This value will not refer solely to value for money but will include value for time and effort spent and value for attention or coverage gained or publicity generated.

The promotional mix

The promotional mix refers to the different promotional options available to the marketer. There are four main elements: advertising, sales promotion, public relations, and personal selling. The essential question for the marketer is, which elements or combination of elements are most appropriate?

It is important that marketing communication activities are integrated. While advertising generally remains the most important communication medium for many FMCG companies, greater sophistication and expectation on the part of consumers, new and fragmenting media and the availability of highly focused communication modes have seen an increase in sales promotion and below-the-line expenditure and a greater use of such instruments as direct mail and sponsorship. This is well illustrated in the case of the H. J. Heinz Company, which spent $1,700 million in marketing its four thousand varieties around the world in 1995 (Smyth, 1996). Heinz cut its purchase of network television advertising but turned to using cable television. The company also used data-based and one-to-one marketing approaches to complement its above-the-line advertising. These included a magazine, *Heinz at Home*, which was posted to four million households in Britain. Public relations activities were used judiciously, as were merchandising and outdoor advertising.

In relation to industrial companies and business-to-business marketers, there is a traditional tendency to use relatively more personal selling than the marketers of consumer goods as a means of communication. Industrial and business-to-business marketers will of course use other forms of communication; the relative mix, as with marketers of consumer goods, will depend on the nature of the product or service.

Above the line and below the line

Above the line is a term generally used to describe advertising; *below the line* is used to describe promotions. In the Irish marketing communication industry, for example, above-the-line suppliers include advertising agencies, media buying specialists, national and regional newspapers, magazines, the broadcast media, mobile advertising, cinema advertising, the internet, and specialist media—in other words, firms involved in the production and transmission of advertising (*Irish Marketing Journal*, 1997).

Below-the-line suppliers include a broad range of companies involved in the creation and implementation of promotional campaigns and activities, such as direct-marketing companies, sales promotion consultants, public relations consultants, conference and event organisers, tele-marketing, in-store promotions and merchandising, press cutting agencies, and promotional merchandise.

Both above-the-line and below-the-line firms use the services of production specialists. The production industry includes a wide variety of companies specialising in such areas as design and graphics, slides, copywriting, typesetting, printing, audiovisual equipment, animation, film and video production, and sound recording.

The distinction between above and below the line is not always clear (sometimes communication that involves a combination of above-the-line and below-the-line activities is known as 'through-the-line'). As the following panel demonstrates, there are ways of communicating about products and services on television that do not involve conventional television advertising.

... AND THERE'S ONE FOR EVERYONE IN THE AUDIENCE

This was the often-heard remark of Gay Byrne, presenter of 'The Late Late Show', the world's longest-running talk show, when giving away products to the studio audience. Such was the nature of the programme that the audience could expect to go home with various products given by manufacturers to gain exposure on this popular programme. This is known as programme enhancement, and it has become an accepted part of radio and television programming.

Usually the give-aways are linked to an event such as a product launch or a company anniversary. In addition, manufacturers or service providers will also sponsor prizes for television and radio shows. On 'The Late Late Show' these usually form the basis of a postal quiz, giving the viewer the chance to win.

Producers consider that such competitions and give-aways complement the entertainment value of their programme. Guidelines exist in television and radio stations so that broadcasters do not show favouritism to particular manufacturers, and programmes do not become over-commercialised. In the case of 'The Late Late Show', give-aways are limited and agreed in advance of the show. From the marketer's viewpoint, programme enhancement does provide an opportunity to communicate and create goodwill. Many marketers consider the exposure to be on a par with or greater than exposure gained through advertising.

Source: Richard Brophy, 'One for everyone in the audience?', *Checkout Ireland*, December 1997.

Product placement on films or television programmes is also a below-the-line activity. In 1998 Harp lager appeared in an episode of the American television series 'Friends' (*Sunday Tribune*, 19 April 1998), in which one of the characters was seen drinking a bottle that Guinness had supplied free of charge to the production company (it being illegal to pay for product placements in the United States).

The increase in below-the-line activity by many marketers caused some to suggest that traditional above-the-line advertising would decline in importance (Fanning, 1997). Below-the-line has certainly increased in importance; other developments—such as direct marketing, new media, a more marketing-aware consumer, and an inability by advertisers to explain the precise effects on sales of a given level of advertising expenditure—have contributed to increased scepticism about advertising. However, advertising power could also be considered to be quite intangible; it can add meaning, add value to products, and create a culture around a brand.

ELEMENTS IN THE PROMOTIONAL MIX

Traditionally the promotional mix includes advertising, promotions, personal selling, and public relations. We will also include sponsorship, which is growing in importance as a communication medium.

ADVERTISING

Advertising can involve the use of the press, publications, poster sites, radio, television, cinema, outdoor advertising, free newspapers and other advertising media to transmit the message. Advertising is therefore a very public form of communication and is suitable for messages that need to be transmitted to a wide audience. Messages can be repeated several times on press, radio or television or can be placed on poster sites for long periods. This increases the opportunity for receivers to see or hear the advertisement. The message can be transmitted using words, pictures, music, characters, and a wide variety of symbols.

Advertising campaigns can be easily costed, as advertising rates and audience details are available. The media buying departments in advertising agencies are skilled at obtaining the best rates available. As rates can vary, for instance on television by time of day, the media buying department will seek to obtain the broadcast times that are most likely to reach the intended audience.

In general, television is the most expensive advertising medium. A critical calculation in determining the advertising medium to use will be the *cost per thousand* (CPT): this is the cost of the advertisement per thousand viewers, listeners, or readers. It is calculated according to the time at which the advertisement is broadcast or published and the nature of the viewers, listeners or readers of the programme or publication.

The annual surveys—Joint National Readership Research (JNRR), Joint National Media Research (JNMR), and Joint National Listenership Research (JNLR)—all provide updated information on the audiences that most of the advertising media reach. In relation to television, the weekly TAM (television audience monitor) ratings give information on the viewership of programmes and commercial break data for the national channels in Ireland and limited data on other channels.

Advertising models

Advertising models are useful attempts at understanding how advertising works. A number of models that have been developed over time are summarised below. These are known as *hierarchy of effects models*, as the stages are hierarchical and follow on from each other. All the models emphasise the role, awareness or attention at the initial stage; awareness is therefore an important precondition for successful advertising. Other models of advertising concentrate more on the qualitative aspects of the advertisement. These suggest that it is factors such as novelty or the emotive aspects that best explain how the advertisement works.

The DAGMAR model

The DAGMAR model (Colley, 1961) suggests that the consumer or receiver moves through a number of states of mind.

Unawareness
↓
Awareness
↓
Comprehension
↓
Conviction
↓
Purchase

The AIDA model

The AIDA model suggests that the individual goes through a number of stages: cognitive, affective, and conative. Attention requires thought processes to engage; these are cognitive. If interest is stimulated it leads to desire, both of which are emotional or affective states. Finally, if desire leads to action, for example purchase, this is conative.

Attention
↓
Interest
↓
Desire
↓
Action

The Lavidge and Steiner model

This model proposed that—following awareness—knowledge, liking and preference led to conviction. Only when the consumer was so convinced would purchasing take place.

Awareness
↓
Knowledge
↓
Liking
↓
Preference
↓
Conviction
↓
Purchase

Ehrenberg's ATR model

This model proposed that there are three essential stages and that the principal role of advertising is to create awareness, which would induce trial. This would act as a reinforcer of behaviour.

None of the advertising models completely explains how advertising works. Each of them may be shown to work in particular settings or with particular individuals, but they are not all-encompassing.

Perhaps it is easier to examine what advertising can achieve to demonstrate its value and importance. Advertising is fundamentally about communicating information. This can be done with words, pictures, music, and other devices. Advertising can create powerful imagery in support of firms, products, or brands. It can emphasise their unique selling points and in so doing strengthen competitive advantage. Brand personality can be communicated and developed through advertising.

Advertising not only influences consumers' behaviour before purchase but also helps to reinforce post-purchase behaviour. Consumers may look to advertising for reassurance after they have bought the product. Advertising can help reduce the post-purchase cognitive dissonance the consumer may be experiencing; this is the discomfort the consumer may experience as a result of conflicting information, which can be particularly apparent after high-involvement purchases. The consumer may experience dissonance, for example, on the basis of information obtained from a competitor's advertising. One study on the effect of written post-purchase communication (Ward and Turley, 1996) showed that it can be effective in increasing post-purchase customer satisfaction.

There is also a strong role for advertising in marketing channels, where it can influence channel members' perceptions and behaviour. Typically, when products or promotions are being launched to the trade, the marketer will also outline the amount of advertising support that will be provided. This may be influential in the trade member's decision to stock the product or take part in the promotion.

TYPES OF ADVERTISING

There are a number of different types of advertising. *Brand advertising* emphasises the features, benefits and image of particular brands. It is important for image-building and will be significant in the decision on brand positioning. Consider the illustration in fig. 9.9 for Siúcra.

Fig. 9.9: Siúcra

Brand advertising is used to create awareness of the brand or to remind consumers to buy. It can be used to stimulate demand for the product or service in general or to encourage selective demand, such as for a special offer or feature. Some brand advertising has even become mini-drama, as the following panel illustrates.

NICOLE, PAPA, AND CLIO

In 1991 Renault launched an advertising campaign in Britain and Ireland for its Clio car model. With her father snoozing quietly in his deck chair, Nicole sneaked off for an afternoon of love, little knowing that Papa had the same idea. This has been the basis for the script ever since, and several commercials have been made. The actors who play the parts have just one word each: 'Papa' and 'Nicole.'

Television advertisements with story lines have proved popular with viewers. Nescafé also had a popular series of advertisements for its Gold Blend product; there was even a Gold Blend book.

Source: *Sunday Times*, 31 May 1998.

Co-operative advertising occurs where two marketers decide to combine resources for a joint advertising campaign. Usually they are not in competition but complement each other. Consider the joint campaign by Ryanair and Boeing in fig 9.10.

Fig. 9.10: Ryanair and Boeing

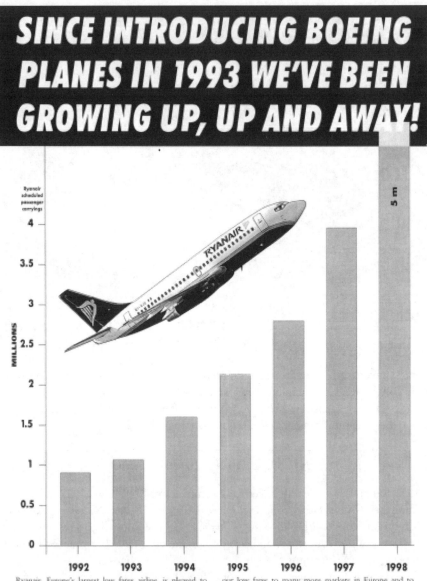

SINCE INTRODUCING BOEING PLANES IN 1993 WE'VE BEEN GROWING UP, UP AND AWAY!

Ryanair, Europe's largest low fares airline, is pleased to announce the acquisition of 45 Next Generation 737-800 series aircraft from Boeing, the world's largest aircraft manufacturer. These aircraft will enable Ryanair to offer our low fares to many more markets in Europe and to continue to expand Europe's largest and most successful low fares airline. Ryanair and Boeing, an unbeatable team!

The microchip manufacturer Intel has also engaged in co-operative advertising with computer manufacturers. The campaign based on the 'Intel inside' message was judged successful and was credited with helping the computer manufacturers Dell and Gateway 2000 in their direct marketing campaigns (Johnson, 1997).

Corporate advertising is used by companies and organisations as a means of building an image and creating a strong corporate identity. This can be important for reinforcing shareholders' confidence in the firm or emphasising particular issues that may be of concern to the firm. It has been argued that corporate advertising is aimed at three specific constituencies: business customers, opinion-formers (investors, politicians, activists, and the media), and employees (*MII News*, May–June 1998). Some companies may use an umbrella corporate advertisement, which is supplemented with additional brand-specific or product-specific advertisements.

DEVELOPING A NEW CORPORATE ADVERTISEMENT

On St Patrick's Day, 1998, Aer Lingus began a national television advertising campaign with a new sixty-second commercial. It was five years since the company had shown a corporate advertisement on television, and it felt that this was unacceptable for a brand of its size and that it needed to get back in touch with its audience. In the intervening period the company had undergone some restructuring and a number of changes, including the launch of a new logo in 1996. The airline was budgeting £3 million over two years for showing the advertisement. A further £300,000 was to be spent on showing a seventy-second cinema version.

Research was commissioned to define the vision and values of the Aer Lingus brand. These were defined as intimacy, intuition, and professionalism. This emphasised what the company considered to be its core brand strength: an ability to be world-class in how it related to air travellers.

With its brand agreed, and clear on the message it wanted to convey, Aer Lingus decided to switch advertising agencies, and put the account out to tender. In the final round it was between McConnell's, DDFH&B, and Irish International, with Irish International being selected. 'Our task was to take the brand essence and to bring it to life in the television advertisement,' said Dave McGloughlin, director of Irish International. 'As much as possible, it needed to give a good sense of the airline and its values.'

The commercial was technically quite complex. A production technique known as 'morphing' was used to create the effects, and quite a lot of post-production work was required. The morphing technique enabled the advertisement to show characters metamorphosing into different versions of themselves. The scenes were shot in a variety of locations, including Croke Park and a warehouse containing a specially constructed aircraft cabin for the flight scenes. The sound track was an Irish instrumental version of the Cyndi Lauper song 'True Colours' performed by traditional musicians. The overall structure of the commercial was an attempt at demonstrating that the airline had the ability to see beyond face value. Scenes that showed a customer lost in a strange terminal or feeling stressed or tired provided an opportunity to demonstrate that the airline could recognise this and deal with it in a human way. The television advertisement will eventually be shown in Britain and the United States.

At the same time as screening the corporate campaign, the company continued to use press advertising to promote particular offers, individual brands, and the airline's frequent-flier scheme, and also to attack competitors. In Britain and on the Continent the company had launched a press campaign using well-known personalities such as the racing driver Eddie Jordan, the folk singer Shane McGowan, and the model Pamela Brannigan. This was part of a planned campaign that would be updated with new personalities over time.

A press campaign on the home market attacked the no-frills airlines head on. Ten advertisements were developed, emphasising, among other things, that Aer Lingus gave pre-assigned seating and had no credit card booking charges.

Sources: Monica Igoe, 'Sky wars', *Business and Finance*, 23 April 1998; 'Aer Lingus', *TAB Network News*, vol. 2, no. 2, April–June 1998.

Corporate bodies know that their image is much more than a corporate logo or advertisement: the image surrounding the message is just as important as the message itself. Just as marketers seek to develop brand personality and identity, so too should it be examined for the company itself. In the early nineties Allied Irish Banks launched a new logo and visual identity. This was part of a process engaged in by the bank symbolising a change in organisational structure and corporate values (Bourke, 1994). A similar exercise was engaged in by the financial services providers Friends Provident and the First National Building Society, both of which decided to change their corporate identity in 1998.

BEING FIRST MAKES AN IMPRESSION

Unknown to each other, two financial institutions decided to test consumer reaction to alternative names as part of a series of steps to create new identities. The two had different motivations but got a similar response: that the word 'first' sent a positive, progressive signal to potential customers.

In early April 1998, First National Building Society announced that, subject to approval by shareholders, it was to become First Active PLC. Three weeks later Eureko and its subsidiaries Friends Provident and Celtic International became Friends First.

First National's primary rationale for a new name was its plan to transform itself from a building society into a public limited company, but there was also some confusion with other financial institutions. There was a First National Bank, a public limited company trading in Belfast, which would have precluded it from being floated on the stock exchange with that name. The company conducted research to find out what consumers wanted, and the response was that the word 'first' was strong, as was the company's beehive device. An international design consultancy was then called on to come up with a new identity. The company immediately launched a new First Active home loan with a £400,000 campaign on radio, 48-sheet poster sites, and bus shelters. It was estimated that it would take approximately eighteen months to change the signage at the company's 170 branches throughout the country. This would cost an additional £1 million.

⚡ Friends First

For Eureko the motivation behind the rebranding was that it had nine separate brands under the group umbrella and it wanted to make a strong statement about the company's existing and future position in the financial services market. Its businesses, which had over 200,000 customers, covered everything from fund management and life insurance to motor and household insurance. It engaged Lansdowne Market Research to talk to brokers and customers, and what emerged was that the strongest brand was Friends Provident. The word 'Friends' was strong, but people did not relate to Provident, which sounded old-fashioned and somewhat cold; by contrast, the word 'First' was considered modern and innovative. A design company was commissioned to come up with a new identity, and this was launched by replacing all letter-headings with new Friends First stationery. Some 8½ million sheets had to be ready for the day. The budget ran to £1.2 million, including a £200,000 advertising campaign, split between television, outdoor and press advertising.

FRIENDS PROVIDENT
LIFE ASSURANCE COMPANY

Source: A. O'Toole, 'Being First makes impression', *Sunday Business Post*, 10 May 1998.

The corporate logo is therefore an important feature of corporate image. Symbols such as the Nike tick and the Coca-Cola typeface may be instantly recognisable, but they also require support in the form of the development of an image and personality. Corporate advertising can play a significant role in this. The corporate image may be a determining factor in the firm's ability to extend into new markets or to develop or extend product ranges. Consumers may prefer to buy from a firm that has a good corporate reputation.

The regulation of advertising

Advertising is generally regulated in most countries, both through public regulation and codes of advertising standards that may be imposed by the advertising profession. In Ireland there is the Advertising Standards Authority, which exists 'to promote and enforce throughout Ireland the highest standards of advertising in all media of communication so as to ensure, in co-operation with all concerned, that no advertising contravenes or offends against these standards having regard inter-alia to the code of advertising standards in Ireland' (Advertising Standards Authority, 1989). The code deals with such issues as the legality, truthfulness, decency and honesty of advertisements. Specific sections deal with advertising to children, comparative advertising, and advertising claims in relation to specific categories, such as health and slimming products, tobacco, and alcohol. The essence of good advertising, as defined in the code, is:

• All advertisements should be legal, decent, honest, and truthful.
• All advertisements should be prepared with a sense of responsibility both to the consumer and to society.

- All advertisements should conform to the principles of fair competition as generally accepted in business.

Each year the Advertising Standards Authority publishes a report on the complaints made by the public or by firms. These complaints are investigated by the authority, and conclusions are drawn. If a complaint is upheld, the authority can request that an advertisement be withdrawn or modified.

ADVERTISING MEDIA

The outdoor sector

The outdoor sector essentially refers to poster sites, which can come in various sizes and are priced accordingly. Sites range from bus shelter sites to larger '48-sheet' and '96-sheet' hoardings and are available throughout the country, enabling marketers to have national campaigns.

The advantages of outdoor advertising are considered to be the number of sites and the fact that posters are on display twenty-four hours a day. Developments in the sector have included new sizes, illuminated sites, and sites that allow a number of posters to be displayed automatically in rotation. Fig 9.11 illustrates some examples of poster campaigns for a number of products.

Fig. 9.11: Outdoor campaigns

Source: *Deadline*

Figures for 1996 show that the top five spenders on outdoor advertising (table 9.1) were brands of alcoholic drink. Some of these brands, such as Hennessy and Smirnoff, being spirits, are prohibited from advertising on television or radio; others use outdoor advertising as part of their total communication strategy.

Table 9.1: Top spenders on outdoor advertising, 1996

1. Bulmer's cider	£524,800
2. Guinness stout	£524,300
3. Hennessy cognac	£456,300
4. Smirnoff vodka	£287,500
5. Cooper's cider	£275,300
6. Coca-Cola	£257,700
7. Bacardi rum	£254,500
8. Dunne's Stores	£253,500
9. Superquinn	£246,200
10. Ritz	£237,300

Source: Advertising Statistics Ireland, 1996.

Television

Television provides advertisers with a powerful medium that allows the use of visual imagery as well as sound track and voice-overs. Television advertising was dominated until the nineties by RTE, which had two channels, RTE1 and Network 2. In 1996 Teilifís na Gaeilge (now TG4) was launched, and in 1998 TV3 was launched, which increased competition in the sector.

Advertising on RTE television is limited to six minutes per hour, while on radio it is four minutes per hour. Television advertising costs depend on the number of times an advertisement is screened and the time of the broadcast. Generally, advertising during the most popular programmes costs more. The costs of advertising are listed on a *rate card*. The media buying departments in advertising agencies are skilled at buying time for television advertising, based on the number and profile of viewers watching at particular times of the day. Media buyers typically negotiate advertising packages with the television stations to ensure that advertisements are broadcast at the times when they are most likely to reach the target audience.

In addition to running its two channels, RTE pays a subvention to TG4 as part of the national station's public service broadcasting obligations. This was £4 million in 1996 and £6 million in 1997.

In Northern Ireland the main terrestrial channels are BBC1 and BBC2, Ulster Television, and Channel 4. Advertising is not available on BBC but is available on Ulster Television, which was received by 74 per cent of Irish homes in 1998. Some advertisers in the Republic use UTV for this reason. Channel 4, along with other channels, such as MTV, Sky, and NBC Europe, have London bases and have various levels of penetration in the Irish market. One channel in Britain, Tara TV, is directed at people of Irish descent living in Britain.

The main challenges in the television industry in the late nineties and the early years of the new century are the launch of TV3 and the impact of digital television.

TV3, which pays an annual rental to RTE for the use of its transmission system, is allowed nine minutes of advertising per hour. The station was established at a cost of between £15 and £20 million by a consortium of private investors. RTE derives approximately one-third of its cash flow from the television licence fee (RTE Annual Report, 1996). TV3 will not receive any licence fee revenue. It will provide more competition for television advertising, and there is also likely to be competition between TV3 and RTE to secure popular British or American programmes. In 1998 RTE's two channels had 45 per cent of the multi-channel audience, and initial indications were that TV3 would be aimed at those watching British television. This channel was also aiming primarily at the 15–44 age group.

Digital television

Digital television is essentially the combination of telephony, computing and television technology. The result is an interactive television that will completely replace existing analogue technology. It is likely to begin to have an impact in the early years of the century (Carter, 1996). There are four main digital broadcasting alternatives: digital terrestrial transmission (DTT), digital cable transmission (DCT), digital satellite transmission (DST), and digital microwave transmission (DMT). Fig. 9.12 illustrates how these can be broadcast to the home.

Fig. 9.12: Digital signals in the home

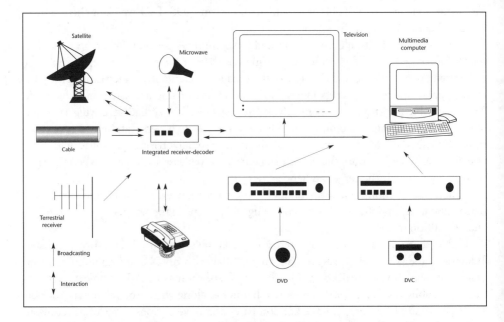

Source: U. Reimers, 'Digital broadcasting: the future of television', *Physics World*, April 1998.

In the late nineties RTE made a submission to the Government on digital television, the total cost of which it estimated at between £35 and £40 million. RTE proposed to establish a digital terrestrial system. A strategic partner was considered essential for this development (*Marketing*, March 1998). TV3 has had digital broadcast facilities from its inception.

By the late nineties approximately 50 per cent of homes had cable television, which in effect meant that 50 per cent of the network for distributing digital television already existed (Cable Communication Association of Ireland, 1997). Satellite penetration has been much lower than for cable, so the impact of DST may be limited as a result. This contrasts with Britain, where British Sky Broadcasting was ready to launch a digital satellite system in 1998 (*Sunday Business Post*, 25 January 1998).

The Office of the Director of Telecommunications Regulation commissioned a report on the technological and economic implications of digital terrestrial television. This was published in 1998 and favoured the use of cable for digital television transmission, as opposed to the DTT system recommended by RTE.

The implications for viewers will be the need to eventually replace their existing television sets with a new generation of wide, flat, wall-screen televisions (*Business and Finance*, 15 May 1997). It will also be possible to buy set-top adapters for existing analogue sets. In addition, the viewer will need to buy a decoder to receive the digital signal. These will be supplied by the broadcaster or cable operator.

Digital television is expected to bring dramatic changes to the content and infrastructure of broadcasting. At the most basic level it allows for many more channels. Lower production costs will mean that regional and local content becomes cheaper to produce. Additional services to the viewer will include near video-on-demand, multimedia and interactive television, more sophisticated home shopping, and internet access.

Whatever the broadcast system chosen, digital television has implications for marketers. There will be a number of opportunities but also threats. If viewers can have a keyboard attached to their television they will be able to respond on line to advertising, special offers, or competitions. Marketers will be able to use this interaction to build databases on viewers: for example, those with special interests could be specifically identified. Interaction means that direct response to advertising may become easier. When advertisements are being shown, for example, an icon could appear on the side of the screen inviting the viewer to click on it and get more information on the product. Advertising for a particular brand could incorporate price promotions, with the viewer again being invited to click on an icon leading to their frequent-shopper card being automatically credited with a discount the next time they buy the product in the supermarket (Branagan, 1997).

There will also be threats. Digital television will mean more choice of channels for the viewer, but the fragmentation that may result could mean that advertising to a national audience may become more difficult. It will also mean more widespread pay-per-view television: in other words, particular programmes or televised events may be available only to subscribers. While in principle this means a more focused audience for an advertiser, it may be a smaller audience if pay-per-view leads to a reduction in the total number of viewers.

Radio

The Joint National Listenership Research of 1997 showed that 89 per cent of adults listened to the radio every weekday. This high level of listenership means that radio is a particularly important medium. There are two state-owned national radio stations, RTE Radio 1 and 2FM. In 1997 an independent station, Radio Ireland, was launched, which was later renamed Today FM. In addition there are twenty-one local stations, each of them holding a franchise for a particular region. A number of community radio stations were also licensed in 1998.

Market shares for radio listenership are calculated according to the total number of minutes spent listening to a particular station. The 1997 JNLR research, for example, showed that the independent stations had a national market share of 43 per cent, while Radio 1 and 2FM had a 33 and 22 per cent share, respectively.

Table 9.2: Radio audiences, 1997

	Market share, 1997 (%)	Market share, 1996 (%)
Highland Radio	73	79
MWR FM	58	61
WLR FM	58	57
South-East Radio	56	52
96 FM	54	55
96/103 FM	52	49
Clare FM	51	46
103 FM	50	45
Radio Kilkenny	44	48
NWR FM	44	47
Radio Kerry	41	54
Tipp FM	41	46
Shannonside/Northern Sound	38	44
LM FM	34	34
Radio 1	33	33
Midlands Radio	32	30
East Coast Radio	31	21
Galway Bay FM	28	33
Tipp Mid-West	25	35
2FM	22	21
CKR FM	19	27
98 FM	16	18
FM 104	16	15

Source: *Deadline*, March 1998 (JNLR-MRBI, 1996, 1997; IRS).

In spite of high levels of listenership, radio tends to get a smaller share of advertisers' expenditure relative to television and outdoor advertising. In 1998 the radio stations agreed to establish a Radio Promotion Bureau to develop the medium as a whole and to promote its strength to audiences and advertisers alike.

In Northern Ireland, BBC Radio Ulster enjoyed the largest market share in 1997, as table 9.3 demonstrates.

Table 9.3: Radio market shares, Northern Ireland, 1996–7

	Market share, 1997 (%)	Market share, 1996 (%)
BBC Radio Ulster	19.2	20.3
Cool FM	18.7	17.1
Downtown	14.4	15
Atlantic 252	9.6	9.1
BBC Radio 1	6.9	8.7
Belfast City Beat	4.2	3.4
BBC Radio 2	3.5	3.6
2FM*	3.5	2
BBC Radio 4	3	3.4
BBC Radio 5 Live	2.8	3.2
RTE1*	2.1	2
Virgin 1215	1.9	1.4
Classic FM	1.5	1.6
Talk Radio	0.5	0.9
BBC Radio 3	0.2	0.2

*RTE comparisons made with statistics from second quarter of 1997.
Source: *Deadline*, March 1998 (AV Browne Advertising-RAJAR, 1997).

Digital radio

As with television, digital technology will also affect radio broadcasting. Digital audio broadcasting (DAB) will provide CD-quality sound, interference-free reception, and a range of multimedia services, including the ability to display a text screen. It will have most impact in the early years of the century, though the first digital service in Britain was expected in 1999 (*Marketing*, February 1998). There will also be implications for radio manufacturers, with the first DAB Walkmans expected by 2005.

Press and magazines

The Joint National Readership Research, conducted by Lansdowne Market Research, is used by media buyers to calculate the most cost-effective way of spending print advertising budgets. In addition to the JNRR figures, circulation figures audited by the Audit Bureau of Circulations (ABC) allow advertisers to calculate the number of readers a publication has per copy.

The readership of individual newspapers and magazines can change, as table 9.4 shows. A particular publication knows that if readership figures are going down, this can affect advertising income. Imported newspapers from Britain also had an impact, though these were not included in the JNRR research. Individual newspapers often highlight the results of the JNRR, as fig 9.13 illustrates.

Table 9.4: Newspaper readership, 1996–7

	1996–7 (thousand)	(A)	1997 (thousand)	(A)	Difference
Sunday Independent	1,152	42	1,126	40	–2%
Sunday World	968	35	977	35	+1%
Irish Independent	612	22	598	21	–2%
RTE Guide	588	21	585	21	–16%
Evening Herald	393	14	379	14	–4%
Star	376	14	373	13	–1%
Irish Farmers' Journal	331	12	337	12	+2%
Irish Times	283	10	286	10	+1%
Sunday Tribune	256	9	261	9	+2%
Woman's Way	241	9	230	8	–5%
Examiner	222	8	219	8	–1%
Image	127	5	116	4	–9%
U	110	4	106	4	–4%
Sunday Business Post	107	4	131	5	+22%
IT	92	3	93	3	+1%
Evening Echo	63	2	67	2	+6%
Hot Press	58	2	44	2	–24%

(A) Percentage of adult readership, June 1996–June 1997.
Source: JNRR-MRBI, 1997.

The importance of regional newspapers should not be underestimated. In 1998 there were 63 regional newspapers in the Republic and 48 in Northern Ireland. The 1997 JNRR survey showed that in the Republic one in every two adults reads a regional weekly newspaper. Readership among younger people was also strong, with 12 per cent of those between 15 and 19 and 17 per cent of those between 25 and 34 reading a local newspaper weekly. Farmers constituted 24 per cent of readership. Thirty-five per cent of the readers of regional newspapers were in Leinster (excluding Dublin).

Public transport

Advertising on the interior and exterior of buses and trains, as well as in railway and bus stations, is handled by a company called TDI. Advertisements can be displayed on designated panels inside or outside the vehicle; in addition, an entire bus can be painted with a logo or advertising message. In Dublin it is also possible to have a design on a whole DART train, as Guinness has done. Developments in the sector have included illuminated advertising panels on the outside of buses, improving the visibility of the advertisements after dark (*Marketing*, January 1998).

Fig. 9.13: The Irish Times

NOT ONLY ARE WE GREAT AT OUR ABC's, NOW WE CAN COUNT ALL THE WAY TO 283,000!

According to the JNRR, 283,000 adults* read The Irish Times each day. That represents a rise of 11,000. Which means there are now even more people in the right place. More women, more housewives, more Dubliners, more under 35 year olds, in fact more of the people you want to reach. So if you want to know the best way to attract ABC1 readers, it's elementary.

*JNRR July 1996 - June 1997

THE IRISH TIMES
THE RIGHT PLACE - THE RIGHT TIMES

Cinema advertising

The cinema enjoyed a renaissance in the mid to late nineties, and by 1998 Ireland had the highest rate of cinema attendance in Europe (*Euromonitor*, March 1998). In 1988 cinema admissions were 6 million; in 1997 the figure was 12 million. The importance of cinema advertising increased as a result, with many marketers using it as part of their advertising mix.

The biggest group of cinema advertisers was the drinks industry, accounting for 45 per cent of advertising revenue in 1997. The top ten cinema advertisers in 1997 are listed in table 9.5. One agency, Carlton Screen Advertising, was responsible for putting commercials on all but three of the 327 screens (223 in the Republic, 104 in Northern Ireland) in 1997.

Table 9.5: Top ten cinema advertisers

January–November 1997

1. Murphy's brewery
2. Showerings
3. Guinness Group Sales
4. Tennents Ireland (Caffrey's)
5. Nike
6. Levi-Strauss
7. Coca-Cola
8. Cadbury
9. Unilever
10. Wrangler

Source: M. Cullen, 'Screen player', *Marketing*, January 1998.

The growth in cinema attendance has been attributed to the age profile of the population and to the arrival of multiplex chains, such as UCI and Virgin. The 15–34 age group is particularly important. People of this age tend to be light television viewers and to want to be out as many nights a week as possible (*Marketing*, January 1998). Standards of customer service have improved, in the form of booking facilities, air-conditioning, digital stereo sound, and smoke-free auditoriums. Advertisers can book advertising on a screen-by-screen basis, which is important when considering geographical campaigns.

The internet

The internet was originally developed in the United States for military purposes but is now a series of linked networks spanning the globe. It can be used by companies and individuals for sending e-mail messages, transferring files, advertising products and services, and carrying out other transactions. As a result its marketing applications are widespread, particularly for research, communication, promotion and sales transactions. The introduction of digital television means that television sets can be interactive, which is a potential threat to the internet.

The use of the internet is considered to have a number of advantages for marketers (Paul, 1996). It presents international communication opportunities, is becoming more accessible as consumers and businesses become more familiar with personal computers, and allows the user to interact with the marketer on line. The main problem has been security; the possibility that transactions, such as the consumer giving a credit card number, can be intercepted by someone else has probably reduced its attractiveness.

The possibilities of the worldwide web for marketers include corporate sites, marketing sites, service sites, and commerce sites (O'Brien, 1997). Corporate web sites can provide basic information about the company, such as financial reports or contacts. The marketing site will usually contain more detailed product information or details of promotions and therefore can be used as an aid to interactive selling. Service web sites could provide the customer with the facility to download programs, provide detailed technical information, or allow the customer to track the progress of their order. Commerce web sites allow commercial transactions to take place, which will involve a financial transaction; banks have been using such sites for international financial transactions.

With the growth in the internet as a communications medium there has been a corresponding growth in the number of internet specialists. These provide a variety of services, including the design of web pages, programming, training, and other internet support services. Worldwide web sites are an important link with consumers; some people argue that they can reduce the traditional problem of advertising waste because they are accessed by people who are directly interested in the company (Heinen, 1996).

Many firms began developing web sites in the late nineties. A number of issues are important in the design of pages. Web sites can perform a public relations role; they can therefore contain information about the company, its staff, and its products. Some firms place press statements or news updates about the company on their web site. Sites can also be used for data-base capture: for example, market research information can be obtained from people using the site. Pre-sales activities, such as requests for information or detailed specifications, can be entered, while post-sales activities, such as feedback on product performance, can be received on line.

Web sites can also play a role in customer loyalty schemes: for example, airlines or supermarkets can provide information on special offers aimed at members. With products such as Waterford crystal, where customers may become collectors of particular suites or ranges, web sites can be used to communicate with potential customers and with customers who have a special interest in the brand. This is particularly so for customers in the United States, who may like to be kept up to date on new items added to the range or on limited editions that are available. Similarly, airlines have been developing web sites for their frequent fliers to provide them with up-to-date information and offers.

Developing a strategy for the worldwide web

The use of the internet as a communications medium should be considered in the context of a company's general business strategy. The internet may have a role in achieving particular marketing objectives. This will depend on the nature of the product or service: for example, the internet may be especially good for reaching market niches. Customers' computer access and proficiency will be important factors; it will also be important to monitor what competitors are doing on their web sites. Web sites need to be maintained and updated; users will become frustrated if information is out of date.

As with advertising, marketers can be creative in the design of web sites, which will help differentiate them from competitors.

In 1998 Proctor and Gamble brought together some of the world's biggest advertisers to assess the use of the internet for advertising. In addition to opportunities, internet advertising presented some threats also.

P&G BRAINSTORMS TO IMPROVE INTERNET ADVERTISING

In August 1998 Proctor and Gamble brought together some of the world's biggest advertisers to see if they could reverse what many saw as a failure of internet advertising up to then. Executives from companies such as Coca-Cola, Unilever, Levi-Strauss and AT&T attended. It was estimated that annual spending on internet advertising in the United States exceeded $1,000 million, which is less than $1^{1}/_{2}$ per cent of expenditure on measured media.

There were several reasons for the meeting. Web 'surfers' were proving more elusive than television viewers. Other difficulties included immature technologies, a lack of agreement on how to measure who was browsing the web, and the very nature of the box-like banner advertisements, which users could easily click past. Many marketers were concerned that the internet would become a medium that supported transactions and that it would therefore be difficult to use for such issues as enhancing the emotional appeal of established brands.

Source: S. Beatty, 'P&G brainstorms to improve internet ads', *Wall Street Journal*, 13 August 1998.

Other advertising media

Additional advertising media range from posters mounted on the back of lorries and vans to light aircraft pulling advertising banners. These services are usually supplied by specialists or by promotional companies.

Ryanair offered advertisers the chance to advertise on the exterior of its aircraft (fig. 9.14). Some advertisers, such as Kilkenny Irish Beer and Jaguar Cars, did so. Kilkenny tied in the introduction of the aircraft advertisement with a promotional campaign for free flights (*Checkout Ireland*, January–February 1998). In December 1997 Ryanair also offered an in-flight television advertising facility on some of its aircraft (*Deadline*, October 1997).

Fig. 9.14: A Ryanair jet

THE RELATIONSHIP BETWEEN ADVERTISING AND SALES

An area of marketing that has been much researched is the link between expenditure on advertising and the sales generated. Some researchers have attempted to establish some mathematical relationship between the two, but the results have been inconclusive. There is no doubt that there can be a relationship, but there is no way of predicting how much should be spent on advertising to help generate sales. Advertising will be only one factor in the relationship; others, such as brand name, channels used, and image, will also . have a part to play. Indeed many products have been successful with very little advertising expenditure.

It is interesting, however, to compare the media expenditure by some of the top grocery brands in Ireland between 1990 and 1996 (table 9.6). The figures certainly show that the top brands—Lyon's tea in 1990 and Coca-Cola in 1996—spent and continued to spend significantly on media but that brands that spent a lot less, such as Dairygold and 7-Up, ended up with comparable sales levels.

Table 9.6: Media expenditure and sales of top grocery brands, 1990–6

	1990	
Brand	*Media expenditure*	*Sales value*
Coca-Cola	£572,000	£16.4 million
Lyon's tea	£515,000	£20.5 million
Kellogg's corn flakes	£370,000	£13.2 million
7-Up	£284,000	£18 million
Pampers	£256,000	£15.5 million

Coca-Cola	£795,000	£34 million+
Lyon's tea	£514,000	£22 million+
Pampers	£305,600	£21 million+
7-Up	£265,000	£22 million+
Dairygold	£ 60,000	£16 million

Top brands are based on value sales at RSP and are only product categories covered by A. C. Nielsen.

Source: Advertising Statistics Ireland; Institute of Advertising Practitioners in Ireland; Irish International Advertising Agency.

Table 9.6 does not, therefore, prove or disprove the contention that expenditure on advertising can be directly related to sales, as other factors have to be taken into account. In the case of Dairygold, for example, the brand engaged in a significant below-the-line promotional campaign with a radio show in 1996 and therefore spent less on above-the-line media (*Sunday Business Post*, 13 July 1997). It is probable that the other brands also engaged in below-the-line campaigns. There is certainly no doubt that none of the brands described would have been so successful and maintained that success without significant advertising and promotional spending.

Table 9.7 examines the individual advertising expenditure in different media.

Table 9.7: Top brands' share of advertising expenditure with media, 1990–6

	1990	1996
RTE television	76.3%	75.1%
Outdoor	10.2%	12.5%
RTE radio	7.4%	7.5%
National press	3.5%	1.3%
Magazines	2.3%	1.1%
Local radio*	0.3%	2.5%
Total expenditure	£11.23 million	£13.45 million

*Dublin and Cork stations only.

Source: Advertising Statistics Ireland; Institute of Advertising Practitioners in Ireland; Irish International Advertising Agency.

RTE television was the dominant medium for these brands, even though multi-channel availability during the period had grown from two-thirds of homes to over 70 per cent, and RTE's share of viewing fell from 51 per cent in peak time to 46 per cent.

EVALUATION AND EFFECTIVENESS OF ADVERTISING

Obviously, sales can be used as a test of the effectiveness of advertising. This is not, however, the only measure. Since the objectives of advertising can be quite broad, the measure of effectiveness must be similarly broad. Advertising research will therefore be important, and it may concentrate on measuring recall, perceptions, or attitudes.

If the objective of an advertising campaign is to change attitudes, these should be measured before and after the campaign to determine whether the advertising has had an influence. Some advertising campaigns attempt to include an interactive element. There has been an increase in the number of advertisements that include a phone number that the viewer can ring for more information (*Marketing*, 26 March 1998). Some advertisers have even incorporated the number in their advertising jingle. The insurance company Guardian Direct used the number 1850 282820 in this way, making it sound like an owl's call (the owl symbol was used by the company in its advertising). This example emphasises the importance of using numbers that are easy to remember or that the viewer can easily associate with the company.

The telecommunications company Esat also used a direct-response commercial in 1998, with positive results.

DIRECT RESPONSE PAYS OFF FOR ESAT

With over five thousand callers after its first airing, the Esat television commercial demonstrated the potential of direct-response television advertising. The commercial, which went out on a Thursday night, featured the chairman of the company, Denis O'Brien, and invited viewers to ring a freephone number if they wanted to switch from Telecom Éireann to Esat Home for international calls. It was claimed that twenty thousand people responded and expressed an interest in switching.

According to the company, it got 40 per cent more business during the month in which the commercial was shown than in the previous month; and 98 per cent of those who called set up an account.

The company decided to use the chairman in the commercial to give the company a human face. The commercial was also shot in the company's offices and used company staff rather than models.

Source: Christine Doherty, 'Direct response pays off for Esat', *Sunday Business Post*, 10 May 1998.

Consumer behaviour emphasises the difference between high-involvement and low-involvement decision-making. The level of involvement can have practical implications for advertisers. One study (Fanning, 1987) suggests that low-involvement theory means that the consumer passively processes advertisements, rather than consciously evaluating them. Behaviour that is often triggered by association of the advertisement with the product at the time of purchase precedes change of attitude. This theory was considered particularly relevant for fast-moving consumer goods. The advertising practitioner may not therefore need to concentrate on bringing the consumer through the traditional hierarchy-of-effects model: instead, the creative role of advertising becomes more important, the hope being that by differentiating and entertainment, people will associate the advertisement with the product. In other words, the more creative the advertising, the more effective it may be. To some extent, advertising in the nineties moved away from a strict statement of unique selling proposition to an approach that sought out inherent consumer needs and appealed to these needs in an entertaining manner.

With regard to research, the main implication of low-involvement theory was the swing away from the use of quantitative measures of advertising, such as recall measures, towards more qualitative approaches, such as focus group discussion. Quantitative measures, such as percentage recall, can measure only one dimension of the effectiveness of advertising: qualitative measures of perceptions or attitudes can yield additional, perhaps more insightful, information.

DEVELOPMENTS IN ADVERTISING

Given the competition for the receiver's attention from different advertisers using different media, there will always be an interest in developments that may attract more attention. In recent years much interest has been expressed in the internet and its use as an advertising medium. In the outdoor sector, new technology has created poster sites that can incorporate several advertisements that change in rotation, and sites with three-dimensional features.

It is probable that there will be increased competition in the television market, especially following the launch of TV3. New integrated media will develop. Internet, satellite and digital technologies will become more important, providing new challenges for conventional television providers. Direct-response television and pay television are also likely to be significant.

THE ROLE OF THE ADVERTISING AGENCY

Advertising agencies are essentially service providers who specialise in media buying and scheduling, the creation of advertising, and providing advice to their customers on their marketing communications. Many advertising agencies have become more integrated and in addition to their traditional role in above-the-line have also become engaged in below-the-line activities. This allows them to offer a more integrated service. In 1998 there were just under eighty advertising agencies in Ireland.

The specialist skills of the agency are in getting the best possible exposure for their clients with creative and attention-getting advertisements. The agency plays an important role in the development of brands. Many brands have been successfully built with advertising support.

SALES PROMOTION

Sales promotion involves the use of incentives to encourage purchase or sales. As a communication activity it is designed to create a sense of immediacy by offering reasons for purchase in the short term. It is therefore useful for stimulating sales. Typical forms of consumer sales promotion include samples, coupons, rebates, price reduction, banded offers, premiums, and competitions.

Promotions may involve product give-aways, and marketers often co-operate in joint promotions: the packet soup manufacturer Erin, for example, engaged in a joint promotion with the National Dairy Council. To encourage consumers to use milk in making packet soups, 250,000 packets of Erin soup were distributed with the morning milk delivery (*Checkout Ireland*, November 1997). Shortly afterwards one of Erin's main competitors, Knorr, launched an on-pack joint promotion with Cityjet involving a competition, the winner having the use of a plane to take fifty people away for a day (*Irish Marketing Journal*, February 1998).

Sales promotions can be aimed at the retailer or other channel members. These may include buying allowances for specified orders, samples, free goods, co-operative advertising support, or sales competitions. Sales promotions are also possible on industrial products and may also involve financial incentives, samples, and competitions.

Sales promotion has become a growth area in marketing practice, with many marketers using it to complement their advertising activity, while for firms with limited resources for advertising it can be an effective means of communication. The principal uses of promotions include attracting new users for the product, rewarding loyal users, and increasing purchasing frequency among occasional users. Sales promotions may help differentiate the product offering, and can be used to counteract competitors' activity.

Marketers launching new products or relaunching existing products may find sales promotions useful. Consider the example of the launch of round tea bags by Lyon's Tetley, where in the short term, at least, sampling coupled with a price promotion did increase market share.

DEVELOPING A ROUNDER TEA

In the mid-eighties Lyon's Tetley was examining the tea market in Britain. At the time it was the number 2 brand, after PG Tips, and it was losing market share to own-label products. Research established that brands of tea bags were being differentiated according to personality. The company began researching potential physical differentiation of the product. A large number of new ideas were generated, and a short-list of the better ideas was qualitatively researched.

This resulted in the identification of round bags as a concept worth being developed. Research on the concept was carried out that involved giving respondents traditional square tea bags to test for one week and then round bags to test for another week. Both square and round bags contained exactly the same quality and amount of tea. The result of the test was a significant preference for round bags, which were perceived as better-tasting and having a stronger flavour.

Further research was undertaken, and by 1989 the company decided to launch the round tea bag. The Tetley brand was relaunched in the southern half of England in July 1989, when 6½ million samples were delivered to households, consisting of sixteen tea bags and a 20p coupon. Almost immediately the brand share in southern England began to rise sharply, with Nielsen research showing that Tetley's market share, which had been 11 per cent in the summer of 1989, increased to 15 per cent by the end of the year.

Source: A. Phillips, J. Parfitt, and I. Prutton, 'Developing a rounder tea', *Esomar*, 1990.

The Tetley example shows how price coupons and free samples can be combined to encourage the trial of a new product. Other consumer promotions can involve the use of coupons inserted in newspapers, magazines, or other publications, coupon booklets, on-pack coupons, or direct-mail coupons. *Price packs* typically involve extra quantities of the product, such as '25 per cent extra free,' or blister packs that may comprise two packs together for a special price. *Cash rebates* could involve the consumer collecting tokens on the product and redeeming them for cash. *Banded offers* might include a free toothbrush on a packet of toothpaste. *Advertising gifts* may involve gift items that the buyer can send away for: thus a brand of breakfast cereal might offer buyers a bowl with its logo on it, or a coffee brand might offer a mug. Promotions can also involve the use of point-of-purchase displays or merchandising that emphasises the nature of the promotion and the offers that are available. *Competitions* for holidays, cars or other prizes may be used to promote the product and create a sense of excitement.

Research conducted in 1997 among grocery shoppers showed that there were high levels of participation in in-store promotions. Seventy-six per cent of respondents had participated in promotions in the past, while sixty per cent had bought grocery items on promotion on their last shopping trip.

As table 9.8 demonstrates, some promotions are more popular than others. The research also showed that women of 25–49 years of age with children are most likely to buy on promotion. Seventy-six per cent of respondents had participated in in-store tastings.

Table 9.8: Most popular promotions

Buy two at reduced price	50%
Extra quantity free	45%
Buy one, get one free	51%
Money-off coupons	42%
Collect tokens for offer	38%
Free gift with groceries	25%

Base: all buying items on promotion.

Source: Lansdowne Market Research; Shopper Focus; *Checkout Ireland*, November 1997.

The effectiveness of sales promotions

As with any form of communication, the marketer needs to assess the effectiveness of sales promotion efforts. Promotions represent a cost to the business, in some cases involving significant price discounts. It is important that promotional campaigns are planned and that specific objectives are set. One study (Wickstrom, 1987) found that the regularity in the consumption of a product group, a product or a brand will determine what type of effects will result from a promotion. Another study (Lambkin and O'Dwyer, 1994) explored the nature of couponing and coupon redemption; it found that coupon redemption rates are influenced by a variety of factors, including the company's promotional strategy, the method of coupon distribution used, the value of the coupon, and the effort and timing of the coupon drop.

Poor planning and wastage were found to be significant problems in the implementation of promotions. Evidence was presented that instant point-of-purchase coupons were more suitable for receiving higher redemption rates, and that ideally coupons should offer a discount of 15 to 20 per cent on the value of the product. The costs of couponing were emphasised, with an example of a 20p coupon that could cost the marketer as much as 43p when such factors as handling charges, distribution and redemption costs were calculated.

Sales promotion agencies

Just as with advertising, there are a number of sales promotion agencies that design and implement promotional campaigns for marketers. These may come up with creative ideas for promotions; they may also undertake the administrative aspects, such as sending out gifts or cash rebates. Other companies specialise in providing personnel for in-store promotions, such as product tastings.

Fulfilment companies specialise purely in the administrative aspects of sales promotion. Consumers may send tokens or coupons to them in exchange for gifts, samples, or rebates. Fulfilment companies should provide the marketer with *top-line reporting*, which involves updates on the proportion of coupons redeemed, gifts despatched, monetary value of the rebates sent out, and stock levels remaining. Profiles of respondents may be possible if some background information has been obtained. Top-line reporting is required if the marketer is to judge the effectiveness of the promotion, and will be required as a financial control where cash rebates are involved.

Planning sales promotions

Sales promotions should be attractive to the consumer, but the marketer needs to avoid the pitfall of discounting sales too heavily, and promotions that have higher costs than benefits. The domestic appliance manufacturer Hoover discovered this to its cost in 1993, when a very successful promotion cost the company more than it expected.

A SUCCESSFUL PROMOTION, BUT AT WHAT COST?

In 1993 the Hoover company began a promotion in Britain. Consumers who spent £100 or more on a Hoover vacuum cleaner were entitled to a voucher for two free transatlantic air tickets. The company calculated that redemption rates on the coupons would be low and that the cost would be more than covered by increased sales of its products.

The promotion worked well, and sales of vacuum cleaners increased substantially—so much so that the manufacturing plant in Scotland went on 24-hour production. Problems emerged, however, when customers began looking for their tickets. So many applied that Hoover's seat allocation with the airlines was quickly used up; complaints began when the company was unable to offer seats. The news media took up the story, and Hoover had to hastily arrange additional seat allocations, at a higher cost. Not enough seats could be secured, and the company was criticised in

Parliament, by the Consumers' Association, and in the media. It had not intended to mislead or disappoint but had been over-ambitious in its promotional planning.

In addition to the costs incurred in running the promotion, sales of Hoover vacuum cleaners declined immediately after the promotion ended. The small ads in local newspapers featured many advertisements offering unwanted new vacuum cleaners.

A similar promotion was run in the Irish market but was limited to a particular product in the Hoover range and involved the customer being able to buy two flights for the price of one.

Source: S. Dibb, L. Simkin, W. Pride, and O. Ferrell, *Marketing: Concepts and Strategies*, New York: Houghton-Mifflin 1997.

An issue that the marketer should consider when designing promotional campaigns is the long-term effects they may have on sales. The Hoover promotion, for example, had a long-term negative effect on sales of vacuum cleaners.

There is a danger inherent in promotions that the consumer will stockpile when the product is on promotion. One research study (Mela, Jedidi, and Bowman, 1998) suggested that stockpiling behaviour has changed over the years. The increased long-term exposure of households to promotions has reduced their likelihood of making category purchases on subsequent shopping trips. The study found an increasing tendency among consumers to 'lie in wait' for especially good promotions. This change could affect profitability in product categories.

Trade promotion is a feature of many marketers' activities. Distributors and retailers may expect buying allowances, free products, advertising and promotional support, contests, or prizes. Business conventions or trade shows may be used to communicate the promotion to the trade, or sales representatives may communicate the promotion directly. Trade promotions will often be undertaken in advance of consumer promotions: marketers may need to communicate to the trade to encourage them to stock the product or to participate in a particular promotion.

PERSONAL SELLING

Personal selling covers a wide variety of areas, including delivery, order-taking, building goodwill, educating customers, and providing technical support. Traditionally it involved interpersonal communication and was therefore useful for dealing with complicated products, where the receiver can ask questions. Usually, consumers are involved in very little direct selling; but there are exceptions. When Daewoo launched its cars in Britain and Ireland it sold directly to customers, using advertising to provide them with the necessary contact information (Simms, 1997).

Increasingly the internet is having an important role in selling. This does not involve the same level of interpersonal contact, but it does allow for interaction. One of the large computer multinationals, Dell, differentiates itself by selling directly to customers using the internet. In 1998 the company was recording worldwide sales of $4 million per day using the internet (O'Dwyer, 1998). The advantages to the company were considered to be a better ability to service and support customers, the ability to build to order, the elimination of unnecessary mark-ups in the distribution channel, a reduction in the time taken to get the product to the market, and a reduction in stock-carrying costs.

It remains to be seen what precise impact electronic sales will have on the personal selling process. It will certainly be an aid in selling products, but it may not be a complete replacement for personal selling. The process itself involves a number of stages, and these are described in the following section.

SETTING THE OBJECTIVES OF THE SALES FORCE

Objectives will vary between companies, but the sales force will usually be expected to perform a number of tasks. These should be specified and might include:

- finding and developing new accounts
- communicating information about the company's products or services
- presenting products
- answering questions
- providing service or support to the buyer
- gathering market intelligence
- preparing sales reports
- involvement in the planning of sales budgets
- dealing with customers' complaints or difficulties.

The objectives of the sales force can therefore be quite broad and are usually much more than simply selling the product, and it is important that sales personnel have a clear understanding of them. The objectives emphasise the importance of the role of the sales force in relationship marketing.

Sales force strategy

The essential element of sales force strategy must be understanding the customer's buying process, which can be quite complex in business-to-business selling. A variety of sales approaches are possible: for example, the salesperson can be an account manager, managing the relationship between company and buyer; other approaches may involve teams of salespeople being responsible for different products or territories. The sales force will usually be expected to engage in identifying new business and in developing existing accounts.

Structure of the sales force

Three main approaches are used in designing the structure of a sales force: territorial, product, and customer.

1. **Territorial structure.** Each salesperson is assigned a geographical area. This is quite a common approach. The salesperson is then responsible for this area and can build close contacts with buyers.
2. **Product structure.** Salespeople specialise in particular products from the company's range. This is commonly used for technical or industrial products.

3. **Customer structure.** Where salespeople sell to specific customers or industries, the sales force may be assigned to particular customers. This can also be a feature of business-to-business selling.

The structure chosen will depend on the nature of the company, its products, markets, and buyers.

Size of the sales force

The size of the sales force will depend on a number of factors, including the number of accounts, number of sales calls expected per day, or type of account. A formula can be used to calculate the required size of a sales force, based on call frequency, the number of customers, and the average number of calls that can be made:

$$N = \frac{1}{K} \; X \; [F1(C1) + F2(C2)]$$

where N = desired number of salespeople
Fn = call frequency required
Cn = number of customers
K = average number of calls the salesperson can make per year.

Suppose a marketer has two groups of customers, supermarkets and TSNs. There are 50 supermarkets and 400 TSNs that salespeople need to call to. Supermarkets require a sales call every two weeks, while TSNs require a weekly call. The average number of calls a salesperson can make per year, given distances to be covered and other factors, is 1,400:

$$N = \frac{1}{1,400} \; X \; [26(50) + 52(400)] = 16$$

In a research study carried out by the UCD Marketing Department in 1991 on the top thousand firms in Ireland it was found that the most common sales force size was between five and ten people (Lambkin and de Búrca, 1993). There were no significant differences between consumer, industrial and service companies in this regard. The average number of calls made by a sales representative was 28 per week. The ratio of sales managers to sales representatives was 1 to 4.

Sales force pay

Generally the pay for sales representatives involves a basic salary together with a mix of other rewards, including company car (including tax, insurance, and fuel), commission or bonus, allowances for entertainment, and other expenses. In most cases salespeople will have sales quotas or targets set for them. These are considered to be motivational and may be the basis for calculating sales bonuses. Quotas or targets should be realistic and fair. If sales are declining, raising the target for salespeople may not be the answer; in many cases declining sales are more a marketing problem than a sales issue.

The UCD study showed that the average basic salary for salespeople in 1991 was £17,750. It estimated that the average total cost of a sales representative to a company was £43,500 a year. The study showed that as a motivating force, pay ranked third for sales personnel, after acknowledgment of effort and the achievement of sales targets.

Sales force selection

Typically there are a number of personality traits that companies will look for in their salespeople: persistence, enthusiasm, attention to detail, initiative, self-confidence, and honesty. As the salesperson will be a communication medium, communication skills will also be important. The UCD research established the selection criteria used by the companies surveyed, and these are listed in table 9.9. Usually when companies are recruiting salespeople, personality tests will form a large part of the assessment.

Table 9.9: Selection criteria for sales force

	Mean score
Personal characteristics	4.6
Ambition or potential	4.5
Sales experience	3.9
Knowledge or experience	3.8
Education level	3.7
Personal mobility	3.8
Age	3.4

Source: 'Profile of a Salesforce', UCD.

A salesperson should be able to demonstrate competence in six basic areas: business knowledge, industry knowledge, company knowledge, product knowledge, sales skills, and attitude (Denny, 1988).

The selling process

There are a number of steps in the selling process.

1. Prospecting and qualifying

Prospecting involves identifying potential customers, for example using trade directories or phone calls to arrange initial meetings. *Qualifying* means screening out poor prospects, for example on grounds of their size, location, or specific needs. This ensures that the salesperson does not waste time prospecting for customers that the company cannot realistically serve.

2. Pre-approach

'Pre-approach' involves learning as much as possible about potential customers before meeting them. The use of secondary research will be particularly useful here. It is important that the salesperson be familiar with the target customer's markets, business, and environment. Secondary research may provide profiles of the business or changes that have taken place in its environment. A salesperson needs to be well informed about these issues, not least because they may identify where sales opportunities exist.

3. Approach

The approach stage involves meeting the potential customer for the first time and getting off to a good start. It is important to build up a professional rapport with potential customers; salespeople should remember the adage that first impressions last. The salesperson should be on time, be dressed appropriately, and have with them all the documents and other material they may require.

4. Presentation and demonstration

The salesperson will usually be given the opportunity to make a presentation. From a communication point of view this is critically important. Use should be made of well-designed and illustrated presentation aids. *Sales presenters* may be used: these have illustrations of the product, variations, and details of price and other specifications. With the advent of multimedia technology, sales presentations can be quite sophisticated. The presentation should be tailored to the potential customer or audience and can be used to emphasise the benefits or features of the product. If using videos or multimedia technology the salesperson should make sure they can obtain access to the required equipment; if not, they will need to bring it with them and allow for setting-up time.

The demonstration stage may be required if the salesperson needs to show how the product works. This may involve the use of the product itself or a demonstration using video or multimedia. Demonstrations may even involve inviting the potential customer to another location.

5. Handling questions

This stage involves clarifying issues about the product and answering any questions the customer may have. If, for some reason, it is not possible to answer the questions on the spot, the salesperson should undertake to provide the answer at a specified time. It will become apparent at this stage whether the potential buyer is interested in the product. This stage allows the salesperson to provide more information and to engage the potential customer in a more detailed discussion about the product.

6. Closing the sale

Closing the sale involves asking the customer for an order. The salesperson must ask for an order; this creates a sense of immediacy. Details of special incentives or promotions that may exist can be included. Prices should be clearly specified, and the buyer should be made aware of the payment terms or options.

7. Follow-up

The objective in selling anything is not just the sale itself. It is important that the salesperson verifies that the order was successfully processed and delivered. Follow-up with the customer is extremely important, especially for building a base for repeat business.

Technology and selling

Direct selling has, over time, been influenced by developments in communications technology. The introduction of the postal service in the nineteenth century and the telephone in the twentieth century enabled marketers to sell directly to more customers. Developments in telecommunications have continued, with tele-marketing and internet marketing becoming more important. Many firms have established tele-marketing centres to serve the domestic and international markets. The Industrial Development Authority identified the sector as one where growth was possible, and by 1997 it had attracted forty-three companies, employing 3,600 people (*Sunday Business Post*, 16 February 1997). Such firms as airlines and financial service providers were attracted to establish call centres in Ireland, mostly for their Continental markets. The quality of the telecommunications system, the use of English and the customer care abilities of staff, together with tax incentives, all encouraged them to establish in Ireland.

Obviously, selling is only one part of the activities that staff in these centres engage in. They are also used to provide customer services, advice, and information. They do, however, demonstrate the ability of a firm to sell products in different markets over the phone.

The internet is also taking on an increasingly important role in sales. As with tele-marketing, selling is only one dimension of the internet, but it is likely to become more important. The interactive nature of the internet allows the sales prospect to look at illustrations of the product, in many cases in virtual reality form. Prospects can request information about the product and even create a virtual product on their computer screen. Products can be ordered and feedback provided on line. To the extent that use of the internet becomes more widespread among firms and consumers, its role in selling will increase.

Relationship marketing and selling

Given the nature of the salesperson's job, their direct contact with customers will mean that they will play an important role in developing relationships with those customers. Salespeople should therefore be familiar with the concept of *relationship marketing*. There are a number of implications. While all customers are important, some may require more time or sales effort. Significant customers may require more contact and special care. The salesperson will therefore have to identify prospects and customers who are most important with regard to relationship effort.

Salespeople also need to build up a rapport with their customers. We rarely buy from people we do not like. Personality clashes between salesperson and customer, for example, can be avoided by attempting to match the salesperson with the particular customer.

Salespeople should not be required to manage too many relationships. The sales manager or other manager should supervise the relationship. Salespeople could provide updates on the quantity and quality of their interactions with customers, and customers could be surveyed to assess their satisfaction with the relationship. In general, salespeople should be encouraged to actively develop relationships with customers. Taking initiatives such as anticipating the customer's needs or problems, keeping them informed or thoughtful gestures may be appreciated and help build the relationship. If the customer perceives the salesperson as someone who only reacts and does not initiate, they may have a less favourable impression.

PUBLIC RELATIONS

Public relations broadly describes attempts to achieve favourable publicity for the product, service, or firm. It can involve a variety of aspects, including press relations with the news media, obtaining publicity for the product, for example for a product launch, internal and external corporate communication, lobbying decision-makers, and advising the company management on public issues and media relations.

Specific tools that are used include press statements to the news media and specialist media, speeches by executives or the company management, special events such as conferences, openings, and photo opportunities, written materials such as annual reports, company profiles, brochures, articles or newsletters, corporate videos, and social or charitable activities. All of these provide communication opportunities and are a means of communicating the message.

The press statement

Press statements are used by firms to convey information to the media. Many of the activities of firms are newsworthy, such as new investment, job creation, the launch of new products, sponsorship of events, management appointments, or marketing activities. Some activities will be newsworthy to the general news media, such as the publication of an annual report or accounts, while other activities will be of more interest to specific media, such as the trade press. Press statements facilitate the media, as they communicate newsworthy items directly, which saves journalists time in investigating or obtaining material; they can be used to fill space in newspapers, magazines or the trade press and will usually be welcomed by journalists. Needless to say, the information in the press statement must be factual and accurate, otherwise journalists will not use it.

Consider the following press statement issued by Aer Lingus. This was released on the worldwide web in addition to being sent to the news media and travel trade.

PRESS RELEASE

Over 100,000 avail of Aer Lingus winter breaks promotion

Bookings up 50 per cent on last year

Aer Lingus described its winter flight breaks promotion as 'hugely successful.' The offer, run in conjunction with Quinnsworth-Crazy Prices outlets throughout the country, will see over 100,000 passengers avail of special return fares on twenty-six Aer Lingus routes to Britain, the Continent, and the United States.

The deal, which offered return fares for two people travelling together between 1 November 1996 and 23 March 1997 from £79 to Britain, £179 to continental Europe, and £379 to the United States, was designed to entice customers to travel at off-peak periods during the winter months.

Commenting on the success of the initiative, the airline's marketing director, David Bunworth, said the offer brought the Aer Lingus brand of service quality to a bargain-conscious market. 'The response to the offer has been phenomenal, and we are delighted that over 100,000 customers will avail of exceptionally good-value promotional fares this winter.'

The offer has enticed over 50 per cent more customers than in 1996, and the airline attributes some of the increase to changes in the structure of the offer. 'This year we included new destinations, such as Chicago and Stansted, and also gave customers the option of travelling abroad themselves or arranging to bring relatives or friends to Ireland. These extra dimensions certainly added to the promotion's attractiveness.'

Further information: contact Aer Lingus web site: http://www.aerlingus.ie

A number of factors should be noted when preparing press statements.

- The statement should be relevant and useful to the publication that receives it. For example, the statement above was used in the national press and trade press.
- The statement may need to have a time embargo placed on it if it is not to be published immediately. For example, the firm may want to issue advance information to the press about a forthcoming product launch or event.
- The statement should begin with a suitable headline. This should describe the general theme of the information and should attract attention.
- The main details should be set out in the first paragraph. The publication may not have space to publish all the information in the statement, and so the most relevant information should be communicated at the beginning.
- The statement should be structured in distinct paragraphs.
- The information in the statement should emphasise facts rather than opinion.
- The style used should be plain and concise. Exaggerated statements should not be made.
- Direct quotations should be used if possible. In the example above, comments are directly attributable to the marketing director.
- The statement should indicate where further information can be obtained. Usually company stationery will be used, giving the address, telephone number, and fax number, or, as in the example above, the worldwide web address.

Public relations planning

Public relations activities should be carefully planned. They are communication opportunities, and, as fig. 9.15 demonstrates, can be used to select different audiences. In this case the cross-border railway project provided a number of different events that required different PR activities. As can be seen from the proposed plan, particular attention was paid to the PR activities, taking into account the cross-border and EU aspects. Different activities were planned with particular audiences in mind: for example, some events were purely local, while others had national or EU significance.

Fig. 9.15: Proposed public relations programme: cross-border rail project

Event	Objective	Proposed PR activity	Target groups or media	Event date
Launch of branding (Enterprise)	Begin public awareness	Event suitable for planned visit by EU Transport Commissioner to Dublin and Belfast	All-Ireland media	1 March 1997
Infrastructure events	Public awareness	Bridge reconstruction	Local and national: important information for intending passengers	Continuous from start of project
Switching on of new signalling system	Alert public to imminence of launch, and publicise EU funding	Option 1: national event with ministers from Republic and Northern Ireland. Statements on EU investment. Option 2: more low-key event carried out by chairmen of the two rail companies	Customers, staff, local communities, opinion-formers, elected representatives, European Commission	May 1997
Opening of renovated Dundalk and Drogheda stations, including upgraded freight depot in Dundalk	Create awareness of the quality of service and customer care to be provided. Publicise EU investment.	Ribbon-cutting and unveiling of plaque; possible ministerial involvement,	Local and national officials	To be confirmed

Literature: brochures, leaflets, and media fact sheets	Hand-outs for events, public and press queries	Quality brochures for information use	As above	Fact sheets: February 1997; brochure: March 1997
Film on project for BBC, RTE, and UTV; similar for radio	Increase awareness	Discuss concept with relevant television and radio head of programmes	Wide general audiences	For broadcast week of launch
Regular feature programmes	Continue awareness	Foster a series of regular feature stories, continuing up to launch	All audiences	Beginning February 1996
Pre-launch proving trials: press and interest groups	Heighten awareness of imminence of new service	Special trains from Dublin and Belfast, presentation on board	General public, trade unions, opinion-formers in area of staff morale. National local and specialist media	Summer 1997
Official launch	All audiences	Launch programme to be developed around Enterprise trains meeting nose to nose. Launch most likely at head of government level if political progress is good.	Britain, Northern Ireland, Republic, EU political leaders, key media personnel	Autumn 1997

Source: Iarnród Éireann, Media and PR Department.

Measuring the effectiveness of public relations

As with any communication exercise, it is important that objectives are set for a company's public relations activities. Equally it is important to measure the results of campaigns. There are no definitive measures of performance. Firms may quantify the amount of positive publicity or coverage they have received; these, however, will give only one dimension of effectiveness. To measure effectiveness more comprehensively, research on perceptions, attitudes or opinions before and after a public relations campaign would be desirable.

It is important that the marketer establishes objectives for the public relations campaign at the outset and that this is used to measure performance. The evaluation of public relations activities can be difficult, given their sometimes intangible nature. The public relations industry has been searching for a standard of measurement, but such a universal system is unlikely to solve the problems of evaluation (Marshall, 1997). One approach (Dubin and Farrell, 1997) suggested tying in a response mechanism to PR activities. This included fine-tuning objectives, making sure news statements actually contain news, being objective in communications, incorporating response mechanisms in PR activity, and reaching out directly to communities. Tying in PR with other marketing activities was also considered important.

The impact of negative publicity

Negative product publicity can be a nightmare for marketers. It almost always leads to a loss in market share; however, there is much evidence to suggest that the way in which the marketer handles the publicity can limit the damage. Typical problems that have faced marketers include the contamination of a product, environmental damage, accidents, or tampering with a product. Faced with such situations, the firm should remember that it is the customer who must come first.

One American study (Weinberger and Romeo, 1989) looked at the negative publicity that surrounded four companies: Ford, Dodge, Proctor and Gamble, and Johnson and Johnson. In the case of Ford and Dodge the negative publicity arose because of safety problems. Both companies lost market share, and in Ford's case the product was ultimately withdrawn. In the case of Proctor and Gamble the results of negative publicity involved an entire product class and affected the brand's market share. The Johnson and Johnson case involved tampering with the product. This did affect market share, but the company's response, involving the recall of 22 million bottles of the product (Tylenol), ultimately restored the brand to the position it held before the crisis.

Marketers want to encourage positive word-of-mouth publicity, but the effects of negative word-of-mouth can be disastrous. Public relations can play a strong role in a crisis, when it is important to communicate to consumers, the media, or other relevant publics. The way in which the crisis is handled can determine how much damage is done to the company and its products.

Advertising can play an important role in post-crisis situations also. Following a contamination scare in 1990, the Perrier brand of mineral water was completely withdrawn from the market. When new stock was on the shelves, the company began an advertising campaign with the line 'Helleau again.' One year later the brand was back as the number 1 mineral water in Britain.

Relations with the media are also important. The media should be considered as customers, and therefore getting to know them and building relationships with them will be important (Matthews, 1994).

SPONSORSHIP

Commercial sponsorship has been defined as an investment in cash or in kind in an activity in return for access to the exploitable commercial potential associated with that activity (Meenaghan, 1994). Sponsorship can have many forms and has grown in importance in marketing communications. The world sponsorship market was estimated to be worth $16,600 million in 1996 (*Marketing*, March 1998).

Sport and sporting events have always been strongly associated with sponsorship activities, and these continue to be important. It has been estimated that football strip sponsorship of English league teams was worth £25 million every year (*Marketing Week*, 26 April 1996). Manchester United alone was receiving £2 million a year from Sharp, the electronics company (*Sunday Business Post*, 26 April 1998). There has also been growth in strip sponsorship in Irish soccer and Gaelic games; it was reported in 1998 that Bank of Ireland was thought to be spending £750,000 on sponsoring the All-Ireland football championship (*Marketing*, January 1998).

Sports are not the only form of sponsorship activity. Firms may become involved in the sponsorship of individuals such as athletes, events such as concerts, and causes such as the environment or charity. Television programmes may also be sponsored. The insurance company PMPA sponsored the twice-weekly serial 'Fair City' on RTE television, while Hibernian Insurance sponsored the monthly 'Crimeline' programme. The cost of such sponsorships is not always revealed; however, in 1998 it was reported that the financial services company Standard Life was paying £300,000 to sponsor a sports programme on Network 2, 'Saturday Sports Live' (*Marketing*, January 1998). The increasing importance of tourism may have been a factor in encouraging the Norwegian company Statoil to begin sponsorship of Dublin's Viking visitor centre (*Sunday Tribune*, 17 May 1998). The company reportedly paid £75,000 for the sponsorship, and it planned to promote the centre at its forecourts and through its loyalty card scheme. It would also be used as a venue for corporate entertainment.

Sponsorship is usually used in addition to other forms of marketing. The Bailey's brand is supported by worldwide advertising and promotion, but the company also sponsors the world figure skating championships.

BAILEY'S GOES ON ICE FOR £5 MILLION

In 1994 R. and A. Bailey signed a five-year sponsorship deal with the International Skating Union to sponsor the world and European ice skating championships. While ice skating is a minority sport in Ireland, women's figure skating ranks as the second most popular sport in the United States, after American football. Bailey had been advertising its product using a 'Bailey's and ice' theme for several years and believed that the sponsorship would be synergistic. It was also considered appropriate, as ice skating was very popular in eastern Europe, which at the time was an emerging market for the product.

To assess the value of the sponsorship, the company carried out a media audit. This involved estimating how many people the brand reached through sponsorship. In 1994 it was estimated at 230 million people in fifteen countries; in 1995 it was 320 million people. All of these were people who had watched a significant number of hours of the championships. The Bailey logo and signage were available for 60 per cent of the time.

The sponsorship has given the brand inroads into markets that are difficult to penetrate. The 1994 world championship was held in Japan, an expensive market to advertise in. However, with the logo prominently displayed around the skating rink, the brand enjoyed its highest sales in Japan immediately after the event.

Source: *Sunday Business Post*, 16 January 1994, 19 March 1995.

Sponsorship is usually used by firms as part of their general communication strategy. In the highly competitive mobile phone market the two principal competitors, Eircell and Esat, have used a variety of sponsorships to help in their battle for market share. Both companies have developed a means of evaluating the effectiveness of their sponsorship.

MOBILE SPONSORS

In 1997 Eircell had over 400,000 customers and Esat Digifone close to 100,000, but the market was considered to have even more potential users of mobile phones. Both companies are now investing in sponsorship deals to attract new subscribers. The companies have been linking their brands to a variety of high-profile events, from horse races and motor-racing to international expeditions.

Even before it was launched, Esat had sponsored the South Aris expedition, which re-created Shackleton's rescue voyage to the South Atlantic in 1908. Since then it has been connected with the Leinster rugby team, the champion stakes, the Jordan Grand Prix, Cork GAA, and the Chamber of Commerce Ireland conference. In 1998 Esat took over the sponsorship of the Young Scientist Exhibition from Aer Lingus.

Esat chose projects that it felt would help it establish a brand identity, reinforce its attributes, select specific market segments, and communicate the company's role as a good corporate citizen. Local sponsorship is important. The deal with Cork GAA tied in with the company's extended coverage in Munster.

Eircell also has a number of sponsorships, including its own 'Smile of Ireland' photographic competition, which built on the company's symbol. Other sponsorships include formula 1 racing and the press photographer of the year award. It is also associate sponsor of Murphy's Irish Open. Eircell is joint sponsor of the Rose of Tralee festival and Enterprise Ireland. In 1997 it took over from Bank of Ireland as sponsor of the GAA All-Stars in a three-year deal.

Eircell considers sponsorship to be a commercial investment, and any new sponsorships must enhance the company's image. The value of sponsorships is evaluated in both a quantitative and a qualitative way, and the company uses these evaluations to decide on future activity and to compare the success or otherwise of the sponsorship. Most sponsorship deals run for three years.

Source: Christine Doherty, 'Mobile moguls set their sights on sponsorship', *Sunday Business Post*, 21 December 1997.

As with all forms of marketing communication, it is important that the marketer evaluates sponsorship activities. In the case of R. and A. Bailey, sponsorship gave it access to viewers that it would have found difficult to reach otherwise. The mobile phone marketers Eircell and Esat evaluate their sponsorships quantitatively, for example the number of viewers a sponsored programme reached, and qualitatively, for example the perceptions or attitudes of the viewers towards the company.

Only a limited amount of research has been carried out on sponsorship. One study (Hoek et al., 1997) did compare sponsorship and advertising within the context of

Ehrenberg's awareness-trial-reinforcement model of advertising. It found that while both advertising and sponsorship stimuli evoked responses consistent with the model with regard to unprompted recall, attitudes, and purchasing probabilities, sponsorship may generate higher levels of awareness and may lead to the association of a wider range of attributes with the promoted brand. Another study, conducted among financial institutions in Britain, sought to identify the contribution of sports sponsorship to achieving particular objectives, and this yielded the results illustrated in table 9.10.

Table 9.10: Contribution of sports sponsorship to achieving objectives

	Mean
Increased corporate awareness	5.9
Increased media attention	5.1
Community involvement	4.9
Corporate hospitality	4.2
Increased sales	4
Change of corporate image	3
Increased product awareness	3
Increased new-product awareness	2.7
Change of product image	2.2

Source: D. Thwaites, 'Corporate sponsorship by the financial services industry', *Journal of Marketing Management*, vol. 10 (1994), no. 8.

The same study also examined influences on the choice of sponsorship activity. These are illustrated in table 9.11.

Table 9.11: Influences on choice of sponsorship activity

	Mean
Sponsor's name can be linked to event	5.9
Event has a clean image	5.5
Sole sponsorship is available	5.3
Provides a good fit with brand or corporate positioning	5.1
Audience profile can be determined	5
Audience size can be measured	4.8
Television coverage is available	4.5
Can be incorporated in mainstream advertising and promotion	4
Little dialogue is necessary with organisers	3.5
Represents a new event	3.2
Contract is available for three years	3.1

Source: D. Thwaites, 'Corporate sponsorship by the financial services industry', *Journal of Marketing Management*, vol. 10 (1994), no. 8.

This research illustrates the role sponsorship can play as part of the firm's communication effort. It also emphasises the need for marketers to establish clear objectives for their sponsorship activities and to evaluate the results. Common forms of evaluation include establishing the number of mentions made of the sponsor, the amount of broadcast time given, or the number of column-inches printed. With regard to the quality of the publicity, it is probable that the marketer will need to consider perceptual and attitudinal research.

While evaluation measures such as awareness levels will be important, it is also necessary that sponsorship be assessed on the broader issues of its effect on brand, product or company image. The planning of sponsorship activities is also important. In 1998 Coca-Cola became the first sponsor for the soccer World Cup competitions of 2002 and 2006. The deal was estimated to cost it $80 million (*Marketing*, March 1998). The sponsors of the 1998 World Cup included Adidas, Anheuser Busch, Canon, Coca-Cola, Gillette, JVC, Fuji Film, Mastercard, McDonald's, Opel, Phillips, and Snickers (*Irish Marketing Journal*, February 1998). This list illustrates the lack of exclusivity that a sponsor can enjoy and the competition that exists between sponsors, particularly for large-scale events. Given the amount of money that companies invest in sponsorship, it is important that planning and forms of evaluation exist.

TECHNOLOGY AND MARKETING COMMUNICATION

Technological developments have affected communication media and led to growth in direct advertising and communication. It is probable that this trend will continue. Important developments in marketing communication technology will include the growth in the internet, multimedia, and digital television and radio.

Multimedia

Multimedia means the combination of different media, including text, pictures, animation, narrative, and music. An important aspect is the ability of the user to interact with it. It can be used for a variety of applications, including training, on-line help, internal company communication, interaction with customers, and promotional activities. The worldwide web is the multimedia layer of the internet.

A study, *Multimedia Ireland: Realising the Potential*, was commissioned by Forbairt to identify the potential for growth in the multimedia industry and the policy initiatives necessary to realise the potential (Forbairt, 1998). The report concluded that the multimedia industry had the potential to create nine thousand jobs by the year 2000. It was expected that multimedia applications would become as pervasive as computerised publication layout had become.

Multimedia falls into three broad categories: hardware and software used to create products; the multimedia products and services themselves; and the technologies used to deliver the content.

Growth has been stimulated by price reductions in hardware and software, improvements in telecommunications infrastructure, and increased demand for video-conferencing and data-conferencing. It was estimated that 2,200 people were employed in the sector in 1998. The multimedia industry uses the skills of producers, designers, localisers, animators, and abstract-writers. It includes the development of everything from computer games to the design of individual web sites.

FURTHER READING

Advertising Standards Authority of Ireland, *Code of Advertising Standards for Ireland*, Dublin: ASAI 1992.
Meenaghan, T., and O'Sullivan, P. (eds.), *Marketing Communications in Ireland*, Dublin: Oak Tree Press 1995.

DISCUSSION QUESTIONS

1. Pick a consumer product, a service and an industrial product and describe the components of the communication model that would apply to each. In your answer, give details of each of the components of the model.
2. Explain how you would design appropriate messages for each of the following:
   —a new brand of frozen pizza
   —a retirement home
   —a campaign to encourage people to donate blood
   —an American football match in Ireland.
3. Prepare a press statement for each of the following:
   —a local sports team that has won a competition
   —a college recruiting business pupils from secondary schools
   —a small manufacturer of home-made pies and cakes that has built new premises.
   In each case you should indicate the appropriate media for your statement.
4. Comment on the effectiveness of sponsorship as a means of communication.
5. Compare and contrast the different elements of the communications mix.
6. Discuss the pros and cons of using internet advertising.

REFERENCES

Advertising Standards Authority of Ireland, *Code of Advertising Standards for Ireland*, Dublin: ASAI 1989.
Bourke, K., 'Corporate culture identity and design: AIB Group', *Irish Marketing Review*, vol. 7 (1994).
Branagan, P., 'Is digital TV good for the advertising industry?', *Irish Marketing Journal*, April 1997.
Carter, M., 'Digital: the future of TV', *Campaign*, 5 July 1996.
Colley, R., *Defining Advertising Goals for Measuring Advertising Effectiveness*, New York: Association of National Advertisers 1961.
Denny, R., *Selling to Win*, London: Kogan Page 1988.
Dubin, S., and Farrell, J., 'Direct response through "direct public relations"', *Direct Marketing*, May 1997.
Ehrenberg, A., 'Repetitive advertising and the consumer', *Journal of Advertising Research*, 14, 1974.

Fanning, J., 'Perspectives on the new advertising', *Irish Marketing Review*, vol. 2 (1987).

Fanning, J., 'Is the end of advertising really all that nigh?', *Irish Marketing Review*, vol. 10 (1997), no. 1.

Forbairt, *Multimedia Ireland: Realising the Potential*, Dublin: Forbairt 1998.

Heinen, L., 'Internet marketing practices', *Information Management and Computer Science*, vol. 4 (1996), no. 5.

Hoek, J., Gendall, P., Jeffcoat, M., and Orsman, D., 'Sponsorship and advertising: a comparison of their effects', *Journal of Marketing Communications*, March 1997.

Irish Marketing Journal, *Guide to Marketing and Advertising Services, 1997*, Dublin: Marketing Information and Communication 1997.

Joachimsthaler, E., and Aaker, D., 'Building brands without mass media', *Harvard Business Review*, January–February 1997.

Johnson, B., 'Intel-ligence inside', *Business Marketing*, August 1997.

Lambkin, M., and de Búrca, S., 'Sales force management in Ireland', *Irish Marketing Review*, vol. 6 (1993).

Lambkin, M., and O'Dwyer, M., 'Couponing and coupon redemption: problems and perspectives', *Irish Marketing Review*, vol. 7 (1994).

Lavidge, R., and Steiner, G., 'A model for predicting measurement of advertising effectiveness', *Journal of Marketing*, 25, October 1961.

Marshall, S., 'A wordy cause?', *Marketing Business*, November 1997.

Matthews, W., 'Do unto media as you shall do unto your customers!', *Communication World*, August 1994.

Meenaghan, J., 'High visibility: celebrities, marketing and image-making', *Irish Marketing Review*, vol. 3 (1988).

Meenaghan, J., 'The role of sponsorship in the marketing communications mix' in *Perspectives on Marketing Management in Ireland*, Dublin: Oak Tree Press 1994.

Mela, C., Jedidi, K., and Bowman, D., 'The long-term impact of promotions on consumer stockpiling behaviour', *Journal of Marketing Research*, May 1998.

O'Brien, B., 'Harnessing the new interactive tools', *Decision*, April 1997.

O'Dwyer, A., 'Perspectives on Developments in Electronic Media and their Implications for Marketing Practice', presentation to conference of Irish Marketing Teachers' Association, National University of Ireland, Cork, May 1998.

Office of the Director of Telecommunication Regulation, *The Future Delivery of Television Services in Ireland*, Dublin: ODTR 1998.

Paul, P., 'Marketing on the internet', *Journal of Consumer Marketing*, vol. 13 (1996), no. 4.

Simms, J., 'A driving force', *Marketing Business*, February 1997.

Smyth, D., 'Integrated marketing communication: H. Heinz Company', *Irish Marketing Review*, vol. 9 (1996).

Ward, R., and Turley, D., 'The effect of post-purchase communication on consumer satisfaction', *Irish Marketing Review*, vol. 9 (1996).

Weinberger, M., and Romeo, J., 'The impact of negative product news', *Business Horizons*, January–February 1989.

Wickstrom, Bo, 'Analysis of the effects of special retail promotions in a consumer perspective', *Irish Marketing Review*, vol. 2 (1987).

10

Marketing Channels

The *marketing channel* is the external contractual organisation that the management operates to achieve its distribution objectives. A *distribution system* is an essential element of the marketing channel; this is the network of people, institutions or agencies involved in the flow of a product to the customer, together with the informational, financial, promotional and other services associated with making the product convenient and attractive to buy and rebuy.

Physical distribution is only one part of marketing channel activities. This chapter explores the nature of marketing channels and the decisions required for the effective flow of the product to the buyer.

The marketing channels selected will play a critical role in the success of a product. On occasion, marketers may seek to adapt their channel strategy to suit their requirements, as the following panel illustrates.

CHOCOLATE KIMBERLEY: SUCCESS IN MARKETING CHANNELS

One of the most successful new FMCG products in the nineteen-nineties was the Chocolate Kimberley brand, launched by Irish Biscuits in 1996. The product was an extension of an existing popular brand; one of the principal differences was its packaging and distribution. Available in individually wrapped form, the product could compete with other countline products in a market where impulse buying was important. As a result, Irish Biscuits paid particular attention to in-store displays, such as counter mounts and selected supermarkets, TSNs, and the catering trade. From the consumer's point of view the brand was therefore widely available and physically positioned in the countline section of the shop rather than the biscuit section.

Source: *Checkout Ireland*, April 1997.

The marketing channel comprises a number of different flows that provide a useful framework for understanding the scope of channel management.

- **Product flows** are the physical movement of the product from the manufacturer to all parties who take physical possession of the product.
- **Negotiation flows** represent the interplay of the buying and selling functions associated with the transfer of title of the product: for example, retailers will seek to negotiate with manufacturers to get preferential prices or promotional deals.

- **Ownership flows** are the movement of the title of the product as it passes through the channel.
- **Information flows** consist of information exchanged by channel members on all aspects of the product: pricing, order sizes, technical details, and other issues.
- **Promotional flows** include the involvement of promotional agencies, such as advertising agencies, sales promotion agencies, and public relations consultants. In relation to many communication campaigns, the marketer may have to rely on the co-operation of channel members: for example, retailers who are expected to redeem coupons or to stock promotional items may need to be encouraged to do so.

THE ROLE OF MARKETING CHANNELS

Marketing channels perform a number of different roles, all of which involve delivering value to the marketer, the channel members, and the customer. Five roles in particular can be identified: the creation of purchase opportunity, communication, service, cost reduction, and control.

Creating purchase opportunity

One of the primary roles of the channel is to make the product readily available and easily accessible to buyers. Marketing channels therefore create place utility for the buyer. Marketers cannot always achieve this on their own, so they rely on channel members to provide their products at appropriate locations and with the necessary support.

Communication role

The channel facilitates the flow of information about the product. Channel members may be asked for advice by buyers, and they may approach potential buyers and be involved in demonstrations of the product. Specific promotional campaigns may be implemented by channel members, which may mean they are expected to stock promotional items, to redeem coupons, or to give rebates.

Service role

Marketing channels involve a service role, whether this means giving advice on using and maintaining the product, providing for repair and spare parts, providing credit, or simply a friendly greeting. Obviously some products will require more service, but in many cases it is the channel member who will be relied on to provide it.

Cost reduction

For many marketers it may be more cost-effective to use 'middlemen' than to establish their own distribution channels. Firms use middlemen because they themselves lack the financial resources to have their own distribution system, and because a middleman who is a specialist in distributing, wholesaling or retailing may be more cost-effective.

Channels can be expensive to establish and maintain. In many cases where marketers have had their own distribution system they may decide to change or adapt it, as Guinness did.

THE GUINNESS SHIPS

In 1995 the last Guinness tanker sailed from City Quay, Dublin, marking the end of an era. Guinness-owned ships had been transporting beer from Dublin since the last century. The company had two vessels, which were used to transport Guinness stout in bulk to the port of Runcorn, Cheshire; from there it was transported to a kegging plant, where it was kegged for onward distribution in the north-east of England and Scotland.

The use of the tanker vessels had required the company to transport the product in road tankers from the brewery in St James's Gate to City Quay, where it was pumped on board the ship. A similar inter-modal transfer was required in Runcorn. The new distribution arrangements involve the use of special container tanks, which can be loaded at the brewery and brought directly to the kegging plant by means of conventional ferries.

Control

Marketers will generally be concerned about the control implications of channel management. The more members there are in the channel the more difficult it can be to maintain control over such factors as distribution coverage, communication, and price.

One of the main disadvantages of using a middleman for distribution is that the company may lose control, and this is why many companies consider it a strategic advantage to have their own distribution system, or to exercise as much control as possible in the channel. Distribution arrangements are protected vigorously.

DEFENDING THE DISTRIBUTION CHANNEL FOR HB ICE CREAM

The HB brand, now owned by the multinational Unilever, has been Ireland's market leader in ice cream for several decades. The company's distribution system was based on supplying retailers with a freezer, which HB owned, stocked, and serviced. Retailers were supplied with a freezer on condition that it was stocked only with HB products. This distribution policy gave HB a strong measure of control in the channel.

In 1990 the Mars range of ice cream products was launched and began to appear in many of the HB-owned freezers. HB reacted by getting a High Court injunction to stop Mars putting products in its freezers. Masterfoods, the owner of the Mars brand, took the case to the European Commission, which took the view that some aspects of HB's practices were anti-competitive.

A compromise was reached, with Unilever agreeing to give rebates to retailers who owned their own freezer and who sold a minimum of £650 worth of HB ice cream a year. This allowed retailers to buy their existing HB freezer cabinet or to buy a new unit from HB in instalments, with the obligation to stock it exclusively with HB products ending when the last payment had been made.

By 1996, however, Mars was still pursuing the case, claiming that Unilever had not done enough to open the market to competition. In February 1997 the European Commission appeared to support this view when it informed Unilever that rules banning retailers from stocking rival ice creams were illegal and in breach of EU competition rules. Inspections had taken place in the market, and the Commission was unhappy with Unilever's pledge not to tie retailers to them.

Sources: *Sunday Business Post*, 9 March 1995; *Irish Times*, 15 October 1996; *Examiner*, 22 February 1997.

FUNCTIONS OF MEMBERS OF THE MARKETING CHANNEL

The firm relies on members of the marketing channel to perform a number of different functions. **Research** information should be available from channel members: for example, retailers meet customers face to face and may be a source of feedback to the marketer who has not got this level of personal contact.

Communication and promotion campaigns may be implemented by channel members; they may be the medium through which the marketer communicates.

Consider the company relying on its distributors in overseas markets, where it may not have the resources to engage in direct advertising campaigns. Channel members will make **contact** with buyers and potential buyers and will be involved in **matching** supply and demand. **Negotiation** may be carried out by channel members on behalf of the marketer, and the physical aspects of distribution, such as **transport and storage**, may be performed by them. **Finance** may be arranged by channel members: for example, car dealers may arrange packages with financial institutions, and they may take the buyer's old car as a trade-in or in partial payment for a new car.

Channel levels

The term *channel levels* refers to the number of possible levels that can exist between the marketer and the consumer. A level 0 channel means that there is no middleman between the marketer and the consumer, while other channels can comprise a number of levels, as shown in fig. 10.1.

Fig. 10.1: Levels in marketing channels

0:	marketer ....customer
1:	airline ....travel agent ....customer
2:	manufacturer ....wholesaler ....retailer ....customer
3:	manufacturer ....export agent..........importer ....retailer ....customer

The number of levels in the channel is determined by the nature of the product and by market conditions. Many products—some services, for example—cannot be distributed through middlemen, while other channels are highly structured and involve several levels, for example hardware. In some cases exporting can involve the use of extra channel members, such as an export or an import agent.

Technological developments have enabled many marketers to reach the customer directly, for example direct banking and insurance services. Customers can get quotations over the phone, transfer funds, or pay for the service with a credit card. These activities were traditionally carried out in the branch or through an agent or broker.

Logistics

Logistics refers to planning, implementing and controlling the physical flow of materials and goods from points of origin to points of use. This is a function of the marketing channel.

There are a number of fundamental components in a logistics system. *Transport* involves physical movement. *Materials-handling* refers to the placement and movement of products in storage areas; while *order-processing* is a significant component at different levels in the distribution channel. *Stock control* attempts to strike a balance between holding the lowest levels of stock and the customers' demands. *Warehousing* involves the storage of raw materials or products.

In addition to these factors, *packaging* affects the other components of the logistics system: for example, it may not be possible to transport some products in their consumer package, and they may need to be transported in bulk or in protective packaging.

A detailed review of each component is beyond the scope of this book; in the following section an overview of the components of the logistics system is given.

THE COMPONENTS OF THE LOGISTICS SYSTEM
Transport

There are a number of different modes of transport, each being particularly suitable for different types of products. In general, air transport has advantages for low-volume, high-margin products, such as flowers or crystal glassware, while rail and water suit higher-volume, low-margin products, such as timber or cement. Road transport will invariably be used for many inter-modal transfers, in addition to being a direct mode.

Ireland's island location means that air or sea must be used for the export and import of most tangible products, while for internal movement road and rail are the main modes. Transport may involve the movement of freight or it may be an element of the product itself, for example a flight to a holiday destination.

Air transport

Air transport in Ireland changed significantly with the advent of European deregulation in 1984. The industry grew rapidly from a single international carrier in 1984 to four international passenger airlines in the nineteen-nineties: Aer Lingus, Ryanair, Cityjet, and Transaer.

By the late nineties Aer Lingus, the state-owned national airline, had scheduled services on several internal routes and routes to Britain, continental Europe, and the United States. In common with strategies being pursued by many airlines in the nineteen-nineties, Aer Lingus entered a strategic partnership with the American carrier Delta in 1997. Under this arrangement the two airlines co-operate on transatlantic routes, allow frequent fliers to collect points on either company's services, and engage in joint marketing activities. In 1998 the Government gave the company permission to seek another strategic partner to widen its routes and services

Ryanair initially developed routes from Ireland to Britain. In 1997 it began services from Dublin to Paris and Brussels. European deregulation, in particular the increased use of 'seventh freedom' rights, allowed airlines to operate outside their own state. This presented opportunities, and in 1997 Ryanair began operating flights from Stanstead in London on a number of Continental routes. Ryanair is one of the principal low-fare airlines in Europe. It is not involved in the cargo business.

Cityjet began operations in 1995 with a service between Dublin and London City airport. In 1997 it launched a service from Dublin to Paris and signed a partnership agreement with the French national airline, Air France. Transaer concentrated on the sun holiday charter market, operating from a number of airports in Ireland and Britain. Neither Cityjet nor Transaer is involved in the cargo business.

Aer Lingus and the specialist cargo airline Aer Turas are the main cargo operators. In addition, cargo services are provided by a number of specialist and international airlines. The volume of air freight between Ireland and other countries has increased significantly: over the five-year period 1992–7, for example, it grew by 70 per cent (Institute of International Trade in Ireland, January 1998). It was estimated in 1998 that 21 per cent of exports was carried by air freight and that the volume of cargo carried by express operators, such as DHL, Federal Express, and UPS, was set to account for 40 per cent of total traffic (*Irish Times*, 13 January 1998). Since the mid-eighties a number of regional airports have been developed, which were used mainly for passenger flights, though some, such as Connacht Regional Airport at Knock, County Mayo, have also developed significant freight traffic.

The Warsaw Convention (1929) established common agreement on the extent of liability of airlines. The Chicago Convention (1944) established the International Civil Aviation Organisation (ICAO) and the 'freedoms of the air'. Originally there were five, but these were subsequently expanded to seven:

1. The privilege of flying over another country's territory without landing.
2. The privilege of landing in another state for non-traffic purposes.
3. The privilege of setting down passengers and cargo in another state.
4. The privilege of picking up passengers and cargo in another state and returning to one's own state.
5. The privilege of picking up passengers and cargo *en route* in a second state and carrying them to a third state.
6. The privilege of picking up passengers and cargo in a second state and carrying them via its own state to a third state.
7. The privilege of operating from a second state to a third state.

(Source: ICAO.)

In the airline business, these freedoms are essentially the means of gaining more routes and the right to serve more markets. They can therefore dictate which markets it is possible to enter, and so are a significant determinant of how competitive a market will be. Normally, bilateral air agreements are established between states, which usually cover the first four freedoms. The other freedoms can be more difficult to achieve. In the European Union, all seven freedoms should eventually apply in all member-states.

The International Air Transport Association (IATA) is a representative body for many of the world's airlines. Before widespread deregulation it was heavily involved in establishing fare policies on routes. Nowadays it has a more important role as a clearing-house for airlines and is involved in making financial settlements with carriers for inter-airline tickets. It is also involved in arranging standardised and interchangeable tickets.

An important element in airline operation and economics is the passenger or cargo load factor. The number of passengers and the amount of cargo available will determine such factors as the type of aircraft that will be used. Operations will therefore be determined by the needs of the passenger or cargo market segments. Capital costs for new aircraft are high, though many manufacturers offer structured financial packages and will often take older aircraft as trade-ins.

High capital costs mean that aircraft are used intensively. An aircraft is only productive when it is in the air. Efficiency is determined by flying times, time on the ground, and other factors, such as connection with other flights. Given the intensive use of equipment, delays due to weather conditions or technical problems can have a consequential effect on subsequent services.

Pricing depends on such factors as the size of the aircraft, route traffic density, the regularity of demand in both directions, and the nature of demand, for example business or leisure. Many aircraft carry cargo in addition to passengers.

A significant trend among airlines since the nineteen-eighties has been the establishment of partnerships and strategic alliances. These agreements involve co-operation in the marketing and development of routes and the co-ordination of operations; they therefore allow airlines to gain access to new routes, provide feeder traffic to each other's services, and enjoy economies of scale. Irish airlines have been involved in this trend.

Rail transport

Ireland's rail network contracted significantly from the nineteen-fifties but had stabilised in the nineties at around 2,000 kilometres. The network is largely radial, with most passenger services operating between Dublin and other centres. Freight services operate over the entire system, including some lines that are used for freight only.

There are two railway operators: Iarnród Éireann and Northern Ireland Railways. Both operate urban and inter-city passenger services; Iarnród Éireann is the only freight operator. Cross-border services are marketed using the 'Enterprise' brand, originally developed in 1947 by the Great Northern Railway. This was relaunched in 1997, when a new cross-border service was introduced.

In relation to freight transport, Iarnród Éireann estimates that rail accounts for 10 per cent of freight movements greater than 50 kilometres. Significant rail traffic includes mineral ore, fertiliser, chemicals, cement, sugarbeet, beer and stout, containers, and timber. Smaller items, such as parcels or packets, are often despatched on passenger trains.

FASTRACK

Fastrack is the brand name used for Iarnród Éireann's express parcel delivery service. Parcels, packets and other items can be checked in at railway stations or, in some towns, collected at company premises; they are then despatched to their destination on the next available passenger train.

Firms that use the service include Ford, which despatches car parts to dealers and garages convenient to the rail network. Many of these parts are high-value items, which dealers may not normally keep in stock. The advantages of the service are that most destinations on the rail network are served by several trains at different times every day, giving customers flexibility and choice.

Source: Iarnród Éireann.

In the late nineties a £275 million investment was made in the railway network. The investment was mainly in track, signalling, and other infrastructure, much of which had been out of date. Continuous welded rail and computer-controlled signalling systems were installed more widely. These allowed for increased operational efficiency and reduced running costs.

Passenger numbers increased in the nineties, particularly on urban services, while the tonnage of freight carried remained fairly constant (CIE Annual Report, 1997).

Railways involve high capital costs, including expenditure on locomotives, rolling stock, track, and signalling. To be economically viable, railways need to carry large volumes of passengers and freight, and rolling stock must be used intensively. This requires quick turnarounds. As with airlines, timetables are dictated by the availability of trains, journey times, and turnaround times. Weather does not disrupt services to the same extent as air or sea transport, but breakdowns or other delays will inevitably disrupt timetables.

It is not uncommon for railway operators to schedule freight trains at night, which allows them to use locomotives for passenger trains during the day and for freight at night. As in most other countries, the cost of running the railway network exceeds income; a state subsidy is therefore provided to make up the shortfall.

Road transport

Road haulage is the dominant means of freight transport within Ireland. It is also the dominant mode to and from ports, airports, and rail freight depots. The Irish Road Hauliers' Association estimated that road transport and distribution employs 66,000 people in the Republic and as a sector accounts for 5 per cent of gross national product.

Significant developments in the sector have included increased European regulation and increased competition, with worldwide courier companies, such as Federal Express and UPS, having a more significant presence in the market. Integration between different modes and the location of transport and storage facilities is a significant objective.

NATIONAL FREIGHT DISTRIBUTION CENTRE

In 1997 planning permission was sought for a national freight distribution centre in Clondalkin in the western suburbs of Dublin. The proposed site is near the orbital M50 motorway and its links with the national road network. It is also near the Dublin–Cork railway line, from which a round-the-clock freight train service would be provided for container traffic to and from Dublin port, while a link would also be provided with the national rail network. Warehousing, office and industrial buildings would be included, creating an integrated transport, transfer and storage centre.

Source: *Irish Times*, 12 March 1997.

The European market for road haulage has become much more competitive. Operators can compete in any of the EU member-states. Road haulage is controlled by various EU requirements, including drivers' hours, the size of vehicles, and driver testing.

Water transport

Internal waterways are no longer used for freight transport in Ireland. Significant amounts of freight are handled by ocean-going vessels. Approximately 79 per cent of the Republic's traded goods are transported by sea. In 1998 the most significant commercial ports by tonnage were Dublin, Cork, Shannon Estuary, Foynes, Waterford, New Ross, Rosslare, and Drogheda (Central Statistics Office). The most important ports in Northern Ireland were Belfast, Larne, and Warrenpoint. Access from ports to the national road and rail networks is important.

PROFILE OF THE PRINCIPAL PORTS

Dublin had the largest throughput in the country in 1997: 16.8 million tonnes of freight—an increase of 1.6 million tonnes on the 1996 figure. The estimated tonnage for 1998 was 18.7 million. The main cargoes handled in 1997 were 8.95 million tonnes RO-RO (378,000 freight units and 93,600 trade cars), 3.85 million tonnes LO-LO, 2.5 million tonnes of bulk liquid, 1.25 million tonnes of bulk solid (e.g. grain and ore), and 220,000 tonnes of break bulk (e.g. timber and paper). Dublin handled 983,000 passengers in 1997.

Belfast claimed 25 per cent of Ireland's total seaborne trade. In 1997 this included 310,000 freight vehicles, 1.1 million containers, 3.1 million tonnes of dry bulk, and 3 million tonnes of liquid bulk. A total of 1.9 million passengers used the port.

Cork recorded 8.5 million tonnes of freight in 1997, with container traffic and bulk liquids the largest categories.

> Shannon Estuary ports include the port of Limerick and a number of specialised facilities at Moneypoint (coal), Tarbert (oil), Shannon Airport (aviation fuel), and Aughinish (alumina). Together these ports handled 8.34 million tonnes in 1997.
>
> Source: 'Ports of Ireland', *Business and Finance*, 23 April 1998.

Freight is generally carried on 'roll-on, roll-off' (RO-RO) or 'lift-on, lift-off' (LO-LO) vessels. RO-RO ferries are widely used into and out of Irish ports. As with aircraft, rail, and road, the essential operational consideration is the maximum utilisation of equipment. This requires round-the-clock sailings and rapid port turnarounds; RO-RO vessels are therefore very suitable for this type of operation. Access from ports to the national road and rail networks is important. Inevitably, weather and tidal conditions can disrupt services or dictate schedules.

New technology and safety have been significant issues in marine transport. Faster vessels, such as high-speed catamarans, have come into service on Irish Sea routes. In the light of a number of ferry disasters in Europe, particularly after the *Herald of Free Enterprise* and *Estonia* disasters, requirements for improved safety and design features on RO-RO ferries have been introduced. The significant design difficulty with RO-RO vessels is that they cannot have internal bulkheads, because they must have open car decks. New regulations were drawn up by the International Maritime Organisation, which will apply to the construction of new vessels. These deal mainly with stability and internal design, and will apply to the Irish Sea routes by 2004.

Materials-handling

Materials-handling comprises the range of activities and equipment involved in the placement and movement of products in storage areas. The principal objectives are to minimise the distances over which products are moved within the storage area, to minimise damage, and to maximise efficiency. Mechanical equipment, such as conveyor-belt systems, computer-aided systems, and fork-lift trucks, may be required. Materials-handling is required at ports, airports, railheads, warehouses, and production plants.

Order-processing

A firm's order-processing system is an important feature of customer service. The principal objective is to minimise the *order cycle time*, which is the time it takes from the customer giving the order to delivery. An important consideration is accuracy. Electronic data interchange (EDI) has been a significant development; this involves the direct transfer of structured data from one firm's computer system to another. If one firm wishes to order from another, the order can be transmitted by electronic data transfer, provided the information can be exchanged to agreed specifications. The same system allows the firm to track a shipment during transport and to get electronic proof of delivery. The more integrated the system, the more advantages firms can derive from it.

Stock control

The main objective of stock control is to hold the lowest level of stock that will enable the firm to meet demand from customers. Stock-carrying costs, such as storage, insurance, and damage, can be quite high. The ideal position is where the firm can keep stock at the lowest possible level while at the same time placing orders for goods in large quantities; this is because average stock costs rise in direct proportion to the level of stock, while order costs decrease in proportion to the size of the order. A trade-off point must be established between these two costs to find the optimum levels for both, and this point is known as the *economic order quantity*. The EOQ can be calculated by using the formula

$$EOQ = \sqrt{\frac{2AS}{i}}$$

where

A = annual usage
S = order set-up cost
i = stock-carrying cost.

For example, if a manufacturer uses 2,000 units of product A in a year, each costing £20, and each order set-up cost is £100 and the carrying cost of stock is 25 per cent, the EOQ is

$$\sqrt{\frac{2 \times 2,000 \times 100}{20 \times 0.25}} = 283 \text{ units}$$

The main problem with the EOQ formula is that the reorder quantity it yields means that more stock is carried than is actually required per day over the complete order cycle (except on the last day). This represents a cost to the business. To overcome this, Japanese industries developed the 'just-in-time' (JIT) approach, whereby small shipments are made frequently to meet the precise time requirements of the user.

Developments in information technology, such as EDI, have facilitated the JIT approach. A retailer, for example, could order on line as demand warranted and could be supplied with the appropriate amount of the product. This eliminates the need to hold stock. Just-in-time approaches obviously need to be supported by an efficient and cost-effective logistics system.

Warehousing

Warehousing describes the holding or storage of products until they are ready to be sold. An important consideration is the location of warehousing facilities, convenient to the road network, ports, airports, or railheads. Many warehouses are equipped with materials-handling systems, which minimise movement of the product through the warehouse and reduce the risk of damage to stock.

Packaging

In general, air cargo packaging costs can be lower than for rail or road, because there is less risk of damage. Special packaging may be required for transport: for example, liquids may be transferred in bulk containers to bottling plants, where they are packed into consumer packages. A significant development in the nineteen-sixties and seventies was the introduction of ISO (international standard) containers. These are manufactured to precise dimensions and are the same throughout the world. They can be carried by road, rail, or water, and variants are used to carry liquids, dry goods, and frozen or refrigerated goods.

DEVELOPING AND MANAGING THE MARKETING CHANNEL

Channel distribution strategy

Channel distribution strategy refers to how resources are deployed to build a channel linking the producer to the consumer. The marketer will be required to make decisions on how the distribution channel will fit in with general organisational strategy and how it may become a strategic tool for the firm.

Fig. 10.2 illustrates the stages in the development and management of the marketing channel.

Fig. 10.2: Developing and managing the marketing channel

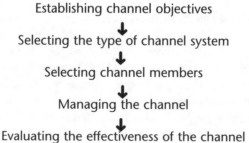

Establishing channel objectives
↓
Selecting the type of channel system
↓
Selecting channel members
↓
Managing the channel
↓
Evaluating the effectiveness of the channel

Channel objectives

In general, the marketer will want to choose the most efficient system possible. Channel objectives will be influenced by general company objectives, the role of distribution in the marketing mix, the channel design, the profile of channel members, and their performance.

The push-pull approach

If the marketer is relying on the *push* approach, this involves the channel members, such as wholesalers or retailers, 'pushing' the product towards the consumer. Incentives may be used to encourage channel members to achieve sales targets, and they may be encouraged to prospect for new business in the market.

The *pull* approach, on the other hand, involves using advertising and promotion to 'pull' the consumer towards the product. The idea is that if consumers have a positive reaction to the advertising and promotion they will be drawn towards the distribution channel to obtain the product. In general, most marketers will use a combination of push and pull approaches; it may be dangerous to rely on one approach alone.

Customer shopping preferences

Consumers have preferences with regard to factors such as time, convenience, availability, price, and the location of distribution outlets.

An issue that has taken on added importance in recent years for channel members, especially retailers, is Sunday trading. Some people argue that changed life-styles and working patterns mean that Sunday trading is a necessity; others argue that it disrupts what is traditionally a family day, especially for retail staff who are required to work. The attitudes of the public are mixed: in a survey in 1996 a majority were opposed to it, as fig. 10.3 shows; however, among younger people there were more in favour than against.

Fig. 10.3: Attitudes to Sunday trading

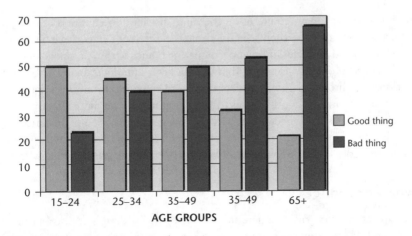

Source: *Checkout Ireland Yearbook and Buyer's Guide, 1996.*

Consumers' shopping preferences vary by product and service but are important considerations in designing channels. It is also important to remember that the atmosphere and image of the outlet should be in line with the customers' self-image. Consumers may prefer to shop where they feel most comfortable and where they feel the outlet reflects something about themselves. The growth of shopping centres in urban areas and the increase in the number of British retailers that have extended their operations to Ireland, such as Debenham's, Boot's, and Argos, have catered for changed preferences in location and variety.

Image

The distribution channel must be consistent with the image projected by the rest of the marketing effort. For example, the Tricot Marine brand of clothing and accessories is sold in its own shops in addition to those of other fashion retailers. The brand is aimed at higher-income customers, and the shop layout also suggests exclusivity and luxury.

While image is important, retailers must concentrate primarily on customer satisfaction. One study examined the relationship between shop image, shop satisfaction, and shop loyalty (Bloemer and de Ruyter, 1998). It found a positive relationship between shop satisfaction and loyalty but no evidence of a direct effect of shop image on loyalty.

Services offered

Members of the marketing channel may have to offer services such as finance, credit, delivery, technical advice, or maintenance and repair. Depending on the nature of the product or service, these services may be quite extensive and may involve high levels of technical expertise. Some outlets offer a limited service, such as supermarkets or discount stores, though several supermarkets have sought to differentiate themselves by using customer service.

Competition

The firm's strategy may require using the same distribution channels as competitors, so that consumers can make their selection from the different competitive offerings. In most supermarkets and groceries in Ireland, competing brands within product categories can be found in close proximity. Ensuring that the marketer's products are available in the same locations and through the same outlets as those of competitors may be a significant aspect of positioning strategy. In other cases the marketer may find it more effective to seek non-conventional distribution channels: in the cosmetics market, for instance, Avon has tended to avoid department stores and pharmacies and has concentrated on direct selling and distribution. The houseware manufacturer Tupperware has done likewise.

Type of product

The type of product will be a determining factor in the design of distribution channels. If the product is a convenience product, for example, it should be widely available; thus marketers such as Cadbury and Nestlé distribute their confectionery products through TSNs, supermarkets, petrol stations, cinemas, restaurants, and vending machines. In cases where products are more expensive or specialised they may be distributed less extensively. Many services and industrial products are distributed directly from the provider to the customer.

Defensive flexibility

If a manufacturer is to have influence in the channel, the channel must value the manufacturer's business. The stronger the value placed on the manufacturer's business, the easier it is to manage the channel.

Trade marketing has taken on added significance as channels become more competitive. Many firms have appointed trade marketing managers to develop and maintain relationships with the trade. Trade members are encouraged to be loyal through a range of marketing activities, such as rebates, price promotions, incentives, and offers.

Channel enslavement

'Channel enslavement' can occur when members make demands for discounts, better margins or preferential treatment and the marketer is obliged to meet these demands because the channel members have sufficient power. Enslavement is obviously something that the marketer should avoid, but it can happen in channels where the balance of power is in the hands of channel members.

Cost

Channel alternatives must be ranked according to costs. These costs refer not just to transport and distribution but also to costs associated with the management of the channel. Channel members will require a margin on sales, which becomes part of the cost structure of the product. If the marketer attempts to reduce the margin, difficulties within the channel can emerge. This was well illustrated in 1997 by the case of the airline Ryanair when it reduced the commission on sales of its tickets through the travel trade.

RYANAIR AND THE TRAVEL TRADE

In 1997 Ryanair announced that it was reducing the commission it paid travel agents on the sale of its tickets, from 9 to 7¹/₂ per cent. This provoked an immediate response from the travel agents, who began a national advertising campaign condemning Ryanair's action. Many agents began to refuse to sell Ryanair tickets.

In the fiercely competitive air market, Ryanair's decision was motivated by a desire to cut costs. The company had also established a call centre where customers could make bookings directly, thus avoiding the middleman and saving the airline the commission that would have to be paid.

The Competition Authority took legal proceedings against the Irish Travel Agents' Association as a result of its campaign against Ryanair. The authority was acting under section 4 of the Competition Act, which deals with collusion by traders to keep prices up or charges down. The association denied that it had promoted collusion, stating that it was common for traders to take their custom elsewhere when prices fell below a certain level.

The case against the IATA was the first such case taken by the Competition Authority under new powers it received in July 1996. These require the authority to enforce competition law. It can act on complaints received from a company or a member of the public; it can also act on its own initiative.

Sources: D. Crowley, 'Travel agents face legal action over alleged Ryanair campaign', *Sunday Business Post*, 12 April 1998; Paul O'Kane, 'Travel agents face court', *Sunday Tribune*, 12 April 1998.

SELECTING THE TYPE OF CHANNEL SYSTEM

After establishing the general channel objectives, the marketer needs to consider the type of channel system required. There are a number of alternatives, ranging from direct selling to more indirect channels.

Direct selling

Direct, face-to-face selling is suitable if a high level of pre-sales and post-sales service is required, if the product is complex, or if order size is large. This will be the case for many industrial products. Airbus Industries, the European manufacturer of aircraft, has a team of sales executives and technical sales personnel who sell directly to airlines around the world. They can provide the potential buyer with comprehensive information on their range of aircraft and on features ranging from different seating configurations to fuel consumption.

Direct selling is also widely used by service providers. Where the service is inseparable from the person providing it, for example consultancy or advice, the marketer will usually sell directly. Other service providers, such as airlines, use a combination of direct selling and sales agents.

Few marketers of consumer goods use direct selling; the majority tend to use middlemen. The impact of the internet could change this, however, and many marketers are investigating using the internet to sell directly. In the United States several companies use the internet to directly sell products, and as the use of the internet increases in Ireland this may also happen here.

Direct marketing

Direct marketing involves the use of various media to interact directly with carefully selected customers. Generally the customer is expected to make a direct response; direct marketing can therefore be a combination of focused communication and distribution. It includes mail order, tele-marketing, invitations to events or launches, free phone advertising, and marketing on the internet. It is gradually becoming more widely used by marketers. To be successfully implemented it requires accurate data-bases of potential targets. The main types of direct marketing include direct mail, catalogue marketing, tele-marketing, and shopping channels on television.

Technology has had an impact, in the form of CD-ROM, the internet, and the use of promotional videos. The internet in particular will take on added significance in direct marketing. The next panel illustrates the results of the first survey conducted on Irish internet usage. While the first users tended to come from a particular demographic and socio-economic segment, it is probable that as the internet diffuses, so too will the profile of users.

THE INTERNET: THE INTERNATIONAL COMPUTER COMMUNICATIONS SYSTEM

One of the main technological advances in communications in the nineteen-nineties has been the internet. In 1997 the first survey of internet usage in Ireland was conducted by the Irish Internet Association, which is the representative association for those doing business on the internet.

Over 2,300 users were surveyed, including members of the public and business users. The survey showed that 94 per cent had used the internet to obtain news, 93 per cent to obtain product information, and 68 per cent to obtain financial information. Forty per cent of those who had used it had made purchases on it.

The great majority of users were male, urban, professional, and well educated. Forty-three per cent had an annual income over £30,000, while 22 per cent were third-level students. Twenty-five per cent of users were female, which was lower than other countries. Of the total, 61 per cent had access to the internet at home and 35 per cent in the office. Only 15 per cent of access was from rural areas.

Source: *Irish Times*, 22 July 1997; *Irish Independent*, 28 July 1997.

The increased use of credit cards by consumers means that payment can be easily made, even by phone, and this has facilitated direct marketing activities.

A number of direct marketing techniques are widely used. Direct mail is useful for letters, samples, or promotional material, which can potentially be sent to every private and business address in the country, An Post operates the 'Postaim' service to facilitate this.

The main difficulty with direct mail is the 'junk mail' tag with which it has come to be associated. This is probably due to poor targeting as much as anything else, with many direct mail campaigns amounting to nothing more than large-scale leaflet drops. Nevertheless in Ireland we are still behind many European countries in the amount of direct mail items received per household, as table 10.1 shows.

Table 10.1: Direct mail in Europe, 1996

Number of addressed direct mail items per household per month

Switzerland	105
Belgium	85
Germany	68
France	65
Sweden	62
Denmark	50
Norway	48
Finland	45
Britain	42
Spain	35
Ireland	**15**
Portugal	10

Source: European Postal Administration, 1996.

Catalogue marketing has traditionally been limited in Ireland to companies such as Family Album, which offer a range of clothes, footwear, and household items. Other marketers, such as the retailer Habitat, which has one retail outlet in the Republic, also use catalogues, which supplement their limited distribution coverage. The British company Argos has also established a number of catalogue stores. Customers select items from a catalogue, and these are obtained from a warehouse. Items are not usually displayed in the shop, which eliminates the need for large areas of shelving and display.

Tele-marketing, which involves direct contact with individuals or organisations, has become a growth area, not least because the Industrial Development Authority began to identify the sector as a potential generator of jobs in the nineteen-nineties. Several multinational firms established their tele-marketing centres in Ireland: for example, American Airlines opened its European call centre in Dublin in 1996, which it used to handle reservations, enquiries and sales to several European countries (*Sunday Tribune*, 17 March 1996).

A related concept is *tele-shopping*, which first came to prominence in the nineteen-seventies. It was thought that it would pose a serious challenge to retailers, and many companies investigated it or began tele-shopping activities in the eighties. While some early entrants did not appear to do very well, others, such as Télétel in France and the Home Shopping network in the United States, prospered (Reynolds, 1990–1).

Owned outlets exist where manufacturers own the retail outlet. These can be good for control purposes: for example, airlines often have their own sales outlets or reservation centres in shopping districts, as has the hand-made chocolate manufacturer Butler. Few firms rely on their own outlets exclusively: airlines, for example, will also sell tickets through travel agents and the internet, and Butler's products are available in supermarkets and duty-free shops. Other companies that distribute some of their products through owned outlets in Ireland include Sony and Levi's.

SELECTING CHANNEL MEMBERS

Given that few manufacturers or service providers own their own distribution outlets, most will use middlemen. The selection of middlemen is an important decision and will be influenced by a number of factors, including the type of product, the amount of service or support required, location, financial security, and willingness to participate in marketing activities. Selection will also be influenced by the degree of exclusivity of the product or the number of outlets actually available to stock it. For many specialist products in a small market like Ireland, there may be only a small number of possible sales outlets.

General criteria for the selection of channel members are:

- market coverage
- customer service ability
- stock and efficiency in order-handling
- credit facilities
- value of the product to them
- willingness to co-operate in marketing activities, for example sales promotions
- ability to provide additional services, for example repair.

The marketer will apply these criteria when assessing individual channel members. They will also be important factors in the development of relationships between the marketer and channel members.

There are different types of channel members. In the following section we examine three broad types, under the headings wholesaling, retailing, and franchising. The criteria listed above can be used in assessing individual members in each case.

Wholesaling

Wholesalers typically function as middlemen between manufacturers and retailers. They deal directly with manufacturers or importers, store products, and provide a range of services to retailers.

The main function of the wholesaler is to buy in bulk from manufacturers and then sell smaller quantities to retailers. In some sectors, such as clothing, where there are many small retailers, the wholesaler is still a strong element in the marketing channel. In other markets, such as the grocery market, the number of smaller retailers has declined and the wholesalers' importance has declined also. Manufacturers and retailers increasingly deal directly, bypassing the wholesaler. Strategically, wholesalers have had to adapt to these changes in the channel system. Some, such as Musgrave, engaged in forward integration by buying the L&N chain of supermarkets in 1995 (*Checkout Ireland*, May 1997); other developments have included wholesalers securing retailing franchises. There were ten major grocery wholesalers in 1997, as shown in table 10.2.

Table 10.2: Irish grocery wholesalers, 1997

Musgrave Ltd; turnover: Republic £607 million, Northern Ireland £46 million, Spain £85 million

BWG Ltd (subsidiary of Irish Distillers Ltd); turnover: Republic £249 million, Northern Ireland £165 million

Punch Holdings Ltd; turnover: £80 million

Mangan Brothers Ltd; turnover: £60 million

Lee and Company Ltd; turnover: £7 million

Associated National Distributors Ltd; turnover: *n.a.*

James A. Barry and Company Ltd; turnover: *n.a.*

E. Fanning and Company Ltd; turnover: *n.a.*

McCambridge's (Galway) Ltd; turnover: *n.a.*

National Wholesale Grocers' Alliance; turnover: *n.a.*

Source: 'Musgrave's and BWG dominate Irish cash and carry business', *Checkout Ireland*, May 1997.

There are also many specialist wholesalers in both consumer and business-to-business product categories.

Retailing

Retailing is the selling of goods or services to the final consumer. Retailers are marketing institutions, members of the marketing channel, and they play an important role in the positioning of the product or service. Retail sales continued to rise in the nineteen-nineties, as table 10.3 shows.

Table 10.3: Retail sales, 1994–7

	1994	1995	1996	1997	1998
Value of sales	118	123.7	134	145.4	159.9
Volume of sales	109.3	112.4	119.4	128.8	140.1

Base: 1990 = 100.
Source: Central Statistics Office.

The retail sector has undergone considerable change in recent decades. Grocery retailing, for example, is concentrated in the hands of a small number of multiples. The following panel, however, suggests that smaller outlets have experienced a revival.

CORNER SHOPS MAKING A COMEBACK

The corner shop has made a comeback in recent years, and independent family-owned retailers, including those belonging to the 'symbol groups'—such as Spar, Mace, Super Valu, and Centra—now account for 45 per cent of the £4,000 million Irish grocery market. This compares favourably with other European countries, where the figure is 35 per cent, and Britain, where it is only 7 per cent.

The turnaround has come about through retailers investing in their shops. The low population density makes small independent outlets particularly suitable. Challenges in the sector include opening hours and Sunday opening.

The symbol groups have grown in importance. These work on a franchise basis, with the franchise-holder buying for the group and providing support services to independent retailers, including technology, marketing, and shop design. Super Valu, Centra and Spar are the biggest participants in the Irish market. Musgrave operates the franchise for 193 Super Valu branches and 268 Centra shops and claims some 20 per cent of the Republic's grocery market. The franchise for the Republic's 320 Spar shops is owned by BWG Ltd, which also holds the Mace franchise for Leinster and Northern Ireland.

An area where development was scheduled to take place was the forecourt market. Mace and Maxol had agreed a forecourt alliance; Spar also developed the forecourt channel but was not aligned with any particular petrol company. Musgrave bought the Northern Ireland chain Wellworths and converted it into Super Valu branches.

The Belfast wholesaler Henderson holds the Spar franchise for Northern Ireland. It also has the VG franchise, and extended its operations into the Republic with the

> Vivo chain. Vantage, another wholesale group, supplies the Cost-Cutter low-price chain of shops.
>
> Source: J. O'Sullivan, 'Corner shops making major comeback', *Irish Times*, 20 February 1998.

There has been an increase in the number of most types of retail outlets. New shopping centres in cities and towns, many of which were encouraged by urban renewal schemes and tax incentives, have seen the retail sector grow in both turnover and jobs.

Many of these new developments have had an effect on existing retailers, not least in the form of competition. Many larger shopping centres were in the outskirts of cities, increasing competition for established retailers in these areas. Some retailers responded to the challenge by improving their own marketing activities. This was the case in Lisburn, County Antrim, where local retailers stepped up their marketing of Lisburn as a shopping location in response to Marks and Spencer's decision to build a 240,000 square feet complex at Sprucefield on the outskirts of the town (Brown, 1988).

An emerging trend in retailing in the nineties was increased internationalisation (Treadgold, 1990–1). In Ireland this manifested itself in the increased presence of British retail chains, attracted by growth in the Irish retail market (*Irish Times*, 18 June 1997). The advent of greater European integration was also expected to lead to change in the sector, though Quinn (1995) maintained that the retail trade had paid very little attention to the views of customers in its approach to the single European market. He suggested that listening to the customer might make the single market a greater reality, and that Superquinn's customers were unhappy at the slow rate of change from local shopping experience to a more 'European' experience. They also perceived a lack of benefit from the increase in competition and from supermarkets failing to cater for the environmental interests of their customers.

In the nineties many retailers concentrated on attempting to differentiate through customer service. One study (Sparks, 1990–1) examined what retailers could do to establish a service strategy, drawing an analogy from the value chain. It looked at the experience of an American retailer, Nordstrom, which had managed to become synonymous with customer service. The lesson for retailers was clear: they could improve customer service by adding value. This could be done by being more responsive to customers' needs, through shop layout and design, staff training, and complaint-handling procedures, and providing services such as children's play areas or home delivery.

Functions of the retailer

In addition to making products or services available to the market, retailers are a source of market information, they play a role in the legal transfer of title, and they implement promotional activities on behalf of marketers. Increasingly, retailers are competing directly with national brands by developing ranges of own-label products.

The development of own-label or retailer brands has been of particular significance in the grocery market. Quinnsworth was the first supermarket chain in Ireland to introduce own-label brands. It did so to offer a cheaper high-quality alternative to its customers, to enhance its price-perception and price-competitiveness, and to improve its profitability

(Pratt, 1994). Retailers may be involved in delivery, offering repair or adjustment services, packaging, or arranging finance.

INFORMATION TECHNOLOGY IN RETAILING

One of the concepts that many retailers concentrated on in the nineteen-nineties was efficient consumer response (ECR). This involved a number of applications that retailers could use to improve service-stock management by constant maintenance of stock levels and increasing the range of goods available. It also involved data warehousing and mining, which concentrates on consumers' preferences and selects specific groups with product or service offerings.

In-store modifications, such as self-scanning and electronic shelf edge labelling, which improved the shopping environment and made more information available to customers, also came under this heading (*Checkout Ireland*, December 1997). Scanning systems had been widely introduced by retailers. These had the advantages of improved stock control, reduced labour costs, increased speed, and improved customer service. These benefits could be reinforced by linking the scanning equipment to head office computers, which can then provide the latest sales and stock figures. Stock control could be implemented for all products, or simply for high-value stock, depending on which option offered the retailer greater added value.

Electronic data interchange

Electronic data interchange (EDI) has had a significant impact on channel relationships. EDI is the transfer of structured data by agreed message standards from computer to computer (Nelson, 1990). In retailing it involves the transmission of orders by means of a computer network from the retailer to the supplier. Large suppliers, such as Musgrave and BWG, have been using this method; every retail unit in the Super Valu chain, for example, is linked to head office through an EDI system. Order confirmations arrive to verify the delivery.

EDI technology can also be used for invoicing, for notifying retailers of price changes or new products, and for payment. It is essential for suppliers who want a central billing facility for all the products they deliver.

Developments in computer systems allow more accurate sales forecasts, more focused promotions, and comparative analysis with similar products. When combined with sales-based ordering or a continuous replenishment programme, such systems will increase the precision with which demand is estimated and stock ordered. This will reduce warehouse storage time, lower stock costs, and improve customer service.

It is also possible for manufacturers to directly manage the retailer's stock. This would largely depend on the closeness of the relationship between the manufacturer and the retailer.

Improved delivery efficiency can be achieved with hand-held terminals, which can be used by delivery drivers. The driver has a programmed terminal containing customers' details, which calculates the amount and any outstanding balance for cash sales. This can be linked to a printer, which can produce a cash invoice or delivery note for credit customers. At the end of the day the delivery information is downloaded to the supplier's computer, and the deliveries made can be checked against remaining stock.

In-store changes

The changes that will have the most immediate effect on customers have been the advances in in-store technology, including electronic shelf edge pricing. This involves an LCD screen built in to the shelf, which can be altered instantly by the in-store computer by means of infra-red or radio frequency transmission, with the check-outs receiving the information simultaneously to give full price agreement. With in-store price changes quite common, such a system would achieve labour savings. The LCD display could also show information on nutrition, unit value, and special offers, and these could be updated easily.

Self-scanning involves giving customers a hand-held scanner, which they can use to scan items as they move through the supermarket. When they reach the check-out, the scanner prints the bill. Self-scanning reduces queuing time. Superquinn has tested these systems among members of its loyalty club. Some supermarkets in Britain have experimented with self-check-outs, which allow shoppers to scan, bag and pay for groceries using a system that incorporates an ATM.

Computerised in-store information kiosks can provide information on special offers, new products, or brands in stock. Bookshops could find such systems beneficial. Other developments include what has been referred to as 'micro-marketing', with electronic screens on trolleys, which can even broadcast personal messages to specific customers. This development may be some years away.

Loyalty schemes

Retailers in the nineteen-nineties enthusiastically embraced the concept of loyalty schemes. Loyalty cards certainly play a role in holding on to customers; they also provide an information data-base on the customer's shopping behaviour. On-line systems mean that points can be recorded or redeemed instantly. (The implications of loyalty schemes for consumers' behaviour are discussed in chapter 6.)

Retailers and the internet

Shopping on the internet will probably grow in importance as use of the internet increases. Some retailers have developed web sites to expand their retailing activities.

The main drawbacks of the internet have been making secure payments and the slowness of downloading information. Improvements in telecommunications technology and improved security software have been developed in an attempt to overcome these problems.

CLASSIFYING RETAIL OUTLETS

Retail outlets can be classified in a number of ways, ranging from self-service to full service and from speciality shops to vending machines. Some outlets are specialist, for example a fishing tackle shop, which specialises in product lines within a particular category. Other outlets, such as supermarkets, convenience stores, and department stores, stock wide ranges of products in many categories. The nature of the product and the customers' requirements will dictate the type of retail outlet used.

Franchising

A franchise is a contractual agreement under which the franchisor sells certain rights to market specified goods or services to the franchisee. Franchises as a form of business activity have grown in Ireland. It was estimated in 1996 that there were six hundred retail franchise units, with a combined turnover of £202 million, including outlets such as Abrakebabra, Golden Discs, and some Bewley's cafés (*Examiner*, 10 May 1996). Many international franchises have developed their operations in Ireland, especially in the fast-food sector, but there are also some Irish examples, as the following panel shows.

DUDS 'N' SUDS

Duds 'n' Suds is a franchisor in Derry specialising in the franchising of launderettes. By 1997 a number of franchises had been established around the country. The estimated total start-up cost of each is £100,000. The franchise itself costs £15,000, and the franchisor assists with the negotiation of leases, purchase of machinery, training, and business advice. Franchisees pay a fixed proportion of turnover each year to the franchisor.

The basics of the business range from offering self-service washing and drying facilities to a full service that includes cleaning, dry-cleaning, drying, and ironing. Clothes are docketed and washed separately according to colour and temperature; a single customer's washing may require the use of five separate machines.

Source: *Examiner*, 10 May 1996.

Franchisors can be classified in a number of ways. Manufacturer-sponsored franchisors exist where manufacturers grant franchises to dealers or retailers. This is common in the motor industry. Manufacturer-sponsored wholesale franchisors include companies such as Coca-Cola, which give franchises to bottlers. Service-sponsored retail franchises include international operations such as McDonald's and Burger King, and the Duds 'n' Suds example described above. There has also been some growth in retail-to-retail franchises: for example, the Body Shop chain in Britain has expanded through franchising new retail outlets in various parts of the world.

With most franchises the product or service will have proved itself in the market before franchising gets under way. The franchisee must have the capital to get the operation off the ground, and the system must be properly supervised. The franchisor must have a continuing interest in the franchisee's success and must give advice and help to the franchisee.

Typically, franchise agreements permit the franchisee to carry on a particular business under a specified name or using a process or equipment belonging to the franchisor. It entitles the franchisor to exercise control over the manner in which the franchisee carries out the business, and it obliges the franchisor to provide the franchisee with assistance in carrying out the business. The agreement obliges the franchisee to periodically pay sums of money in consideration for the franchise.

The benefits of franchising to the franchisor are an expanded distribution system without the need for large-scale capital investment, a guaranteed income—which can range from 5 to 15 per cent of the franchisee's turnover—and the onus on the franchisee to run the franchise smoothly (MTS, 1992). In some cases franchisors charge a fixed annual fee or royalty, though in other cases financial arrangements vary. The ice cream manufacturer Häagen-Dazs, for example, established a number of café franchises in Europe. The cafés served a range of ice creams, sorbets, gourmet coffees, patisserie, and sweets, and represented an extension for the brand. They charge an initial flat fee for each franchise of between £60,000 and £100,000 and after that take a proportion from the ice cream and other products on sale. The company established its first Irish operation in Belfast in 1998 (Sunday Business Post, 12 April 1998).

Franchisees usually pay an advertising levy, which can vary between 1 and 6 per cent of turnover. In return the franchisee has the benefit of advertising and promotional campaigns that would cost them more if they were financing them on their own. The franchisee will get the benefit of the support and assistance of the franchisor, a proven product or service, and the benefits of the franchisor's research and development. Usually a high level of interdependence will develop between the franchisor and the franchisee. Business failure rates for franchisees in start-up ventures may therefore be lower.

Channel management

Relationship marketing plays an important role in marketing channel management. Relationships should be mutually beneficial. Relationships may also be influenced by the level of power held by the marketer or a channel member.

If a manufacturer or marketer is to give a lead to co-ordinating channel members, they must possess and exercise the requisite amount of power. The essence of power is having access to resources needed by others. Leadership in a channel results if the marketer can command the loyalty of the channel members. Power can have a number of bases:

1. **Coercive power**—the ability to harm the interests of the other party in the relationship: for example, the manufacturer could slow down deliveries to retailers.
2. **Reward power**—the ability to withhold or bestow some material reward on the other party in the relationship, for example price discounts.
3. **Legitimised power**—the extent to which the commands of a particular member of the channel are obligatory, for example under contract.
4. **Manipulative power**—resourcefulness in the use of credibility and attractiveness.

A source of high credibility convinces, while a source of high attractiveness persuades.

The different power bases can have varying degrees of effectiveness. Coercive power is generally the least effective, in that it achieves minimal compliance. People do not like being coerced, and coercion tends to fuel resentment. This is not a basis for developing channel relationships.

Reward power gets results in line with the magnitude of the reward. Reward power in channels will usually be based on the profitability of individual products or the volumes ordered. The more sales effort expended by the channel member the higher the potential reward. The difficulty with reward power arises when competition or other environmental forces limit the channel member's ability to achieve the reward. Successfully achieving rewards encourages the tendency to expect more and better rewards the next time. Marketers have not got unlimited resources with which to reward channel members.

Legitimised power generally results in no higher level of performance than is formally needed to signify compliance. In other words, channel members may fulfil their contractual obligations and no more.

Manipulative power is regarded by many as the most effective. The power of persuasion can deliver the desired results. This may be a feature of developing relationships.

Motivating channel members

Motivation of channel members will be an important part of the channel management process if channel relationships are to be maintained. There are many ways in which to motivate, and the way chosen will depend primarily on the needs of the channel member.

The use of power in the channel will also be important. Support can be offered to channel members in the form of co-operative arrangements, partnerships, and strategic alliances. In addition, some firms use distribution programming. This has been defined as a comprehensive set of policies for the promotion of the product through the channel (McCammon, 1970); a frame of reference for it is illustrated in fig. 10.4.

Fig. 10.4: Frame of reference for distribution programming

Manufacturer's marketing goals
Based on careful analysis of
>   corporate capability
>   competition
>   demand
>   cost-volume relationships
>   legal considerations
>   reseller capability

and stated in terms of
>   sales (cash and unit)
>   market share
>   contribution to overhead
>   rate of return on investment
>   customer attitude, preference and 'readiness-to-buy' indices.

Manufacturer's channel requirements

Reseller support needed to achieve marketing goals stated in terms of
- coverage ratio
- amount and location of display space
- level and composition of stock investment
- service capability and standards
- advertising, sales promotion, and personal selling support
- market development activities.

Retailer's requirements

Compensation expected for required support stated in terms of
- managerial aspirations
- trade preferences
- financial goals
- rate of stock turnover
- rate of return on investment
- gross margin (cash and percentage)
- contribution to overhead (cash and percentage)
- gross margin and contribution to overhead per pound invested in stock
- gross margin and contribution to overhead per unit of space
- non-financial goals.

Distribution policies

- price concessions
- financial assistance
- protective provisions.

Source: Bucklin, *Vertical Marketing Systems* (1970).

In addition to distribution programming, co-operative arrangements might include co-operative advertising, in-store promotional materials, coupon-handling allowances, prizes for competitions, training, research, and discounts. The principles underlying partnerships and strategic allowances will be fundamentally based on the principles of relationship marketing. (These are described in chapter 15.)

Assessing the effectiveness of channel members

Rosenbloom (1995) recommends that firms conduct periodic and comprehensive performance audits of channel members. Criteria that could be used to measure effectiveness include sales performance, stock maintenance, attitudes of channel members, competition, general growth prospects, and other relevant criteria, such as the channel members' financial status, their reputation, and the quality of their service. To a large extent these criteria derive from the criteria used in the initial process of selecting channel members. These criteria can be developed into a weighted credit system for evaluating each member's performance, as shown in table 10.4.

Table 10.4: Weighted credit method for assessing performance of channel members

Criteria	Criteria weights (A)	Criteria scores (B) (out of 10)	Weighted score (A X B)
Sales performance	0.5	7	3.5
Stock maintenance	0.2	6	1.2
Selling capability	0.15	6	0.9
Attitudes	0.1	5	0.5
Growth prospects	0.05	3	0.15
Overall performance rating			6.25

The marketer can therefore assess each channel member using this system. The relative weightings indicate the importance attached to a particular criterion: thus sales performance is judged to be the most important in the table above. The weighted credit method is one way to assess performance. It is useful as it provides an overall rating; low scores on individual criteria can be examined in further detail.

FURTHER READING

Christopher, M., *Logistics and Supply Chain Management*, London: FT Pitman 1992.
Rosenbloom, B., *Marketing Channels: A Management View* (fifth edition), Hinsdale (Ill.): Dryden Press 1995.
Stern, L., el-Ansery, A., and Coughlan, A., *Marketing Channels*, Englewood Cliffs (NJ): Prentice-Hall 1996.

DISCUSSION QUESTIONS

1. Do you think that developments in technology, such as the internet, will make marketing channels more direct? Give reasons for your answer.
2. Write a profile of the marketing channel components for each of the following:
   —Coca-Cola
   —a small hotel
   —a Mexican restaurant
   —lawnmowers
   —fishing trawlers.
3. Explain the term *franchising*. Can you identify any franchising opportunities in Ireland that have not yet been exploited?
4. Comment on the reasons why retailers need to pay careful attention to customer service.
5. Explain why relationship marketing is important in the management of marketing channels.

Marketing Channels   319

REFERENCES

Bloemer, J., and de Ruyter, K., 'On the relationship between store image, store satisfaction and store loyalty', *European Journal of Marketing*, vol. 32 (1998), no. 5–6.

Brown, S., 'Out of town shopping development: a case history in retail innovation', *Irish Marketing Review*, vol. 3 (1988).

Bucklin, L. (ed.), Vertical Marketing Systems, Glenview (Ill.): Scott Foresman 1970.

MTS, *Franchising in Ireland Survey*, Dublin: Bank of Ireland 1992.

Nelson, C., *EDI: The Key to Business Success*, Dublin: Eirtrade 1990.

Pratt, Maurice, 'Own Brands: The Benefits' (paper presented to National Marketing Conference), *Business and Finance*, October 1994.

Quinn, Feargal, 'A case for the customer', *European Superstore Decisions*, spring 1995.

Reynolds, J., 'Is there a market for teleshopping?', *Irish Marketing Review*, vol. 5 (1990–1), no. 2.

Rosenbloom, B., *Marketing Channels: A Management View* (fifth edition), Hinsdale (Ill.): Dryden Press 1995.

Sparks, L., 'Retailing in the 1990s: differentiation through customer service?', *Irish Marketing Review*, vol. 5 (1990–1), no. 2.

Treadgold, A., 'The emerging internationalisation of retailing: present status and future prospects', *Irish Marketing Review*, vol. 5 (1990–1), no. 2.

CASE STUDIES

These cases were developed as a basis for class discussion rather than to illustrate either effective or ineffective handling of an administrative situation. The market shares and prices used are for illustration purposes only.

AGFA AND THE AUDIOCASSETTE AND VIDEOCASSETTE MARKET

The Irish market for blank audiocassette and videocassettes was very competitive. Manufacturers and distributors fought for market share, and the market became extremely price-sensitive. Against this background one of the leading manufacturers, Agfa, faced a dilemma. It had a fairly significant market share in both markets, but in spite of volume sales increasing in line with market growth, sales income was static. The company's brands were under intense price pressure. The management of the company was considering how to develop a marketing strategy that would improve its sales position.

Agfa-Gevaert

Agfa-Gevaert had come into existence when the German company Agfa and the Belgian company Gevaert combined in the mid-sixties. The company produced a wide range of products, including photographic film, audiocassettes and videocassettes, photocopiers, and film-processing equipment. The company had at one time produced cameras but had decided to get out of the market in the nineteen-eighties when competition intensified. It was the market leader in many product categories in Europe and also had significant markets in other countries.

The company's Irish operation involved the distribution of most of the parent group's products. Agfa film was widely distributed through camera shops, pharmacies, and other retailers. Audiocassettes and videocassettes were also widely distributed, sold under the Agfa brand.

In common with other European markets, competition in the Irish audiocassette and videocassette market was intensifying. The senior management in Leverkusen, Germany, began a review of the company's performance in this product category throughout its European markets.

The audiocassette market

The audiocassette market was estimated to be worth approximately £5 million. The market had been increasing in volume by 2–3 per cent per year, but increases in income had been much lower. There were seven significant brands on the market, as shown in table 10A.1.

Table 10A.1: Audiocassette brands by market share

Agfa	16%
Maxell	15%
Sony	14%
TDK	12%
BASF	10%
That's	10%
Fuji	8%
Others	15%

Most competitors produced a number of cassette types, ranging from basic ferromagnetic ('ferro') to high-quality chromium dioxide ('chrome'). Agfa was the dominant brand in the ferromagnetic category and had also introduced a range of high-quality chromium dioxide cassettes. The highest-quality chromium dioxide cassettes guaranteed the best sound quality but occupied a niche position, accounting for 1 or 2 per cent of sales. Most cassettes sold were in the ferromagnetic or lower-quality chromium dioxide categories and were generally bought in multiple packs, containing three or five cassettes.

With regard to quality, research showed that Sony, TDK, That's and Maxell were considered to offer the highest sound quality. Agfa was perceived as offering a lower quality, even though there were few if any complaints from consumers or retailers. It was thought that its price positioning had a strong influence on this perception.

Users fell into three broad age groups: teenagers (11–18), young adults (19–25), and adults (26+). Teenagers and young adults accounted for roughly two-thirds of sales, with the remaining third spread over a much wider age profile. Consumers did not differentiate strongly between brands on grounds of quality: research showed that they considered the main brands to be fairly similar on sound quality. They did, however, differentiate on price. Few consumers were loyal to a particular brand: the majority responded to price promotions and would switch brands on this basis.

Few brands did any significant advertising; most communication was concentrated on in-store promotions, which were heavily price-based. Agfa was considered one of the most price-competitive brands on the market. TDK and Maxell were the only brands to engage in any significant advertising. TDK concentrated on outdoor poster campaigns, while Maxell had done some radio advertising. Agfa concentrated on on-pack promotions.

Agfa audiocassettes were distributed mainly through record and music shops, including a large number of small privately owned shops as well as outlets in department stores such as Clery's and Arnott's. Outlets that stocked Agfa film, such as the HCR chain of pharmacies, were also significant.

The other brands on the market also enjoyed significant nationwide distribution. BASF was distributed through the Golden Discs chain, which had the distribution rights for this product in Ireland. Sony had a strong presence in electrical retailers, where it complemented the company's other products; and Fuji tended to appear in shops that also stocked Fuji film. Some of the larger music shops, such as HMV, stocked up to four of the leading brands. Smaller outlets stocked one or two at the most.

The search for new distributors was intensive, and some competitors adopted a 'sell to anyone' approach. Supermarkets and discount stores began to stock the product, though this tended to annoy existing channel members, who complained that they could not buy the same volume as supermarkets. They also argued that it would be bad for the image of the product to be associated with discount stores.

The videocassette market

The blank videocassette market exhibited similar characteristics to the audiocassette market, except that competition was even more intense. The market was estimated to be worth £8 million and had grown in line with increased ownership of videocassette recorders. Seventy per cent of Irish homes owned a video machine in the mid-nineties. Growth in the market could also be stimulated by particular events: for example, sales increased significantly during the soccer World Cup competitions in 1990 and 1994, as a result of the involvement of the Irish team.

The mass production of cassettes had become a feature of the industry, especially in Asia; and one company, Saehan Media, established a manufacturing plant in Sligo to serve the European market. At one time in the early nineties there were at least twenty-five brands on the market. Many of these were transient, but between them they accounted for over a third of the market. The top nine brands are listed in table 10A.2.

Table 10A.2: Videocassette brands by market share

JVC	11%
Sony	10%
Agfa	9%
Maxell	9%
Memorex	9%
BASF	6%
Fuji	5%
Scotch	4%
PDM	3%
Others	34%

The main competitors in the videocassette market produced products of different quality ranges. The higher-quality products tended to be used by video professionals. With regard to the standard VHS cassette, which accounted for up to 90 per cent of consumer market sales,

Agfa was considered to produce one of the best and most competitive products.

As with the audiocassette market, however, consumers were not especially loyal to particular brands, and there was little or no brand advertising. On-pack promotions were common, which included competitions and banded offers. Agfa used some banded offers, which had included a roll of film banded to multi-packs of videocassettes. The highly competitive nature of the market and high advertising costs meant that manufacturers and distributors were reluctant to invest in brand advertising.

The PDM brand had benefited from that company's sponsorship of cycling. One of Ireland's leading cyclists in the nineteen-eighties and early nineties, Seán Kelly, had been sponsored by PDM. In spite of this, the brand had a small market share.

Cassettes were typically sold in packs of three or five, with a significant price discount. Only 20 per cent of sales were of a single cassette.

Distribution for most brands was through the same outlets as audiocassettes, with the addition of video rental shops. Some of these, such as the Xtra-Vision chain, had introduced an own-label cassette. Retailers considered that the best form of promotion was a good in-store display. Agfa had produced free-standing and counter displays for its audiocassettes and its videocassettes, and these had been well received by retailers.

A feature of the videocassette market was the sporadic appearance of relatively obscure brands, usually imported from Asia and sold mainly through discount stores and smaller music outlets. These did not develop a foothold in the market but had the effect of creating brand confusion among consumers and causing downward pressure on prices. The effects of this activity in the distribution channels could be severe at times, with retailers using it as a means of getting better price deals from the main manufacturers and distributors.

Pricing structures

The following tables show the pricing structure for the mainstream audiocassettes (table 10A.3) and videocassettes (table 10A.4). These were estimated to account for 90 per cent of sales in both categories.

Audiocassettes come in two categories, giving sixty minutes' or ninety minutes' recording time. 60 per cent of purchases were of sixty-minute cassettes and 40 per cent were of ninety-minute cassettes.

Table 10A.3: Pricing structure, audiocassettes

Product group: ferromagnetic (type I)

Brand	Size	Trade price	Average selling price
Agfa FDX1	60	£0.50	£0.90
	90	£0.75	£1.10
BASF FE	60	£0.45	£0.95
	90	£0.70	£1.05
Fuji FR	60	£0.55	£0.99
	90	£0.85	£1.39

Maxell UDIS	60	£0.60	£1.10
	90	£0.89	£1.79
Sony HF-S	60	£0.60	£1.09
	90	£0.89	£1.69
TDK AR	60	£0.75	£1.55
	90	£0.99	£1.99
That's	60	£0.69	£1.29
	90	£0.89	£1.79

Videocassettes are sold in two main categories: E180, giving three hours' recording, and E240, giving four hours. E180 cassettes accounted for 90 per cent of sales.

Table 10A.4: Pricing structure, videocassettes

Product group: VHS standard

Brand	*Size*	*Trade price*	*Average selling price*
Agfa	E180	£2.30	£3.99
BASF ER	E180	£2.10	£3.99
	E240	£3	£5.99
Bush	E180	£1.80	£2.99
Fuji HQ	E180	£2.40	£4.99
High Colour	E240	£3	£4.99
JVC	E180	£2	£3.99
Lloytron	E180	£1.60	£2.99
Maxell	E180	£2.35	£4.29
	E240	£3.40	£5.99
Memorex	E180	£2.19	£3.99
	E240	£3.59	£5.19
PDM	E180	£2	£3.95
	E240	£3	£5.95
Premium	E180	£1.80	£2.99
Sony DX	E180	£2.20	£3.99
	E240	£3.50	£5.99
TDK HS	E180	£2.45	£4.99
	E240	£3.50	£6.99

THE MANAGEMENT DECISION

Agfa's Irish management were required to prepare a marketing plan for the company's marketing director in Leverkusen. They were asked specifically to emphasise a pricing strategy for the Irish market that would increase sales income by 5 per cent.

As they considered their options they were aware that in a fiercely competitive market any increase in price could meet resistance. There was also the problem of the reaction of the trade: if they did not get the price deal they wanted, experience had shown that they would switch to another brand. The sluggish sales growth in the market meant that funds for advertising were limited, though there could be an opportunity for an innovative sales promotion.

As the management deliberated they were also aware of the company's response to the increased competition in the camera market in the nineteen-eighties.

DISCUSSION QUESTIONS

1. Are there ways in which purchasers of audiocassettes and videocassettes can be encouraged to be more loyal to a particular brand?
2. Advise the management on their pricing decision. Should prices be increased? If so, by how much?
3. Develop a proposal for a price promotional strategy that will meet the head office's objectives.

KEELINGS: MAKING STRATEGY VISIBLE THROUGH IDENTITY

Keelings is one of Ireland's leading importers and distributors of fresh fruit, flowers, and vegetables. It is a private company with a strong family ethos and a full-time staff of more than two hundred.

Until 1997 the Keelings group consisted of a number of individually named companies. Some of these included the family name Keelings, while others retained the names of the companies it had acquired over the years. In Britain a buyer in Tesco might have dealt with J. K. Peters in Glasgow or Emsley and Collins in Dewsbury, while in Ireland buyers might have dealt with Keelings (Fruit) Ltd, Amalgamated Fruit, Patrick Bolger, Greengrow, Dan O'Sullivan, Healthworks, or Keelings (Flowers) Ltd.

A changing retail environment in Ireland and Britain, and a more competitive market for suppliers of fresh produce, required Keelings to reposition at home and abroad.

The business objectives of an identity change

- To deal with the concept of a Keelings Group as the core of the business. This would help make it clear to partners and customers that they are dealing with one company, as opposed to many unrelated companies.
- To communicate the essential attributes of Keelings, such as its concentration on quality, professionalism, and trustworthiness.
- To raise awareness among the trade and ensure that leading suppliers and customers from abroad will want to do even more business with Keelings.
- To strengthen the position of Keelings as one of Ireland's top two distributors of fresh produce.
- To reaffirm the position of Keelings as the banana ripener and distributor with the highest standards in Britain and Ireland.
- To make the Keelings vision tangible for staff and consistent throughout the group.
- To build the corporate brand so as to help cement relationships with leading retailers and suppliers and to give Keelings a competitive edge in a rapidly changing market.
- To establish an identity system that would lead to time and cost efficiencies as well as a greater level of professionalism.

The external environment

The Irish and British retail trades have undergone significant change in the nineties. For Keelings the following issues have had most impact.

Central purchasing has become the norm: gone are the days when each retail outlet placed its orders with its preferred suppliers. Buyers in these centralised purchasing departments now wield significant power, and they have the ability to determine the success or failure of their suppliers. Suppliers are expected to supply products to retailers that conform to rigorous quality specifications, while at the same time keeping prices low.

The arrival of Tesco in Ireland has reaffirmed the changes that have been taking place and has underlined the adage that only the fittest can survive.

Retailers' own brands are gaining respectability and in many cases are beating established brands. This is also true of fresh produce; and, with the exception of some brands (such as Chiquita and Fyffes), retailers are requiring suppliers to pack fruit and vegetables in own-brand packaging.

The identity brief

In September 1996 Keelings appointed the Identity Business, a firm of identity specialists, to create a new identity for the group. At the outset the requirement was for a design solution that would deal with the concept of a Keelings Group as being at the centre of the firm. Therefore an identity system was required to embrace all aspects of Keelings and its related business units. The solution would be required to work alongside other trade marks and symbols, including ISO 9002, Chiquita, and other suppliers' logos. A stated requirement was to visualise how the proposed identity would work on stationery, packaging, signage, and vehicle livery. A recommended house style was to be documented.

In essence, therefore, the objective of the design project was to create an identity that would reflect the nature of the core business and provide a coherent corporate structure and house style to allow for present and future needs.

The design solution

Detailed interviews were conducted by the Identity Business with staff, the group's biggest retail customers in Ireland and Britain and the suppliers ENZA and Chiquita to get a detailed understanding of Keelings and the main issues.

The roles and values of the firm were clarified with the chief executive and his team.

Keelings (Fruit) Ltd, Amalgamated Fruit and Greengrow became Keelings Ltd. Emsley and Collins became Keelings (Dewsbury) Ltd; J. K. Peters became Keelings (Scotland) Ltd; Healthworks became Keelings (Catering) Ltd. Keelings (Flowers) Ltd remained unchanged. Patrick Bolger and Dan O'Sullivan also remained unchanged, because of the reputation and goodwill associated with the individuals concerned.

An extensive audit of buildings, vehicles, stationery, labels and boxes was carried out.

Creating the identity

Sketch proposals were developed and reduced to the final direction in consultation with the chief executive and corporate identity manager. This was then developed and tested against a set of criteria.

The Keelings name was hand-drawn to give an organic feel to the brand. A gradation was incorporated to give an impression of the natural ripening process, while the leaves denote freshness.

The slogan *Naturally fresh* captures the essence of all their produce, making Keelings the natural choice for consumers.

Developing the identity

The Identity Business conducted an audit of all existing communications aimed at staff, suppliers, and customers, which enabled them to establish a communications structure, which involved

- promoting the Keelings brand
- developing a visual style owned by Keelings
- rationalising the range of forms
- developing a suite of stationery and templates for all staff to ensure that the entire firm is communicating in one voice
- designing a system for signage and vehicle livery.

Launching the new identity

The new identity was implemented consistently and effectively throughout all communications. Tailored launch letters were sent to three audiences: staff, customers, and suppliers. Advertisements were placed in the British trade press.

Point-of-sale material, including labels and boxes, was redesigned. One stationery design replaced eight distinct types. Standardised layouts were applied to letter-headings, compliments slips, and business cards. Templates for all word-processed documents were installed on staff computers.

A stunning forty-foot vehicle was designed; the design has subsequently been implemented on all vehicles. A signage system was launched at five locations in Ireland and Britain.

IDENTITY MANAGEMENT

The Identity Business established a number of controls to help Keelings protect their investment. Before any item was printed, proofs were produced on various types of paper. Master artwork was produced in various sizes and versions. A corporate typeface was selected, and standards were set for its use. This typeface was installed on all computers, and all other typefaces were removed. Guidelines were compiled on the use of the Keelings identity throughout all applications, including signage and vehicle livery.

The outcome for marketing and business objectives

Having consolidated the Keelings name and created an identity that expresses its core values, the group is well placed to perform in a demanding, competitive market. Keelings is now communicating in one voice, and time and cost efficiencies have been realised.

From the customer's point of view, it is now much easier to contact Keelings, because there has been total clarification around the name. This makes Keelings' strength more apparent. British retailers have complimented Keelings on this change.

Using the new identity, a press advertisement was placed in the British trade press. It generated twenty times the response to previous advertising.

In 1972 Keelings had introduced its first vehicle livery. Latterly it had received many negative comments about it. Since the launch of the new livery, suppliers and customers throughout Europe placed calls with the management of Keelings to tell them of the impact it had on them; in some cases it reminded past acquaintances to renew contact with them.

A poster campaign in bus shelters has been promoting kiwi fruit, and the advertisement is endorsed by a Keelings logo. The man on the street is now recognising a previously hidden Keelings.

One design has been adopted for letter-headings, compliments slips, business cards, and other stationery items. Printing costs are reduced, because the only changes are in relation to address details.

Fax, memo and letter-heading templates have been installed throughout the company. This reduces time spent on re-inventing the wheel every time a member of the staff writes a fax. The quality of these items further reinforces Keelings' strengthened professionalism.

DISCUSSION QUESTIONS

1. Consider the environmental issues that can force a company to reposition itself, and examine how a change in identity can play a vital role in this task.
2. Discuss the implications of a change in identity for the staff, and consider how such a change can improve efficiency and work practices.
3. Consider how a change in identity can help customers.

OKI SYSTEMS (IRELAND) LTD

Oki Systems (Ireland) Ltd was established in 1991 by Oki Europe Ltd to offer products and support to customers throughout Ireland. Oki Europe Ltd is part of the Oki Data Corporation, which in turn is a wholly owned subsidiary of Oki Electric Industry Ltd in Japan.

The Oki Electric group decided to form Oki Data Corporation in 1994 during a reorganisation of the company. As the worldwide computer peripheral market was continuing to grow at an increasingly rapid pace, it was decided to create a subsidiary that would concentrate on R&D, manufacturing, sales and marketing of fax machines, printers and multi-function products throughout the world.

By 1996 Oki Electric Industries had grown into a Fortune 500 company with worldwide sales of over $7,000 million and more than twenty thousand employees working in thirty-eight countries.

Oki Systems Ireland Ltd

The growth of the Irish economy has led to a surge in the market for computers and peripherals. Business at Oki Ireland is growing quickly, and the company continues to expand its product line. It now sells a range of printers and fax machines both to the business market and to retailers. Oki is the largest seller of dot-matrix and inkjet printers in Ireland and has a well-developed and integrated distribution network. The main European manufacturing plant is in Cumberland, Scotland, so products are readily accessible to the Irish customer.

Oki Ireland recently entered into an agreement with Viking Components Inc., which sells computer system enhancements. Viking Components recently established a manufacturing plant in the Citywest industrial estate in County Dublin. It chose Oki Ireland to promote and distribute its memory upgrades and connectivity products throughout Ireland.

In 1998 Oki Systems opened an office in Northern Ireland to service the six counties with a full range of printers and fax machines. Oki is aggressively seeking to build business in Northern Ireland by being close to its customers. Its Northern Ireland manager, Paul Cinnamond, commented: 'We appear to be the first major printer manufacturer to have invested in a sales and support presence in the province.'

Fig. 10A.1: Printers and fax product line

Dot-matrix printers

Page printers

Inkjet printers

Thermal POS printers

Printronix printers

Okifax machines

Scanners

In addition to fax machines and printers, Oki Ireland also has a large portion of the lucrative computer support business. It markets IT services, including a technical support desk, with troubleshooting capabilities for customers. It also installs and maintains computer hardware, including networks. The computer support business adds a synergistic effect to Oki's business range, as the fax and printer businesses feed off computer services, and vice versa.

Sales force organisation

With the growth in the printer and fax business at Oki Ireland, the sales manager was concerned that all areas of the market should receive the coverage required to maintain sales and market share. He was well aware that during economic upturns many smaller customers might not get the attention they deserved. He decided to reorganise the sales force. Instead of the sales force selling to all types of customer, he decided to reorganise the selling effort of printers and fax machines to concentrate on two broad customer types. The company created an additional sales position in Tallaght, County Dublin, to concentrate solely on the fast-growing reseller market. The resellers—such as ESB shops, Dixon's, and PC World—provide direct access to the burgeoning consumer market. While the outlets are smaller in number and more geographically dispersed in comparison with the trade segment, they do potentially provide a significant quantity of business, which warrants more dedicated attention.

Fig. 10A.2: OKI Systems (Ireland) Ltd

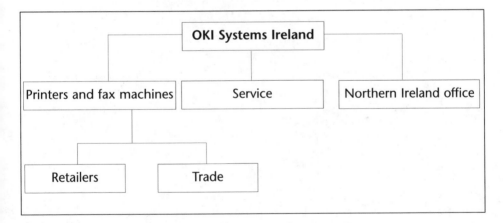

The newly hired salesperson was given all the reseller accounts in Ireland, and sales targets and a sales budget were established. On-the-job and formal sales training was provided, and the new salesperson was soon calling on both established and potential retailer customers.

Organising the sales force to mirror the company's objectives and the dynamics of the market is a continual concern for the sales manager. It is highly probable that there will be another reorganisation of the sales force in the near future. Customers' expectations and demands, changes in the economy, competitors' moves and marketing and sales objectives will all stimulate the necessity to reorganise the sales force.

DISCUSSION QUESTIONS

1. Comment on the factors that should be taken into account in any attempt to reorganise the Oki sales force.
2. Evaluate the pros and cons of using a direct marketing approach.

SMITHWICKS: GENTLE TONE OF ADS WINS BACK DRINKERS

Smithwicks is an important and profitable brand in the Guinness Ireland Group range and is the company's third-largest brand in the Republic. Its sales had been declining in the nineteen-eighties and early nineties, leading to the adoption in 1994 of a brand strategy aimed at retaining existing drinkers and halting the rate of decline.

The situation in the eighties

In the nineteen-seventies the Irish beer market was dominated by three brands: Guinness, Smithwicks, and Harp. However, in the eighties Smithwicks was suddenly out of place. Younger people became more assertive, ambitious and self-confident about their Irishness, while also becoming more aware of and open to international influences. Although it was Irish, Smithwicks could not achieve the success of Guinness, which had been repositioned over the years and had been successfully aimed at younger drinkers, while retaining its older, loyal consumers.

Smithwicks therefore fell between the growing desire to experience the world outside Ireland—manifested in the growth of lager brands such as Heineken, Budweiser, and Carlsberg—and an Irish icon to whose stature it could never aspire. Consequently the Smithwicks brand share halved during the mid-eighties.

Advertising strategy

Smithwicks decided to mount an advertising campaign in an attempt to halt the decline. In 1984 the first series of commercials produced by its advertising agency, McConnell's, featured the brand in a gritty city-centre setting. It featured a group of fairly 'hard' men. Research revealed within a year or two that, although some aspects of the campaign were liked, in general it was not sufficiently aspirational.

The next series of commercials—more or less the same genre as the first series—moved 'upmarket' in location and cast. These were followed by another series, entitled 'Homecoming', 'All heart', and 'Missing pint'. In spite of these campaigns, the brand continued to decline.

In 1988 McConnell's produced a commercial that essentially answered the 1984 brief in every respect, with urban credibility in abundance but with a cast that related to all social groups. This commercial had high-quality production values and a superb music track. It was an immediate success with an increasingly advertising-aware target audience. The campaign did not, however, have any impact in attracting new drinkers. The gap between the sophistication of the commercial and the reality of the Smithwicks brand image was becoming a serious problem. A series of commercials entitled 'Get into it' served to underline this point further.

In 1995 an unapologetically single-minded strategy was adopted to consolidate the existing brand loyalists and slow the rate of decline. Detailed market research led to an important insight into the target audience: Smithwicks-drinkers were predominantly male and saw themselves as unpretentious, down-to-earth people who were in their own way quietly self-confident. To them a pint of beer was a social lubricant, not a deeply meaningful statement about themselves. They enjoyed a social night out and despised ostentation.

The advertising proposition had to faithfully reflect this quiet self-confidence. It would also have to present the brand as 'the beer that's essential to easy, relaxed social drinking'. 'Easy drinking' was always to be understood as applying to both the product experience and the sociability of the drinking occasion. The campaign would also have to be 'big' enough to facilitate other essential media support, most importantly local radio, outdoor, and press.

In 1995 the first 'Locals' television campaign was introduced with four executions. Up to late 1998 there were twelve executions in the full television campaign, including a tactical commercial that helped to successfully launch a new Smithwicks brew with a longer-lasting head. The 'Locals' campaign had an immediate effect on the Smithwicks brand. Millward Brown Research indicated that ale drinkers felt that

- 'Locals' was about Smithwicks drinkers and made them feel more like drinking Smithwicks
- 74 per cent of the drinkers rated the 'Locals' as better than most drink advertisements
- 51 per cent of the drinkers believed the 'Locals' campaign would make more people feel differently about Smithwicks.

Crucially, the image of Smithwicks also improved as 'a beer people like to be seen drinking' and 'a beer people believe is becoming more popular.' Qualitative group research results were also very positive.

At last Smithwicks advertising was seen to be developing a consistent shape and style, rather than bouncing all over the place. This led to a sense of consolidation and stability at brand level, which reinforced the steadfastness of existing drinkers. Respondents across the board understood the intended message of the campaign: easy drinking. The gentle tone was appreciated as cuing an easy drinking atmosphere.

The overall effect of the campaign for drinkers and competitors alike was to consolidate the brand's positioning; Smithwicks was perceived as the embodiment of easy drinking—relaxed, convivial, and genial. But the most encouraging result of all was that from the introduction of the 'Locals' campaign the rate of decline of Smithwicks slowed down, from 11.3 per cent in 1993 to 1.6 per cent towards the end of 1998. Despite the formidable challenges of a highly competitive beer market, the 'Locals' campaign successfully turned around the Smithwick's image and all but halted the decline in sales.

Source: This is an edited case study of a campaign that won gold for Guinness and its advertising agency, McConnell's, in the long-term campaign category in the Institute of Advertising Practitioners' advertising effectiveness awards. Published in the *Sunday Business Post*, 6 December 1998.

DISCUSSION QUESTIONS

1. Comment on the reasons why the advertising campaigns for Smithwick's in the nineteen-eighties and early nineties appeared to have little success.

2. Can advertising ever damage a brand? Use evidence from the case to support your answer.
3. Why is it important for marketers to develop close relationships with their advertising agencies? Do the principles of relationship marketing provide any guidance?
4. What advice would you give to Guinness and McConnell's for the future development of this brand?

PART 4

Marketing Applications

11

The Marketing of Services

Marketing theory has developed mainly on the basis of product marketing. However, a significant share of the economic activity of most industrialised countries is accounted for by services. Services marketing has increased in importance as marketers come to operate in an increasingly competitive services environment.

The same basic principles of marketing products apply also to the marketing of services, but the characteristics of services imply that some adaptation in marketing practice is required. This chapter explores the nature of services and examines how they are marketed.

THE NATURE OF SERVICES

A service is any activity or benefit that is largely intangible in nature. While products are physical things, objects, or devices, services tend to be deeds, efforts, or performances. Berry (1980) argued that three broad characteristics of services distinguish them from products: they are more intangible than tangible; they are more likely to involve simultaneous production and consumption; and they are less standardised and uniform.

If a person flies from Dublin to London, they buy not just a flight but a bundle of benefits, including how they are treated by check-in staff, the time they save by flying, the in-flight service, and the comfort and convenience of the flight. These can be quite intangible. To avail of the flight the customer has to be physically present: the service is therefore produced and consumed simultaneously. While every passenger on the plane has bought a transport service, some may be travelling business class and may therefore have bought a more customised service in the form of a flexible ticket and in-flight service.

A service customer may therefore experience a number of elements of the service. If any one element gives rise to dissatisfaction, this can influence the customer's general perception of the service offering. The challenge for the service marketer is to ensure that all the elements of the service are consistent with the customer's expectations.

Obviously, a product marketer can experience similar challenges. However, the highly intangible nature of many services implies that service marketers have to adapt their marketing mix in an attempt to manage intangibility.

Services in general can be considered to be intangible, inseparable, perishable, and variable. As we have seen, *intangibility* refers to services being deeds, performances or efforts rather than tangible things. Inseparability means that many services cannot be separated from the person providing the service—for example a visit to a hairdresser; we

339

rely on the skills and ability of the person performing the service. Services are *perishable* if they cannot be stored: for example, if a flight takes off with empty seats, the opportunity to sell those seats is gone for ever. Given that many services are dependent on humans, the outcome can be more variable than if machines are involved. Thus in the case of visiting a hairdresser, if the person is not concentrating on their work the result may not be satisfying to the customer.

THE IMPORTANCE OF SERVICES IN IRELAND

Services are of particular importance to the Irish economy. In 1996 the Central Statistics Office labour force survey showed that 787,000 people worked in services; this means that approximately three out of every five people who work do so in services. These services include building, utilities, financial services, transport, and public administration.

A service economy is defined as one in which more than half the work force are working in services; the Irish economy would therefore come under this description. Under the Programme for Competitiveness and Work in the nineteen-nineties the Government established a target of 117,000 jobs in the service sector by the year 2001 (Stationery Office, 1995). The CSO survey showed that within the labour force there were increases in the numbers working in commercial or financial services, retailing, and personal, social and professional services. Services are largely dependent on people providing them; they therefore have good potential for creating employment.

In Ireland, services represent approximately 53 per cent of gross domestic product. This is made up of distribution, transport, and communication (19 per cent), public administration and defence (6 per cent), and other services (28 per cent). Services such as tourism, transport, training and consultancy are important earners of foreign currency.

Tourism is a particularly important service industry in Ireland and is a good example of the marketing of both the tangible and the intangible. The tourism industry grew rapidly in the nineties, and employment in the sector grew from 91,000 in 1994 to a planned 126,000 in 1999 (Stationery Office, 1994). The following panel gives some idea of the performance of the sector.

IRELAND'S TOURISM PERFORMANCE

In the nineties the performance of tourism in Ireland was far ahead of the European and world averages. In 1996 tourists spent almost £1,900 million, and the number of visitors grew by 11 per cent, the fifth successive year of growth. The World Tourism Organisation's estimates for Europe showed an increase of 3.6 per cent in arrivals and 5.9 per cent in income for 1996. Ireland more than exceeded these estimates.

Tourism provides significant economic benefits. The total tourism industry, including international and domestic tourism, was estimated to be £2,500 million in 1996. The Government, through direct and indirect taxes on tourism expenditure, received £1,300 million of this. Tourism provided 108,700 jobs in 1996, or 8.3 per cent of total employment. An additional 35,000 jobs are planned by 1999.

Consumption of the tourism product takes place where the service is available, and tourism activities are particularly concentrated in areas that lack an industrial base. It can therefore have a regional distribution effect.

Tourists to Ireland come from a variety of countries. Britain is the largest market, followed by the United States, Germany, and France. American and Continental visitors generate proportionately more income.

Tourism numbers and income

	1988	1993	1994	1995	1996
			(thousand)		
Britain	1,508	1,857	2,038	2,285	2,590
United States	385	377	449	587	660
Germany	113	265	269	319	339
France	111	242	231	234	262
Australia and New Zealand	46	56	68	89	88
Netherlands	38	69	80	94	109
Spain	34	57	59	67	66
Canada	34	45	45	54	69
Switzerland	24	40	62	62	62
Italy	21	116	121	112	119
Belgium and Luxembourg	20	41	41	53	60
Denmark	14	17	19	22	23
Japan	n.a.	18	22	30	33
Norway and Sweden	12	32	33	46	55
Other Europe	21	66	73	93	83
Other overseas	44	50	69	85	65
Total	2,425	3,348	3,679	4,231	4,682

Income

	1988	1993	1994	1995	1996
			(£ million)		
Britain	267	375.1	451.9	501.2	574
North America	165.5	182.1	213.4	275	316.6
Germany	35.9	117.3	110.4	122.4	148.9
France	31	91.5	74.4	83.8	88.1
Italy	6.9	51.1	46.3	42.4	53.5
Netherlands	n.a.	n.a.	n.a.	n.a.	35.4
Other Europe	49.9	141.7	140.5	165.1	140.7
Other overseas	37.6	54.7	77.2	96.5	93.8
Total	593.8	1,013.5	1,114.1	1,286.4	1,451

Source: Bord Fáilte Éireann, Tourism Facts, 1996.

The development of the International Financial Services Centre in Custom House Dock, Dublin, in the early nineties was a catalyst for growth in the sector generally. Many providers of financial services established operations, and benefited from special tax advantages by doing so. Other sectors that increased in importance include airlines, retailing, fast-food franchising, and tele-marketing and tele-sales.

In March 1997 Forbairt, the development agency with responsibility for indigenous enterprise, launched a Services Development Programme (*Irish Independent*, 14 March 1997). This provided seed capital, management development grants, feasibility study grants and a graduate placement scheme to suitable service providers. The scheme was aimed at internationally traded services, such as software development, tele-services, and media services.

In the world as a whole, while trade in services is approximately one-fifth the size of trade in goods, during the nineteen-eighties and into the nineties trade in services increased twice as fast (GATT, 1988–9).

REASONS FOR GROWTH IN SERVICES

New services to meet new needs

Changing consumer and organisational needs contributed to the growth in services. Consumers' consciousness of the importance of health and leisure meant an increase in demand for associated services. Increased leisure time was spent on travel, eating out, health clubs, and fitness. Firms require new computer systems and programs, while training and re-training needs also increased.

Increased world trade and investment contributed to the demand for financial services. The growth in electronic commerce also required creation and support services. Any increase in commercial activity usually means an increased demand for business-to-business services, such as the marketing services provided by advertising agencies and market research companies. In some cases old service ideas are resurrected, such as the plan to build a light rail or tramway system in Dublin. (Trams were a feature of public transport in Dublin from the nineteenth century, but the network was dismantled in 1949.)

Social trends

More women in the work force, increased leisure time and increased consumer sophistication have all contributed to increases in the demand for services. Services such as child-minding, 'ethnic' restaurants and home delivery all increased in importance. Increased travel means increased use of transport, accommodation, and associated agency services. More emphasis is being placed by consumers on convenience, and in many cases it is more convenient to use a service than to do the work oneself.

Demographic trends

Increased life expectancy, lower marriage rates and smaller family sizes mean that people are living longer and have more disposable income. In industrialised countries, when people have more money to spend they will be more likely to buy non-essential items, and many services have benefited as a result.

CHARACTERISTICS OF SERVICES

Intangibility

Products are physical objects that can be seen, touched, heard, or smelt. Services, on the other hand, are intangible and are more likely to involve feelings or emotions. The degree of intangibility can vary, as demonstrated in fig. 11.1.

Fig. 11.1: Relative tangibility and intangibility

While many product marketers try to attribute intangible aspects to their products in order to differentiate them from competitors' offerings, service marketers often try to attribute tangible aspects to their service so that the customer can relate to them. For example, credit card companies that are providing consumers with the benefits of flexibility, convenience and an interest-free credit period relate these to a small plastic card.

Customer involvement in production

Customers are more likely to be involved in the production of a service than in the production of a product. A customer who visits a hairdresser or self-service restaurant has to physically take part in the production of the service; in all such cases the customer must be present. This is not so for most products, where the finished product can be selected from the shelf, without the customer becoming involved in the production process.

Quality control

Many services are produced and consumed simultaneously. Unlike products, where quality control techniques are used before they leave the factory, services can have a variable outcome, which can be difficult to control. This is so because for most services the marketer is relying on people to deliver the service. The variability in service quality can occur for many reasons, including poor training, poor communication, and the mood of the service provider.

A marketer needs to make sure that service quality is consistent, otherwise the consumer may not return. As people are an integral part of the production of the service, quality control must be through people. An interesting research study in Britain examined how service quality could affect blood donations (Newman and Payne, 1997). The study examined the motivations for giving blood, the reasons why people stopped giving, and the reasons why the majority of people eligible to donate don't do so. It concluded that there were important customer service and service quality issues to be addressed.

The benefits to firms of improving service quality are well documented. They include greater customer satisfaction, customer retention and improved company profitability as direct benefits, and attracting new customers as well as inducing customers to increase their use of the service (Danaher et al., 1996). One Irish study (Carson and Gilmore, 1993) examined how the ferry company Stena Sealink enhanced service quality on its Ireland–Scotland route. The result was a significant reduction in the number of complaints by customers.

Another study (Quinn, 1994) proposed the 'PROMPT' approach to service quality. This provides managers with a guide to improving service quality. It has six components:

- Prioritising customers' needs
- Reliable and fast delivery of service
- Organising for customers
- Measuring customers' satisfaction
- Personnel training
- Technology-focusing.

The PROMPT approach involves establishing what customers' needs are and giving priority to the most important ones. Reliable and fast delivery of the service is considered to be crucial. Firms need to be organised around the customer, not around particular managers.

The chief executive of Scandinavian Airlines, Jan Carlson, recommended the inverted pyramid as the basis for organisation design (Carlson, 1987). When a company is being organised it should be borne in mind that personnel who come in contact with the customer are more likely to interact with the customer than higher-level management.

Customer satisfaction can be measured using research techniques. If a company is seeking to improve customer service, measurement means that comparisons can be made before and after. The training of people is obviously part of the process, as is the use of technology that can provide faster, more efficient or more reliable service.

One technique for measuring service quality that became widely used was 'Servqual' (Parasuraman and Berry, 1986). The model measured consumers' perceptions of five areas of service: tangibles, reliability, responsiveness, assurance, and empathy. *Tangibles* refers to the appearance of physical facilities, equipment, personnel, and communications. *Reliability* is the ability to perform the promised service dependably and accurately. *Responsiveness* requires the service provider to be willing to help customers and to provide prompt service; while *assurance* is the knowledge and courtesy of employees and their ability to convey trust and confidence. *Empathy* refers to the service provider's ability to be caring and to provide individualised attention to customers.

Quality or, more specifically, *quality management* became a much-researched and documented topic from the nineteen-eighties. *Total quality management* (TQM) developed to become a significant influence on product and service organisations in the nineties. The process of introducing TQM in a service industry requires the management to be conscious of service gaps that may emerge (Candlin and Day, 1993). Service gaps may come about from not knowing what customers expect, having the wrong quality standards, service performance not living up to expectations, or promises not being met. A conceptual model of service quality is illustrated in fig. 11.2.

Fig. 11.2: Conceptual model of service quality

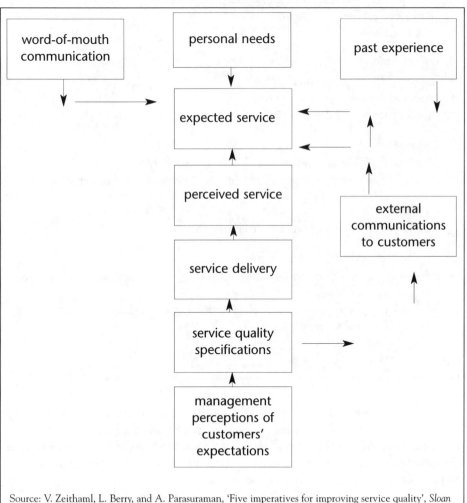

Source: V. Zeithaml, L. Berry, and A. Parasuraman, 'Five imperatives for improving service quality', *Sloan Management Review*, summer 1990.

Quality, whether of products or services, became an important differentiation tool. Aer Lingus introduced a 'Programme for a better airline' as part of a quality initiative, as shown in the following panel. This concentrates on five main areas: in-flight service, better airport facilities, punctuality of flights, less queuing, and faster baggage delivery. The company also emphasised this policy in its advertising.

AER LINGUS: PROGRAMME FOR A BETTER AIRLINE

In-flight service:

- professional, friendly and intuitive staff on all flights
- allocation of seats before boarding
- complimentary meals or snacks and drinks on most flights
- assistance for customers with special needs
- smoke-free cabins on all flights
- duty-free sales.

Better airport facilities:

- improved check-in facilities
- improved customer service and ticketing
- upgraded lounges and waiting areas.

Flight punctuality:

- 85 per cent of Aer Lingus flights to depart on time
- 95 per cent of flights to depart within fifteen minutes of specified departure time.

Less queuing:

- secure more space in airports for check-in desks.

Quicker baggage delivery:

- premier passengers' bags to be delivered to baggage reclaim area within fifteen minutes of aircraft's arrival
- all other passengers' bags to be delivered to baggage reclaim area within thirty minutes of aircraft's arrival.

Source: Aer Lingus web site (www.aerlingus.ie).

In each of these areas, specific service targets were set; these become what the consumer could expect when buying the service. In a fiercely competitive environment, the airline planned that these service levels would differentiate it from its competitors. The programme demonstrates the need for firms to constantly strive to improve their product, bearing in mind the needs of the customer.

Stock

In general, services cannot be stored easily, if at all. Staff and equipment can be held in readiness to produce the service, but unused capacity—for example one empty seat on an aircraft—is lost for ever. An important task for the service marketer is to smooth demand levels to match supply. The marketer must establish what the patterns of demand are and then adopt strategies that attempt to change these patterns to make them more favourable. Price is often used as a means of achieving this, for example offering reduced prices at times when demand is lowest to encourage people to change their usage patterns of the service.

Distribution channels

Typically, services are distributed through people—for example a solicitor or a dentist—rather than through physical distribution channels. There are exceptions: some services, such as cash lodgment and withdrawal, are now highly mechanised through ATMs. Developments in technology, such as the internet and EDI, are having an increased impact. Information services can be easily accessed on the internet, and orders, reservations and payments can be made. In general, the distribution channels for services will be shorter and will not involve as many levels as those for products.

THE SERVICES MARKETING ENVIRONMENT

The services marketer will have to continuously monitor the micro and macro-forces in the environment that affect the business and to react by providing a competitive service that meets the needs of the customer. The following panel shows how one firm reacted to changing environmental trends.

PREMIER BANKING: ADAPTING TO CHANGING CUSTOMER NEEDS

The market for personal banking services has developed considerably in recent years. Customers' changing life-styles have meant that the traditional branch banking services were not always convenient or accessible, especially for busy career people. Premier Banking was established in 1990 by Bank of Ireland and was the country's first direct bank.

With direct banking, almost all business can be conducted by phone. Business hours are longer than branch opening hours, and the service can be provided throughout the country from one location. Premier Banking provides a service from 8 a.m. to 8 p.m. Monday to Friday and 10 a.m. to 2 p.m. on Saturdays. The services offered are limited to personal loans (£1,000 to £10,000), mortgages (in conjunction with ICS Building Society), and deposits. Customers must be over twenty-one, in full-time employment, and earning over £12,000 a year. All customers are screened before acceptance, and proof of income and other details have to be provided.

Premier Banking spends heavily on press and radio advertising, which has proved effective in reaching its target market. Each customer is asked where they heard about the service, so that the effectiveness of different media can be monitored. Since the launch of Premier Banking, AIB has also entered the market with a direct banking service, and it is probable that the market will expand further.

Source: Premier Banking.

In the nineties there were many indications that such elements in the service environment as speed, quality, price-competitiveness and reliability were the main factors used by customers to judge service offerings. Society became more convenience-oriented, presenting opportunities for service marketers. This had been forecast by the Henley Centre of Ireland (1992), which had predicted an increase in demand for ready meals, for example, and a growing demand for delivery to the home. It was also expected that consumers would spend more on services and leisure following trends in more affluent countries.

THE SERVICES MARKETING MIX

The marketing mix for services is basically the same as that for products, namely product, price, promotion, and place. Many marketing theorists would argue, however, that the traditional 'four Ps' framework needs to be expanded for services so as to include an additional P: people. Certainly the provision of services is normally people-intensive; in many cases the service cannot be separated from the person providing it. We will include people as a fifth P in the services marketing mix. Other theorists consider that addition Ps, such as *process* and *physical evicence*, should be included. These are also considered in context.

Product

In relation to services, *product* is used broadly to describe the offering that is being made to the customer. The service product will have *core*, *actual*, *augmented* and *potential* features.

On page 340 we looked at the importance of the tourism product in Ireland. Consider the following panel, which examines the levels of that product.

IRELAND: A TOURISM PRODUCT

Tourism is one of Ireland's most important economic activities, accounting for over 60 per cent of the country's exports of services. At the core, visitors to Ireland are buying a number of benefits. Their visit is an experience that can include a wide variety of elements: relaxation, excitement, peace of mind, friendship, a different pace of life. Tourists are attracted by the country's greenness, clean air, pure water and unspoilt landscape as well as the activities they can engage in, such as golf, water sports, and angling. These, as well as accommodation, food, and drink, are all part of the tangible aspects of the product.

When they are here, visitors have expectations about the augmented aspects of the tourism product. They expect to get value for money and good-quality service and to have a guarantee that any problems or difficulties that might affect their enjoyment of a visit will be sorted out satisfactorily. The *potential product* describes what Ireland could possibly become from a tourist point of view. This would include the development of particular attractions or facilities that are different from or enhance the existing product offering.

One of the main considerations for the marketer is the degree of intangibility involved in the service. The marketer may try to associate something tangible with the service so that the consumer can relate to it or can easily recognise what the service will offer.

Branding may play a part by giving the service added value and providing a recognisable cue for the consumer. Many service marketers have invested substantially in their brands; McDonald's, SDS, Access, Jury's, Golden Discs and JWT are all recognisable brands regarding whose quality, value and standards of service the customer has definite expectations. As with the marketing of products, the services marketer can use branding to differentiate the service offering. Consider fig. 11.3, where the ICC Bank seeks to distinguish itself by concentrating on a particular financial product.

Fig. 11.3: ICC Bank

Why rob Peter to pay Paul when you've got Noel to pay Bills?

**Manage your cash flow better with
Supplier Payline from ICC Bank.**

- No insurance premiums
- No annual fee
- No unexpected charges
- You only pay when you us the facility

- Allows you make payments to meet your trade cycle
- Improves your purchasing power
- More credit and better discounts from suppliers

ICC BANK

To arrange a Supplier Payline for your business, phone Noel MacMahon at 1850 73 2000. He'll look after Peter and Paul for you.

▶ SUPPLIER PAYLINE ◀

LENDING CRITERIA AND TERMS AND CONDITIONS APPLY

Price

The relationship between price and quality can have great significance in the marketing of services. Price will form the cue the consumer uses to compare different service offerings. Given the intangibility of services, the consumer may use the price of the service as an indication of the level of quality they can expect. It is important therefore that the services marketer has a clear idea of what the consumer's perception of the price actually is.

Berry and Yadav (1996) recommended three broad strategies for service pricing. *Satisfaction-based pricing* could include, for example, a guarantee that if the customer is not happy they will receive a refund. *Benefit-driven prices* would depend on the benefits the buyer required from the service—the more benefits, the higher the price—while flat-rate pricing would involve the same price being charged to everyone for the same service.

Costing a service can be more difficult than costing a product, because of its intangibility. How do you price the services of a medical specialist? It is inherently difficult to place a value on something intangible. The tangible costs incurred in providing the service—for example the materials or equipment used—can be computed, but the value of time or advice is more difficult to calculate. A cost-plus pricing approach may be used where the tangible costs are computed. A cost is added for the intangible aspects, such as time, and then a mark-up is added.

In many cases service providers will price on a *going-rate basis* or on what they estimate the market will bear. A *rate of return* approach may also be used: for example, an airline that has a large investment in aircraft and ground equipment might use a pricing approach based on a target rate of return on its investment.

Price is an important tool for the services marketer, as it can be used to influence the patterns of demand for the service. This will be especially relevant where demand reaches peaks at certain times but is lower at other times. In off-peak times, price will be reduced in an attempt to stimulate demand: thus cinemas offer reduced rates for afternoon showings, and transport companies offer reduced fares at off-peak times. In fig. 11.4 an example of off-peak promotion is given; in this case people travelling by bus in the off-peak period could avail of a reduced fare.

Promotion

The general objectives in promoting services will be much the same as in the promotion of products. The principles of the communication model (chapter 10) should be adhered to. The marketer should identify the audience, determine what the promotional objectives are, develop the message, and decide which element or combinations of elements of the promotional mix should be used.

The nature of the service may sometimes limit the type of promotional activity that can be undertaken. Unless something tangible can be associated with the service, the consumer may have difficulty visualising it. Promotion may therefore have to emphasise tangible cues.

All the elements of the promotions mix can be used by the services marketer. Advertising is widely used and is good for creating a strong visual image. Organisations like Bord Fáilte rely heavily on television and print advertising to create an impression of what Ireland has to offer; similarly, financial services companies use television, radio and print to inform and in many cases explain what can be quite complicated products. Fig. 11.5 shows how one market research company promotes its services to business, while fig. 11.6 shows how Telecom Éireann promotes itself to the business community. In both cases the print media are used to explain the nature of the service and to create an identity for the companies. Both advertisements appeared in business publications.

Fig. 11.4: Bus Éireann

BUS ÉIREANN

FARES

Our fares are excellent value for money and some examples are shown below. Remember that if you travel Tuesday, Wednesday, or Thursday our **Midweek Return** ticket covers a return journey within one month at a discounted fare, thus you save money by travelling outside the peak weekend period.

Midweek adult return fares from Dublin *--valid for one month*

Ballina	IR£ 9.00	Limerick	IR£ 11.00
Clonmel	IR£ 9.00	Rosslare Harbour	IR£ 10.00
Cork	IR£ 13.00	Sligo	IR£ 9.00
Donegal	IR£ 11.00	Tralee	IR£ 15.50
Galway	IR£ 9.00	Waterford	IR£ 7.00
Letterkenny	IR£ 11.00	Westport	IR£ 12.00

Enquire at booking offices and travel centres for details of mid-week return fares to other locations.
*Special student fares are available to holders of valid **International Student Identity Cards (ISIC)** with current **Travelsave Stamp** issued by the **Union of Students of Ireland Travel (USIT)**.*
Special Day Return Tickets available on most routes at single fare.

Our **Rambler and Rover** tickets which allow you to travel on any part of our network are especially good value.

Travel to *or* from Ireland by coach with **Bus Éireann** and **Eurolines**:

eg. London/Dublin Adult fares from **IR£15 single / IR£29 return**.

There's no better value way of travelling to Ireland.

Bus Éireann/Euroline Services

Fig. 11.5: Irish Marketing Surveys

Personal selling is particularly important for services because of the high involvement of people in delivering the service. As with products, the person selling the service will be seen to represent the service provider and will therefore create an image in the mind of the customer. Personal selling is good for explaining the nature of the service, answering questions, and learning about customers and their needs. It is widely used by financial services companies, as it enables them to explain the range of options available, and customers can ask questions about what can be quite complicated products.

Sales promotion can be used to provide incentives to buy. Discounts or special offers can be used to encourage trial or repeat purchases. Given the importance of price as a means of attempting to change demand patterns for services, sales promotions involving special prices are quite common.

Public relations can be a useful medium for newsworthy aspects of the service. The use of press statements, or coverage of conferences or sponsorship events, can help to communicate a message about the firm. Banks use public relations opportunities to communicate, among other things, the strength of their financial performance. They will usually place particular emphasis on the publication of their annual report and results.

In general, direct sale is the most common method of service distribution. Channels are therefore short:

service provider → consumer

Intermediaries can be involved: for example, airline and holiday services can be sold through travel agents. Franchising has also been used successfully by many service providers, ranging from fast food and launderettes to printing and financial services.

Fig. 11.6: Telecom Éireann

A Telecom Eireann *charge***card** will make a significant change to the way you make business calls.

When you're travelling around a lot at home or abroad and need to stay in touch, a Telecom Eireann *charge***card** will save you the bother of finding loose change to make your phone calls.

This new telephone charge card lets you make local, national and international calls from wherever you are, without the loose change.

Calls from most phones are automatic, otherwise an Irish operator will process the call. And because it's a telephone charge card, the cost of the call will be charged to your home or office telephone bill.

To apply for a Telecom Eireann *charge***card**, call **FREEFONE 1800 580 500** or drop into your nearest TeleCentre.

TELECOM EIREANN

CASHLESS CALLS FROM WHEREVER YOU ARE.

The service may be distributed totally through people, but technological changes have presented more opportunities to marketers. Information-based services, such as Aertel (on television) and Weatherline (delivered by phone), provided new distribution channels. The growth in use of the internet increased the possibilities considerably and improved marketers' ability to provide interactive services.

Place

The location of the service provider can vary in importance according to the nature of the service. For a car breakdown service, location is not important, as the customer will use a phone to summon help; in the case of a restaurant, however, location will be very important.

Modern telecommunications technology and data transfer mean that the location of the service provider may be irrelevant. The IDA has identified international tele-marketing as a new service that can be established, using Ireland as a base for marketing products to consumers in other countries by phone. A good telecommunications network and low-cost international phone calls are the main considerations for these companies. Several companies were attracted to Ireland during the nineties, one such being American Airlines, which established its European call centre in Dublin in 1996, creating 220 jobs (*Sunday Tribune*, 17 March 1996). By 1997 the IDA had attracted forty-three companies, and 3,600 were employed in the sector (*Sunday Business Post*, 16 February 1997). The fact that costs were 30 per cent lower than alternative sites was considered to be Ireland's competitive advantage.

Ireland is well placed to compete in international service markets, as one indigenous enterprise, the Foreign Exchange Company of Ireland, has demonstrated.

THE FOREIGN EXCHANGE COMPANY

The Foreign Exchange Company of Ireland was established in Killorglin, County Kerry, in the early eighties and began by operating a number of foreign exchange bureaus around the country. The opportunity for this business had been spotted by the company's founder and managing director, Brian McCarthy, who had previously worked as a bank official. He noticed that tourists were frequently frustrated at the limited opening times of the banks, so he applied for a licence from the Central Bank to operate exchange bureaus. This business developed, but the company was keen to exploit its opportunities, and did so with Cashback.

Cashback was established to process and refund VAT payments to overseas visitors, who are entitled to claim back the VAT they have paid on purchases made while in Ireland. At the time, the processing was being done by retailers, who found it costly and time-consuming. Cashback took over this task and provided a service whereby visitors were able to claim their refund directly, or have it forwarded to them; retailers in turn paid Cashback for the service. The business relied on the development of data-processing technology and good telecommunications, which enabled the company to process potentially millions of claims at its premises in Killorglin. Location was not a disadvantage, and Cashback expanded rapidly, selling its service to practically all the large retailers in Ireland. In Britain, retailers such as Harrod's use the service, and Cashback has expanded to corner a significant share of the market.

In 1998 the company opened a new £5 million information technology and tele-services building in Killorglin, and it now employs 350 people. Its services include the Cashback VAT repayments service to tourists, Western Union cash transfers, and investments in the prize bonds scheme. It also operates a freephone information service for Coca-Cola. In 1998 it estimated that it would process £200 million worth of Western Union business from Britain, £110 million from Spain, and £12 million from Ireland. The company receives between a third and a half of the 7 to 8 per cent commission paid.

The VAT refund business handles about two million refunds per year. The average fee charged is £5 per transaction. The company hopes to launch a new VAT refund service on investments in 1998.

Source: T. Harding, 'Fexco plans VAT refund service', *Sunday Business Post*, 8 February 1998.

People

People are an important part of the services marketing mix, as in many cases the service cannot be separated from the person providing it. The problem for marketers is that it can be difficult to ensure uniformity in quality of service. With manufactured products, uniformity can be achieved with quality control techniques, which in many cases can be highly mechanised. In the case of services, quality control can be achieved through supervision, motivation, and training, and these need to be carefully organised to ensure that the consumer gets the level of service they expect. Many service marketers, for example airlines, banks, and hotels, use the quality of their staff as part of their promotional campaigns. Fig. 11.7 illustrates how one company used the quality of its staff to promote its services.

Increasingly, service providers are coming to recognise that competitive advantage can be gained through the quality of their staff. This implies a need for adequate training, especially for those who come in contact with customers. Service strategy can be seen as a combination of a firm's marketing and human resource strategies. This can be categorised as either a relationship-based marketing strategy, which emphasises customers' loyalty to the firm, or, in contrast, a *transaction-based* strategy, which emphasises volume, resulting in lots of customers with no expectation of loyalty (Dearick et al., 1997). It is possible to consider a mixed strategy, for example taking a transaction-based approach with customers and a relationship-based approach with employees, or vice versa. Determining which strategy to pursue will depend on the nature of the customers, the type of service or product, and the firm's ability to attract and retain competent employees.

A service company's corporate culture should be supportive of staff and should help to motivate them to provide the best service possible. The firm's culture refers to the shared experiences, beliefs and actions that characterise the firm. All employees of the American airline Delta are expected to help get the job done; if passengers' luggage is being delayed, managers are expected to help out in physically dealing with the problem. The core policy is that the customer should not be inconvenienced and should receive the best possible service.

Fig. 11.7: The use of people in service promotion

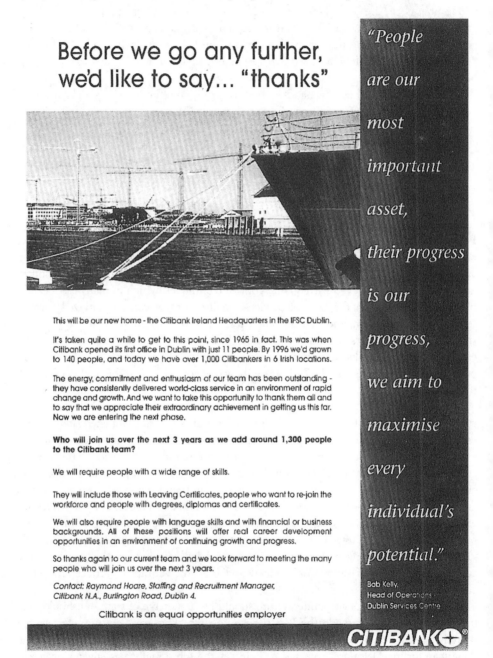

Before we go any further, we'd like to say... "thanks"

This will be our new home - the Citibank Ireland Headquarters in the IFSC Dublin.

It's taken quite a while to get to this point, since 1965 in fact. This was when Citibank opened its first office in Dublin with just 11 people. By 1996 we'd grown to 140 people, and today we have over 1,000 Citibankers in 6 Irish locations.

The energy, commitment and enthusiasm of our team has been outstanding - they have consistently delivered world-class service in an environment of rapid change and growth. And we want to take this opportunity to thank them all and to say that we appreciate their extraordinary achievement in getting us this far. Now we are entering the next phase.

Who will join us over the next 3 years as we add around 1,300 people to the Citibank team?

We will require people with a wide range of skills.

They will include those with Leaving Certificates, people who want to re-join the workforce and people with degrees, diplomas and certificates.

We will also require people with language skills and with financial or business backgrounds. All of these positions will offer real career development opportunities in an environment of continuing growth and progress.

So thanks again to our current team and we look forward to meeting the many people who will join us over the next 3 years.

Contact: Raymond Hoare, Staffing and Recruitment Manager, Citibank N.A., Burlington Road, Dublin 4.

Citibank is an equal opportunities employer

"People are our most important asset, their progress is our progress, we aim to maximise every individual's potential."

Bob Kelly,
Head of Operations
Dublin Services Centre

CITIBANK

Internal marketing means applying the marketing policy to people within the firm so that they come to appreciate the importance of the customer and of how the performance of their job is directly related to customer satisfaction. Internal marketing should be practised by all firms, but service marketers need to be especially aware of its benefits. Internal marketing can contribute to the firm's corporate culture by facilitating a positive spirit in the company, and this in turn will affect the attitudes and motivation of employees.

The recruitment and training of staff are important elements. At the recruitment stage, such factors as the aptitude and personality of the applicant must be taken into account: the company needs to make sure that the people being recruited are capable of delivering the service in the desired manner. They will be trained to deliver the service, to dress in the required manner and to deal with people but also to appreciate the importance of service quality.

Many service companies have recognised the importance of involving their employees in decision-making. The Scandinavian airline SAS believes that its front-line staff need to be empowered to make decisions. Individual customer requirements imply that staff need to be able to react quickly to a situation and make a decision that is in the best interests of the customer.

DELIVERING CUSTOMER SERVICE

Customer care

The role of marketing is not just to create customers but also to initiate and develop a relationship with those customers from the first stage of contact and throughout a series of different transactions. Customer relationships are a marketing asset, to be cultivated and maintained.

One study, which examined how a customer care improvement scheme was developed by Northern Ireland Electricity (Carson and Gilmore, 1989), set out a model for customer care and examined the quantitative issues involved, such as speed of delivery, and the qualitative issues, such as courtesy. The study suggests that rules and procedures are common for the former but that in the qualitative or psychological areas it is the perceptions, attitudes and behaviour of staff who come into contact with customers that are important. Obviously these are areas where marketing managers can have an impact or can implement improvements.

Increasingly, consumers are demanding higher levels of service and have expectations about the quality of service they expect. Service marketers can use this to advantage by seeking to deliver these standards and by differentiating themselves on the basis of their service quality.

Among the factors that should be taken into account when considering customer service are the following:

- Customers' enquiries and questions should be dealt with as comprehensively as possible.
- Customers' orders should be accepted, processed and delivered in an efficient manner.
- Time deadlines should always be met.

- All complaints, comments or suggestions should be dealt with.
- Service providers should seek to understand their customers' requirements and seek to add value in their dealings with the customer.

In his book *Crowning the Customer*, Feargal Quinn, the owner of Superquinn supermarkets, stated that customer service would be the competitive battleground for business in the nineties. He described some of the policies and practices that helped make Superquinn a successful business and a recognised provider of good customer service, including getting a feel for the market, listening effectively to the customer, and the use of consumer panels.

The services mission statement

The mission statement is the starting point for any organisation, as it indicates its purpose, beliefs, values, and strategies. A good mission statement should give direction to the business and its employees, and will also indicate how that business will operate.

MARKS AND SPENCER'S MISSION STATEMENT

Offer customers, under the company's brand name St Michael, a selected range of high-quality, well-designed and attractive merchandise at reasonable prices which represent good value.

Encourage suppliers to use the most modern and efficient techniques of production, based on the latest developments in science and technology.

With the co-operation of our suppliers, enforce high standards of quality control.

Wherever possible, find UK sources of supply.

Simplify operational procedures so that the business operates reasonably efficiently.

Foster good human relations with staff, customers, and suppliers.

This statement gives a good indication of Marks and Spencer's business policy: the provision of quality products and customer service. The core ideal is that all elements of the company should be concentrated on quality, whether dealing with suppliers, staff, or customers. To be successful, the company must operate according to the mission statement; therefore the people who work for the company must be aware of the mission statement, must implement it, and must see it being implemented by others.

High-contact services

High-contact services are those where there is a high degree of contact between the service provider and the customer, for example in health care. The quality of the service is therefore inseparable from the service provider. Marketers need to be sure they have the right service personnel to provide the level of service the customer expects. They must also devote resources to the training and development of their service personnel.

Understanding what motivates people is important for all firms; the service marketer, who must rely on people to deliver the service, must be especially aware of this. Service companies can find, for example, that because demands for the service can vary during different periods of the day, they can introduce flexible working hours for employees. Employees may therefore feel that the company is accommodating them in allowing them to work their preferred working hours, and their attitude to the employer may therefore improve.

Internal marketing is also important for service providers. The services marketer needs to remember that they must market the job to the employee before they can expect the employee to market it to the customer.

The physical services environment

In cases where the production and consumption of the service happen simultaneously—for example in a restaurant or a dentist's surgery—the physical environment is important, as this will convey an image of the service provider to the customer. In many restaurants the customer can see the food being prepared behind the counter, and so the kitchen area must be well maintained. The layout of the seating area, the cleanliness of toilets and the facilities for children will also be noted by the discerning customer. Banks, which traditionally provided their service across counters lined with metal bars or thick glass, have changed their layouts, and in many cases business is now conducted without physical barriers, so that customers do not feel intimidated. In the waiting areas of doctors' and dentists' surgeries some have started to provide play areas for children. Retailers pay particular attention to shop design and layout and to providing added value in the form of someone to pack the shopping at the check-out, someone to help the customer to their car, or simply the umbrellas that are kept at the check-out for customers to borrow.

All these examples illustrate attempts by service providers to improve their physical environment and to create a distinctive image for themselves.

Reshaping supply and demand

This may be required because of fluctuating demand patterns for the service. Demand can be reshaped using price incentives to encourage people to use the service when demand is normally lower.

Reshaping supply can take the form of using part-time staff to cater for the increased demand at peak times, or having employees do more than one job so that they can be moved to other jobs as demand for the service requires. It is possible to automate some services, for example food and beverage dispensers or cash-dispensing with ATMs.

DISCUSSION QUESTIONS

1. Describe the areas that you feel will provide opportunities for marketers of services in the next five years. Give reasons in support of your answer.
2. Compare and contrast the differences in marketing practice between each of the following:
   —Jury's Hotels v. Tayto

　　—ESB v. Ballygowan
　　—McDonald's v. Sony Walkman
　　—Aer Lingus v. Guinness.
3. Describe how developments in technology will assist in the development of the services sector.
4. Tourism in Ireland grew rapidly in the nineties. Are there any disadvantages of this growth?
5. Comment on the importance of relationship marketing to services marketers. What role does customer service play in this relationship?

FURTHER READING

Bateson, J., *Managing Services Marketing* (third edition), Hinsdale (Ill.): Dryden 1996.

Glynn, W., and Barnes, J. (eds.), *Understanding Services Management*, Dublin: Oak Tree Press 1995.

Lovelock, C., *Services Marketing* (second edition), Englewood Cliffs (NJ): Prentice-Hall, 1991.

Palmer, A., *Essentials of Services Marketing*, New York: McGraw-Hill, 1998.

REFERENCES

Berry, L., 'Service marketing is different', *Business Magazine*, May–June 1980.

Berry, L., and Yadav, M., 'Capture and communicate value in the pricing of services', *Sloan Management Review*, summer 1996.

Candlin, D., and Day, P., 'Introducing TQM in a service industry', *Quality Forum*, September 1993.

Carlson, J., *Moments of Truth*, Cambridge (Mass.): Ballinger 1987.

Carson, D., and Gilmore, A., 'Customer care: the neglected domain', *Irish Marketing Review*, vol. 4 (1989), no. 3.

Carson, D., and Gilmore, A., 'Enhancing service quality: the case of Stena Sealink', *Irish Marketing Review*, vol. 6 (1993).

Central Statistics Office, *Labour Force Survey, 1996*, Dublin: Stationery Office 1996.

Danaher, P., Rust, R., Easton, G., and Sullivan, M., 'Indirect financial benefits from service quality', *Quality Management Journal*, vol. 3 (1996), no. 2.

Dearick, D., McAfee, R., and Glassman, M., '"Customers for life": does it fit your culture?', *Business Horizons*, July–August 1997.

Henley Centre of Ireland, *Planning For Social Change: Report*, Dublin: Henley Centre of Ireland 1992.

International Trade, vol. 1 (1988–9).

Newman, K., and Payne, T., 'Service quality and blood donors: a marketing perspective', *Journal of Marketing Management*, August 1997.

Parasuraman, A., and Berry, L., *Servqual: Multiple Item Scale for Measuring Customer Perceptions of Service Quality Research*, Cambridge (Mass.): Marketing Science Institute 1986.

Quinn, M., 'Winning service quality: the PROMPT approach', *Irish Marketing Review*, vol. 7 (1994).

Stationery Office, *The Second Operational Programme for Tourism*, Dublin: Stationery Office 1994.

Stationery Office, *Programme for Competitiveness and Work*, Dublin: Stationery Office 1995.

12

International Marketing

This chapter explores the nature of international marketing and the adaptations to marketing practice that may be required when a business operates in more than one country. International marketing is of particular relevance to Ireland, because of its high dependence on trade; Ireland is one of the most trade-dependent countries in the world.

Between the nineteen-sixties and nineties the Irish economy was transformed. It went from being largely agricultural, with only 22 per cent of merchandise exports consisting of manufactured goods, to a technology-based economy, with manufactured goods accounting for 70 per cent of merchandise exports.

According to the Irish Trade Board, over the years 1994–6 Ireland achieved the highest average export growth in the European Union, and its exports outpaced growth in world trade by a ratio of 3:1. By the late nineties Ireland was the second-largest computer software exporter in the world, after the United States.

Because of the limited size of the home market, Irish companies tend to look towards international markets for expansion. Jury's Hotels launched a budget hotel chain, Jury's Inns, in 1993. Six were established. To expand its budget hotel business the company looked to Britain and planned three inns there, one each in London, Edinburgh, and Manchester (*Sunday Business Post*, 1998). Jury's already had four hotels in London but had not been competing in the budget hotel market.

For marketers in the Republic, Northern Ireland may represent the closest external market. There can be advantages for businesses in developing business there, as Renley Ltd discovered.

RENLEY LTD WINS PRESTIGIOUS BUSINESS AWARD

Renley Ltd of County Kildare is a designer and manufacturer of electrical engineering switchgear products. In 1998 it was awarded the Compaq Ireland Trade Award for small businesses; this is given to companies that have contributed significantly to the development of trade and business links between the North and South of Ireland. The company had won a £500,000 contract from Northern Ireland Electricity to supply cable distribution cabinets. This was its first order from Northern Ireland.

As with most small companies, the domestic market was the traditional focus for Renley until the early nineties. However, investment in the company by its two new owners, ESB International and Pauwels Ltd, increased its export potential significantly. Entering foreign markets became a fundamental objective for the long-term development of the company. The markets selected included Britain, Africa, the

Middle East, south-east Asia, and Australia.

Renley is the sole manufacturer of many of its products. Its main products include fuse combination units, low-voltage fuse panels, traditional pole-mounted cut-outs, and cable distribution cabinets for use on low-voltage electricity distribution networks. The company had always been strongly committed to quality and was awarded recognition under the ISO quality system for its operations in 1992.

Source: Irish Trade Board web site (www.irish-trade.ie).

The main difference between marketing in the home country and in international markets is the marketing environment. In International markets the environment can be less certain; and the more international markets the business is involved in, the greater the potential uncertainty.

Uncertainty arises for many reasons, not least the fact that international markets can be physically and culturally removed from the home market. These differences may require adapting the marketing practice for different markets.

INTERNATIONAL TRADE

Countries trade because few, if any, can be completely self-sufficient. Generally, countries will concentrate their productive effort on the products they can produce best and that give them a competitive advantage.

The 1996 annual report of the Irish Trade Board showed that Ireland was the third-largest exporter in the world per capita, after Singapore and Belgium. It expected that the greatest expansion would be in European markets. Ireland had a trade surplus of £7.9 million in 1996, as table 12.1 shows. Since 1990 the surplus has grown by an average of 30 per cent per year. Britain was still the largest export market, with 22 per cent of exports, followed by the rest of the European Union, with 44 per cent. Exports to the United States increased by 30 per cent in 1996.

Exports of industrial goods and traded services were especially strong. Most of the goods exported were manufactured products, while goods imported were related to Ireland's limited natural resources and the number of foreign-owned firms established here, which needed to import much of their raw materials.

Table 12.1: Balance of trade, 1986–97

	Imports	Exports (£million)	Balance
1986	8.6	9.4	0.8
1987	9.2	10.7	1.6
1988	10.2	12.3	2.1
1989	12.3	14.6	2.3
1990	12.5	14.3	1.9
1991	12.9	15	2.2

1992	13.2	16.7	3.5
1993	14.9	19.8	4.9
1994	17.3	22.8	5.5
1995	20.7	27.8	7.2
1996	22.5	30.4	7.9

Source: Central Statistics Office.

The Irish Trade Board and Enterprise Ireland

Since it was established in the late nineteen-forties, the Irish Trade Board played a significant role in Ireland's international marketing activities. In 1998 the board was merged with the Industrial Development Authority and Forbairt to form Enterprise Ireland. The following panel outlines the main functions of the board, which will continue to be performed.

THE ROLE OF THE IRISH TRADE BOARD

The Irish Trade Board existed to help develop Ireland's exports. It did this by helping companies to identify profitable opportunities and to win business against international competition. The board invested in three main areas: market support, finance for new exporting initiatives, and the promotion of Ireland internationally. After 1998 the functions of the board continue to be performed by Enterprise Ireland.

Market support involved providing support services and in-market activities, including the identification of customers, profiling of competitors, market intelligence, planning distribution channels, establishing a direct market presence, trade fairs, conferences and seminars, and translating and interpreting. Many of these support services wee provided through a network of overseas offices.

Finance was provided in two main areas. Smaller exporters (with exports of less than £1 million) that were planning new initiatives with substantial growth potential could apply for limited non-repayable grants. Eligible companies could apply each year, for a maximum of three years, for support towards half the eligible expenditure detailed in an agreed marketing plan. The other area was the targeted marketing consultancy (TMC) programme. Under this scheme up to 66 per cent of the agreed marketing costs of a five-year project could be subsidised. This was repayable, with repayments linked to sales performance. The TMC programme was designed to enable companies to take advantage of significant business opportunities that would not otherwise be tapped.

The board also marketed Ireland internationally to those seeking suppliers, including multinational manufacturers, distributors, public sector organisations, and international retailers. It researched their requirements and briefed them on the capabilities of relevant Irish companies. The internet was used extensively as a communications medium.

Source: Irish Trade Board web site (www.irish-trade.ie).

Important factors in world trade

There has been rapid growth in world trade and investment, and this is forecast to continue. Since the nineteen-eighties the United States has been running an unfavourable balance of trade, and it is anxious to deal with this. One of the main motivations behind the American position in the Uruguay round of the General Agreement on Tariffs and Trade (GATT) in 1994 was ways of tackling this imbalance. Japan has become a stronger economic power and, unlike the United States, has a large trade surplus.

Oil prices can fluctuate and can have inflationary effects on the economy of countries. Prices have remained relatively stable since the eighties, as there are now more countries producing oil. New markets have opened up, including the former Soviet Union, eastern Europe, and China.

Some countries have experienced severe debt problems. Poland and Mexico had their debts rescheduled in the eighties. Many non-industrialised countries have significant debts, leading to calls by many people for industrialised countries to waive the debt as a means of stimulating growth.

CAMPAIGN TO WAIVE WORLD DEBT

The statistics of world debt are staggering. Non-industrialised countries owe western banks more than $2.1 billion. Everywhere health and education schemes are being cut so that debt repayments can be met. These countries repay four times as much in debt as they receive in aid. African governments transfer to creditors in the northern hemisphere four times the amount they spend on health. According to aid agencies and churches, the crisis is adding to poverty and environmental destruction and fuelling the drugs trade.

Many relief agencies began lobbying for a radical once-off solution to the problem. The Jubilee campaign (so called after the Biblical concept in which slaves are freed and debts written off every fifty years) is calling for the cancellation of all unpayable debt by the year 2000. Campaigners want the remission of debt linked to promises by the governments of those countries that they will spend any money that becomes available on good development projects and not on arms or prestige projects.

Banks are keenly aware of the crisis, and many have already written off debts that they realise will not be repaid. The World Bank and the International Monetary Fund have not forgotten the fright they received in 1982 when Mexico announced that it could not repay its debts, and only the provision of new short-term loans staved off a financial disaster. The problem for many countries is that debts are passed on from generation to generation.

Source: Paul Cullen, 'Campaigners want Third World to go into millennium without debt burden', *Irish Times*, 8 May 1998.

The Uruguay round of the GATT was completed in 1994, which led to changes in industrial tariffs, agricultural subsidies, import barriers, intellectual property, and textile and clothing quotas and tariffs. In addition there were clearer rules on dumping, and a permanent world trade body was established to implement the results of the agreement.

A new North American Free Trade Agreement (NAFTA) between the United States, Canada and Mexico also came into force in the nineteen-nineties. These countries will become a more significant trading bloc as a result.

The international marketing environment

International marketers have to take into account conditions in the different marketing environments in which they operate. While some conditions, such as physical proximity or language differences, may be quite apparent, others may be less so and will need to be researched before a company enters that market. As in the home market, the company must keep abreast of environmental changes and their implications.

The economic environment

The economic strength of the particular country or market will dictate such factors as wealth and disposable income. The economies of countries can be classified as subsistence, raw-material-exporting, industrialising, and industrial. *Subsistence economies* are those of countries such as Ethiopia or Somalia, where the majority of the population subsist on very low levels of income; the consumer market will therefore be relatively undeveloped. *Raw-material-exporting countries*, such as Nigeria, typically have natural resources such as mineral ore, oil or food commodities that account for the bulk of their exports. These may be exported in their raw state without any further processing or added value in the country of origin. There are usually low levels of industrial and commercial development, and consumers have low levels of disposable income. *Industrialising countries*, such as Egypt, are attempting to build up an industrial base. This may involve attracting internationally mobile investment by means of tax incentives and low labour costs. Consumers may have higher levels of disposable income. In *industrial countries*, significant value-adding activities take place, and consumers have the highest levels of disposable income.

The classification of an economy is based on income; and how income is distributed in a particular country is an important economic indicator. It is also a determinant of the size and nature of the consumer market.

The political and legal environment

Ireland and other member-states of the European Union have seen significant developments in the harmonisation of laws and regulations. A fundamental principle of the Treaty of Rome is the free movement of products, people and capital between member-states. Many of the directives issued by the European Commission have been aimed at the removal of laws or regulations that hinder the free movement of goods or trade between states. As a result, it is easier for Irish companies to do business in Europe, and, similarly, the Irish market has opened up to more competition.

In relation to trade outside the European Union, regulations, tariffs and quotas may govern whether and how much trade can take place between Ireland and other countries. Members of GATT, for example, agree tariffs and quotas; these then determine how much trade can be done between states.

Political and legal considerations may determine whether any trade can take place. The United Nations may impose trade sanctions against particular countries. Such sanctions were imposed against Iraq in 1990, which affected a number of Irish companies that had been involved in exporting food products and medical services to Iraq. Similar sanctions were imposed against Libya in the past, and this also affected Irish companies doing business there.

While trade barriers are being lowered around the world, there are still many countries that may not have positive attitudes towards foreign marketers. These attitudes may be based on a desire to protect the market for indigenous suppliers, or they may be based on political, social or religious grounds. The result can be laws or regulations that prevent or limit the activities of foreign marketers.

Regulations and bureaucracy are an inevitable part of exporting. In the European Union efforts have been made to reduce aspects of regulation and bureaucracy that had the effect of slowing down or hindering the movement of products. Regulations exist governing, among other things, how products are to be transported between countries, safety issues, and the components and ingredients of products. These exist to prevent disease, accidents, and contamination. Customs examination, which usually takes place at the point of entry, involves administration and may lead to delays. Monetary regulations may prevent the marketer repatriating profits, while exchange controls may place limitations on the financial transactions associated with trade.

Political stability is important for trade to flourish; instability creates uncertainty and increases the risk associated with exporting. In general, industrialised countries tend to be politically stable; difficulties tend to emerge in countries where there is significant political or social unrest.

The cultural environment

The way in which foreign consumers think about certain products must be clearly understood. Cultural conditions can influence whether or not the product will be considered by consumers in the overseas market. Not all products or services are cross-cultural, though several, such as Coca-Cola, Levi's, and McDonald's hamburgers, are sold virtually throughout the world. Irish products such as Waterford Crystal and Bailey's Irish Cream also have cross-cultural characteristics.

Factors that influence how a product is perceived in a particular cultural setting include the nature of the product and the needs and motives of buyers. Language differences can also affect how the product is communicated in the market. In less developed markets, consumers may have little or no familiarity with certain products or the concepts underlying them. The rate of literacy may be low, and pictures or symbols may therefore be more important than text; this can have implications for packaging and advertising.

Marketers need to understand something of the psyche of consumers in overseas markets. Consider the example in the following panel, which shows how consumers' attitudes changed in nineteen-nineties Britain, Ireland's biggest trading partner.

THE BRITISH CONSUMER PSYCHE

In the early nineties the Chartered Institute of Marketing asked the Henley Centre to study the implications of recession on marketing in Britain. The eighties had seen high levels of consumer confidence and spending; then recession followed in the nineties, and all this changed. In the late eighties people had borrowed on the strength of their housing assets to pay for everything. With recession, many witnessed significant losses in real or perceived wealth, and the concept of 'negative equity' became a reality for some.

Needless to say, the Henley research showed changed consumer attitudes towards borrowing, with consumers becoming much more circumspect. The research also showed that, in an environment where retailers were heavily promoting their own brands, consumers were questioning the value for money they received from manufacturers' brands. There were also changes in the perceived relationship between price and quality. In relation to categories such as cosmetics, fresh food, packaged food, and durables, such as microwave ovens and cassette recorders, there was a long-term decline in the number of people agreeing that highest price means best quality.

The research showed that consumers had relatively unchanged attitudes to savings, the majority of them intending to build them up. Their optimism about investing in housing was also undiminished, in spite of the recession. Service was still considered important, with consumers indicating a desire for improved service throughout a range of sectors. Quality was also important, and this made value for money the main marketing emphasis.

Demographically, the young adults of the sixties represent an important marketing opportunity in the nineties. By the year 2000 those aged between 45 and 59 will represent nearly a fifth of the total population. They are adventurous and have the highest levels of disposable income, and their experience will add to the mature, sensible and more marketing-aware feel of the nineties.

The Henley research predicted that the marketing environment for the rest of the decade would be more competitive. There would be more restrained economic growth and more muted consumer spending. More spending would be directed to things previously provided by the state, such as health and education. The research also suggested that there would be a reducing core of affluent consumers as the number of relatively poor households grew. There would be a reducing mass market as income distribution stretched, and consumers would be much more cautious. It was expected that they would also be more 'marketing-literate'. While tastes would continue to fragment and consumers would become more perceptive, the Henley centre expected that there would be a requirement for more, not less, marketing. Each marketing pound would have to work harder, with marketing budgets and personnel becoming more accountable.

Source: A. Beale, 'Chartered Institute of Marketing', *European Marketing Confederation Gold Book*, 1994.

Irish marketers attempting to position products in the British market in the nineties would have found the results of the Henley research of interest. To some it may have helped determine how they would approach that market, for example launching their own brand or becoming a contracted manufacturer of own-label products for one or more of the large retail chains. One of Ireland's manufacturers of dairy products, Town of Monaghan Co-operative, had launched a range of yoghurt and desserts under the Mona brand in 1983. However, when the company began exporting to Britain it did so principally with own-label products, which it produced for a number of retailers.

Consumers' behaviour and purchasing patterns vary in different markets. Ireland and Britain, for example, have the highest consumption per capita of chocolate and sweets in Europe, as fig. 12.1 shows. These figures mean that the average Irish person spends over £68 a year on chocolate and sweets. There is no difference in consumption patterns between men and women. Cadbury, which accounts for over 50 per cent of the Irish market, attributes this level of consumption to the climate, the number of small sweet-shops, and an increase in snacking (*Sunday Tribune*, 18 January 1998).

Fig. 12.1: Chocolate and sweet consumption: some international comparisons, 1997 (kg per capita)

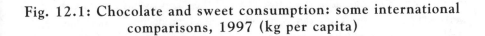

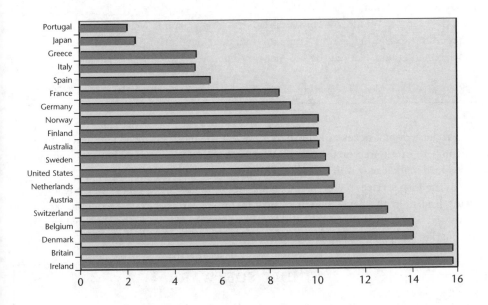

Source: *Confectionery Review*, 1997.

Cultural change can present opportunities for marketers. In China, government policy has limited families to one child each. The result was the creation of a generation of young people who were well educated and prosperous, materialistic, and accepting of western culture (Barnathan et al., 1994). This group of younger consumers were described by some marketers as 'the little emperors' (Wei, 1997).

Technological environment

Technology is a possible source of competitive advantage; in international markets, technology developed in one country may give it an advantage over other countries. Consider the example of Bantry Bay Mussels, which developed process technology to give it an advantage in selected export markets.

BANTRY BAY MUSSELS

Bantry Bay Mussels, established in 1991 to harvest fresh mussels, has patented a process for producing frozen vacuum-packed mussels for export. France became the company's largest market, accounting for 70 per cent of sales; the remainder went to Italy, Germany, and Britain.

In addition to supplying fresh produce, the company began to investigate the production of processed mussel products to boost sales. These would have the advantage of a longer shelf life. The result was the development of a process for freezing and vacuum-packing the mussels, which the company has used successfully, as well as licensing the technology to other mussel producers. Other value-added products include the development of mussels frozen with a variety of sauces so that they will keep for eighteen months.

In 1996 the company was awarded the AIB Capital Markets Export Award. According to the judges, the company had developed an intimate knowledge of its target market and adapted the product range accordingly.

Sources: *Irish Independent*, 31 October 1996; *Sunday Business Post*, 23 February 1997.

Products do not necessarily have to represent the most advanced technology in order to compete in international markets. What is considered a low level of technology in a developed market may well be high technology in a developing market.

In the Irish services sector, many companies have created a competitive advantage by being leaders in the development of new technology. Consider the example of Kindle Software, which used the ability and creativity of people to compete internationally in the market for specialist banking software.

KINDLE SOFTWARE

Kindle began life in 1979 as a sub-contractor working with a hardware manufacturer. Up to then computers were sold without business applications to large firms, which then employed their own staff to develop schemes for harnessing the computer to do jobs. In the early years the company worked with the construction industry and the legal profession, but it was the banking industry, with its need for software and automation, that attracted it most. Its business was information, which was a central competitive weapon, as was the ability of automation to allow it to undertake and manage certain activities and deliver new services to customers.

Kindle developed a standard product, called Bankmaster, which it licensed to banks. The original customers were Irish, and these were followed by customers in London and Jersey. Kindle was reliant on computers supplied by ICL, with which it entered on a co-operative marketing arrangement. This gave it access to ICL's customers throughout the world, and the company expanded rapidly. In the mid-eighties the company bought an American banking software company, which it hoped would give it access to the many small banks that existed there. This did not prove successful: the banks tended to buy systems on the basis of lowest price rather than those with the best-quality solutions. The American business was sold in 1988.

The company then began to develop systems to run on personal computers, and a PC version of Bankmaster was launched, which involved establishing a link with Microsoft and Novell, which flourished in the nineteen-nineties. The number of Kindle's customers around the world expanded, annual sales growth was 40 per cent, and the company employed several thousand people in Ireland.

According to the company's chairman, software is a value-added business. Virtually no raw materials are used, and there are no imports. Almost all expenditure is on people, getting them in front of customers and keeping them in contact with customers. It is an ideal business to conduct from a base in Ireland, and location is not a disadvantage. The business must be organised around a core product team at a single location and involves continual travel out to the market and from the market back to the core to examine and verify.

Source: T. Kilduff, chairman, Relfex Group, National Marketing Conference, October 1993.

Competitive environment

A profile of competitors in the overseas market will be required, with information on who they are, what range they offer, how widespread their distribution coverage is, and how they promote their products.

If competitors enjoy the benefits of protection in the foreign market, this can be a significant disadvantage for a company trying to establish there. Marketers will seek to create a competitive advantage over rivals in the market, as Waterford Wedgwood did with the development of the Marquis range of glassware, which it used to widen its product base. Waterford Wedgwood's strategy in developing this product, which was obtained from other European countries, such as the Czech Republic, was to fill the gap in price segments it had vacated when it had increased the price of its classic hand-cut range. In the crucial American market the product achieved sixth place in sales in higher-priced crystal (Galvin, 1993).

MARKETING DECISIONS IN INTERNATIONAL MARKETS

Research

Research is vital for making decisions, especially if the decisions are being made on markets with which the business has little familiarity. The research process will be the same for international markets as for the home market. Enterprise Ireland, which provides assistance to Irish business, has a market information library, which provides various profiles, reports and figures on overseas markets.

The benefits of conducting international market research were demonstrated by the experiences of Tyrone Crystal in the Japanese market (Bell and Brown, 1989). The research showed that there were few official impediments to entering the market but that many of the design qualities prized in other markets were incompatible with prevailing Japanese tastes. In spite of this, the study identified some concrete opportunities within specific market segments.

Developing the product for international markets

A classic example of the development of a product for international markets comes from the nineteen-sixties and the development of the Kerrygold brand.

IRELAND IS KERRYGOLD COUNTRY

In 1961 the Irish Dairy Board was established as the central export marketing organisation of the dairy industry. In 1962 the British market was the successful launching-pad for Kerrygold butter. A number of factors can be attributed to the success of the launch, such as product quality, distinctive packaging, a higher-priced pricing policy, and a television campaign that presented strong visual images of the green pasturelands of Ireland.

The strategy for the launch of the product in the German market in 1972 echoed the British formula, namely providing a high-quality butter tailored to consumers' tastes. Once again the advertising emphasised the country of origin, the green island with the clean and unspoilt nature. '*Das gold der grünen insel*' was the theme with which the advertising would become associated for twenty years.

With the success of Kerrygold butter the logical progression was to capitalise on brand awareness and to extend the range to include 'light' butter and a range of natural cheeses.

The key to developing Kerrygold branded sales in Belgium has been the role played by the board's subsidiary, IDB Benelux, which imports and distributes products from eight European countries, including Ireland. This has given Kerrygold improved access to the Belgian trade and a greater presence in retail outlets for both butter and Kerrygold cheddar in blocks and pre-pack form. Support for both product categories ranges through television and press advertising and sales promotions directed at the trade and the consumer. IDB Benelux also developed a successful 'Green Flag' brand for a range of higher-priced European fine foods, including Irish smoked salmon, breakfast bacon and salmon spread and the Greek speciality tzatziki, as well as a range of pre-packed convenience foods.

In Greece, Kerrygold was the first branded cheese on the market in 1980, and Kerrygold Regato became the largest cheese brand in the country. Again the brand was supported by a significant expenditure on advertising and promotion. Television commercials demonstrated the versatility of the cheese by incorporating it in traditional Greek recipes as well as in new, imaginative dishes.

The Irish Dairy Board attributes the success of the Kerrygold brand around the world to a number of factors:

- All the products marketed under the Kerrygold brand are of the highest quality, and many are demonstrably superior to the competition.
- The board has a total commitment to branding in the long term and a heavy investment in achieving national distribution, including maximising consumers' awareness through above and below-the-line support.
- An attractive brand name is enhanced by the positive image towards its country of origin: 'Ireland, the food garden of Europe.'
- Regular innovation allows the board to capitalise on the Kerrygold brand name with a complementary product line.

Notwithstanding the fact that the different countries demand marketing tactics to suit their various individual requirements, the core communication values of Kerrygold remain constant in all markets served by the board. In that regard Kerrygold has become a Eurobrand and will, through time, become a truly international brand.

Source: Caroline Palmer, 'Irish Dairy Board', *European Marketing Confederation Gold Book*, 1994.

The development of the Kerrygold brand demonstrates some of the prerequisites for success in international markets. Another significant Irish success has been Bailey's Irish Cream, which has become a leading world brand in the drinks market.

BAILEY'S IRISH CREAM: THE WORLD'S TOP-SELLING LIQUEUR

Since it was launched in 1974 on the Irish market and in 1975 on the international market, Bailey's Irish Cream has become an international brand success story. It created a completely new market where no products had existed before and is one of the top twenty spirit brands in the world. Annual sales are more than 50 million bottles, and the product is manufactured in Ireland from locally obtained raw materials.

The ten leading markets are the United States, Germany, Spain, Britain, Italy, France, Canada, Australia, the Netherlands, and duty-free outlets. Developing new markets and acquiring new consumers is still an objective, and Latin America, the Far East and eastern Europe are considered to be the main prospects.

The brand has consistently been supported by advertising and promotional campaigns, the themes of which have varied over the years. The core proposition has remained the same: an original product, and a taste of Ireland.

Bailey's Irish Cream was named the world's top-selling liqueur brand by *Drinks International* in February 1998. 4.1 million cases (49.2 million bottles) were sold, its nearest rival being De Kuypers, a schnapps-style liqueur, which sold 4.06 million cases. Bailey had increased its sales in 1997 by 3.8 per cent.

The top ten world liqueurs were:

		million cases
1.	Bailey's (Diageo)	4.1
2.	De Kuyper	4.06
3.	Kahlua (Allied Domecq)	2.45
4.	Southern Comfort (Brown Forman)	2.23
5.	Malibu (Diageo)	1.7
6.	Amaretto (ILLVA)	1.61
7.	Marie Brizzard	1.4
8.	Bols (Bols International)	1.4
9.	Grand Marnier (Marnier Lapostolle)	1.35
10.	Cointreau (Rémy Cointreau)	1.06

Source: Paul O'Kane, 'Bailey's tops world sales chart', *Sunday Tribune*, 22 February 1998; *Sunday Business Post*, 16 March 1997, 13 July 1997.

There are three distinct categories of global brand: long-term international brands, such as Ford or McDonald's; brands created for the global market, such as the Sony Playstation; and exported brands (Byfield and Caller, 1996). It is probably true to say that Bailey's Irish Cream is Ireland's main global brand. Most of Ireland's international efforts have been concentrated on exported brands. Two-thirds of Irish exports are to other EU member-states.

While brands like Kerrygold and Kindle software have been very successful in many markets, there are of course many other products and services that may be less well known but have been successfully marketed in many overseas markets. The successful development of a product or service for the international market must take account of the needs of buyers in those markets, and there must also be a competitive advantage.

New ranges may need to be developed to suit changes that have taken place in international markets. This was the case for Waterford Wedgwood, which, as seen earlier, developed the Marquis brand in the early nineties.

CREATING A NEW INTERNATIONAL BRAND

In the early nineteen-nineties Waterford Wedgwood was faced with significant problems. There was a recession in its main market, the United States, with the result that its high-income potential customers were trading down to lower-priced crystal. There was also a change in tastes.

Waterford Wedgwood responded with the launch of a new brand, Marquis, designed in a more contemporary or transitional way and positioned in a lower price tier of the higher-priced crystal market. The new brand moved quickly into the number 6 sales position in the United States. This was achieved not only at great speed but also without cannibalising sales of the parent brand, Waterford Crystal, which was repositioned adroitly at the same time to increase market share in an essentially static market.

Source: R. O'Donoghue, 'Marquis by Waterford: creating a new international brand', *Irish Marketing Review*, vol. 7 (1994).

Not all products can be successfully internationalised. Exporting the product that is being supplied to the home market is not always possible, and adaptation of the product may be required. Irish Biscuits, for example, may find it difficult to internationalise its successful Kimberly, Mikado and Coconut Cream brands. All three products are soft-textured biscuits, and while these have been successful in Ireland, they may not fare so well in markets such as Britain, where consumers prefer crisp-textured products. The existing product may have to be adapted to the particular tastes and needs of the overseas market, or a completely new product may have to be developed.

In some cases a product developed for the international market may ultimately be launched on the home market. For many years the Kilkenny brand of ale, developed by Guinness for the international market, was available only outside Ireland, but it was subsequently launched on the home market.

The home market may provide a good testing-ground for the product before its international launch. Waterford Wedgwood launched the John Rocha range of crystal on the Irish market in 1997. Inspired by the dress designer John Rocha, the range was designed to bring the Waterford brand to a younger, more contemporary market that had not previously been buying Waterford. The range, which included bowls, glasses, and vases, was designed to be more simple than traditional Waterford. With sales of £1.1 million in its first year in Ireland, it was planned to launch it in Britain, the United States, Singapore, Hong Kong and Australia in 1998 (*Sunday Tribune*, 18 January 1998).

Some companies try to have a standard product for all markets. In 1988 the Ford Motor Company made a strategic decision to launch a global car. Similarities between the various markets were growing as legislation reached new levels of harmony; car buyers in various continents found their motoring needs less different than they had been in the past. The company spent over $6,000 million on the development and manufacture of the Mondeo, an international design team having carried out extensive research into customers' needs, desires, and aspirations (Nolan, 1993). In 1998 Ford began to implement a value-engineering programme designed to eliminate excess cost from the Fiesta, which was a popular European brand. The company found that it was making 27 million differently specified Fiestas: there were 132 different door trims alone. The scheme had as its target a reduction to about 10,000 different specifications (*Sunday Times*, 18 January 1998). Obviously such drives to simplify production, reduce manufacturing costs and create a globally competitive product cannot be at the expense of product quality.

Products and culture

A product has both tangible and intangible features. Much of the importance of the intangible benefits is attributed by the values and customs within a culture, and it is important to understand how consumers will perceive products or communications about them in international markets. One successful export in the nineteen-nineties was the 'Irish pub', which had tangible and intangible aspects. Guinness had a pivotal role in the concept, along with firms such as the Irish Pub Company, a Dublin design and building firm. Irish-themed pubs spread throughout Europe, and a number were also established in Asia (Prystay, 1997; Jones, 1997).

The semiotics of the product or the message may dictate a need for change or modification. The personalities, colours, settings, characters and advertising copy used will all need to be scrutinised to make sure they cannot be misinterpreted or misunderstood. In China, alphanumeric brand names are popular with consumers, because of the impact of Chinese lucky and unlucky numbers (Ang, 1997).

Some cultures are very receptive to products and brands from other countries. In many markets there is widespread consumer acceptance of and desire for American brands (Taninecz, 1997). This is certainly shown in Ireland, where products such as Coca-Cola have gone from strength to strength, as the following panel illustrates. Irish marketing organisations such as Bord Fáilte and An Bord Bia attempt to build on the positive perceptions of Ireland as a holiday destination and as a source of quality food products. Enterprise Ireland attempts to build a positive perception of Ireland as a country to invest in.

COCA-COLA: CROSSING THE BOUNDARIES

Some 98 per cent of the growth in cola sales last year was taken by Coca-Cola, strong evidence of how it is defeating competitors in the Irish market. Coca-Cola's marketing strategy of getting customers to consider having a Coca-Cola at almost any time of the day appears to be paying off, as it achieved an 18 per cent increase in volume sales last year, accounting for a 4.3 per cent gain in market share.

Irish consumers drink an average of 92.9 litres of Coca-Cola per year, compared with an American average of 173.2 litres. Seventy per cent of all purchases of carbonated soft drinks in Ireland are unplanned. An analysis of the commercial beverage market since 1985 has shown that the consumption of milk has remained almost static, as have the sales of coffee and tea, but the sale of soft drinks has increased from 220 million litres in 1985 to 535 million litres in 1997. Because of this growth, 72 per cent of people aged between twelve and forty-nine in Northern Ireland consume Coca-Cola or Diet Coke daily, while the figure for the Republic is 48 per cent.

Source: Richard Curran, 'Coca-Cola strategy pays off', *Sunday Tribune*, 12 April 1998.

The country of origin of a product can affect consumers' evaluation of it. One research study (Schafer, 1997) evaluated the potential impact of British consumers' age, sex and socio-economic background on the magnitude of the effects of country of origin on the purchase of lager and sparkling wine. It found that older consumers in particular showed stronger effects of country of origin. The AB socio-economic group had stronger effects for sparkling wine, while the C1C2 group had stronger effects for lager. The sex of the respondents had no impact on the magnitude of effect. The image of the country of origin may therefore be linked to brands. This has probably benefited brands such as Bailey's Irish Cream.

One study (Kim and Chung, 1997) emphasised the importance of international marketers taking country image into account in their competitive analysis. Another research study, conducted among industrial buyers in Britain and Germany (Corrigan,

1996), ranked Ireland fourth and second, respectively, in 'environmental friendliness'. To the extent that this is considered an important purchasing criterion, this was a significant finding.

Sometimes products can take time to be successfully adopted in overseas markets. The rate of diffusion will be affected by such factors as age and income but also by familiarity with the product concept, communication, and distribution.

Promotion

In the development of an effective promotional strategy for international markets, the same principles apply as for the home market. However, the same promotional mix or the same content may not be appropriate. Cultural factors will be important here.

Marketers need to be particularly careful with the language used. A small number of companies, such as Coca-Cola and Pepsi, use global advertising campaigns. Most marketers have to adapt campaigns at a basic level to incorporate different language voice-overs and, at a more advanced level, to have completely different campaigns for individual markets.

Global advertising and promotional campaigns have the advantage of being more cost-effective than developing separate campaigns for each market. British Airways unveiled a new corporate identity in 1997, incorporating fifty world images, which would be incorporated in its signage, stationery, and aircraft (Marsh, 1997). Some of the images were commissioned from designers; in other cases the company held competitions in different countries to select a suitable image.

If market or competitive conditions dictate, separate campaigns will have to be used. In some cases the same product is known by a different name in different markets.

The imagery used may also be very different. Bord Fáilte has developed an image of Ireland that, while not radically different, has subtle differences in different markets. Advertising standards and the rules governing the promotion of products can vary from country to country, and advertisements may have to be modified accordingly.

As with the product decision, a vital question in international promotion is whether a standardised promotion strategy can be developed for all international markets or whether it is necessary to customise to meet needs in different markets. Language will certainly play a part. One American study (Ueltschy and Ryans, 1997) investigated the extent to which standardised advertising could be effectively employed in the United States and Mexico. The research concentrated on consumers' attitudes to different versions of print advertisements designed to test the impact of language and cultural differences. The conclusion was that respondents in both countries preferred total customisation of the advertisement.

Many marketers are interested in developing pan-European advertising campaigns. There are difficulties, however, in getting pan-European media that will deliver the audience the marketer requires. Television channels such as MTV and Eurosport do reach pan-European audiences, but they have their limitations. MTV has lost some of its position, because countries such as Britain and France are launching competitive domestic channels; and Eurosport has a predominantly male audience (Barrett, 1997).

Language is also an issue. Consistency in advertising campaigns may not come from words but rather from a consistent image. This may mean.that direct translations, which can sometimes be unfortunate, can be avoided. It was found that Wrigley's Spearmint gum, for example, would have a direct translation in some eastern European markets as 'shark's sperm', while Mitsubishi realised it could not launch the Pajero brand in Spain, where this word would have an offensive meaning (Barrett, 1997).

This demonstrates that it is not easy to develop standardised promotional campaigns. There are few marketers that can successfully promote their product in the same way in all markets.

Opportunities can also be found in the use of language, as an Irish crisps and snack manufacturer discovered.

USING THE RIGHT LANGUAGE TO BOOST SALES

Largo Foods was established in 1982 to produce potato crisps and snacks, and by the late nineties it had an estimated 30 per cent share of the Irish market with brands including Mr Perri, Hunky Dorys, and Cottage Crisps. In 1997 the company won a £1.1 million contract in Russia. It had already had sales in Russia and had begun to print its packaging in Russian. This contrasted with its competitors Pepsico and Estrella, which simply stuck a label with the ingredients in Russian onto existing packages.

Source: *Sunday Tribune*, 21 December 1997.

Pricing

When the price of the product to consumers in the overseas market is being calculated, it must be remembered that there are additional costs to be taken into account when marketing in international markets. Such costs as transport and the margins required by middlemen have to be included in any cost calculations. When Avonmore launched its Country Ladle soup on the Scottish market in 1994 it retailed at the equivalent of 99p, while it was selling in the home market at 89p at the time.

Some companies adopt a variable-cost pricing approach, which means they cost goods on the basis of the marginal or incremental cost of production: they do not include any fixed costs in their calculations (these fixed costs are covered by sales in the home market).The danger with this approach is that the business can be accused of dumping and could face anti-dumping penalties. Products will therefore be costed on a full-cost basis, which means that each product will bear a portion of the fixed and variable costs incurred in its production.

Other important factors that have to be taken into account are exchange rate fluctuations, inflation, and VAT or local taxes.

Distribution

Distribution channels can be longer in international markets, as illustrated in the diagram. Indeed some markets may have many more levels than the five illustrated.

manufacturer ➜ exporter ➜ importer ➜ wholesaler ➜ retailer ➜ **consumer**

An important aspect of the distribution of the product is the assessment of middlemen in international markets. Prospective middlemen should be assessed according to the same factors used in the home market but bearing in mind the unique features of the overseas market. The difficulty for the marketer is that control can become more difficult in international channels. Many international marketers have used franchising as the means of expanding into international markets and alleviating the control problems. Whatever the nature of the distribution channel, a formal agreement or contract is desirable. Considerations that should be taken into account in assessing international channel alternatives include productivity or volume, financial strength, market coverage, managerial stability and capability, and the nature and reputation of the business.

Customer service issues, such as the availability of information, spare parts, and a procedure for handling complaints, also need to be addressed.

EXPORTING

Exporting is one aspect of international marketing, concerned with the supply of finished or semi-finished goods from one country to one or more foreign countries. It is therefore an operational aspect of international marketing. The principal objective in exporting is to get goods or services from the manufacturer or service provider to the market with the minimum cost and delay and the maximum efficiency.

Exporting can be direct, through the firm's own channels or through middlemen; it can also be indirect, for example using a professional exporter or trading house.

The principal issues in exporting

As countries are keen to keep statistics of imports and exports, products are classified, with each product given a tariff code number, in the Irish case by the Central Statistics Office. This allows them to maintain records and to produce quarterly trade statistics. Tariff codes are useful when market research is being conducted, as they give details of the quantities of the product exported or imported.

Export controls may exist in the home country: in Ireland, for example, export licences are required for certain agricultural products and for works of art. Import controls in a country may limit or place restrictions on the amount of a particular product that can be imported. As part of the GATT, for example, quotas and limits were negotiated and agreed between participating states.

Some goods may have import duties imposed on them, and these are usually payable at the point of entry. The valuation for duty can vary: for alcoholic products, for example, the duty is calculated on the percentage alcohol content; thus the duty on wine is usually lower than on whiskey. Whether the goods are delivered *free on board* (FOB) or with *cost, insurance and freight* (CIF) paid will also determine how much duty is to be paid.

Exporting requires familiarity with any regulations that may exist. Some of these may be temporary: some countries imposed a temporary ban on the importing of Irish beef, for example, following the BSE outbreak in the nineteen-nineties. Typically there are regulations governing the exporting of dangerous goods, drugs and medicines, and foodstuffs. Regulations require that the product's origin be clearly stated. This is particularly important if the product has come by way of another country. Other regulations govern product samples and weights and measures.

Exporting involves several risks, not least when there are difficulties in receiving payment. Generally *letters of credit* or *bills of exchange* are considered the safest method. The bill of exchange is an unconditional order in writing, signed by the person giving it, requiring the person to whom it is addressed to pay a sum of money on demand or on a specified date. This will be underwritten by a bank or financial institution, thus minimising the risk. Banks or financial institutions may *discount* the bill of exchange, thus providing a source of finance to the holder. Other methods of payment, such as *cash against documents* or *open account*, may be more risky or difficult to administer.

Exporting may also involve dealing with special packaging requirements. It may not be possible to transport the product in its retail pack, and therefore a transit pack may be required. This provides maximum protection during transport. On arrival, the product can be packaged for sale in the market.

Entering international markets

Direct export involves the company establishing its own export division, selecting and managing the channel, and possibly engaging in advertising and promotional activities in the market. This is an expensive option, which may require significant investment. *Indirect exporting* usually involves using professional exporters or trading houses. The company supplies the product to them and they manage the channel and the marketing activities.

Large companies or existing multinationals typically use *wholly owned subsidiaries* or *foreign direct investment*. In Ireland, HB and Goodall are wholly owned subsidiaries of Van den Bergh Foods and CPC Foods, respectively. Irish companies have entered markets in this way also: for example, Wedgwood China is a wholly owned subsidiary of Waterford Wedgwood, and First Maryland Bank Corporation in the United States is a subsidiary of AIB Bank. Foreign direct investment may involve the establishment of manufacturing facilities in other markets: for example, Guinness established breweries overseas in countries such as Nigeria and Malaysia.

Licensing and royalty agreements reduce the cost of owned subsidiaries or direct investment. Typically the licenser will sign an agreement with a local manufacturer, which may involve the licensing of patents and will involve the payment of royalties, disclosure fees, and possibly payments for management or technical assistance. The licenser is therefore guaranteed an income and typically a certain proportion of turnover, without the risk of investment. In the early nineteen-seventies Waterford Co-operative signed a licensing agreement with a French company, Sodial, to produce Yoplait yoghurt in Ireland; this subsequently became the market leader in the sector. Franchises are a common form of licensing agreement and have been used extensively by firms to expand into international markets.

Contract manufacture involves arranging for a manufacturer to produce the product in the overseas market. This may allow for speedy entry to the market but must be tightly controlled to ensure that quality levels are maintained. Waterford Wedgwood produces the Marquis range of glassware using contract manufacturers in eastern European countries; and the frozen food manufacturer Bird's Eye has used contract manufacture to produce some of its Menumaster range in Ireland.

In joint ventures the firm may identify suitable local partners and develop the market jointly with them. This may or may not involve the purchase of an interest in the company. Joint ventures will be governed by an agreement on such issues as the allocation of dividends and commercial policy. In 1997 Ballygowan entered a three-year agreement with Scottish Courage, the largest brewing company in Britain, to consolidate its position in the British licensed trade (*Deadline*, November 1997). The company already had a similar agreement with Bass breweries in Britain. The concept of joint venture has been extended to include strategic alliances and partnerships. Aer Lingus has partnership agreements with several airlines, including the American airline Delta. Under the agreement Delta sells a number of seats on Aer Lingus's transatlantic services; this gives Delta access to routes it does not serve itself, and also guarantees the sale of the seats to Aer Lingus.

Which market to enter?

The ultimate decision in international marketing may be which market to enter. Most businesses have limited resources; therefore the most attractive market should be picked. Target markets should generally be assessed according to

- estimates of the existing market potential
- estimates of future market potential and risk
- forecasts of sales potential
- forecasts of sales and profit for five years
- estimates of the rate of return on investment.

Markets should be thoroughly researched before a decision is made. Given development costs associated with entry to a market, it can be several years before a company realises a return on its international markets. A commitment to international marketing is therefore required.

FURTHER READING

Ball, Donald, and McCulloch, W., *International Business* (fourth edition), Homewood (Ill.): Irwin 1990.
Cateora, P., *International Marketing* (eighth edition), Homewood (Ill.): Irwin, 1990.

DISCUSSION QUESTIONS

1. Pick an Irish product that has been successfully internationalised, such as Bailey's Irish Cream or Waterford Crystal, and describe the environmental forces it must contend with in its international markets.
2. Identify an Irish product or service that is not internationally traded as present but has the potential to be. Give reasons for your choice.

3. Explain why an understanding of cultural differences is important for the international marketer.
4. Do you think there is a potential for more global brands? Give some examples to illustrate your answer.
5. Describe how relationship marketing can be relevant to international marketers. What role can strategic alliances play in this?

REFERENCES

Ang, S., 'Chinese consumers' perceptions of alpha-numeric brand names', *Journal of Consumer Marketing*, vol. 14 (1997), no. 3.

Barnathan, J., Comes, F., Roberts, D., Einhorn, B., Roy, E., and Moore, J., 'China's youth: a new generation leaves tradition behind', *Business Week*, 14 July 1994.

Barrett, P., 'Abroad-minded', *Marketing*, 24 April 1997.

Bell, J., and Brown, S., 'Tyrone Crystal: striking out in Japan', *Irish Marketing Review*, vol. 4 (1989), no. 2.

Byfield, S., and Caller, L., 'Building brands across borders', *Admap*, June 1996.

Corrigan, J., 'How a green image can drive Irish export growth', *Greener Management International*, October 1994.

Galvin, P., 'The Turnaround at Waterford Crystal', National Marketing Conference, October 1993.

Jones, A., 'Éire apparent', *Marketing Week*, 7 February 1997.

Kim, C. K., and Chung, J. Y., 'Brand popularity, country image and market share: an empirical study', *Journal of International Business Studies*, second quarter, 1997.

Marsh, H., 'Why BA has designs on a global brand', *Marketing*, 12 June 1997.

Nolan, E., 'Launching a New Product in a Hostile Environment', National Marketing Conference, October 1993.

Prystay, C., 'Betting on the luck of the Irish', *Asian Business*, July 1997.

Schafer, A., 'Do demographics have an impact on country of origin effects?', *Journal of Marketing Management*, November 1997.

Taninecz, G., 'Global grocers', *Industry Week*, 17 March 1997.

Ueltschy, L., and Ryans, J., 'Employing standardised promotion strategies in Mexico: the impact of language and cultural differences', *International Executive*, July–August 1997.

Wei, R., 'Emerging lifestyles in China and consequences for perception of advertising, buying behaviour and consumption preferences', *International Journal of Advertising*, vol. 16 (1997), no. 4.

Business-to-Business Marketing

Business-to-business marketing covers all activities involved in the marketing of products and services to firms that use them in the production of consumer or industrial goods and services. The fundamentals of marketing are essentially the same; however, there are a number of important distinguishing aspects of business-to-business marketing. In this chapter the nature of business-to-business marketing is reviewed and examples of business-to-business marketing practice are given.

THE NATURE OF BUSINESS-TO-BUSINESS MARKETING

Industrial markets are relatively concentrated. As a result, individual orders can be quite large. Consider the world airline market, where there are a small number of producers and where individual orders from airlines can be very significant. As the following panel illustrates, when airlines engage in aircraft replacement, very often there are economies in replacing an entire fleet.

AIRBUS WINS $2,500 MILLION AIRLINE AGREEMENT

Airbus Industrie, the European aircraft manufacturer, secured its largest European deal in February 1998 with a $2,500 million agreement to supply Iberia, the Spanish state airline, with at least fifty new planes.

Iberia was buying from the A320 range of single-aisle planes to replace ageing McDonnell-Douglas aircraft, Boeing 727s, and Airbus A300s. The order will see thirty-one A320s and nineteen A321s delivered from 1999.

Iberia had an option to buy a further twenty-six aircraft, increasing the value of the order by $1,300 million. An industry source said that Iberia had operated planes from too wide a range of manufacturers in the past, which kept servicing and training costs high.

Source: A. Jones, 'Airbus wins $2.5 billion airline agreement', *Times*, 4 February 1998.

Ryanair announced a similarly large-scale purchase from Airbus's main rival, Boeing, in 1998. The company planned to replace its fleet of Boeing 737-200s, which it had bought second hand from a number of other airlines, with a fleet of new Boeing 737-800s. The initial order for twenty-five aircraft was worth £1,400 million; the company also had an option on another twenty aircraft. The fleet replacement was part of the company's plans to develop new European routes and was to be partly financed by the company's flotation on the New York stock exchange.

The concentrated nature of business-to-business markets means that relationship marketing is important. Marketers in business-to-business markets may have a smaller number of customers to develop relationships with, a significant advantage when compared with many consumer marketers.

As with many services, distribution channels in business-to-business markets tend to be shorter, and in many cases products are sold without intermediaries. For many Irish companies, however, additional levels will be added in international markets, as Unilokomotiv of Galway found.

UNILOKOMOTIV

Unilokomotiv is a Galway manufacturer of rail shunting vehicles, which are used to move railway wagons around marshalling yards and industrial complexes. The limited potential of the home market—its only Irish customers being Irish Steel and Tara Mines—means that it had to develop export markets. In addition to European markets, the company has built export markets in Pakistan, China, Malaysia, and Bangladesh. It competes in international markets with producers from Germany, Italy, and the United States.

The company concentrated on developing a network of local agents in these markets, estimating that it took nine months to appoint an agent and a further six months before there were any tangible results. Bureaucracy was certainly an issue. When tendering for contracts, the company had to supply bid bonds; and when it was awarded the contract, performance bonds had to be obtained. When the vehicles were being prepared for delivery, guarantee bonds had to be issued. All of these required a lot of paperwork and an appropriate level of financial backing. Unilokomotiv built a close relationship with its bankers, which was necessary in order to have access to bond facilities and international sources of credit. An Bord Tráchtála were also instrumental in providing market information.

Local agents gave the company the advantage of being able to conduct business at the right pace. It also ensured that due attention was paid to social norms. Gaining knowledge of what might appear to westerners to be more complex social structures within Far East markets was also important.

Source: M. Downes, 'Galway firm wins £500,000 orders', *Sunday Business Post*, 9 May 1993; E. Hughes, 'Local agents: key to eastern markets', *Sunday Business Post*, 3 November 1996.

Ultimately, the demand for business-to-business products and services is derived from the consumer. If consumers' demand for a product or service increases, then the demand for the raw materials, services and equipment necessary to produce and deliver that product or service will also increase. This is known as *derived demand*. The concept of derived demand means that the business-to-business marketer has to monitor trends in the consumer market. Opportunities may present themselves from doing so: for example,

Moffett Engineering spotted an opportunity to develop an innovative fork-lift truck as the distribution industry increased in importance.

MOFFETT ENGINEERING

In September 1997 it was announced that Powerscreen International was buying a County Monaghan engineering company, Moffett Engineering, for £25 million. Moffett had been a family-owned business, established in the nineteen-forties to manufacture and repair agricultural machinery. The company was innovative in product development, which culminated in the development of the Moffett Mounty, a truck-mounted fork-lift, which became the company's main product line. Orders for the product increased in line with increases in the distribution sector.

Moffett Engineering had been run by Carol Moffett, who had taken control of the company at the age of nineteen on the death of her father. The company established a strong customer base among co-operatives and had built significant export markets, the Mounty being sold in thirty countries.

Powerscreen is a large industrial concern involved in screening, crushing, and materials-handling. It had grown through acquisition and had a highly developed global distribution network. This would provide new markets for the Mounty.

Source: Richard Curran, 'Ms Moffett's bread and butter', *Sunday Tribune*, 14 September 1997; Paul O'Kane, 'Powerscreen consolidates its Irish market', *Sunday Tribune*, 14 September 1997.

In other cases, increases in consumer demand can have implications for business-to-business marketers, as the American aircraft manufacturer Boeing discovered in 1998.

PRODUCTION PROBLEMS AT BOEING

Boeing, the world's largest aerospace group, hit fresh production problems in 1998, which have delayed the delivery of aircraft worth more than $1,400 million. It was the second time in six months that Boeing had suffered from severe bottlenecks.

The problem was caused by parts shortages and demands by American and European regulators for additional modifications. This slowed down the assembly lines for the 737 model. In October 1997 the 737 lines had to be closed down for a month while production problems were sorted out. As a result, Boeing had to take charges of $2,600 million to pay for restructuring and late deliveries. Renewed delays could cause further charges.

Boeing was scheduled to double production in the spring of 1998 to satisfy soaring demand. The problems further undermine airlines' confidence in Boeing's ability to deliver on time.

Source: O. August, 'Boeing hit by further bottlenecks', *Times*, 24 March 1998.

Myopia

Industrial marketers can be especially prone to 'marketing myopia' if they become too caught up in the technological aspects of their product and forget about customers' needs. This can be compounded by the nature of derived demand if they lose sight of the needs of the ultimate consumer.

Many industrial companies are very product-oriented. One research study conducted among manufacturers in Scotland (Donaldson, 1995) suggested that many industrial companies were not following the principles of customer service for their business customers. It recommended that managers become more customer-driven by concentrating on three central issues: business vision, service implementation, and a commitment to quality.

Differences between consumer and business-to-business markets

There are a number of broad differences between business-to-business and consumer markets, as illustrated in fig. 13.1. These differences demonstrate the ways in which marketing practice and activities may need to be adapted to suit the type of product or service being marketed.

Fig. 13.1: Broad differences between business-to-business and consumer markets

	Business-to-business	Consumer
Market structure	Concentrated; fewer buyers; e.g. Irish airline market	Dispersed mass markets, e.g. Irish lager market
Buyer behaviour	Functional involvement, e.g. production manager	Family involvement, e.g. housewife
	Rational or task motives, e.g. packaging machine	Social or psychological motives, e.g. after-shave
	Technical expertise, e.g. technical manager	Less technical expertise, e.g. child operating video
	Interpersonal, e.g. technical sales representative	Non-personal, e.g. vending machine
Decision-making	Distinct or observable stages, e.g. management meetings	Unobservable or mental stages, e.g. 'black-box' decision-making

Products	Technical or complex, customised, e.g. drilling equipment	Standardised, e.g. television set
Distribution channels	Short and direct, e.g. car ferry	Longer and less direct, e.g. breakfast cereal
Promotion	Personal selling, e.g. Moffett Engineering	Advertising, e.g. Calvin Klein
Price	Bidding, negotiation, tenders, e.g. public contract	List price, e.g. supermarket

The nature of industrial buying

The buying process in business-to-business markets can be more complex than in consumer markets. Consumers can of course face highly involved decisions; and levels of involvement will vary for different products and buying situations. In business-to-business markets there will typically be more functional involvement in the purchasing decision. If a company is considering a purchase, different people will usually have influence. This influence is usually determined by their position within the company.

Business-to-business buyers tend to be well informed and highly organised. This is, after all, their job. They are unlikely to buy on impulse, as in consumer markets, and will pay particular attention to the detail of product and service specifications and quality. Sophisticated buying techniques, such as value analysis, may be used to assess products; this involves the systematic appraisal of an item's design, quality and performance requirements in an effort to minimise costs. It includes an analysis of the extent to which the product can be redesigned, standardised or processed using less expensive production methods.

Cost analysis will also be part of the process. This seeks to determine what it costs a supplier to produce the item, and the results may be used to obtain more favourable prices from suppliers.

Given that it is the business that is making a purchase, multiple influencers will usually exist, offering different points of view on the purchasing decision. An analogy can be drawn with family buying, where different family members have different relative amounts of influence. In the business-to-business setting, different personnel may perform different buying roles and have different amounts of influence.

There are, typically, five buying roles: *decider, influencer, user, buyer,* and *gatekeeper.* These roles may be performed by different individuals in the firm, or an individual may have more than one role. The marketer or salesperson needs to determine who precisely performs these roles.

One of the principal tasks the marketer or business-to-business salesperson has to determine is who is in the *decision-making unit* in the prospect firm. The buying roles will determine the amount of influence or decision-making ability an individual possesses. The most important or primary decision roles will usually be the deciders and influences, while the users, buyers and gatekeepers may be considered to have secondary roles.

Users are those in the firm who will actually use the product: for example, the operator of a packaging machine may have some influence on the purchase of a particular type of packaging material used.

Influencers are those who provide information on the product and who have a particular expertise. The information will be used in the evaluation of the product; influencers will therefore have a technical or professional expertise, as for example a technical manager or cost accountant.

Gatekeepers control the flow of information to others. The gatekeeper could therefore be a secretary or personal assistant who arranges meetings for their superior, or a purchasing or functional manager.

Buyers are those who actually buy the product: for example, most of the multiple supermarkets have specialist buyers in different product categories. The buyer's influence depends on the amount of decision-making autonomy they enjoy. In some cases their influence may be limited by specifications or organisational requirements. Most public service organisations are required to seek tenders for purchases.

Deciders are those who have the power and authority to make decisions. In most companies this describes the board of directors or senior managers. Naturally, the senior management or directors will not be involved in every organisational purchasing decision: responsibilities will be devolved to others.

The role of quality

Quality standards are of considerable importance in many business-to-business relationships, as the next panel illustrates. Holding a recognised quality mark, such as an ISO quality designation, may be a prerequisite.

KERRY DIE PRODUCTS

Kerry Die Products manufactures a range of pellet mill dies and rolls, mainly for use in animal feed and associated industries. The company has been in business since 1980, serving home and foreign markets.

In 1990 a salmonella outbreak in Britain almost killed off an important market, while the BSE outbreak later in the nineties also led to a fall in demand for feed products. The company countered this by concentrating on developing its export market. It had exported to the Netherlands, France, Italy, and Germany, and began forging links with Scandinavia, Spain, and Portugal.

Excellence in quality and service was crucial to being able to compete in these markets. ISO 9002 registration and product diversification were cited by the company's owner as the two important tools that enabled it to compete successfully. The company considers high quality standards, price-competitiveness and service to be its main strengths. ISO 9002 introduced the concept of quality as a production tool throughout the company but particularly in the manufacturing end. The company also introduced new complementary products to its range.

In 1997 the company was one of five finalists in the DHL export awards.

Sources: Commercial profile, 'Kerry Die Products', *Sunday Business Post*, 15 June 1997; B. O'Halloran, 'Dedication pays off for engineering firm', *Examiner*, 20 August 1997.

Quality standards also present opportunities. One of the conditions for obtaining recognition under the ISO 14001 environmental standard is that a certain amount of goods must be transported by rail. CPC Foods, which markets brands such as Knorr and Hellmans, increased the quantity of its products transported by train by 60 per cent in order to attain this standard (Ahern, 1998).

The buy grid model

One model that has been developed to illustrate the buying process in industrial markets is the 'buy grid' model, illustrated in table 13.1. This model proposes that three broad buying situations face the industrial marketer. 'New task' means that the product has not been bought before; 'modified rebuy' means that modifications are required to a product that has been bought before; 'straight rebuy' is a simple repeat purchase.

The model proposes that there are eight stages through which the buyer may progress. The speed of progress and the number of stages will depend on the nature of the buying task. Thus in the 'new buy' situation it is probable that more time will be spent and that each stage will be gone through. The 'modified rebuy' usually occurs where the need remains unchanged but there is a desire to modify the buying task because of quality or price, for example. In the 'straight rebuy' situation the search, analysis, evaluation and selection stages may be skipped.

Table 13.1: The buy grid model

	New task	Modified rebuy	Straight rebuy
1. Need recognition	✓	✓	✓
2. Determine quantity	✓	✓	✓
3. Describe quantity	✓	✓	✓
4. Search for quantity	✓	✓	
5. Analysis of proposals	✓	✓	
6. Evaluation	✓	✓	
7. Selection	✓	✓	
8. Performance feedback and evaluation	✓	✓	✓

Source: P. Robinson, C. Faris, and Y. Wind, *Industrial Buying and Creative Marketing*, Boston: Allyn and Bacon 1967.

The influence of purchasing on buyer behaviour

Material requirements planning (MRP) refers to the co-ordination of purchasing with production scheduling. Raw materials, sub-assemblies, parts and components should be available to be incorporated in the production process. The purchasing department or manager will liaise with the manufacturing or production department to plan purchasing requirements.

A significant influence on MRP has been the 'just-in-time' approach developed by Japanese industry, based on the idea that wherever possible no activity should take place in a system until there is a demand for it. This should eliminate the need to hold stock, which ties up working capital. The just-in-time approach can therefore have implications for business-to-business marketers if customers require products and services just in time to be incorporated in their production process.

Just-in-time operations require careful co-ordination. They can also lead to the development of closer relationships between the marketer and the customer. The use of new technology, in particular electronic data interchange (EDI), will usually have a significant role.

In attempting to sell to the purchasing department in a firm, the marketer or business-to-business salesperson should be familiar with the reporting relationships and the level of involvement that individuals have in the purchasing decision. The purchasing manager may perform the buying role described on page 387. It will be important to determine whether they perform any of the other roles. It is necessary to determine who performs the buying decision roles so that communications can be aimed at them.

MARKETING RESEARCH

The principles of conducting marketing research will be the same for business-to-business products and services. If these have a technical orientation, that will be reflected in the research. The concentrated nature of business-to-business markets may mean that there is also concentrated access to information. If, for example, research was being conducted among cement producers, there are only three possible companies that could be interviewed: Irish Cement, Seán Quinn Group, and Blue Circle Cement. The small population size in business-to-business research may also affect respondents' willingness to participate. Respondents may fear that their views or opinions could be easily identified when the population of interest is so small.

The research techniques used will also be determined by the size of the population. In the case of research on cement production, for example, it is probable that personal interviews with particular people would be sought, rather than using a postal questionnaire. In this case personal interviews would be feasible with regard to timing: the researcher would have to alleviate respondents' fears of identification.

Technical research may need to be conducted by specialist researchers. Respondents will expect the researcher to understand the research topic.

SEGMENTATION VARIABLES

The basis for market segmentation may be different in business-to-business markets. Consumer markets are very often segmented according to demographic or psychographic variables. Factors such as life-style, for example, may have little relevance in a business-to-business context. It is more probable that the following bases would be used:

- **industry**—for example agriculture, mining, light engineering
- **organisational characteristics**—for example number of employees
- **plant characteristics**—for example assembly, finishing
- **location of plant**

- **customers' industry**—for example freight v. passenger transport
- **purchasing**—for example centralised in the company's head office or decentralised at branch level.

THE BUSINESS-TO-BUSINESS MARKETING MIX

Product

The industrial or business-to-business product may be more technically complex than many consumer products. However, factors such as branding, quality and the development of product extensions will be just as important.

Branding can be as much a source of competitive advantage to business-to-business marketers as to consumer marketers. One research study (Mudambi, Doyle, and Wong, 1997) suggested a conceptual framework for brand value in industrial markets. This comprises four performance components: distribution, the product, support service, and the company itself. This demonstrates a number of salient considerations for business-to-business marketers. Relationship marketing will be important in managing the marketing channels and the provision of support service. Product quality will be an important prerequisite, and the reputation of the business will be strongly linked to the brand.

Another study (Thompson, Knox and Mitchell, 1997–8) concluded that business-to-business branding was a potentially powerful differentiation and communication tool. It considered that business-to-business branding could play a strong role in an environment where there were changing work practices, globalisation, and new technology.

The role of packaging may vary somewhat for business-to-business products. Products may be transported in bulk, and the main functions of the packaging used will be protection and economy rather than promotion. Specialist packaging or containers may be required to transport the product.

Given the technical nature of many business-to-business products, new-product research and development activities may be more technical in orientation. New consumer products may also be developed from technical research; but many new consumer products have been based on the development of less technical factors, for example the change from square to round tea-bags. Such innovations may be less apparent with many business-to-business products.

MARKETING COMMUNICATION IN BUSINESS-TO-BUSINESS MARKETS

The principles of communication apply regardless of product or service type. In business-to-business markets the relative use of components of the communication mix can vary. In general, specialist media rather than general consumer media will be used, and there tends to be a greater emphasis on personal selling than there is in consumer markets.

Advertising

Business-to-business marketers tend to use specialist advertising media, such as trade magazines and journals. They rarely use consumer media, though marketers such as

Airbus have advertised in consumer media, as fig. 13.2 shows. Such advertising can be considered important for corporate image and identity. In the case of Airbus, the brand is sold directly to consumers. By advertising directly to the consumer the company may have hoped to build awareness levels for the product and to stimulate demand in the ultimate market.

Fig. 13.2: Airbus
'If you want to fly comfortably, we recommend an Airbus'

Business-to-business advertising can appear in general business and trade publications. Trade directories, such as Kompass directories, are also used. Generally, advertising for industrial products emphasises such factors as technical description and detail rather than life-style or image, which is more common in consumer advertising. There can be exceptions, of course, but advertising will usually be a reflection of the product it seeks to portray. A purchasing manager in a target firm may be more interested in cost and quality than in image.

Business-to-business branding is of course important, and advertising can play a role in support of this. Consider the example of the Bank of Ireland business-to-business advertisement in fig. 13.3.

Fig. 13.3: Bank of Ireland Business Banking

Sales promotion

Sales promotion may be a feature of business-to-business communication, though the type of promotion will vary from those used by consumer marketers. In-store promotions will not usually be significant if the channels used are direct. Price promotions are often used and may be a feature of competitive strategy. These are typically related to sales volume: the bigger the order, the higher the promotional discount.

Direct marketing

Direct marketing and communication has also had an impact. Most business firms are used to being selected by tele-marketers and may be less suspicious than consumers, who are much less likely to be the target. Developments in the internet and in multimedia offer significant opportunities for business-to-business marketers. It is possible to show diagrams or even products in virtual reality form and to give detailed specifications on line.

Sponsorship

Sponsorship has been used by some business-to-business marketers as a means of building a profile, associating the product with particular causes and events, and developing corporate image. Some sponsorship activities have been at local level, for example the sponsoring of local sports teams. Television programmes have also been sponsored: the American comedy series 'Frasier' was sponsored on British television by Ericsson, which, in addition to consumer products, is a significant business-to-business marketer. In Ireland a number of GAA county football teams were sponsored by largely business-to-business firms, including the meat-processors Kepak (Meath) and the engineering company Sperrin Metal (Derry). Business-to-business marketers also appear as sponsors in large-scale international events: for example the stockbrokers NCB sponsored a yacht, *NCB Ireland*, in the round-the-world yacht race in 1994. Sponsorship events may also be used by business-to-business marketers to entertain corporate customers.

Trade shows

Trade shows are widely used by business-to-business marketers, as they reach a relatively large and specialised audience. Usually trade shows are organised by particular industries or professions; the audience is therefore quite focused and specialist. A trade show may reduce the number of sales calls the firm has to make, especially if it attracts large numbers of home and overseas sales prospects.

Participation in trade shows can be expensive. Costs usually include floor space and rental of the stand, the provision of presentation and audiovisual equipment, catalogues, leaflets, staffing costs, and entertainment expenses. Overseas trade shows will be more expensive when travel costs are added to this.

If participating in a trade show, marketers must set clear objectives. The trade show is an opportunity to communicate with a target audience; it is therefore vital to follow the stages in the communication model. It is also important to measure and evaluate the trade show as a communication activity. Typical objectives for participating in a trade show include:

- reaching new sales prospects
- selling the product
- launching a new product or brand extension
- distributing promotional material
- publishing a new or updated catalogue
- conducting research among those attending
- entertaining existing or potential customers
- enhancing corporate image
- introducing new personnel to the trade
- the opportunity to update the company's data-base
- publicity opportunities in general or specialist media.

While selling the product may be an objective, it may not actually happen at the trade show if buyers need time to evaluate or discuss the product within their own firms. Sales leads generated at the trade show should be followed up.

If clear objectives have been set, methods of evaluation should follow. The marketer should seek to measure the response they obtain. If sales have been an objective, these can be measured. If selling is an objective, sales personnel should realise that they may have limited time to engage people attending the show (Kaydo, 1996).

Attempts should be made to measure the quality of communication at the show. Simply handing out publicity material may not be enough; engaging people who attend the show, seeking opinions or inviting questions will yield more information. It is important therefore that the company personnel manning the stand are good communicators, can answer questions, and can gather market intelligence (McCune, 1993). In measuring the effectiveness of trade shows, activities that could be evaluated include pre-show promotion, the size and prominence of the stand, and the number of staff on the stand. In addition, the type of show and size of show should also be evaluated (Dekimpe et al., 1997).

Trade shows also provide an opportunity to monitor what competitors are doing. The presence of competitors also emphasises the comparisons that people attending the show will make. If the business is considering international markets, the trade show can be used as a means of gaining access to market information and to decision-makers in those markets (O'Hara et al., 1993). It can also be used to find potential distributors or other channel members.

Planning for international shows should involve studying the criteria for selecting which shows to attend. It is recommended that the planning process begin at least a year before the show (Vanderleest, 1994). Enterprise Ireland provides advice and assistance to companies planning or preparing for overseas trade shows.

The trade show is like a shop window or shelf: poor presentation may lead to the prospect passing on to the next stand or to a competitor. In many industries the annual trade show may be the most significant marketing communication event. It is important to plan and evaluate carefully (Blythe, 1997). Developments in technology have provided more communication alternatives for trade shows: for example, the use of interactive technology on stands or displays can augment other forms of communication (Shaw, 1994).

Public relations

Public relations may not be as widely used in business-to-business marketing, but it can be useful in developing corporate image and identity, media and press relations, and product launches and other events. Business-to-business marketers should consider public relations opportunities in the context of their general communication plans.

Pricing

Pricing decisions for business-to-business marketers will be based on the same process that applies to consumer marketers. The nature of demand, price elasticity, cost calculation, competitors' prices and environmental influences will all be taken into account in the pricing decision. Pricing methods will also be the same. Less emphasis may be put on concepts such as loss leaders or special-event pricing.

If the business-to-business product or service is to be incorporated as a component cost, issues such as operational costs will be significant. The customer may judge on the basis of keeping operational costs optimised. The benefits of the product or service, such as its functional or design features, may play a significant role in price positioning. These may be assessed relative to the price and corresponding price-benefit ratios calculated.

The nature of derived demand means that there may be a more indirect relationship between price and quality. The buyer of a piece of production machinery, for example, will know that the quality of the finished product will be partly determined by the machine and its features.

If marketers are buying in large quantities they will calculate the economies of scale from doing so. The price per unit may therefore be lower if larger amounts are ordered, and this will have an impact on the total cost of production.

The close interpersonal relationships in business-to-business markets can lead to greater co-operation, which may mean reduced costs. It is not uncommon for suppliers to attempt to show customers where they can reduce costs; in some cases this may mean that the customer ends up buying less of the product. While this may not appear very sensible from the sales point of view, from the point of view of building a relationship and demonstrating that the marketer has the customer's interests at heart it may make a lot of sense. Will the customer perceive a difference between someone who identifies where they can cut costs and someone who tries to sell them more?

MARKETING CHANNELS

The channels used by business-to-business marketers tend to be more direct than those used by consumer marketers. The same product, information, ownership and promotional flows will take place. The smaller number of larger customers that may exist means that it is easier to design more direct channels. It also facilitates the development of relationship marketing. Where middlemen or intermediaries are used, the same selection and management criteria will apply.

If business-to-business channels are more direct, the need for wholesalers and retailers may be eliminated. There can, however, be business-to-business wholesalers and retailers. There are several building materials wholesalers; and many of the franchised printing services, such as Prontaprint and Snap, count many businesses among their customers.

BUSINESSLINK

Businesslink was a joint venture between the South County Dublin Enterprise Board and the South Dublin Chamber of Commerce. It provided a business information service, training services and information technology services to business and enterprises.

A walk-in centre was provided in the centre of Tallaght, which gave visibility and was convenient to surrounding industrial and commercial premises. It was in effect a retail outlet. Members of the staff could provide secretarial services in addition to training services, such as use of the internet, export and trade information, and data on chamber members.

Source: Businesslink.

Information technology, such as the use of EDI and the ability to transfer data directly from the marketer to the business-to-business customer, has had an impact on channels. EDI could be used by purchasing managers, for example, to transfer data and to receive information from suppliers. Advances in EDI technology allow such transactions to be conducted over the internet, and this reduces investment requirements and running costs (Stafford-Jones, 1997). EDI can play an important role in making possible just-in-time ordering and supply.

As with all technology, marketers need to carefully assess the implications of using EDI. One study (Banfield, 1994) found that the companies they researched had to make radical changes to their own systems in order to implement an EDI system with the retailers they served.

Franchising can also be a feature of business-to-business contexts. Franchising can apply to processes as well as to products and services; it is possible for the franchisee to franchise the know-how for producing a business-to-business product or service that may be incorporated in the production or operations of their customers.

FURTHER READING

Brierty, E., Eckles, R., and Reeder, R., *Business Marketing Management* (third edition), Englewood Cliffs (NJ): Prentice-Hall 1998.

DISCUSSION QUESTIONS

1. Describe how marketing practice may differ for each of the following:
   —a motorway construction contractor v. Goodfellas pizza

—Tetra Pak (suppliers of packaging machinery) v. the Doyle Hotel Group
—Airbus Industrie v. McDonald's
—Unilokomotiv v. Bailey's Irish Cream.
2. Compare buyers' decision roles in business-to-business markets and consumer markets.
3. Describe the issues that should be considered in developing a business-to-business brand.
4. Explain how relationship marketing can benefit business-to-business marketers.
5. Profile the elements in the communication mix for each of the following:
—Irish Cement
—Irish Glass Bottle
—Tara Mines.

REFERENCES

Ahern, W., 'Distribution within Ireland: the potential for Irish Rail', term paper, Institute of Technology, Tallaght, May 1998.

Banfield, J., 'Implementing EDI', *Logistics Information Management*, vol. 7 (1994), no. 1.

Blythe, J. 'Does size matter?: objectives and measures at UK trade exhibitions', *Journal of Marketing Communications*, March 1997.

Dekimpe, M., François, P., Gopalakrishna, S., Lilien, G., and van den Bulte, C., 'Generalising about trade show effectiveness: a cross-national comparison', *Journal of Marketing*, October 1990.

Donaldson, W., 'Manufacturers need to show greater commitment to customer service', *Industrial Marketing Management*, October 1995.

Kaydo, C., 'Don't waste a minute', *Sales and Marketing Management*, November 1996.

McCune, J., 'On with the show!', *Management Review*, May 1993.

Mudambi, S., Doyle, P., and Wong, V., 'An exploration of branding in industrial markets', *Industrial Marketing Management*, September 1997.

O'Hara, B., Palumbo, F., and Herbig, P., 'Industrial trade shows abroad', *Industrial Marketing Management*, August 1993.

Shaw, R., 'Trade shows "go interactive"', *Business Marketing*, January 1994.

Stafford-Jones, A., 'Electronic commerce: the future with EDI', *Logistics Focus*, November 1997.

Thompson, K., Knox, S., and Mitchell, H., 'Business to business brand attributes in a changing purchasing environment', *Irish Marketing Review*, vol. 10 (1997–8), no. 2.

Vanderleest, H., 'Planning for international trade show participation: a practitioner's perspective', *SAM Advanced Management Journal*, autumn 1994.

14

Marketing for Non-Profit Organisations

The principles of marketing are equally applicable to non-profit-making organisations. Non-profit organisations typically include charities, museums, art galleries and other bodies where it is not expected that a profit, in the accepted business sense, will be made. They can also include large commercial organisations, such as the Voluntary Health Insurance (VHI) Board, which is involved in the health insurance business.

In recent years many non-profit organisations have become more marketing-oriented, with many employing full-time managers or organisers. Many non-profit organisations are substantial businesses and are subject to the same environmental forces as profit-making concerns.

TYPICAL PROBLEMS FACED BY NON-PROFIT ORGANISATIONS

In many cases, non-profit marketers do not see themselves as business activities. As a result they may be slow to adopt marketing or management techniques. In some cases the organisation may be run completely by volunteers, so that there is no full-time marketing or administrative staff.

With regard to mission, many non-profit organisations are based more on good intentions than on good organisation. The organisation may have been established to support a worthy cause or to campaign on a particular issue, and these become the central objectives. If, however, there is poor organisation, this may lead to inefficiencies and make the organisation less effective.

Some non-profit organisations may look on the notion of being a business with disdain: they do not want to be tainted, as they might see it, by commercialism. They would rather concentrate on their activities—for example the arts, for the sake of art alone. One study on charities in Britain (Balabanis et al., 1997) identified a reluctance among larger charities to adopt a strategy based on market orientation, largely for ideological reasons.

Given the voluntary nature of many non-profit organisations, there may be a poor knowledge of marketing. Marketing may be associated purely with selling or advertising; they may not appreciate its role in understanding the nature of the exchange process they are engaged in. The principles of relationship marketing may not be applied. One research study (Lindsay and Murphy, 1996) found that the donors to a British charity, the National Society for the Prevention of Cruelty to Children, were confused about its work. It suggested that the charity could learn from the theory of relationship marketing and should place greater emphasis on product attributes and brand image.

Political interference can be a problem for some non-profit organisations and may impede or prevent them carrying out their functions. Many relief agencies have found that in attempting to assist victims of famine or war in certain countries they ran into difficulties with the political authorities.

A perennial problem for non-profit organisations is securing adequate funds for their work. While other marketers produce continuously a product or service that is priced and sold, yielding a steady income stream, non-profit organisations may not have this continuous income flow. They may be reliant on sporadic donations or sponsorship and as a result find it difficult to plan and budget. Many smaller charities and charities in less attractive areas, for example those dealing with drug abuse, can find the fund-raising task even more difficult (Hirst, 1997).

Non-profit organisations may take up causes that society pays little attention to or chooses to ignore. Children of Chernobyl is an organisation that sought to provide medical care, relief and support to children who suffered the effects of the nuclear accident at Chernobyl in 1988. The organisation exists because of a lack of resources to deal with the after-effects of the accident.

Given the number of volunteers who may be involved, there can be too many committees in some non-profit organisations. This can slow down or even prevent decision-making. While committees can be essential, they must also be effective. The problem can be alleviated if the principles of organisation typically used in commercial firms are applied.

Some non-profit organisations are dominated by older people, who may not encourage the involvement of younger volunteers, managers, or organisers. This can pose a threat to the organisation's survival.

Sometimes organisations that are based on noble intentions may not have a coherent strategy or direction. As with all organisations, there should be a mission and objectives, and these should translate into specific strategies and plans.

Marketing management issues

According to Shapiro (1973), four principal business concepts provide the basis for marketing thought and action in the non-profit environment: self-interest, the marketing task, the marketing mix, and distinctive competence. The *self-interest* aspect describes the nature of the exchange, whereby both the buyer and the seller believe they are receiving greater value than they are giving up. The *marketing task* is to satisfy the customer's need; and the *marketing mix* consists of the tools that the non-profit marketer will use to achieve the marketing objectives. The *distinctive competence* describes what the organisation does best. These four factors are of course central to any marketing, whether for profit or not, but may need to be emphasised to the non-profit marketer.

According to Shapiro, the principal tasks for the marketing manager of a non-profit organisation will be attracting resources, allocating resources, and persuasion.

Attracting resources

The main issue in attracting resources is determining the correct appeal. Guilt, fear and pride tend to be the dominant themes. Attracting resources implies a need to examine issues such as seeking sponsorship, using advertising and public relations, and personal selling.

Donors and potential donors can be segmented. A school or university might segment on the basis of

- graduates—appealing to a sense of pride or loyalty
- parents of present-day students—interested in better facilities and profile for the university
- business or industry—interested in skilled graduates, tax advantages, and making a contribution to society.

Allocating resources

The resource allocation decision will be analogous to product policy. In other words, resources will be allocated on the basis of the business the organisation is engaged in. The organisation therefore needs to define its business or area of operation. An orchestra may be in the entertainment business, but it also exists to promote and preserve particular types of music; the Irish Heart Foundation exists to educate the public about heart disease and to promote a healthy diet and life-style.

Persuasion

Persuasion involves persuading donors or buyers; it may also involve persuading people to use the non-profit service or product. Sometimes this involves convincing them to do something that the organisation desires but that makes no direct contribution to the organisation itself, for example anti-litter campaigns, or campaigns to encourage people to put themselves on the electoral register, to go for cancer screening or cholesterol testing, or avoid getting AIDS.

THE MARKETING MIX

The following section describes the principal elements of the marketing mix for non-profit organisations. The elements of the mix are broadly similar to the marketing mix for any product, but, given the importance of people in non-profit organisations, as with the services marketing mix, we will include people as a separate element.

People

In marketing services, a lot of emphasis is put on the people element of the marketing mix. It is equally important for many non-profit organisations. Many non-profit bodies have found that they cannot be effectively run by part-timers, and therefore full-time administrative and marketing staff are required. The Irish Heart Foundation and Crumlin

Children's Hospital, Dublin, have full-time marketing and support staff to implement marketing plans and activities. There will still be a good deal of reliance on volunteers: indeed voluntary effort helps keep the administrative costs of the organisation low. Volunteers may have plenty of enthusiasm—an important trait—but they may also require some training. The training of volunteers may concentrate on skills such as responsibility, participation, decision-making, and accountability. These will be important where volunteers are required to take responsibility for aspects of the organisation's work and where they have access to donations or the organisation's funds.

Many non-profit organisations rely on people to deliver the benefit, for example counselling or guidance. For an organisation like the Samaritans the training and support given to its volunteers is very important. The service cannot be separated from the person providing it, who needs very special psychological skills and a strong ability to empathise with the caller.

The role of people is particularly relevant, given the importance of personal selling to many non-profit bodies, whether from door to door, in street collections, or in approaches to businesses for donations. They will need communication and presentation skills and to be able to clearly explain the nature of the organisation they represent.

The product

The non-profit organisation may need to have two sets of product policies, one for donors and one for beneficiaries. In both cases non-profit marketers should seek to define the different product levels they are marketing (see chapter 7).

The product from the donor's viewpoint

The definition of the product from the donor's viewpoint can be quite loose, for example personal satisfaction, a sense of belonging or pride, a sense of right or duty, or a sense of involvement. It is probably not surprising that many appeals to donors concentrate on moral or public-spirit grounds. Lindsay and Murphy (1996), for example, recommended that charities should engage in 'relationship fund-raising', in other words lead donors through a life-cycle from small donations to larger donations to ultimately leaving the charity a legacy.

In relation to corporate donations, there are strong financial and marketing advantages to be derived from giving. Non-profit marketers can use this in selecting and convincing corporate donors. The financial advantages derive largely from the tax relief a company can obtain from donations to charitable causes. Consider the example of the advertisement placed in the business press by the Society of St Vincent de Paul (fig. 14.1).

Fig. 14.1: Society of St Vincent de Paul

PUT A SMILE ON THE FACE OF THE TIGER

Tough times - but good - in the
land of the Celtic Tiger.
For some.
Now thanks to a change in Tax law,
your company can help put a smile
on faces who've only seen the tough.

Give to our work and then deduct what
you give from your profits -
anything between £250 and £10,000.

You pay less tax. We raise more funds.
We know where the need is greatest.

Act now. Talk to your tax adviser.
For smiles all round.

Society of St. Vincent de Paul, 8 New Cabra Road, Dublin 7. Tel: (01) 838 4164 / 838 0527. Fax: (01) 838 7355

The marketing advantages derive from being associated with a cause and being perceived as a good corporate citizen. Corporate philanthropy has been defined (Carrigan, 1997) as an investment of support (financial or otherwise) for an event or activity where the returns are primarily expected to society but are of ultimate long-term value to the company itself. The non-profit marketer needs to be aware that companies can have different reasons for getting involved in corporate philanthropy and should monitor and evaluate it and make contributions in different ways.

Needless to say, it is not just non-profit bodies that may be beneficiaries: corporate philanthropy may extend to encouraging enterprise development, as is the case with the Plato programme and First Step (see chapter 2). If the non-profit marketer can present reasons why they could develop a mutually beneficial relationship with a corporate body, this may be a significant part of the augmented product.

In some cases the activities of non-profit organisations are designed to encourage consumers to engage in a particular behaviour. Organisations such as Oxfam, for example, sell products under the Fair Trade label. These have been obtained from suppliers who guarantee that producers and workers have been paid a fair price and that the products have been produced in an environmentally responsible way. The difficulties with the Fair Trade approach appear to be a lack of recognition by consumers and a lack of extensive distribution channels (Strong, 1997).

The product from the recipient's viewpoint

The product provided to recipients can be quite simple, for example meals on wheels or financial support, or more complex, for example advice, guidance, or counselling. The Irish Cancer Society is involved in a number of activities, including financing research into cancer and cancer treatment, providing information to the public and to specialist publics such as the medical profession, raising funds from the general and corporate public, and lobbying decision-makers or influencers. There may therefore be a need to organise priorities. Funds will not be unlimited, and this will dictate where resources can be allocated.

In relation to product policy it may also be important to associate something tangible with the intangible. The Irish Cancer Society, the Irish Heart Foundation and the Irish Kidney Association use tangible symbols in the form of artificial daffodils, heart badges, and forget-me-nots. These have come to be associated with particular days or weekends during the year. Other symbols have taken on an international significance, such as the red ribbon for AIDS Day.

Institutions such as museums and art galleries could consider themselves as being in the business of selling an experience to the visitor. Consider the example of the National Museum of Ireland at Collins Barracks, Dublin.

THE NATIONAL MUSEUM OF IRELAND AT COLLINS BARRACKS

In November 1997 the National Museum of Ireland opened a new museum in the former Collins Barracks, Dublin. This became the third part in a trio of museums, which includes the National Museum in Kildare Street and the Natural History Museum in Merrion Square. The museum is operated by the Heritage Service under the Department of Arts, Heritage, Gaeltacht, and the Islands.

Collins Barracks positioned itself away from its sister museums as offering something new and different from traditional museums. Many of the displays have never been seen in public before, and the visitor experience is meant to be more informal and accessible than is usual in museums. Computer technology is used so that the visitor can obtain information on the displays. These include tools and utensils and a collection of craftwork over the years from 1600 onwards.

As with the other national museums, admission is free, on the grounds that as a national institution it should be accessible to everyone. The museum relies principally on state financing, though it also plans to develop a Friends Society to encourage sponsorship and corporate and private donations.

Creating awareness of the museum's location is probably one of the most significant issues to be tackled in initial communications. Emphasising the uniqueness of the museum and its collections to tourists and natives alike will be a continuing communication strategy.

Source: Based on A. Fitzgerald, C. Graham, and C. Toolis, 'A Report on the Marketing of an Irish Non-Profit Organisation', term report, Institute of Technology, Tallaght, May 1998.

Pricing

In a profit-making organisation, price links the allocation of resources to resource attraction. If the product is no longer in demand, or if demand is declining, resources will usually be diverted to other, more profitable products or activities. This may not be the case for non-profit organisations: for example, a counselling service may need to be provided whether there is a handful of users or many users.

Some non-profit organisations do charge for their services, in most cases to reach a break-even point. Credit unions, for example, charge interest on loans but, as the following panel illustrates, do not charge for services in the way that banks and other financial service providers do.

THE CREDIT UNION MOVEMENT

The Credit Union Act (1997) granted substantial new powers to credit unions, including the right to lend money for longer periods. It also provided the movement with a platform for expanding beyond its traditional savings and loans services.

A credit union is a financial co-operative owned and democratically controlled by its members. It exists to serve its members, not to make a profit. Members can invest in savings or shares, which earn them a dividend; and only members may get a loan. Credit unions do not impose charges for operating accounts, but interest on loans is charged at 1 per cent per month on the outstanding balance; any surplus made is ploughed back into the credit union.

The credit union movement in Ireland grew rapidly from the nineteen-fifties and sixties and became very strong among communities, occupations, and associations. In 1998 there were 536 autonomous credit unions in Ireland, and it was estimated that 34 per cent of the population were credit union members. Sixteen thousand volunteers were involved in the movement, in addition to the 1,800 administrative staff. Annual growth in the nineteen-nineties was 25 per cent.

Credit unions are supervised by the Registrar of Friendly Societies. The registrar has various powers under the act, including the power to give directives on credit union advertising.

The 1997 act allowed credit unions to get into new markets, such as insurance, credit cards, and mortgages. They will also be allowed to offer support to small and medium-sized businesses. It was probable that one effect of the act would be the emergence of credit unions as a more competitive force in the banking market. Some credit unions had begun offering ATM services, facilities for electronic funds transfer, and foreign exchange services. Banks are often criticised for their perceived anti-consumer bias, but no-one has ever lost money through a credit union. The strength of the movement has been that it is based on a common bond and is operated on a non-profit basis.

Source: A. Coffey, 'Credit unions: banking's biggest threat', *Business and Finance*, 16 April 1998.

Some non-profit organisations receive state subvention, for example relief agencies at times of disasters, but must still carry out fund-raising activities to keep going.

Important considerations in pricing are both monetary and non-monetary. Monetary considerations include donations, admission charges or charges for the service provided. The factors affecting the pricing decision outlined in chapter 8 will be relevant. The non-profit marketer will have to be aware of the nature of demand, the costs associated with providing the product or service, consumer price elasticity, and pricing methods.

Non-monetary pricing considerations include such factors as time, advice, friendship, and support. These intangible aspects may be difficult to cost, and in this regard there are strong similarities with the costing decision faced by services marketers. Intangibility is difficult to cost.

With regard to pricing policy, many of the non-profit bodies that introduced fund-raising activities around special badges charge a fixed price of £1 per badge. This not only presents the contributor with the opportunity to support a cause for a relatively small amount but also guarantees a price per unit and is an aid to stock control. The non-profit organisation can readily assess sales on the basis of the number of units sent out to collectors and on the income and unsold units returned.

MARKETING COMMUNICATION

Most non-profit marketers use a variety of marketing communication tools. The main difficulty they have is typically a lack of resources to finance sustained communication campaigns. Many organisations may not be able to spare scarce resources for any media-based campaigns. Whether the organisation has the resources or not, the principles of communication will still be important; indeed it may be possible to have someone else finance the costs of communication.

Advertising

Some non-profit organisations use the mass media fairly extensively, for example the relief agencies Concern and Trócaire. Consider the examples of press campaigns mounted by these organisations (fig. 14.2 and fig. 14.3). Advertising agencies will usually give discounts to charitable concerns.

Fig. 14.2: Concern

Fig. 14.3: Trócaire

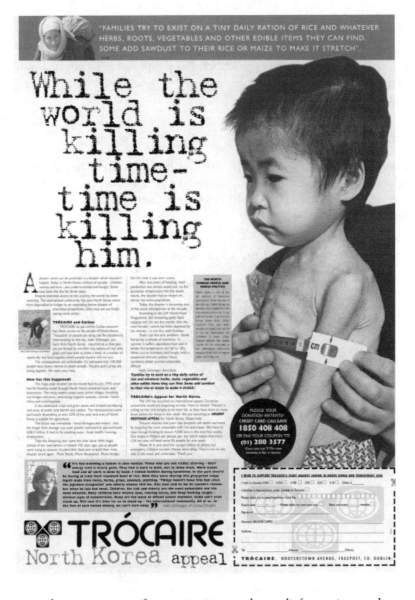

Advertising for many non-profit organisations, such as relief agencies, tends to veer towards a strong moral appeal, attempting to appeal to the receivers' sense of right. Other appeals can be more rational, as with the advertisement for credit unions in fig. 14.4; while the poster advertisement for the National Museum at Collins Barracks in fig. 14.5 seeks to inform and differentiate.

Fig. 14.4: The credit union movement

TUI CREDIT UNION

John McCarthy, Chief Executive, Guaranteed Irish, presents the "Guaranteed Irish" certificate to Austin Stewart, Chairperson, Teachers' Union of Ireland, Credit Union

"We are pleased to support and be part of Guaranteed Irish"

Austin Stewart, Chairperson TUI Credit Union

"The TUI Credit Union is the first Credit Union in Ireland to receive the Guaranteed Irish status."

John McCarthy Chief Executive Guaranteed Irish

Loans and Saving Enquiries contact Ciara / Madeleine

☎ *(01) 4922355 (Dublin)*
1850 741600 (Outside Dublin)
Fax: (01) 4929865

Lending Criteria and Terms & Conditions apply

Fig. 14.5: The National Museum at Collins Barracks

The use of data-bases and newer means of communication, such as the internet, can have a significant role in the communication of the non-profit organisation's message. Data can be compiled on previous donors, and this can be used in direct marketing campaigns. Similarly, the development of a web site allows the organisation to communicate and interact with potential donors or specific targets.

Other means of communication, such as direct mail and magazines or newsletters for members, can also be used. It is important for the non-profit marketer to stay in touch with previous donors, and this is fundamental to the development of a relationship with them.

In some cases the use of public figures to endorse the organisation will be emphasised in advertising: for example, the broadcaster Gay Byrne has endorsed the Irish Cancer Society, and the actor Geraldine Plunkett has endorsed the Special Olympics.

Personal selling

Personal selling can be quite important for many non-profit marketers. The main difference between personal selling in the profit and non-profit worlds is that the non-profit marketer may have to rely heavily on volunteers to do the actual selling. Personal selling will cover everything from selling lines or badges to selecting large organisations to ask for donations.

Personal selling is highly suitable for a small target audience, such as seeking donations or sponsorship from the corporate sector. In this case the stages in the selling process described in chapter 9 will be relevant.

Sponsorship

As described in chapter 9, sponsorship is becoming a more significant element of marketing communication. It can be particularly important for non-profit marketers, especially where they are aiming at the corporate sector for funds or support. Sponsorship of a non-profit organisation, cause or event will be considered by companies on a number of grounds. There may be a genuine desire to support a worthy cause, but there will also be marketing advantages from being seen to do so. As a result, companies will assess their sponsorship activities to find those that best meet their criteria. This may mean that there can be competition between non-profit organisations for the corporate sponsor.

An interesting research exercise on sponsorship of the arts was conducted in 1994. This provided some indication to would-be sponsors on the age and socio-economic profile of people who attend particular events and also their attitude towards the sponsorship of such events.

SPONSORSHIP OF THE ARTS

As sponsorship activities have increased in importance, many marketers have looked towards the arts as a possible sponsorship activity. In making decisions about this, marketers needed to know the type of events that people are attending and what they think about sponsorship.

In 1994 AGB Adelaide carried out some market research to determine who the arts appealed to and whether or not respondents thought sponsorship of the arts a good thing. The first table shows which arts functions people regularly attended.

	Total	Age 15–18	19–34	35–54	55+
Cinema	15%	29%	26%	8%	2%
Pop or rock concert	6%	16%	13%	2%	—
Opera or classical music	2%	1%	1%	2%	2%
Ballet or dancing	1%	1%	—	1%	1%
Theatre	5%	6%	5%	5%	4%
Art or craft	4%	3%	4%	4%	4%
Museums and exhibitions	2%	1%	2%	2%	2%

There is, of course, a difference between events that are regularly attended and events that the person has ever attended. Not surprisingly, when people were asked which of these events they ever went to, the results were higher, as the next table shows.

	Total	Age 15–18	19–34	35–54	55+
Cinema	54%	89%	76%	46%	20%
Pop or rock concert	30%	69%	53%	15%	2%
Opera or classical music	16%	9%	11%	19%	20%
Ballet or dancing	9%	9%	9%	10%	6%
Theatre	44%	41%	45%	30%	38%
Art or craft	28%	33%	30%	32%	19%
Museums and exhibitions	26%	34%	28%	26%	20%

The results by socio-economic group are illustrated in the following table.

	Total	AB	C1	C2	DE	F
Cinema	54%	77%	67%	59%	44%	32%
Pop or rock concert	30%	35%	39%	33%	26%	18%
Opera or classical music	16%	42%	21%	11%	11%	7%
Ballet or dancing	9%	19%	12%	8%	6%	4%
Theatre	44%	70%	56%	44%	33%	33%
Art or craft	28%	56%	45%	23%	18%	17%
Museums and exhibitions	26%	52%	37%	23%	17%	16%

Respondents were also asked whether or not they thought sponsorship of the arts by companies was a good thing. As the next table shows, the majority of respondents in all social classes thought that it was.

	Total	AB	C1	C2	DE	F
A very good thing	44%	55%	48%	39%	45%	36%
A fairly good thing	35%	31%	36%	40%	30%	34%
A fairly bad thing	2%	3%	2%	2%	2%	3%
A very bad thing	1%	—	2%	1%	1%	1%
No opinion	11%	6%	7%	12%	13%	14%
Don't know	7%	5%	5%	5%	8%	13%

Source: Bell Advertising, *Marketing and Creative Synergy*, November 1994.

Public relations

Public relations can be especially important for non-profit organisations. The chance to obtain publicity, to publicise a particular cause or issue to the media or to gain coverage for an event or launch should not be missed. Public relations has played an important part in the case of Goal, the relief and development agency, as the following panel illustrates.

EFFECTIVE USE OF PUBLIC RELATIONS

Goal is a non-profit organisation involved in relief and development projects. It was founded by John O'Shea, who was a sports journalist. Not surprisingly, many well-known figures in the sports world, including Jack Charlton, Stephen Roche, Seán Kelly, and Niall Quinn, have endorsed the organisation's work and appear at charity events and fund-raisers. This helps guarantee media coverage. John O'Shea himself is well known and accessible to the media, which helps gain coverage for the organisation's activities, including its annual St Patrick's Day collection, when it sells shamrock pins.

The work the organisation has done to alleviate poverty and provide relief is well recognised. In 1994 the organisation received a strong public endorsement by the President of Ireland, Mary Robinson.

The nineteen-nineties also witnessed the development of 'telethons', when television channels devoted considerable time to particular causes. In Ireland the annual 'People in Need' telethon was televised on RTE; this involved various television presenters and members of the public raising funds for worthy causes. Many organisations seek to be associated with the event by giving donations or products, both for philanthropic and publicity reasons.

Channels

The marketing channels for non-profit organisations serve the same broad functions as channels for other marketers. They may involve different levels, although, like services and business-to-business channels, they tend to be short. The channels should facilitate provision of the service, facilitate donations, and facilitate volunteers.

Provision of the service

The non-profit organisation may distribute its service in a set place, such as a museum or art gallery, or it may involve the provision of a service that the consumer can gain access to anywhere, for example telephone help lines. If a fixed place is used the consumer may need to be made aware of its location and how to get there. If the organisation operates a telephone help line, important criteria will include emphasising awareness of the number and possibly arranging for the provision of a 24-hour service.

Facilitating donations

It should be easy and convenient for people to make donations. This may mean having donation points in many places, for example shopping centres, door-to-door collections, or dedicated telephone lines where credit card donations can be made. In the case of nationwide appeals or campaigns this may require the involvement of thousands of individual collectors. The Irish Heart Foundation selects retailers, pubs, restaurants, factories and other business premises, using point-of-sale displays. Stocks of heart emblems are provided, together with a collection box, which can be placed on the counter or beside the check-out.

Facilitating volunteers

The facilitation of volunteers is analogous to the sales territory decision. Volunteers can cover their own localities, which is not only convenient but is also important for trust and credibility. People will be more likely to give to or support someone they know.

PLANNING AND STRATEGY

Drucker (1989) in his research into non-profit organisations in the United States found that the most successful had a clear mission statement. He also found that some of the organisations had much better management structures than their profit-making counterparts. The mission statements Drucker came across include:

Salvation Army: 'To turn society's rejects, alcoholics, derelicts and convicts into citizens.'

Scouts and Guides: 'To help young people become confident and capable, to respect themselves and others.'

Nature Conservancy: 'To preserve the diversity of nature's flora and fauna.'

The benefits of strategic planning for non-profit organisations were emphasised by the World Wildlife Fund, which introduced strategic planning in 1978 (Medley, 1988). In the following nine years, as the result of planned actions, cohesive teamwork, and clear objectives, the organisation increased its net funds by a factor of five and its productivity by a factor of six. It simply followed the planning process, carrying out a SWOT analysis (see chapter 15), developing strategies and action plans designed to achieve and implement the strategies.

Distinctive competence

Shapiro (1973) drew attention to the importance of non-profit bodies establishing what their distinctive competence was and sticking to it. Generally, the competitive system in free-market countries means that companies prosper when they meet customers' needs but fail when they do not. In other words, they establish a competitive advantage; if this disappears or is eroded, they may disappear.

This self-regulating mechanism is not as significant for non-profit organisations, for a number of reasons. Many needs are so great that people cannot choose between competitors: they have to take what is available, for example counselling. Demand for the products or services often exceeds supply. For many non-profit organisations, financial viability depends on the attraction rather than the allocation of resources. Market forces may not prevail in the allocation of resources; they may be allocated to highly intangible projects, for example the preservation of historic buildings, which will not be judged by criteria such as market share leadership.

Many non-profit organisations do evaluate the service they give, and co-operate with each other to ensure that no two organisations are seeking to serve the same need. There can still be duplication—a criticism that is often levelled at the charities involved in development aid and disaster relief, with several organisations competing for donations from the public for the same relief effort.

The launch of the National Lottery in 1986 had an impact on many charities. As a certain proportion of the lottery's income goes to such causes, many people perceived that they were in effect giving to charity by buying a lottery ticket. Some charities noticed a decline in donations. Many, however, responded in kind; and it is no coincidence that the number of organisations promoting the sale of £1 badges on particular days of the year has increased: these were priced at the same price as a lottery ticket or scratch card.

FURTHER READING

Hannagan, T., *Marketing for the Non-Profit Sector*, London: Macmillan 1992.

DISCUSSION QUESTIONS

1. Compare and contrast marketing practice in profit-making companies with that of non-profit-making organisations.
2. Do you think people can become apathetic about the marketing activities of charities or cause-related organisations? Give reasons for your answer.
3. Comment on the reasons why many non-profit organisations are reluctant to take marketing principles into account. Is there an inherent contradiction in their reluctance?
4. Describe the elements of the marketing mix for each of the following:
   —GOAL
   —the Blood Transfusion Service
   —Bord na Gaeilge
   —the Royal British Legion in Ireland.

5. Explain why many large corporations engage in philanthropy. How can this benefit non-profit-making organisations?

REFERENCES

Balabanis, G., Stables, R., and Phillips, H., 'Market orientation in the top 200 British charity organisations and its impact on their performance', *European Journal of Marketing*, vol. 31 (1997), no. 8.

Carrigan, M., 'The great corporate give-away: can marketing do good for the do-gooders?', *European Business Journal*, vol. 9 (1997), no. 4.

Drucker, P., 'What business can learn from non-profits', *Harvard Business Review*, July–August 1989.

Hirst, J., 'Charities with attitude', *Marketing Business*, June 1997.

Lindsay, G., and Murphy, A., 'NSPCC: marketing the solution not the problem', *Journal of Marketing Management*, November 1996.

Medley, G., 'Strategic planning for the World Wildlife Fund', *Long-Range Planning*, February 1988.

Shapiro, B., 'Marketing for non-profit organisations', *Harvard Business Review*, September–October 1973.

Strong, C., 'The problem of translating fair trade principles into consumer purchase behaviour', *Market Intelligence and Planning*, vol. 15 (1997), no. 1.

CASE STUDY

This case study was prepared as a basis for class discussion rather than to illustrate either effective or ineffective handling of an administrative situation.

IARNRÓD ÉIREANN

Faced with the challenge of increasing competition from road and air for the lucrative business travel market on the Dublin–Cork route, Iarnród Éireann decided to investigate the possibility of providing an improved service to business travellers in order to win new customers and retain existing users.

Inter-City

'Inter-City' is the brand name used by Iarnród Éireann for its network of passenger services, linking Dublin with the other main population centres. Inter-City services operate all year round (except on Christmas Day and St Stephen's Day). Most trains comprise air-conditioned carriages and have a catering service offering snacks and in many cases full meals. All have standard-class seating; in addition, some have 'super-standard' class, which is a section of the train that offers passengers greater comfort, seat reservation, and a meal and bar service brought to passengers in their seats. Super-standard class costs more, and is used mostly by business travellers.

After many decades of decline, rail travel began to increase in the nineteen-eighties and nineties. By the mid-nineties Inter-City recorded over 8 million passenger-journeys; in the mid-eighties the figure had been $5^{1}/_{2}$ million. The main reasons for this growth were the introduction of newer, faster trains on many routes, more price promotions, and improved frequency. New services had been developed, for example 'Railbreaks', which offered short holiday breaks by rail to different destinations. These proved extremely popular, and Iarnród Éireann became the biggest generator of bed-nights in the home holiday market. The company had also placed a greater emphasis on researching the needs of individual market segments and developing products on this basis.

Market research indicated that Inter-City was used mostly for long-distance journeys. The market share for Inter-City relative to other modes of transport is shown in table 14A.1.

Table 14A.1: Market share for long-distance journeys

Car	65%
Train	21%
Bus	8%
Private bus	5%
Air	1%

People have various reasons for using Inter-City, as shown in table 14A.2.

Table 14A.2: Reasons for travelling by Inter-City

Visiting family or friends	35%
Holiday	20%
Shopping trip	19%
Business	10%
Sporting trip	9%
Other	9%

Business travel

Business travel accounts for 10 per cent of all Inter-City journeys. The number of business travellers is highest on the Dublin–Cork–Limerick and the Dublin–Belfast routes. (All Dublin–Cork trains provide a connection for Limerick at Limerick Junction; there are only a small number of direct Dublin–Limerick trains.) Dublin, Cork, Limerick and Belfast are centres of high population and have a high concentration of industrial and business activity. As a result, Inter-City offered high service frequencies on these routes.

Business travellers are an important segment of the market, because

(a) they tend to travel frequently (an average of four or five return rail trips per year);
(b) they tend to use super-standard class, which produces more income;
(c) they are high spenders on meals and bar service.

Business travellers also have high expectations of service quality and a low tolerance for delays and disruptions.

In the early nineties, Iarnród Éireann began to review its services on the main business routes. The Dublin–Belfast route was to be improved, with new track, signals, and rolling stock, as part of an EU transport initiative, involving a high level of cross-border co-operation between Iarnród Éireann and Northern Ireland Railways. This co-operation culminated in the launch of a new service, branded as the 'Enterprise'. The company therefore concentrated on the Dublin–Cork route.

The Dublin–Cork route

On the Dublin–Cork route there were nine trains in each direction every weekday, each of which also provided a connection for Limerick. The busiest trains in number of business travellers were the early morning and early evening departures. The typical business traveller on a day trip took the 7:30 a.m. train and returned on the 5:30 p.m. departure. These peak business departures offered comfortable super-standard carriages, which had fewer seats than standard class and therefore provided some additional space, as well as an advance reservation service and a full catering and bar service.

Research studies on the route were conducted in the early nineties. The research approach was a combination of surveys conducted on the train and focus groups of business travellers. Among the findings of these studies were the following:

- The Dublin–Cork route carried the highest number of business travellers of all Inter-City routes (60 per cent). The addition of Limerick passengers at Limerick Junction increases this figure to 70 per cent.
- 75 per cent of business travellers were male, and most came from ABC1 backgrounds.
- The majority of business travellers were aged thirty-five or over.
- The main reasons given for using the train included frequency of service, comfort, the ability to work while travelling, the ability to relax, and the availability of catering.
- Almost two-thirds of regular travellers also used car or air for some of their trips on the route.

When asked about the existing super-standard service, business travellers felt that it could be improved. Suggestions included:

- Providing more comfortable and wider seats, with more leg room.
- Providing for more privacy, i.e. greater space between seats.
- Providing facilities such as phones, better reading-lights, and a personal stereo system.
- Providing a wider menu selection.

A consistent research finding was that an improved service would lead to business travellers making more trips by rail and fewer by car or plane.

The Inter-City management decided to investigate the possibility of improving the service on the Dublin–Cork route for business travellers as a means of attracting additional passengers and more income. Details of the research were given to a task force within the company, which set about designing a new interior for the super-standard carriage and began putting together a marketing plan for the new service.

THE NEW SERVICE PROPOSAL

The product

The product proposed by the task force was luxury 48-seat carriages, which would have wide reclining seats, a personal stereo facility for each seat, more leg room, better reading-lights, and greater privacy. All the carpets and other materials used would blend together to create an impression of sophistication and luxury. The carriages could be completed in the company's workshops and would simply involve installing new interiors in existing vehicles. Ergonomically designed seats would be supplied by the manufacturer that provided the first-class seats for the French high-speed train (TGV).

A phone and fax service would be available, and a steward would be on hand to greet passengers, show them to their seats, distribute free newspapers, and generally attend to them. A comprehensive menu would be available, offering a wide range of snacks and full meals.

The new carriages would be used on the peak business trains at 7:30 a.m. and 5:30 p.m. in each direction and also on one midday train each way. A connection would be provided for Limerick passengers at Limerick Junction.

Branding

The existing super-standard name was not considered appropriate for the new service. A list of brand names was drawn up that were designed to reflect the quality of the new service, including 'Premier Class', 'Executive Class', and 'Gold Class'. The preferred brand name in research trials was 'Citygold'.

Price

The price charged had to reflect the fact that a better service would be available, and had to take into account the cost of the investment in upgrading the carriages. The existing fare on the Dublin–Cork route was £47.50 for a super-standard day return. The air fare charged by Aer Lingus on the Dublin–Cork route ranged from £79 (with restrictions) to £99 (no restrictions). Mileage allowances by companies ranged from 25p to 50p per mile (the Dublin–Cork round trip is 320 miles). Price-sensitivity research indicated that business travellers would be willing to pay up to £60 for the proposed service. This price would also give the company a positive return on its investment.

Promotion

A promotional campaign would be needed to inform existing customers about the new service and to create awareness among the business community in Dublin, Cork, and Limerick. It was proposed to run this campaign in newspapers and business magazines. Public relations opportunities would also be required.

Distribution

Tickets for Citygold would be bought at railway stations and travel agents. Credit card reservations could be made on a dedicated phone line.

Product launch

Given the results of the research and the proposed upgrading of the carriages, the management sought board approval for the necessary investment in Citygold. This approval was received, and the management began the task of preparing for the launch of the new service.

DISCUSSION QUESTIONS

1. What are the tangible and intangible aspects of Citygold?
2. In deciding to travel on the Dublin–Cork route, what factors might a business traveller take into account when evaluating the different modes available?
3. What are the unique selling points for Citygold?
4. How should Citygold be promoted? What should the message be? What public relations possibilities might there be?

PART 5

Marketing Strategy and Planning

15

Marketing Strategy and Planning

A *strategy* provides a logic that integrates the different functions of the business and points them in the same direction. A strategy is simply what you do to achieve your objectives.

Firms cannot afford to adopt a trial-and-error approach to planning—in other words, continuing with schemes that seem to be working and eliminating those that are not. Rapid environmental change means that this approach can be costly in the form of missed opportunities, and it means that the business may be unprepared for the future.

Planning does not mean that the future becomes any more certain, nor does it mean that future events or developments can be predicted with certainty. What it does do is force the business to consider its future and how it will achieve continued success.

STRATEGIC PLANNING

There are four distinguishing features of strategic planning: an external orientation, a process for formulating strategies, methods for analysing strategic alternatives, and a commitment to action (Day, 1984).

An external orientation

Having examined the forces in the marketing environment (chapter 3), we should not be surprised to learn that firms need to look continuously outwards at what is happening in the environment. The changing environment presents both opportunities and threats; the business must monitor trends and prepare for change. Consider the example of the market for bottled mineral water. Companies in the sector that monitored changing consumer tastes and distribution channels found opportunities for the development of new products and channels.

CHANGES IN THE BOTTLED MINERAL WATER MARKET

Up to the mid-eighties the Irish market for bottled mineral water was very much a niche market, served by imported brands such as Perrier. With the arrival of the Ballygowan brand, the market increased considerably in size. This growth was principally due to life-style factors: consumers became more interested in the health benefits of drinking water; it also became socially more acceptable to drink water than alcoholic drinks. The Ballygowan brand was readily adopted as a result.

To some extent the Irish market was just catching up on consumption levels in other European countries, though, as the table below shows, consumption by the mid-nineties was still lower than in most European countries.

European bottled water consumption per capita

Italy	118 litres
Belgium	106 litres
Germany	92 litres
France	82 litres
Spain	50 litres
Netherlands	14 litres
Britain	14 litres
Ireland	**11.5 litres**

The market1 had exhibited steady growth throughout the nineties. Within the Irish market there had been a number of changes, principally a change from sparkling to still water, largely as a result of consumers' perception that sparkling was unnatural.

Share of sales by type of water, 1991–6

	1991	1992	1993	1994	1995	1996	
Sparkling	74%	61%	57%	53%	45%	39%	(–10.4%)
Still	26%	39%	43%	47%	55%	61%	(+11%)

Ballygowan was brand leader in the sector, with an estimated market share of 35 per cent in 1997. Several other brands had followed Ballygowan into the market. In addition, between the mid-eighties and mid-nineties the market experienced several changes. As already described, a significant change was a switch from sparkling to still water. Distribution also changed. By 1996 the highest growth in distribution was in the dispenser sector, as the next table illustrates.

Sales volume by trade sector, 1996

	Volume	Share of volume	Share of growth
On-trade	4.4 million litres	11%	–15%
Off-trade	28.3 million litres	71%	–3%
Dispenser	7.3 million litres	18%	+28%

Consumer tastes also veered towards flavoured waters, with several brands appearing in the late eighties and early nineties, including Kerry Spring and Nash's Irish Spring.

Source: *Checkout Ireland*, May 1997.

The danger for companies that did not monitor these changes was that they would fail to innovate and would get left behind. An external orientation implied monitoring the changes and taking action. Ballygowan, the market leader, offered both still and sparkling variants, flavoured waters, and dispensers for offices and other locations.

A process for formulating strategies

The process for formulating strategies implies that the marketer has a structured planning process. From this, a clearer picture of what strategies are appropriate should emerge. The process consists of four principal stages:

1. Assessment:
    - present business position
    - environmental situation
    - analysis of competitors.
2. Strategy generation:
    - strategic options
    - sources of competitive advantage.
3. Strategy selection:
    - rewards and risks
    - objectives
    - allocation of resources.
4. Implementation:
    - programme
    - budgets.

Situation assessment

The situation assessment will involve a thorough review of the firm's present business position, the forces in its environment, and an analysis of competitors.

THE IRISH TRAVEL TRADE

The nineteen-nineties saw a complete change in the ownership of the principal tour operators in the Irish travel trade. By 1997 almost 80 per cent of sales were controlled by large British-owned companies, a complete reversal of the situation that had existed in the eighties. The main competitors by the late nineties were Budget Travel and JWT. Both companies had been in the market for several decades; however, Budget had been bought by Thomson Holidays, and JWT's sun holiday business had been bought by another British company, First Choice, which also owned the Falcon chain. In 1997 Budget-Thomson was estimated to have a 41 per cent share of the chartered sun holiday market, with JWT-Falcon having an estimated 33 per cent.

The change in ownership heralded increased competition in the charter market, known for its tight profit margins. The large British operators could get significantly more economies of scale, which enabled them to offer more competitive prices than the smaller Irish operators. Some of the large British operators even had their own charter airlines, giving them increased operational synergy. Price promotions, particularly aimed at the consumer who booked early in the year, included special family fares and free places for children and grandparents. In a market where demand peaks in July and August, the operators are anxious to fill their seats continuously.

Source: *Irish Times*, 19 August 1997.

While the sun charter market was fiercely competitive and required economies of scale to survive, smaller operators concentrated on niches in the market, such as special interests or particular destinations. The travel trade had therefore changed significantly. Small independent agents found it more difficult to compete. A situation analysis for them emphasised a need to identify specialist niches and to develop their relationship with customers for survival. A useful tool for assessing situational variables is the SWOT analysis.

The SWOT analysis

The SWOT analysis (an acronym for 'strengths, weaknesses, opportunities, and threats') is fundamental to the formulation of strategy. It can be used in situation assessment as an analytical tool.

Strengths and weaknesses will be identified in any internal analysis conducted by the company. Strengths typically derive from skills and capabilities that enable the firm to develop and implement strategies. Weaknesses will exist where skills and abilities do not allow the company to achieve its objectives.

Opportunities and threats exist in the external environment. (Chapter 3 described the forces in the environment.) Opportunities and threats analysis will be based on an external environmental analysis. Opportunities may exist to develop markets or segments or to produce new products or variations of existing products. In other words, opportunities are phenomena or events that, if exploited, may improve the firm's performance.

Threats are the opposite: they are phenomena or events that may make it difficult or impossible for the firm to achieve its objectives. Porter (1980) suggested that in any industry the opportunities and threats can be analysed according to the 'five forces': the level of competitive rivalry, the power of suppliers, the power of consumers, the threat of substitutes, and the threat of new entrants. The higher these are, the more threats in the industry there will be.

Strategy generation

In generating strategic alternatives, it is useful to examine the work of Porter (1980) and of Myles and Snow (1978). Porter described three generic strategic options available to firms at the business level: differentiation, cost leadership, and focus. Myles and Snow developed a typology of four broad business-level strategies: *prospector*, *defender*, *analyser*, and *reactor* (fig. 15.1). Porter argued that firms should choose one of these three strategies and concentrate on implementing it.

Fig. 15.1: Porter's generic strategies

	Definition	Examples
Differentiation	The business seeks to distinguish itself from competitors through the quality of its products or services.	Rolex watches; Cross pens; the Westbury Hotel; Lir Chocolates; Waterford Crystal
Cost leadership	The business attempts to gain a competitive advantage by reducing its cost below the costs of competing firms	Ryanair; Dunne's Stores; credit unions; Budget Travel
Focus	The business concentrates on a specific regional market, product line, or group of buyers.	Macardle's ale; regional newspapers; Beamish stout; Superquinn

The Myles and Snow typology suggests that firms should pick one of four possible strategies (fig. 15.2). Once again it is possible to suggest some examples of firms following these broad strategies.

Fig. 15.2: Myles and Snow typology

	Definition	Examples
Prospector	Constantly seeking out new markets and opportunities; is oriented towards risk-taking.	Seán Quinn Group
Defender	Concentrates on defending its present markets, maintaining stable growth, and serving present customers.	Clery's department store
Analyser	Maintains market share and seeks to be innovative, but not as innovative as the prospector.	HB ice cream

| Reactor | No consistent strategic approach; drifts with environmental events, and is only able to react to them. | Possibly some public service organisations; many small enterprises |

Sources of competitive advantage

There are two possible sources of competitive advantage: skills and resources. If a business is assessing which strategy to pursue, it will find that its skills and resources will be a major determinant.

Skills

Skills cover a wide variety of expertise and applications. They include:

- specialised knowledge of segment needs
- customer service orientation
- design expertise
- applications expertise
- trade relationships
- the ability to use relevant technologies
- systems design capability.

Marketing is obviously an essential business skill. The ability to employ the skills of research, communication and planning, for example, will be critical to success.

Skills are people-based, and therefore there are implications for recruitment, training, and development; individual managers or individuals with particular skills or experience will be in demand. In 1996, for example, the former chief executive of Aer Lingus, David Kennedy, became chief operating officer of the American airline TWA (*Sunday Times*, 26 January 1997). He was recruited as part of an initiative to tackle the airline's financial problems. TWA was the sixth-largest airline in the United States but had been in financial difficulties for several years.

Resources

Organisational resources will also determine strategic choice, as they have a significant bearing on the ability to use the skills described above. Resources could include:

- distribution coverage
- financial structure and access to capital
- shared experience with a related business
- low-cost manufacturing and distribution
- production capacity
- ownership of sources of raw material or long-term supply contracts
- brands
- corporate identity.

Firms will often seek to buy the resources they require to effectively compete in the market. Consider the example of Adidas, which took over the French ski-maker Salomon. As one company, it will have significant resources with which to compete.

ADIDAS PASSES REEBOK AND GAINS ON NIKE

The German company Adidas AG announced in September 1997 that it would take control of the French ski-maker Salomon SA in a deal valued at about £900 million. The new group, which envisages renaming itself Adidas-Salomon AG, would have global sales of more than £2,300 million; that would make it number 2, behind Nike but ahead of Reebok.

The deal underlines a shift in an industry that has concentrated on squeezing higher sales out of sports shoes and T-shirts. There has been a clear trend towards mergers of companies dealing in 'soft' goods, such as shoes and apparel, and 'hard' goods, such as skis and snowboards.

Nike invested in companies that make winter sports equipment and in-line skates, while the Benetton Group of Italy has built a range of brands, from Rollerblade to Nordica. Nike began diversifying into non-footwear sporting goods in the mid-nineties, producing a range that included sports watches, eyewear, and in-line skates. Nike's worldwide non-footwear sales totalled $2,500 million in 1996. Reebok had a few difficult years but had made a comeback in the United States with the launch of the DMX range of sports shoes.

Adidas had pulled back from the brink of bankruptcy in 1993. The company was successfully turned around by removing management, cutting costs, and increasing marketing expenditure. As with other manufacturers in the industry, most production was transferred to Asia.

Sources: C. Wallace and P. Sellers, 'Adidas: back in the game', *Fortune*, 18 August 1997; B. Mitchener and A. Barrett, 'Adidas passes Reebok and gains on Nike', *Sunday Business Post*, 21 September 1997.

Strategy selection

Which strategy to select will depend on a number of considerations. An assessment of the rewards and risks associated with a particular strategy will be made. The strategy will also have to fit in with the general objectives of the business, and the firm will have to have the resources to devote to it.

The implications of a particular strategy will therefore need to be assessed in terms of sales and profits and the firm's operations. If the business has particular objectives—for example if it is following a differentiation strategy—this will determine what it is feasible to consider. Porter, for example, warned against companies attempting to implement more than one generic strategy.

Sometimes large companies will have different strategies for different businesses. In its hand-cut higher-priced crystal business, Waterford Wedgwood has maintained a differentiation strategy. It has also produced a separate range, under the Marquis brand, designed to compete in more price-sensitive segments of the higher-priced market.

British Airways launched a low-cost airline, Go, in 1998, which pursued a cost leadership strategy, while British Airways continued to follow a differentiation strategy.

Implementation

The implementation of strategy will require a detailed programme or plan. This will be accompanied by cost and revenue budgets. The programmes will include all the marketing, operational, financial and human resource requirements. From the marketing viewpoint, a marketing plan will form the basis of the marketing programme.

The marketing plan

The marketing plan is a written document containing details of how the firm's marketing will be done. It will include the assumptions the management has made about its environment and details of the objectives and activities the company will engage in. The plan will be set in the context of the general corporate mission. Plans may be quite detailed documents: they are usually prepared for at least one year and probably two or three years ahead.

Contents of the marketing plan

1. Management or executive summary
2. Marketing objectives
   (a) Company mission statement
   (b) Detailed company objectives
   (c) Product group goals
3. Product or market background
   (a) Product range and explanation
   (b) Market overview and sales summary
4. Marketing analyses
   (a) Marketing environment and trends
   (b) Customer needs and segments
   (c) Competition and competitors' strategy
   (d) SWOT analysis
5. Marketing strategies
   (a) Core target markets (segments)
   (b) Basis for competing or differential advantage
   (c) Desired product or brand positioning
6. Statement of expected sales forecasts and results
7. Marketing programmes for implementation
   (a) Marketing mixes
   (b) Tasks and responsibilities
8. Controls and evaluation: monitoring of performance
9. Financial implications or required budgets
   (a) Delineation of costs

(b) Expected returns on investment for implementing the marketing plan
10. Operational considerations
    (a) Personnel and internal communications
    (b) Research and development and production needs
    (c) Marketing information system
11. Appendixes
    (a) SWOT analysis details
    (b) Background data and information
    (c) Marketing research findings

Source: S. Dibb, L. Simkin, W. Pride, and O. Ferrell, *Marketing: Concepts and Strategies* (third European edition): Boston (Mass.): Houghton-Mifflin 1997.

Analysis of strategic situations and alternatives

Having assessed the environmental forces, the marketer has to evaluate possible courses of action. This is facilitated by a number of planning concepts and techniques and analytical planning methods. Two of these—the BCG matrix and the General Electric business screen—are considered.

The BCG matrix

The Boston Consulting Group matrix (1970) evaluates businesses or products relative to the growth rate of their market and the firms' share of the market (fig. 15.3); it provides a framework for evaluating the relative performance of businesses or products within a portfolio.

Fig. 15.3: The BCG matrix

| | Market share | |
	High	Low
Market growth — High	**Star** High growth, high market share. Will require marketing investment for more growth.	**Question mark** Low market share in a high-growth market. Product may need to be redeveloped or changed.
Market growth — Low	**Cash cow** Holds significant market share in a low-growth market. Generates cash for investment in other products, especially 'stars'.	**Dog** May not have a very long future. Could be sold or allowed to fade away.

The BCG matrix may therefore be useful for companies that market several products or have several different businesses. Many larger companies, such as Guinness, Lever Brothers, or Proctor and Gamble, will have products or brands that could be evaluated on the basis of their market share relative to growth in the market. Strategies may be developed on the basis of the product or brand position in the matrix. 'Star' products will require marketing investment in the form of positioning, communication, and distribution, while 'cash cows' will need to be managed to continue the cash surplus required for investment in other products.

'Question mark' and 'dog' products pose a challenge. For a product to be classified as a 'question mark' it must not be meeting customers' needs, relative to competitors. If the product is not changed or repositioned, it may become a drain on the company's resources. 'Dog' products generally have not got much of a future; they may, however, have a small loyal user base, which the marketer may wish to hold on to. On the other hand, if possible, they may be sold off.

The General Electric business screen

The General Electric 'business screen' (fig. 15.4) was developed to assess business performance on the basis of industry attractiveness and competitive position (Hofer and Schendel, 1978). *Competitive position* is determined by a number of factors, including market share, technological know-how, product quality, service network, price competitiveness, and operating costs. *Industry attractiveness* is determined by market growth, market size, capital requirements, and competitive intensity. Just as with the BCG matrix, the position of the business in the matrix will determine the strategy the firm should pursue.

Fig. 15.4: The General Electric business screen

Industry Attractiveness / *Competitive position*

	Good	Medium	Poor
High	Winner	Winner	Question mark
Medium	Winner	Average business	Loser
Low	Profit-producer	Loser	Loser

Commitment to action

A commitment to action means that the firm is prepared to take action on its plans. Strategy implies action. The company will have to ensure that managers and those who will be required to implement the strategy are aware of and understand what the strategy is about.

There is therefore a need for top-down and bottom-up dialogue. In other words, strategies will usually be developed by senior management; these should be communicated to managers and other staff at lower levels, who should have an opportunity to provide feedback. If, for example, a strategy had implications for product sales strategy, the views of the sales staff should be sought. Their reaction, questions or observations would be useful in assessing how the strategy would be implemented.

All operational managers must understand why a strategic direction was chosen. Strategies will have implications not just for marketing but for production, personnel, and finance.

DEFINING THE BUSINESS

Central to the concept of strategy is the business definition, as this specifies the arena in which the business will compete. As we have seen, the business definition is a fundamental determinant of the company's plans. It should direct attention to the true function of the business, establish the boundaries of the business, and provide a basis for detailed strategy analysis.

Multi-dimensional business definition

The scope of the business can be defined as *multi-dimensional*. There are three principal dimensions: *customer function*, *technology*, and *segments*. These act as parameters within which the business can be defined.

Customer function

Customer function describes what benefits the product provides to customers: for example, the customer buying detergent is obviously looking for the benefit of cleanliness but may also look for other benefits, such as value for money or a product that can get rid of stubborn stains, that leaves a pleasant fragrance, or that does not damage clothes.

Most products and services can provide several benefits. Research and product development can show where additional benefits can be added. The Swiss manufacturer of the Swatch watch, for example, realised that the benefit the customer was looking for was a bit more than something that told the time: watches were fashion accessories and could be offered in different shapes and styles and for different occasions. In the milk market, products have been developed with new benefits, as the next panel illustrates.

ADDING BENEFITS TO MILK

The Irish milk market was valued at £330 million in 1997, with a volume of 115 million gallons. Standard milk accounted for 78 per cent of sales; the remainder was accounted for by low-fat (14 per cent), fortified (5 per cent) and skimmed milk (2 per cent). These categories had grown in importance among increasingly diet-conscious and health-conscious consumers. Milk producers had innovated and produced low-fat and fortified products, which had the benefit of fewer calories and added ingredients, such as vitamins, folic acid, and calcium.

All brands advertised and promoted their own ranges; in addition, generic advertising reminded the consumer of the benefits of milk, particularly the fortified varieties.

Source: J. Lenihan, 'The milky way', *Checkout Ireland*, May 1997.

Technology dimension

The *technology dimension* describes the alternative ways in which the particular function can be performed. A courier service, for example, can provide delivery using bicycles, motorcycles, vans, ships, or aircraft. In other words, there are several ways in which to carry out the service; the technology used will depend on customers' requirements and the company's ability to meet them.

Customer segments

As we saw in chapter 5, customers' needs can differ. Marketers will therefore divide the market into *segments*, or groups of customers sharing particular characteristics and looking for similar benefits. A courier company, for example, might segment its market geographically and by different business or organisational types. Companies such as Federal Express, UPS and DHL emphasise the fact that they can provide a worldwide service using different technologies. Smaller courier operations may operate within the confines of the main business or commercial districts in a particular city or may specialise in providing a service to particular customers, for example delivering legal documents.

The multi-dimensional definition can be illustrated graphically, as shown in the following panel.

MULTI-DIMENSIONAL DEFINITION FOR PET FOOD

The market for pet food in Ireland is estimated to be worth £50 million. The Irish have the highest dog ownership per capita in Europe: 45 per cent of households own a dog. Cat ownership is lower, at 22 per cent of households.

The standard of pet care, however, has been low. Until recent years the majority of domestic animals were fed scraps. An examination of the pet food business reveals a number of customer segments, several technologies employed to produce products, and a number of benefits sought by pet-owners.

Consumers have, however, become more educated about the importance of animal nutrition and diet. Manufacturers have eagerly assisted in the process by providing feeding guides and pet care information on their packaging.

With regard to market segments, an obvious basis for segmentation is between dog-owners and cat-owners. Within each of these are the owners of dogs and cats of different sizes and ages. Foods are therefore formulated for dogs or cats, with variations for puppies and kittens, growing animals, and even the mature animal. The benefits sought by pet-owners include basic nutrition, a balanced diet, and treats. Different formulations are available, from basic low-price ranges to higher-priced ranges of complete meals. Treats are catered for by a variety of products, ranging from dog biscuits to cat snacks.

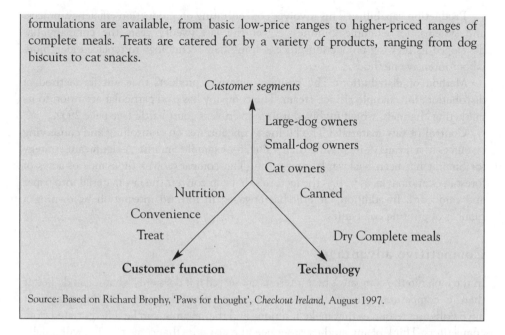

Source: Based on Richard Brophy, 'Paws for thought', *Checkout Ireland*, August 1997.

The three-dimensional definition emphasises the importance of the customer in the definition of the business. In the case of the pet food market it also shows where new functions, segments and technologies can be applied. As pets play a central role in many people's lives, and pet ownership has been linked to the alleviation of stress and loneliness, the importance of pet nutrition has increased. By using the multi-dimensional definition, the marketer of pet foods can assess how they perform on these criteria and where opportunities may exist to develop new segments, serve new needs, or employ new technologies. Possibly the market may become more segmented by animal age; new benefits sought might include low-cholesterol products; and technology might be employed to provide chilled or frozen pet food.

Understanding what drives the business

Marketing theory suggests that businesses are driven by customers' needs and by profit. There are many ways to achieve these objectives, and different firms can place a different emphasis on the means of doing so. A number of possible driving forces can be considered (Day, 1984).

Products offered: The business continues to produce similar products but continually seeks new markets for these products, for example small Irish crystal companies. Few have the resources to compete in overseas markets, so companies concentrate on serving niches, such as the corporate market.

Market-needs-driven: The business continually seeks alternative ways of satisfying market needs, for example Superquinn. The company is needs-focused and has developed its reputation for customer service on this basis.

Technology-driven: The company produces only products that can apply the firm's technological capabilities, for example Iona Technologies, which specialises in the creation of specialist software.

Production capability: This involves concentrating on production efficiency, process and systems, for example Guinness. Over the last twenty years the company has developed its brewing production process, using new technology to replace older, more labour-intensive methods.

Method of distribution: The business promotes products that suit its method of distribution, for example HB ice cream. The company has paid particular attention to its marketing channels, which involved it in a seven-year court battle (see page 293).

Control of raw materials: The business concentrates on controlling and conserving resources as a means of increasing their value, for example Smurfit. A significant strategy for Smurfit has been backwards integration. The company owns thousands of acres of forest in Scandinavia, as well as the factories that can convert the raw material into paper and cardboard. In addition, Smurfit has engaged in forward integration by owning a number of printing companies.

Competitive advantage

In the long run the company's best interests are served if it does only what it can do better than its competitors. This is the nature of competitive advantage. The business must have skills and resources that make it unique and that mean it can be differentiated from competitors. Think of any product or service; the first ones that come to mind will usually have some characteristic that separates them from competing products.

Sometimes companies can achieve a competitive edge by challenging the conventional wisdom in the market. This has been referred to as 'disruption theory' (*Marketing*, 13 February 1997). In other words, every assumption about a market should be questioned. In some industries it was considered that being large and enjoying economies of scale would be a significant barrier to entry, deterring competitors from entering the industry. In the cement market, Irish Cement dominated sales until the arrival of the Seán Quinn Group, as the next panel illustrates. Care needs to be exercised: disruption theory does not mean making reckless or foolish decisions.

CHALLENGING THE CONVENTIONAL WISDOM

The Seán Quinn Group planned to open a new glassmaking factory in County Fermanagh in 1998. Employing 330 people, it would compete principally with Irish Glass Bottle, which had a significant share of the Irish market. The group's entry into glassmaking is almost a carbon copy of its entry into the cement market in the early nineties. Then, also from a plant in County Fermanagh, it took on the market leader in that sector, Irish Cement. The company successfully launched its product and established a strong presence in the cement market.

Source: 'Quinn creates 330 jobs', *Times*, 3 March 1998.

Sustaining competitive advantage

Competitive advantage can be rather transient. The business may introduce a new product or develop a market segment, as Ballygowan did (see page 423); but there will be many imitations. Whether a competitive advantage endures depends on how the marketer reacts to environmental or competitive forces. The resources, skills and strategies of the competitors and the ease with which they can copy or improve on the product will be significant factors.

In attempting to ensure that the competitive advantage survives, the marketer may consider a number of issues. *Patent protection* should be considered, especially in the case of innovative products. Patents provide legal protection and may slow down the process of imitation or ensure that competitors can enter the market only with difficulty. Similarly, the development of brands and registering them as trade-marks can also provide protection. Brands are a source of competitive advantage; well-established brands can have a strong buyer franchise, and this should be sustained.

Another way of sustaining competitive advantage is keeping up to date with the changing needs and requirements of customers. This goes back to the fundamental principle of what marketing is about.

Investment may be required, for example in new technology, to maintain the advantage. This may be in production, communication, pricing, or distribution. Many soft-drinks manufacturers have invested in new-product development but also in the use of vending machines, which can provide the consumer with a chilled drink in an instant.

Research and development into new or existing products or processes may be required. In the oral hygiene market, the leading competitors have all invested in research and development on toothpaste, mouthwashes, and toothbrush design.

RESEARCH AND DEVELOPMENT IN ORAL HYGIENE

The first toothpastes were developed in the nineteenth century. Colgate toothpaste (in a jar) was introduced in the United States in 1873 and in Ireland shortly after the First World War. Toothpaste remained something of a niche product until the nineteen-sixties, when fluoride was added. Subsequent innovations included reformulations that added the ability to resist decay and gum disease and had cosmetic qualities, such as providing fresh breath and whitening of teeth. Mouthwashes were also developed, which also had protective and cosmetic qualities.

The ergonomics of toothbrushes have been extensively researched, resulting in new shapes, designs, and sizes.

In Ireland the toothpaste market was valued at £18 million in 1997, the toothbrush market at £4.6 million, and the mouthwash market at £3 million. The market has been growing as people become more concerned with dental care, although, in spite of the best efforts of toothbrush designers and marketers alike, the average Irish person gets through only 1.1 toothbrushes per year; a change of toothbrush every three months is generally held to be the ideal.

Source: *Checkout Ireland*, March and April 1997.

Organisational mission and objectives

The mission statement should indicate what the company's purpose is. It has a dual communication role, to both staff and customers (Child, 1997). Mission statements give an insight into what makes the company tick; they also provide an indication of what the company can be expected to do, as the example of the Kerry Group illustrates.

MISSION ACCOMPLISHED

The opening sentence in the mission statement of the Kerry Group in the early nineties was: 'The Kerry Group will become a major international food and food ingredient corporation, with significant market share in both Europe and the USA.' The company achieved this objective by acquisition, and in 1998 the Kerry Group became the largest food ingredients manufacturer in the world when it took over the ingredients business of the British company Dalgety for £400 million. By that time half the company's income was derived from its food ingredients business.

The Kerry Group had begun the development of the food ingredients side of its business in 1987 when it made its first acquisition in the United States. Since then it made a number of further acquisitions, including Primas Foods (1988), Beatreme Foods (1988), Dairyland Products Minnesota (1991), and DCA (1994). Other North American acquisitions included the Canadian company Malcolm Research Foods (1992) and the Mexican company Productos UPM (1994). European acquisitions included the German company Millac (1990) and the British companies A. E. Button (1990), Millers and Robirch (1990), Tingles (1993), and Mattesson Walls (1994).

Source: *Checkout Ireland*, January–February 1998.

Strategic goals and objectives

Strategic goals and objectives will emphasise the specific aspects of strategy that will be concentrated on. They should provide guidance and a unified direction for the company, facilitate planning, motivate and inspire, and be an aid in evaluation and control. Typical examples include statements about

- market share leadership
- innovation
- productivity
- financial resources
- profitability
- workers' performance and attitude
- social responsibility.

Consider the corporate objectives of the Campbell Bewley Group. Note, for example, the last objective, of developing the international business interests of the group. Throughout the nineteen-nineties Campbell Bewley made acquisitions abroad. It was also involved in franchising and developed catering operations in many countries, including a contract to provide catering services at both ends of the Channel Tunnel. The company does not give priority to these objectives: it puts equal emphasis on each of them.

CORPORATE OBJECTIVES, CAMPBELL BEWLEY GROUP LTD

1. To offer excellent value and quality products and services to our customers.
2. To provide a reasonable return for the shareholders while maintaining financial stability for long-term growth and survival.
3. To provide an opportunity for all employees to develop to their full potential, and to reward them fairly.
4. To be a good corporate citizen in relation to environmental and social issues.
5. To foster innovation, enterprise and new developments.
6. To preserve the good, essential and unique traditions and practices of the group.
7. To develop the international dimensions of the group.

Source: P. Campbell, 'Bringing the Shareholder Close to the Customer', presentation to the Marketing Institute and Institute of Directors, 29 March 1994.

Tactical goals and objectives

Tactical goals and objectives follow from the strategic goals. For example, a tactical goal of the Campbell Bewley Group might have been to scan markets in Europe or the United States for acquisition opportunities or potential contracts. Tactical goals might also include new-product development, positioning strategy, and brand development.

Operational goals and objectives

Operational goals and objectives will be specific to individual departments. For example, if a company plans to sell more of a product, the sales or marketing department will receive specific targets. Targets will also be set for production or operations departments to make sure the sales targets can be met.

Strategic co-operation

Strategic marketing does not mean that the firm has to go it alone. In the nineteen-nineties much emphasis was placed on the concept of strategic alliances and the development of strategies based on the relationship that firms had developed together. Strategic alliances typically involve horizontal co-operation between competitors or firms engaged in similar activities, while strategies based on relationship marketing are more likely to involve vertical co-operation, for example between manufacturers and retailers.

Strategic alliances

Strategic alliances or partnerships between independent firms are entered into for a number of reasons. As trade barriers have been gradually eroded, competition in the global market has become a reality for many businesses. Environmental changes, keeping up with developments in technology and the lack of skills or resources for going it alone have also been motivations.

Many Irish companies have been quick to enter alliances. In the early nineteen-eighties Aer Rianta, the airport management company, entered into an alliance with Aeroflot, the state airline of the Soviet Union (Keogh, 1990–1). Their relationship developed from what was essentially a barter agreement—of aviation fuel for landing rights at Shannon—to the expansion of Aer Rianta's business ventures in the Soviet Union in the nineties. Alliances are not without potential problems: in the alliance of Aer Rianta with Aeroflot the understanding of concepts of service and quality in the Soviet Union was an issue.

In the late nineties another state company, Telecom Éireann, agreed a strategic partnership with two European partners. As the following panel indicates, the alliance covered a comprehensive list of business areas, in which the three companies agreed to co-operate.

TELECOM ÉIREANN LAUNCHES STRATEGIC ALLIANCE PARTNERSHIP

In January 1997 Telecom Éireann launched a strategic alliance partnership with the Dutch and Swedish telecommunications companies KPN and Telia. The companies signed a comprehensive strategic co-operation agreement containing eighty-five separate initiatives, grouped under the following headings:

- development of the Irish market
- international competitiveness
- the transformation of Telecom Éireann
- the transfer of advanced technologies
- the development of operational support systems
- support in developing the mobile communications business
- development of the multimedia market
- employment-creation initiatives
- joint research and development and purchasing
- international investment opportunities.

The strategic alliance will be significant in the light of the deregulation of the European telecommunications industry. The alliance involved three non-executive appointments to the board of Telecom Éireann by the two partner companies and three executive appointments to the management board. The partners were chosen on the grounds of their strategic fit with Telecom Éireann's business. It was also meant to be a catalyst for telecommunications development.

Source: Telecom Éireann web site (www.telecom.ie).

The move towards strategic alliances was spurred by globalisation and a desire by companies to compete on a wider world stage. It became common in the nineteen-nineties among airlines: consider the examples of Star Alliance, established by United, Air Canada, Thai, Varig, SAS, and Lufthansa, or Oneworld, established by British Airways, American Airlines, Canadian Airlines, Cathay Pacific, and Qantas.

Relationship marketing and strategy

As described in chapter 1, relationship marketing is an important concept in the company's general approach to marketing and in the management of the value-added chain. The development of mutually beneficial relationships will usually be a significant aspect of marketing strategy. Consider the example of the relationship between Boyne Valley Foods and the Superquinn supermarket chain; this proved to be extremely beneficial for both companies, and shows that co-operation in the market can yield positive results.

A MUTUALLY BENEFICIAL RELATIONSHIP

Boyne Valley markets a diverse range of products. Honey is the best-known product, but it also includes cereals, Irish Breeze, Lakeshore, and Lifeforce. The Irish Breeze brand, which covers cotton wool and soap products, was the first winner of the Superquinn Irish Competitiveness Award. The award scheme was launched to recognise success in competing against overseas suppliers in the grocery trade. The criteria included product innovation, market share achieved, and the ability to compete against imported products.

In 1993 all cotton wool was imported; by 1998 Irish Breeze supplied 75 per cent of the market and exported to Britain and Sweden. The competitiveness award included a month-long promotion in Superquinn branches and an introduction to the Continental buying group Associated Marketing Services, which has members in eleven EU countries and access to 23,000 shops, using the Euroshopper brand.

Superquinn had been marking Irish goods on its shelves with a shamrock emblem. It also showed customers on their receipts how much they had spent on Irish goods. By 1998, 60 per cent of all goods sold in Superquinn were produced in Ireland.

Sources: Christine Doherty, 'Honey of an opportunity at Boyne Valley', *Sunday Business Post*, 8 February 1998; 'Irish Breeze takes competitiveness award', *Enterprise and Innovation*, March 1998.

Strategic brand alliances involve one brand name being joined with another as part of a promotional campaign (Rao, 1997). The motivations for entering such alliances include cost-effectiveness, competitive market conditions, and customers' needs. Certainly if companies are pursuing strategies of enhancing product attributes or improved market credibility, a strategic alliance may be helpful. Strategic brand alliances have been entered into by various marketers, including washing-machine manufacturers and detergent companies. Joint advertising can be engaged in, resulting in further economies. In some cases the alliance has translated into new-product development, as when the electrical manufacturer Black and Decker and the paint manufacturer Dulux developed an electric painter.

Marketing organisation and control

One of the generally accepted functions of a manager is organisation. The marketing function needs to be organised so that the company's plans and marketing activities can be effectively carried out.

Companies may approach the organising of the marketing function in different ways. Going back to the earlier example of the Campbell Bewley Group, we can see that it organises its marketing into divisions, as shown in fig. 15.5.

Fig. 15.5: Marketing structures at Campbell Bewley

	A. Products	B. Service
1. Commercial and institutional	1A. Coffee and tea to hotels, caterers, and institutions	1B. Contract catering for work-places and institutions.
2. Retail	2A. Coffee, tea and confectionery to the retail trade (including Bewley's cafés and shops).	2B. Cafés, shops, restaurants etc. in towns, shopping centres, airports, etc.

Source: P. Campbell, 'Bringing the Shareholder Close to the Customer', presentation to the Marketing Institute and Institute of Directors, 29 March 1994.

Some companies organise their marketing function on the basis of their products. Product management structures imply that managers are assigned to specific products or brands, and they look after the marketing and development of these. Product management was originally implemented by Proctor and Gamble in the nineteen-sixties, and it tends to suit companies with a range of products.

If there is a small number of customers, as in many business-to-business markets, the company may organise its marketing function on the basis of customers. Companies like the shipbuilders Harland and Wolf may organise on this basis, such as passenger vessels, cargo or tanker vessels, military or patrol vessels, and oil or gas exploration platforms. Another possibility is geographical organisation: this would apply where the company markets its products in international or regional markets and the marketing function is organised to serve these.

The Campbell Bewley structure recognises that the company markets both to consumers and to firms directly. Many other companies in the food and beverage sector would have similar customer profiles; this can lead to the establishment of separate consumer and trade marketing divisions.

The marketing audit

Firms need to evaluate their marketing ability and performance. Environmental changes and the need to ensure that the firm's competitive advantage is sustained and developed imply a need for an objective assessment. A useful tool for doing this is the *marketing audit*. This is an assessment of the effectiveness and efficiency of the firm's marketing policies, strategies and procedures compared with its opportunities, objectives, and resources. It is a comprehensive, systematic, independent and periodic examination of the company's or business unit's marketing environment, objectives, strategies, and activities, with a view to determining problem areas and opportunities and recommending a plan of action to improve marketing performance.

An audit should be broad rather than narrow in focus and should cover all aspects of the company's marketing. Ideally it should be conducted by someone who is independent of the firm, which should ensure a greater degree of objectivity. The audit should be systematic: in other words, it should follow a prescribed form. It should be conducted periodically and should not just be a once-off event.

COMPONENTS OF THE MARKETING AUDIT

Marketing environment audit
The marketing environment audit should be a comprehensive overview of the forces in the firm's macro and micro-environment. (These are described in chapter 3.) The person conducting the audit should question the assumptions the company has made about its environment

Marketing strategy audit
The marketing objectives and strategies should be assessed in the light of the opportunities or problems facing the company.

Marketing organisation audit
This involves an examination of the way in which marketing is organised as a function and how it interacts with other functions in the business. The marketing function may be headed by a marketing manager, to whom a number of product managers or marketing executives may report. On the other hand, in smaller firms there may be only one person who has responsibility for marketing.

Marketing systems audit
'Marketing systems' describes four broad areas: the marketing information system, the marketing planning system, the marketing control system, and the new-product development system. It is important that the company has systems that support its marketing activities.

Marketing productivity audit
The result of the company's marketing activities can be measured in a number of ways. Satisfied customers who have provided a profit for the business will be an important measure. Research should provide an indication of customer satisfaction; the critical financial measure will be the profits made. Profitability analysis will concentrate on the

profits of the product, product lines, or individual brands. An assessment will also be made of the cost-effectiveness of the company's marketing activities.

The marketing functions audit
The marketing functions audit will involve an assessment of each aspect of the company's marketing mix. This will be assessed to ensure that they are integrated and that clear strategies exist for the products, pricing, promotion and place elements.

Source: P. Kotler, W. Gregor, and W. Rodgers, 'The marketing audit comes of age', *Sloan Management Review*, Winter 1977.

FURTHER READING

Day, G., *Strategic Market Planning: The Pursuit of Competitive Advantage*, St Paul (Minn.): West 1984.

Murray, J., and O'Driscoll, A., *Marketing Management: Concepts and Irish Cases*, Dublin: Gill and Macmillan 1993.

Porter, M., *Competitive Strategy*, New York: Free Press 1980.

DISCUSSION QUESTIONS

1. Describe the implications of the four distinguishing features of strategic planning for each of the following:
   —Irish Biscuits
   —the Educational Building Society
   —Harland and Wolf
   —a third-level college
   —the Abbey Theatre.
2. Comment on the relationship between goals and planning. Are they symbiotic?
3. Explain the importance of establishing a competitive advantage. How does competitive advantage affect the design and implementation of strategy?
4. Describe the competitive advantage you perceive that the following firms have:
   —Nike
   —Abrakebabra
   —Murphy's stout
   —Cityjet
   —Destination Killarney.
5. Select a firm and carry out a marketing audit on it. If you cannot get access to a firm directly, conduct your audit using secondary sources of information.

REFERENCES

Boston Consulting Group, *The Product Portfolio Matrix*, Boston: BCG 1970.
Child, L., 'Mission statements: an inspiration for us all?', *Admap*, January 1997.

Day, G., *Strategic Market Planning: The Pursuit of Competitive Advantage*, St Paul (Minn.): West 1984.

Hofer, C., and Schendel, D., *Strategy Formulation: Analytical Concepts*, St Paul (Minn.): West 1978.

Keogh, D., 'Strategic alliances in practice: the case of Aer Rianta and Aeroflot', *Irish Marketing Review*, vol. 5 (1990–1), no. 3.

Miles, R., and Snow, C., *Organisational Strategy, Structure and Process*, New York: McGraw-Hill 1978.

Porter, M., *Competitive Strategy*, New York: Free Press 1980.

Rao, A., 'Strategic brand alliances', *Journal of Brand Management*, November 1997.

CASE STUDY

CHEEVERSTOWN INDUSTRIES LTD

This case was developed as a basis for class discussion rather than to illustrate either effective or ineffective handling of an administrative situation.

Early in 1997 John Madden, the manager of Cheeverstown Industries Ltd, was contemplating the future. He had been manager for three years and was preparing a proposal for the board of Cheeverstown House on the development of a range of hand-made porcelain and stoneware buttons. The buttons had been a successful product development for Cheeverstown—so much so that maximum production capacity had been reached.

The work force was a group of ninety-three trainees with varying degrees of mental and physical handicap, some of whom were involved in the production of buttons. The buttons were a high-value-added product that provided valuable job-related skills to the trainees involved in their manufacture. A proposal to increase the production capacity would meet the twofold objectives of involving more trainees in the venture and enabling Cheeverstown to identify new customers. Increasing production would also have investment implications, for which the board would expect justification.

Cheeverstown Industries Ltd came under the umbrella of Cheeverstown House, which for many years had been involved in the care and support of the mentally handicapped. It operated a residential centre, a training centre, and an enterprise unit. Cheeverstown Industries Ltd, the commercial division of Cheeverstown House, was established as a company limited by guarantee not having share capital. The objectives of the company, as stated in the memorandum of association, were:

- to promote, on a non-profit-making basis, the education, training and mental welfare of mentally handicapped persons, to provide employment with particular reference to persons with a mental handicap;
- to engage in the manufacture, crafting, production, preparation, processing, warehousing, repairing, maintenance, packaging and ancillary processes of all types of goods and materials on behalf of persons with a physical or mental handicap; and in the conducting of the aforementioned activities, the recruitment of staff, management of facilities and establishment of premises.

The role of the company was to seek commercial opportunities that would meet the objectives of providing supportive employment to people with learning disabilities while competing in the market with products and services. Cheeverstown Industries engaged in a number of activities, including the button production division, which was a small manufacturing enterprise based in the training centre at Airton Road, Tallaght, County Dublin. The participants in the enterprise were mildly to moderately mentally handicapped. Commercial button production began in 1992, and Cheeverstown Industries established its product successfully in both corporate and consumer markets.

Cheeverstown Industries' primary responsibility was to its trainees, providing the education, training and personal development required to enable them to reach their full potential. Each of the trainee's needs was addressed with a comprehensive programme that included speech therapy, reading, writing, numeracy, sports and leisure activities, and, where possible, the development of job-related skills. Cheeverstown's specialist care and educational facilities achieved what trainees' parents and the conventional education system were not equipped to provide.

Training was provided in a variety of areas, including catering, horticulture, and office management, with some time being spent on placement in external firms. Some trainees found external employment, while others moved to the enterprise centre and became involved in the commercial activities of Cheeverstown House.

Commercial activities

The rather broad objectives of Cheeverstown Industries were translated into a number of business activities. The company had a contract with Aer Lingus that involved repackaging head-sets used by passengers on transatlantic flights. These were sent to Cheeverstown Industries, where the foam covers on the ear-pieces were replaced and the unit was repacked in Cellophane, a task that suited trainees with limited dexterity. Similar low-value-added contracts involved gathering and packing printed materials for local printers and manufacturers, including Smurfit Packaging.

More able trainees worked on the production of hand-made porcelain and stoneware buttons. These were first produced on trial in the late nineteen-eighties after the donation of a kiln to the organisation. Samples of buttons and other attachments for garments were prepared, and the views of buyers in clothing manufacturers and retail outlets were sought. Based on this, Cheeverstown Industries decided to concentrate on the production of buttons, and a manufacturing facility was established in the training centre in 1992.

The board of Cheeverstown decided that this was the kind of value-added product it would like to develop. While lower-value-added activities suited some trainees, there were many who had the ability and aptitude for more complex tasks. The reaction to the buttons from manufacturers and retailers had been very positive, and the skills involved suited trainees with higher levels of dexterity and ability.

The market for buttons

The Irish market for buttons comprised two distinct segments: clothing manufacturers and consumers. Research carried out for Cheeverstown estimated that the market for all buttons was approximately 60 million a year, with clothing manufacturers accounting for roughly 95 per cent of the total.

Clothing manufacturers

There were 400 clothing manufacturers in the Republic in 1996. Several button suppliers existed; these, together with their estimated market shares, are listed in table 15A.1. The small market share for Cheeverstown must be considered in the light of the fact that its buttons were a specialist niche product suitable only for certain fabrics and manufacturing processes.

Table 15A.1: Market share of button suppliers to clothing manufacturers

Gallagher and Johnston Allen	50%
Irish Button Company	13%
Leinster Button Company	10%
Morgan Products	5%
Smallwares Ltd	5%
Cork Button Company	4%
Dublin Button Company	3%
Others (including Cheeverstown)	10%

Source: Company estimates.

Cheeverstown Industries was the only Irish manufacturer of buttons: all the other suppliers were importers. The largest supplier, Gallagher and Johnston Allen, offered a wide range of buttons suitable for many garments. Some of the suppliers included porcelain and stoneware buttons in their range; however, Cheeverstown Industries had the largest market share in this category.

Buttons were used on garments either as fastening devices or as a decorative feature. They could be made from a variety of materials, including different types of plastic, metal, leather, wood, and other natural materials, including pottery clay.

Porcelain and stoneware buttons are not suitable for machine-stitching, because they tend to break in the machine, whereas most other buttons can be machine-stitched. This required additional finishing time for such garments. As the buttons were hand-made, each one was slightly different and so they fell outside the very small tolerance allowed for automated stitching. As a result, many of the larger and highly mechanised clothing manufacturers would not use them. Research conducted for Cheeverstown Industries suggested that approximately 150 clothing manufacturers were involved in hand-stitching buttons and therefore were potential users of the Cheeverstown product.

A button can be a significant design feature of a garment. The quantities used by different manufacturers varied according to the type of garment being produced. The demand for different types of button also varied as fashions changed. The Cheeverstown product had been used by a variety of smaller specialist manufacturers.

Avoca Handweavers produced a range of knitwear for the home and export market. The Cheeverstown buttons were used on women's hand-knitted chenille jackets. The hand-made buttons were especially suitable, as their size and weight were ideal for this light wool. The product was sold on both the Irish and export markets, and the range produced appealed to women of all ages.

Bray Knitwear used the hand-made buttons on a range of women's mohair cardigans that had particular appeal for the tourist market. They also exported. The company mechanised its production process in 1996 and as a result discontinued its use of the hand-made buttons.

Clio Ireland produced workwear for a range of companies, including financial services, retailing, and administration. Cheeverstown buttons were mainly used on women's woollen jackets.

Porterhouse was a manufacturer of fabrics and garments, using mainly wool and chenille. The Cheeverstown buttons were used on waistcoats, jackets and coats that were sold on the home and export market. In 1996 Porterhouse had also bought from Cheeverstown 25,000 specially manufactured brooches based on the Tara Brooch. These brooches, three inches in diameter, had been used to enhance garments being sold through an American home shopping channel. This was a special order and represented a diversification for Cheeverstown Industries. It had been very successful, and Porterhouse planned additional orders.

The Bray Knitwear experience emphasised a dilemma for John Madden. The company had been a regular customer and was very satisfied with quality and design, but technological change meant that the Cheeverstown product was no longer suitable. On the other hand, the Tara Brooch order for Porterhouse identified an opportunity to expand the product range.

Cheeverstown Industries had built a good reputation among clothing manufacturers for its design, quality, and delivery, factors that ranked high in manufacturers' buying decisions. Price was not as highly ranked by manufacturers who bought Cheeverstown's products, given the exclusive nature of the garments they produced. Stoneware and porcelain buttons competed largely with buttons made from natural raw materials, such as leather.

The consumer market

The consumer market for buttons was approximately 5 per cent of the total market. The consumer was primarily female, aged thirty and over, who knitted for herself or her immediate or extended family. Typical purchases were small and infrequent. The consumer usually bought buttons for hand-made knitwear, though they could also be stitched onto other garments, such as blouses.

Buttons were sold through a variety of knitwear shops, fabric shops, department stores, and clothing retailers. Trends in the market indicated a decline in sales of buttons in all outlets. This was attributed to a general decline in knitting and the fact that buttons were often included with wool and patterns in pre-packaged knitting kits.

A number of brands existed, including Button Box, Dill, and Vogue Star. Cheeverstown Industries had developed the Tara brand, which was sold mounted on cards displayed on racks. There was very little brand advertising or promotion.

THE MARKETING MIX FOR CHEEVERSTOWN INDUSTRIES

The product

The Cheeverstown product was produced from pottery clay, which was formed, cut, fired, and then decorated. Cheeverstown double-fired its buttons, which produced a more durable and colour-fast product. The pottery clay and ceramic paint were imported from Britain. The forming and cutting process was relatively straightforward, while the decorating process was the most time-consuming and required the highest skill.

Different designs were used for the buttons. Clothing manufacturers co-operated closely in the selection of designs and colours and made suggestions for new designs.

Two kilns were available, giving an average production of six thousand buttons per week. Eight trainees and one supervisor were involved in the production of buttons. The trainees had varying degrees of disability, including Down's syndrome.

Price

Prices for buttons varied considerably. The price clothing manufacturers paid could vary from a fraction of a penny for mass-produced cheaper buttons up to £1.50 for more expensive lines. Generally, buttons made from natural materials commanded the highest prices. Where wholesalers were involved, their mark-up could represent up to 50 per cent of this price. In the retail market, retailers bought from an equally wide price range, starting at 2p and going up to £1.50 each. The mark-up on these was usually 100 per cent.

The price range for Cheeverstown Industries' stoneware and porcelain buttons is given in table 15A.2. Stoneware accounted for 95 per cent of sales; the quantities sold in each size were roughly equal. The Tara Brooch produced for Porterhouse was priced at 50p each.

Table 15A.2: Price per unit for Cheeverstown Industries buttons

	18 mm	22 mm	35 mm
Stoneware	20p	25p	30p
Porcelain	40p	45p	50p

Promotion

Trade promotion involved the use of trade fairs, in particular the Showcase trade fair, held every year in January. This four-day show, for the trade only, attracted a wide variety of fashion industry suppliers, designers, manufacturers and retailers and had been a useful means of establishing contacts with buyers. In many cases, however, Cheeverstown Industries had not been able to follow up all contacts, because of limited time and resources.

A smaller event was the Stitching and Knitting Show, held every year in November. In addition to the trade, this was open to the public. Button sales at this show had been good.

The main promotional device used by Cheeverstown Industries was a colour brochure with illustrations of the range of buttons available. The company had not undertaken promotional activities in retail outlets.

Place

The distribution of buttons to clothing manufacturers was heavily concentrated among wholesalers, who also supplied other materials, such as thread. Cheeverstown Industries sold directly to manufacturers and had not used any wholesalers; this allowed the company to build a direct relationship with manufacturers, and also provided it with a higher margin.

In relation to the consumer market, buttons were sold through a range of specialist fabric shops, knitting supply shops, and clothing retailers. The Nielsen Retail Census in 1991 showed that there were 4,039 drapery shops and boutiques in the Republic. Cheeverstown Industries estimated that approximately 10 per cent of these were potential stockists for its buttons. Early in 1997 the company was supplying only twenty outlets, limited to the area covered by their salesman.

The company used an independent salesman who supplied a range of buttons, thread and other sewing and knitting items to retailers. Retailers that stocked the Cheeverstown product included Hickey's Fabrics, Singer Shops, and Arnott's department store in Dublin. In addition, a small number of clothing retailers, drapery shops and knitting shops in some towns also stocked the product. Distribution was not wide and was largely limited to the area covered by the salesman. The product was generally considered to be a small, specialist line by retailers who stocked it.

One outlet where sales had been especially good was Kerry Woollen Mills, whose customers were predominantly tourists. Sales here were much higher than the average for other retailers. Up to this time Cheeverstown Industries had not done any research on this particular market. An interesting development in Dublin had been a specialist button shop that had opened in 1996 in the Royal Hibernian Way shopping centre, stocking a wide range of styles and sizes.

In general, retailers bought buttons from a small number of suppliers. Three suppliers in particular—F. L. O'Dwyer, Hickey and Company, and Woollen Mills Ltd—accounted for 90 per cent of the market. Most retailers expected suppliers to provide display units for buttons, which the suppliers' merchandisers were expected to restock regularly.

SITUATION ASSESSMENT

John Madden had identified the principal elements in the environment that affected button sales. The fact that the product was hand-made from natural raw materials and that designs could be changed to suit individual customers' requirements had proved a considerable strength. The association with Cheeverstown and its work with mentally handicapped people was also thought to be a benefit. Price was not as important a consideration, as the product was aimed at a specialist niche that was not particularly price-conscious.

The button business was only a small portion of Madden's responsibility. Contracts with other organisations and the day-to-day running of a training and enterprise centre took up a considerable amount of time. While his supervisors concentrated on training and production, he was responsible for sales and marketing, and he was conscious that if the button business was to expand, more time would have to be devoted to it. There were opportunities to increase orders from manufacturers and retailers, but this would require a greater time commitment.

While some previous customers, such as Bray Knitwear, had automated their manufacturing process, there was no immediate indication that others were likely to follow suit. Many of the manufacturers that Cheeverstown Industries could serve were small in scale and specialist in output.

Sales to retailers represented a small proportion of total sales; however, only a limited number of retailers were served, and Madden wondered whether it would be worth while attempting to expand this.

Measuring success

As a non-profit-making organisation, Cheeverstown Industries measured success in a number of ways. Financially it was required to cover 35 per cent of the costs of commercial activities, the remainder being financed by training and development grants. The decision, however, was much more than a financial one. The board, while it would expect financial justification, was also interested in the more intangible measures of success. Cheeverstown Industries provided trainees with an opportunity for personal and social development, something that would not be provided to mentally handicapped people in most organisations. The success of the porcelain and stoneware buttons demonstrated an ability to produce a high-quality product and to compete effectively. The fact that the product was produced by mentally handicapped people was as important a measure of success as the sales of the product had been.

In all its activities, Cheeverstown Industries had enabled Cheeverstown House to achieve significant objectives. Trainees were given an opportunity, in a supportive environment, to prove their ability and in so doing to learn valuable skills that they could bring either to supportive employment or, ideally, to independent employment. The buttons had been the most successful venture so far.

The proposal

The success of Cheeverstown Industries' button business convinced John Madden that he had reached the critical market breakthrough stage. The company was supplying a relatively small number of manufacturers and retailers; he was convinced that it was possible to build on this. Production, however, had reached capacity level, and without additional facilities and investment it would be difficult to develop further. Clothing manufacturers were receptive to new designs and ranges, and the Tara Brooch product, which had sold well for Porterhouse, convinced him that there were opportunities for diversification.

Development would move the business forward from its present basis as a cottage industry to a stronger footing as a small or medium-sized enterprise. In the longer term, Madden considered it possible to become an independent enterprise, without relying on grant aid. The manufacturing unit was unsuitable for expansion; to justify larger premises he estimated that production would need to be doubled. This would require new kilns and new preparation and finishing equipment. The number of trainees would also be doubled, requiring additional trainers or supervisors. Increased production capacity would also need to be used continuously, which emphasised the importance of scheduling orders with production. Unlike many conventional firms, overtime was not something that could be built in to schedules.

From a marketing point of view there were a number of issues, the pros and cons of which Madden felt he needed to address.

- Should Cheeverstown Industries continue direct supply to clothing manufacturers, or should it seek a suitable wholesaler?
- Was there an opportunity to diversify further, given the successful experience with Porterhouse?
- Were there opportunities to expand distribution in the retail sector?
- Should Cheeverstown Industries seek to improve its position in the consumer market? Should the brand be developed? What promotion and publicity opportunities should be considered?
- Should a marketing or sales executive be hired to prospect for new business, to service accounts, and to provide marketing support?
- Should export possibilities be investigated as a longer-term option?
- Should expansion be in stoneware or in porcelain buttons?

Finance for the proposal would have to be sought by the board. Application could be made for grants of up to 65 per cent of the project cost under the EU Horizon programme; the remainder would have to come from sales income.

The proposal would also be framed in the context of Cheeverstown Industries' unique employee profile, and the priority would be the trainees' educational and training needs. The history of the product so far demonstrated their skills and abilities and the ability of Cheeverstown Industries to meet the quality and supply criteria demanded by its customers.

Index

Swatch watches, 123
SWOT analysis, 414–15, 426, 430–431

tangible symbols, 404
target marketing *see also* product positioning,
    128–131
target profit pricing, 225–6
targeted marketing consultancy programme,
    364
targeting, 16
taxes, 70–71, 72, 73, 227–8
tea market, 30, 185
tea market, British, 271–2
technological environment, 76–9
technology, 73
    and competitive advantage, 16
    and customer service, 27
    effects on market, 76–7, 78–9
    and international trade, 370
    and marketing, 24–5
    and marketing communication, 288
    and product innovation, 205
    retail, 4
    and selling, 279
technology dimension, 434, 435
tele-marketing, 16, 279, 306, 308, 354–5, 394
Telecom Éireann, 351, 353, 440
telecommunications, 76, 77, 354
telephone interview, 109
Telesis report (1982), 22, 34
television, 248, 251, 257–9, 269–8, 351
    shopping channels, 306, 308
    and sponsorship, 394
Telifís na Gaeilge, 82, 151
Tellis's taxonomy of pricing strategies, 229–30
Tesco Ireland, 19–20, 171–3
test-marketing, 209–10
Tetley's tea, 271–2
Thermo King, 81
third-level colleges, 47, 50–51
Tidy Towns organisation, 9
timing and new product release, 210–212
tobacco marketing, 80–81
toiletry consumption in Ireland, male, 155–6
top-line reporting, 273
total quality management, 10, 27–9, 345
    core concepts, 28–9
tourism, world incomes, 340–341
tourism product, 348–9

tourism source markets, 122
trade barriers, 367
trade directories, 393
trade fairs, 244
trade marketing, 63
trade marketing managers, 304–5
trade marks, 185
trade promotions, 274, 450
trade publications, 391–2
trade shows, 394–6
training
    and customer service, 27
    in enterprise development, 7
    staff, 401–2
transaction-based strategy, 355
transactions, 9
transport *see* logistics
Trócaire, 408
turnarounds, company, 49, 52–4

UCI cinemas mystery visitor scheme, 109–10
undifferentiated marketing, 128–9
unemployment trends, 74, 75
Unilever, 185, 293–4
Unilokomotiv, 384
unique selling propositions, 15
universities, 47, 50–51
urbanisation, 68–9
usage occasion, 134
user type, 135

value
    for business, 8–9
    customer, 7–8
value-adding process, 8–9, 25, 59–60
value chain analysis, 62
variable-cost pricing approach, 378
variable costs, 223, 225–6
venture capital funds, 47
VHI, 63, 134, 399
videocassette market, 322–3, 324–5
volunteers, 400, 401–2, 414

warehousing, 295, 301
water transport, 299–300
Waterford Stanley, 53–4
Waterford Wedgewood, 23, 371, 375, 429
weighted credit method, 318
whiskey brands, 184, 189, 190–191, 199

ACKNOWLEDGMENTS

The publishers are grateful to the following for permission to reproduce advertisements in the book and for providing the material.

Fig. 4.2 Iarnod Éireann; Fig. 5.3 Aer Lingus and Irish International Advertising; Fig. 5.4 NordicTrack; Fig. 5.5 VHI; Fig. 5.6 Breitling and Smartprint & Design Ltd; 5.7 Cadbury's; Fig. 5.8 Kellogg's and McConnell's Advertising; Fig. 6.2 Dulux Paints Ireland Ltd; Fig. 6.6 Masterfoods and Dimensions; Fig. 6.9 Brown Thomas and DesignWorks; Fig. 8.1 Bus Éireann; Fig. 9.2 R.A. Bailey & Co. and Dimensions; Fig. 9.5 ESB; Fig. 9.6 Procter and Gamble; Fig. 9.7 Drinks Industry Group and Stacey Marketing Services; Fig. 9.8 National Lottery; Fig. 9.9 Irish Sugar and DDFH & B; Figs 9.10 and Fig. 9.14 Ryanair; Fig. 9.11 Poster Management Ltd; Fig. 9.13 The Irish Times; Logos on page 255 Friends First; Fig. 11.3 ICC Bank and Arks Advertising; Fig. 11.4 Bus Éireann; Fig. 11.5 Irish Marketing Surveys; Fig. 11.6 Telecom Éireann; Fig. 11.7 Citibank and Rubicon Advertising; Fig. 13.2 Airbus Industrie; Fig. 13.3 Bank of Ireland and McCann-Erickson Ltd; Fig. 14.1 St Vincent de Paul Society; 14.2 Concern and Doherty Advertising; Fig. 14.3 Trocaire and Public Communications Centre; Fig. 14.4 TUI Credit Union and Typecraft Ltd; Fig. 14.5 National Museum of Ireland and DesignWorks.